In Memory of

Helen K. Wolf Mills '23

Dedicated by the

Carleton Alumni Association

Yale Historical Publications

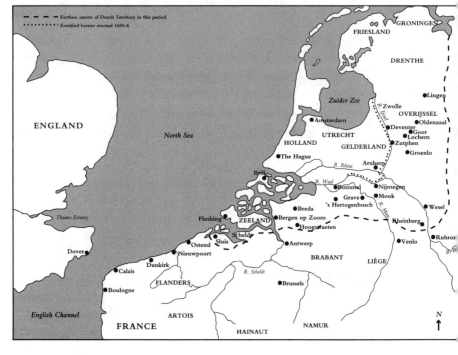

Map of the Low Countries

Philip III

and the

Pax Hispanica,

1598–1621

❖ ❖ ❖

The Failure of Grand Strategy

❖ ❖ ❖

PAUL C. ALLEN

Yale University Press New Haven & London

Published under the direction of the Department of History of Yale University with assistance from the income of the Frederick John Kingsbury Memorial Fund.

Designed by James J. Johnson and set in Bembo Roman and Shelly Volante Script type by Tseng Information Systems, Durham, North Carolina.
Printed in the United States of America by Vail-Ballou Press, Binghamton, New York.

Library of Congress Cataloging-in-Publication Data

Allen, Paul C., 1964–
Philip III and the Pax Hispanica, 1598–1621 : the failure of grand strategy / Paul C. Allen.
p.   cm. — (Yale historical publications)
Includes bibliographical references and index.
ISBN 0–300–07682–7 (alk. paper)

1. Spain—Politics and government—1598–1621.   2. Spain—Foreign relations—Europe.   3. Spain—Foreign relations—1598–1621.   4. Spain—Foreign relations—Treaties.   5. Europe—Foreign relations—Spain.
6. Philip III, King of Spain, 1578–1621.   7. Peace.   I. Title.   II. Series.
DP183.A45   2000
946'.051 — dc21   99-40557

A catalogue record for this book is available from the British Library.

Contents

Preface

The Treaty of the Truce of Flanders made of late between Philip
the Third King of Spain, together with the Arch-Dukes, Albertus and
Isabella, and the States General of the United Provinces of these
Countreys, may doubtlesly be numbered amongst the most memorable
affairs of our time. If we consider the time therein imploy'd, it was above
two years; if the Princes who intervened therein, all the chiefest of Europe
had therein their share; if the difficulties which were to be overcome,
these were never any greater met withall in any negotiation: and lastly,
if we will consider the effects which ensued thereupon, nothing
could be of more importance to the publick affairs of Christendom,
then the 12 years cessation of those arms, which had so long troubled
almost whole Europe with the bitter Wars of Flanders.

—CARDINAL GUIDO BENTIVOGLIO
Historical Relations

On 9 April 1609, in the once great commercial city of Antwerp,
commissioners from Spain, the Spanish Netherlands, and the
United Provinces formally concluded a truce that would end
the fighting between the Habsburgs and their rebellious Dutch subjects
for a period of twelve years. This settlement had been reached only after
more than a decade of diplomatic maneuvering involving not only the
Spanish Habsburgs and the Dutch but also the English and the French.

The Twelve Years' Truce, as the treaty is known to posterity, represented the final act in the implementation of the so-called Pax Hispanica
(Spanish Peace), whose beginnings had been laid with the Franco-Spanish
Treaty of Vervins in 1598, and consolidated with the Anglo-Spanish
Treaty of London in 1604. Although these three treaties constituted the
most significant diplomatic activity of the age and ushered in the age of
high-profile peace conferences, scholars have devoted little attention to

this decade-long period of peacemaking (1598–1609). Instead, modern historians have limited their discussions of the period to brief accounts in broad historical surveys of the Eighty Years' War and of the rise of the Dutch Republic.[1]

Yet the idea that wars could be terminated by means of long-term negotiation and bargaining was a seminal development in the field of international relations and one that proved less than easy. In a remarkable turn of events, Spain, the dominant European power, made peace with three of its enemies, even though no clear victor had emerged in any of the conflicts. Because they could not quite understand this, contemporaries viewed this Spanish peacemaking not as the sign of the decline of the Spanish empire that historians have considered it to be but rather as a subtle device to gain even more power over its rivals. This residual element of distrust concerning why any government would *choose* to end a conflict made early-modern war termination a complicated matter dependent upon much more than the mere desire for peace. That the belligerents did make peace in 1598, 1604, and 1609 despite this distrust was therefore an extraordinary achievement.

For while people today tend to regard peace as an ideal goal to be attained merely for the intrinsic benefits it brings to humankind, it was not always so. Foreign-policy makers around the turn of the seventeenth century viewed peace very differently. Although they theoretically subscribed to the medieval universalist concept of peace as something beneficial to all Christendom, in practice they regarded it as merely another component of strategy, a continuation of war by other means. As such, ministers looked upon peace as something both militarily useful, if promoted by oneself, and dangerous, if promoted by one's rival. Their concept was analogous to Ambrose Bierce's cynical definition of peace as "a period of cheating between two periods of fighting."[2]

Indeed, many ministers of state believed that peace could actually be a destructive force in a world in which conflict was endemic. So dangerous did these seventeenth-century statesmen consider peace that they called negotiators "peacemongers," a word that carried all the reprobation of the modern equivalent, "warmongers."[3] It was this distrust of peace that inspired Sir Thomas Edmondes's remark regarding the impending treaty negotiations with the Dutch: "Those which better know what advantage Princes do win upon a people by that degree of their coming once to taste of the benefits of a truce, will not believe that the States will commit such an incongruity against reason of state."[4] And it was fear of the dangers of peace that underlay the complaint of the great Irish rebel leader Hugh O'Neill, earl of Tyrone, that English desires for peace were an underhanded way to weaken the force of the Irish rebellion and its Spanish supporters. "The English themselves," he fumed, "using the name of peace as a deception, teach us this manner of feigned friendship and of destruction by peace."[5] In other words, peace made one's enemy weak and oneself strong. The idea was to proffer the laurels of peace to your opponents and persuade them to abandon their military pursuits for a time, while simultaneously maintaining your own military establishment, thereby weakening them seriously in the event of a future engagement.

This was the clearly stated goal of the strategy formulated by Spanish ministers toward their rivals in the first decade of the reign of Philip III. Contrary to the widespread belief among modern historians of the reign —most notably expressed by Jonathan Israel in *The Dutch Republic and the Hispanic World*—Spanish ministers under Philip III did not want permanent peace (*paz*).[6] In accordance with their view of peace as an extension of strategy, from the outset they sought a *limited* peace—a long-term truce (*tregua*)—to weaken their opponents and give Spanish arms and finances time to recover before the resumption of war. The reasons for this were clear. In a meeting in 1600 concerning opening negotiations for a truce with their rebellious Dutch subjects, the Council of State, Philip III's chief policy-making body, suggested that such a course of action would have two effects essential for the eventual defeat of the rebels: "One, that it would divert the rebels from arms and undermine the authority of those who by their guidance hold the government of the provinces in tyranny; and two, that, should the natives once begin to enjoy the advantages of quietude and of commerce that would follow, it would be much easier to reduce them to their true obedience." Or, in the more succinct words of Juan de Idiáquez, one of Philip's foremost councilors: "With the armistice we assure ourselves against [the] danger [of having to withdraw our troops], give ourselves time to breathe after such excessive expenses and travails, and weaken the rebels militarily while they attend to the rewards of trade and commerce."[7]

The Spanish peace strategy was designed, then, to lull their opponents into a false sense of security, while simultaneously allowing the *monarquía española* (the Spanish monarchy—the collection of territories ruled individually by the king) to rejuvenate and stockpile its military resources.

And their contemporaries recognized this fact. William Camden, in his renowned history of the reign of Queen Elizabeth, believed that the motive
behind Spanish desires for peace was the hope that "the English would by
little and little neglect their shipping and navigations, when [until] they
could no longer increase their wealth with the spoils of the Spaniards,
and at the length whilest they slept securely in peace, discontinuing their
following of the warres by sea and land, they might be surprized at un-
awares." Philip's decision to resume the war against the Dutch at the end
of the Twelve Years' Truce in 1621 and Spain's subsequent involvement in
wars with England and France were not, therefore, the product of the
failure of the Spanish peace policy but were rather conscious decisions to
carry out the grand strategy that the king and his ministers had conceived
at the beginning of the century. This strategy had always entailed seeking a final victory over the Dutch rebels, insuring the continuing vitality
of the Catholic faith in Protestant territories, and maintaining Spanish
preponderance on the continent. The difference was that now war was
merely one means to those ends; peace, albeit temporary, was another.[8]

To be sure, the strategy of the Pax Hispanica was one forced upon
Philip III and his advisers by the circumstances in which the Spanish monarchy found itself at the close of the sixteenth century. Economically exhausted by more than a hundred years of empire building, and facing increasingly powerful enemies willing and able to strike at it in all parts of
the globe, the monarchy had to begin adjusting its strategies to fit its circumstances. This it would do, but in a way that I believe set it apart from
the other countries of western Europe and that may have contributed to
its loss of predominance on the continent.

No detailed treatment of Spanish grand strategy in northwestern Eu-
rope during the initiation of the Pax Hispanica has been attempted using
Spanish sources.[9] The most comprehensive account of the period is in
the fourth book of John Lothrop Motley's magisterial *History of the United
Netherlands* (1867). But lacking direct access to the major Spanish archives,
Motley depended on contemporary secondary works on the history of the
Dutch revolt for much of his analysis of Spanish policy making. Others
have followed in his stead. Jonathan Israel's new history, *The Dutch Republic: Its Rise, Greatness, and Fall, 1477–1806* (Oxford, 1995), likewise relies
almost entirely on non-Spanish sources for the discussion of the period of
peacemaking after the accession of Philip III. Accordingly, little is known
about who formulated Spanish grand strategy, on what criteria it was

based, or how it was carried out.[10] My work seeks to fill part of the gap in our understanding of Spanish foreign policy during this critical period in the history of the Spanish monarchy, but it makes no claim to be a complete history of international relations for these years. A task of that magnitude would entail years of research in all the major archives. Instead, this is a study of early seventeenth-century war and diplomacy viewed from the perspective of the Spanish monarch and his ministers. To paraphrase Wallace MacCaffrey in his own recent work on Elizabeth I's foreign policy, it is an effort to explore the ways the Spanish leaders went about the task of maintaining their empire—of defining their goals and of finding ways to realize them, using the information and resources available to them.[11]

Acknowledgments

I have incurred many debts during the course of this work. First, I would like to thank the institutions and foundations that have provided generous monetary support for my research on this project: Yale University; the Commission for Educational Exchange between the United States of America and Spain; the Program for Cultural Cooperation between Spain's Ministry of Culture and United States' Universities; and the Andrew W. Mellon Foundation.

In addition I wish to thank all the individuals who have made this project both viable and enjoyable: Isabel Aguirre Landa and Agustín Carreras of the Archivo General de Simancas, for providing an atmosphere of warmth and friendship in which to work; Miguel Valdivielso, Carmen Sandin, and Fernando San José Sánchez, for taking me under their wing; James Boyden and Geoffrey Parker, my dissertation advisers and mentors, for sharing their enthusiasm for, and immense understanding of, early modern Europe and Spain; Bob Goldberg and Dean May, my friends at the University of Utah, for welcoming me, giving me valuable advice, and helping me in innumerable ways; my daughters, Kate and Meghan, for making the time spent outside this project so rewarding and fun; and Susan et al., who read the manuscript, in whole or in part, and provided advice and support whenever it was needed.

Notes on Terminology, Dates, and Currency

Terms: This work relies heavily on original documentation from four countries, each with its own language. Throughout I have tried to use the individuals' names as they wrote them, except where overriding familiarity with one form of a name exists. Where the orthography has been standardized, I have adopted modern spellings for personal names. I have not added accents to titles or quotations from Spanish documents unless they occur in the original, nor have I modernized spelling in these instances.

Although the term "Low Countries" refers to all of the provinces of the Netherlands once under the control of the Habsburg empire, I use Flanders to refer to the Spanish Netherlands, since this is how the Spaniards, English, and Italians used the term. Where I mean specifically the province of Flanders, I so indicate. For the seventeen northern provinces of the Netherlands I have chosen the terms "United Provinces," "Provinces," or "States" (for States-General). "Habsburg" and "Catholic" are adjectives I often use to refer to the people or army of the southern provinces under the control of the Spanish monarchy. "Spain" and "Spanish" refer to the governing kingdoms (Castile and Aragon) and peoples of the *monarquía española,* that conglomerate of territories akin to an empire over which the Castillian monarch ruled. "Dutch" refers specifically to the people of the northern provinces.

The Spanish terms *suspensión de armas* (cease-fire), *tregua* (truce or armistice), and *paz* (peace) pose some difficulties when translated into modern English. A *suspensión de armas* was a temporary cessation of (usually land) hostilities that was called while details for a conference of delegates from the opposing sides was worked out. A *tregua,* on the other hand, was a cessation of hostilities for a longer period, though it did not entail the withdrawal of troops from the war zone. In effect it was a limited or proscribed peace in which neither side was forced to give up its ultimate demands. Finally, *paz,* or permanent peace, for Spain meant the recovery of the northern provinces, whereas for the United Provinces it meant independence and the expulsion of all foreign troops from Netherlands soil. It must be noted, however, that at times the three terms are interchangeable, and one must rely on context to determine which meaning is intended. All translations are my own except where indicated.

Dates: Dates, including those in the documentation, are for the most part new style (the year beginning with January 1); old-style dates are indicated by the abbreviation o.s.

Currency: The diverse currencies used and the differing rates of exchange in the various theaters of war make exact comparisons difficult. In Spain and in the Spanish army the principal unit of account was the *escudo* (a currency unit based on silver). The *maravedí* was used for normal transactions in Spain. The *ducat*, a gold coin originally issued by Ferdinand and Isabella, was still used as a standard unit of account (but no longer as a coin). In the Netherlands the principal unit of account was the *pattard*. English documents refer both to shillings and to pounds. During the period of this study, monies were exchanged at approximately the following rates:

1 ducat = 375 maravedís	1 escudo = 400 maravedís	1 florin = 20 pattards
= 47 pattards	= 50 pattards	= 3.3 shillings
= 2.35 florins	= 2.5 florins	= 0.43 ducats
= 0.9 escudos	= 1.1 ducats	= 0.40 escudos
= 5 shillings	= 5.25 shillings	

Introduction:
The Making of Strategy
at the Court of Philip III

❧ ❧ ❧

The young King of Spain will show himself to the world.
—JOHN COLVILLE TO LORD DOUGLAS
10 April 1599

To begin to understand the adjustments to Spanish strategy begun by Philip III and his advisers, we must know a little about how his policies related to those of his predecessors and how the changes the new monarch introduced affected decisions made by the new regime.

As Geoffrey Parker has recently shown, the Spanish Habsburgs, and in particular Philip II, did indeed have the elements of a grand strategy. Initially these consisted of an unwillingness to surrender any territory previously acquired, the priority of the Iberian peninsula's security over any other problem, a determination to regain control of the Mediterranean and eastern Christian lands from the Ottoman Turks, and the intention of keeping Italy under Spanish control.[1]

The rise of a strong Protestant camp in Europe after the 1530s and Philip II's acquisition of the Portuguese empire in 1580 added two other elements to these traditional Castilian goals: the defense of Catholicism in Europe and the defense of the Spanish monopoly in the East and West Indies, both of which changed the focus of Spanish strategy from the Mediterranean to the northern Atlantic. Following the accession of the Protestant Queen Elizabeth in 1558, Philip found himself drawn into increasing confrontations with England over economic and religious issues, culminating, in 1585, in outright war and a resolution to conquer the island kingdom. And in 1566 the political, economic, and religious revolt of the Netherlands against Philip further complicated Spanish strategy in northern Europe.[2] For defensive and religious reasons Spain could not abandon the provinces; to have done so would have set off a domino effect, inspiring similar revolts in other Spanish possessions and undermining Catholic authority throughout the empire. As the century drew to a close, these two enemies of Spain, increasingly powerful at sea and allied in their antagonism against the Habsburgs, began striking effectively at Spain's vulnerable flanks, the Atlantic and Pacific trade routes to the Spanish and Portuguese Indies. These struggles became linked to a third in the 1590s. To prevent a Protestant succession to the French throne after the death of Henry III, Philip thrust his northern forces into the French civil war on the side of the Catholic League against the Protestant claimant, Henry of Navarre.

Intransigence—religious, political, and economic—became the leitmotif of Philip II's strategy. Believing himself to be acting in the service of God, he brought all of Spain's resources to bear against his religious and political enemies. In the process he jeopardized the traditional long-term strategic goals of the monarchy and brought Spain to virtual financial ruin. By 1598, after twenty-five years of massive military outlays—to reconquer the Low Countries, send three expensive armadas against England, and put a Spanish candidate on the French throne—the crown's debt stood at eighty-five million ducats (almost ten times its annual revenue) and Spanish hegemony in Europe seemed shattered.[3] A careful reconsideration of Spain's long-term strategy was needed. But Philip II was running out of time. All he could do was attempt stop-gap measures designed to minimize the damages and provide a breathing space for Spanish arms. On 2 May 1598 he made peace with the (now Catholic) French king, Henry IV, and just four days later, in the vain hope of ameliorating Dutch resistance, bestowed his title to the Netherlands on his oldest daughter, Isabel Clara Eugenia and her betrothed, Cardinal-Archduke Albert of Austria, the nephew Philip II had personally groomed for high office. With these acts completed, he lapsed into his final illness and died four months later, leaving his twenty-year-old son to redefine Spanish strategy.

Was Philip III ready for such an undertaking? Despite the general view of historians, the new king was not inexperienced in matters of state when he assumed the throne.[4] As early as 1593, when the prince was only fifteen years old, Philip II had initiated him into government affairs "in order to inculcate his son with the ideas that inspired his policies and to make the ministers that were serving him agreeable also to the prince."[5] From that year on, the young prince sat almost daily at meetings of the expanded Consejo de Estado (Council of State), the body responsible for foreign affairs; attended meetings of the Consejo Real (Royal Council), the chief domestic affairs body; and sat in for the king at first audiences with papal *nuncios* and ambassadors.[6] These activities gave the prince valuable experience in a whole range of foreign policy and strategic issues.

According to the papal nuncio (ambassador), Camillio Borghese, the Council of State in this period dealt with dispatching viceroys, governors, and ambassadors; answering foreign correspondence; the acquisition of new territories and defense of old; the enlistment of soldiers; and royal finances. And Luis Cabrera de Córdoba, biographer of Philip II and chronicler of the reign of Philip III, relates that in 1597, the king, needing the council to take more of the weight of administration from him, attempted to enhance its abilities by adding the marquis of Velada, *mayordomo mayor* (grand master of the household) of the prince, and the count of Fuensalida, his own most senior mayordomo. Thus strengthened, and under the direction of the prince, the council began to treat "carefully and understandingly the war that was being carried on against so many enemies, preserving both reputation and the State." Indeed, after September 1597 the prince was even signing official papers, his father having become too weak to continue annotating everything in his usual manner.[7]

But perhaps the most important component of the prince's training came when, for three hours every day, he was present at meetings of the Junta de Noche, an extra-official cabinet-type body that met in the prince's quarters and was made up of Philip II's chief advisers: Cristóbal de Moura, Philip II's grand chamberlain; Diego de Fernández de Cabrera y Bobadilla, count of Chinchón; Juan de Idíaquez, the Comendador Mayor (Grand Commander) of León; Gómez Dávila y Toledo, marquis of Velada; and—until his departure to govern the Low Countries in 1595—Cardinal-Archduke Albert.[8] During the life of this junta, the young prince would have been exposed to a myriad of state matters, including "the King's many wars on sea and land in Europe, with such a variety of outcomes, violent deaths of the powerful for the mistreatment of their king and the death of a humble friar, leagues in favor of religion, battles, skirmishes, invasions, retreats, conquests of strong forts, resolutions, private affairs and civil wars, secret pretensions and public aims, aspiration to the Crown [of

France], pontifical and royal legations for election of the King [Henry IV],
his pardon, aid to cities with various outcomes, sudden deaths and elections of Popes, various accords and resolutions fitting for the times, strata-
gems, powerful armadas with bad or little effect on friends and enemies,
attack of corsairs, and suspicions of potentates of whom it was arbiter, of
all of which there were relations."[9]

Thus the prince received extensive formal training in the workings
of the council and junta and became familiar with the senior ministers
of his father, "avoiding only the irritation that his father encountered in
reading the consultas and dispatches."[10] Firsthand knowledge of the ministers was perhaps the most important aspect of the training, in that he
would depend upon them for advice. In the codicil of his will, Philip II
advised his son to use the members of this junta as advisers, with the intention that they function as a sort of regency government while his son
gained experience.[11] By 1598, when Philip III assumed the throne at the
age of twenty, he was therefore experienced in the particulars of policy
making and would have had a clear notion of the problems besetting the
monarchy and of his father's responses to them.

This is not to say that the new king started his reign with a clear
notion of how he would respond to the challenges facing him. And it
must be remembered that Philip's foreign policy was not entirely of his
own making. Various individuals and groups formed the policy-making
apparatus in the Spanish court, each with a particular agenda: the king;
the king's chief ministers; the members of the Council of State; secretaries
of state; other ministers; and various ordinary and special ambassadors.
The sheer number of people involved often makes it difficult to trace the
decision-making process. Moreover, although the Spanish monarchy left
the most extensive paper records of any early modern state, a great number of the letters to and from the court or between courtiers have long
since been lost or are housed in uncatalogued private libraries. Even if this
were not so, the seventeenth century was still a period in which the majority of political decisions took place *a boca* (literally, by mouth) in the
corridors of power that surrounded the monarchs, conversations that left
no physical evidence.

There is no doubt that Philip III took a less active part in the foreign-
policy decision-making process than his father had done, but this does
not mean that he was, in the words of John Lynch, "the laziest king is
Spanish history."[12] Rather, he chose to make use of the experience avail-

able to him in the administrative structure. Almost immediately upon assuming the throne, he made clear that he would not be ruled by his father's ministers, replacing Cristóbal de Moura and disbanding the junta de noche. Thereafter he relied heavily on an expanded Council of State to provide him with the information he needed to make strategic decisions (see Chapter 2).

The Council of State was an august body made up of senior ministers, influential aristocrats, and men with extensive experience in the military high command. It met regularly to discuss important matters contained in the dispatches of ambassadors and the advice papers of spies, retainers, courtiers, and what would today be called lobbyists—individuals who, like Father Joseph Creswell of the English Catholic college in Valladolid, took it upon themselves to act as spokespersons for a particular group. Secretaries assisted the Council, sifting through incoming correspondence and setting the agenda for council meetings, sometimes in consultation with the king's senior ministers. After discussing issues in absolute secrecy, councillors offered their recommendations, which were recorded by the secretaries and later written up as an advice paper, or *consulta*.[13] The consulta was then sent to the king, who reviewed the recommendations and decided future actions accordingly.

Philip III depended on this council to debate all the possible options open to the monarchy and to provide him with their expert opinions about which policies to pursue. At times he even refused to make a decision unless his most trusted ministers had reviewed the situation. When a consulta concerned with mutinies in the Army of Flanders in 1600 went before Philip without the opinion of the count of Miranda, who had been absent, he returned it with a note asking that Miranda see the consulta and give his advice.[14] Such dependence on the councils astounded Philip's contemporaries, who tended to look upon it as weakness. "The thing that is strange about Spain," wrote one traveler, "is that, having absolute government in their hands, the kings still do not do anything without Councils, nor sign anything without them."[15] But the consultas produced by this council were still merely papers of advice; the councillors did not set policy. Because Philip trusted his councillors, most of his replies to the consultas, in contrast to his father's, were short and unilluminating: "Do as the Council sees fit"; or "This is okay." On one consulta he even lazily traced his rubric over and over, suggesting that he may have been just a little bored. After his first year on the throne, he seldom appeared in council. And when he did so, it was because major decisions regarding his pet projects (Ireland, the English succession, and later Flanders) were to be made.[16]

But such terse replies and apparent lack of interest do not mean that Philip left control in the hands of his ministers; it is clear that the king had the final say over which strategies to implement. As R. B. Wernham has pointed out, "Control of foreign policy, control over the dealings with fellow monarchs and governments, was the last thing any monarch would willingly give up."[17] And at times the king would even bypass the council altogether. In January 1600 he sent a note to one of his secretaries requesting that "the matter of [the dispute between Federico Spínola and the archduke Albert] not be read in the Council, but instead shown to the marquis of Denia and to don Juan [de Idiáquez] so that they can respond as they see fit."[18] At any rate, not all of Philip's comments were so accommodating toward the ministers. On important consultas he often gave fairly long and detailed decisions, sometimes enlarging on the council's suggestions and sometimes directly repudiating the advice given him.

Moreover, Philip had a strong sense of his own authority with respect to the council's. In 1603, worried about the length of time Philip was taking to respond to important letters concerning negotiations in England, council members requested permission to allow the secretary of the council, Andrés de Prada, to use his discretion in sending dispatches on to the king. The king, however, would have none of this, angrily replying that "Prada knows the procedure and standing order he has of sending the letters to my hands so that I might see them first and order them sent on how I see fit, and however long they are delayed in arriving this is still less than they would be by any other way, and so you are reminded for whatever similar occasions may arise."[19] In one instance in 1605 the council, displeased with one of Philip's decisions regarding the *veedor general* (military inspector general) for Flanders, asked that he look at the matter again. Philip's impatient reply shows that he was no mere cipher when it came to decision making: "Order him to depart immediately for Flanders; moreover I find it very inconvenient to keep returning so many times to things which have already been decided, and too much time is lost on all sides in these repetitions." Still not satisfied, the council again tried to change his mind. Philip's reply was a terse "Execute what I have ordered." Although younger and less experienced than his councillors, Philip was still the king and knew it.[20]

The question that remains, however, is: Were Philip's decisions truly his own? For if it is hard to separate the policy-making apparatus into its constituent parts, it is even harder to separate Philip III's role in policy making from that of the duke of Lerma's.

Francisco Gómez de Sandoval y Rojas, fifth marquis of Denia and fourth count of Lerma (he was made duke of Lerma in 1599 during the king's progress in the east), is perhaps one of the most enigmatic political figures to strut across the seventeenth-century stage. Unlike his contemporaries, the duke of Sully and the count of Richelieu, he left neither memoirs nor an apology of his rule. Consequently, we do not know, in his own words, what his aims were, in either domestic or foreign policy. What is more, few of his own papers about his *valimiento* (favoriteship) survive, having probably been burned, and to assess his role we depend upon a relative few pieces of correspondence and some often obscure *billetes,* or notes, to various other ministers and functionaries. But although this lack of a paper trail is a result, partly, of the capriciousness of time and man, it is even more a result of the method of rule employed by Lerma. As Bernardo Garcia has pointed out, Lerma was an experienced courtier who made tremendous use of "face-to-face negotiations, confidences conveniently eliminated, and executive structures parallel to the organs of the ordinary administration."[21] If in fact he ruled all, he did so by often quite nebulous personal ties, the granting or withholding of favors, and the whispered word.

Scion of a great, but destitute, noble household, Lerma had officially entered the prince's service in 1597, when Philip II made him the heir's *caballerizo mayor* (master of horse). The then marquis, more than twice the age of his charge, soon achieved a position of dominance within the prince's household. Soon after his accession to the throne, Philip III allowed Lerma to assume many of the functions of government, thus instituting the office of *valido* (favorite). Over the course of the next few years he gradually arrogated many of the major household offices and much of the patronage power formerly dispersed throughout the court, becoming extremely rich in the process. Eventually, through patronage and family ties, most of the members of the king's court owed the duke allegiance, prompting most historians to think that he came to determine all the policies emanating from the center of politics: "Lerma had a role equal to or greater than his lord in the making of decisions."[22]

Yet while this may be true with respect to domestic affairs, where

Lerma had much to gain and lose in terms of patronage power, it has yet to be proven with respect to the monarchy's foreign policies. Lerma was no more active a participant in the sessions of the Council of State than his master, attending only twenty-two of the 739 sessions held during the years he was in control.[23] It is true that in times of crisis he would step in, but his opinion was often at odds with those of the other councillors and in some cases the king would not agree with his first minister's recommendations. In the fall and winter of 1607–8, at the height of the crisis in Flanders, Lerma even considered retiring because of the criticism being heaped on him by members of the court.[24] Antonio Feros's argument that Lerma could control the opinions given to the king through the use of the junta created in 1601 is not convincing. The junta was composed variously of the count of Miranda; Juan de Idiáquez; the marquis of Velada; the king's confessor, Father Gaspar de Córdoba; and Pedro de Franqueza, count of Villalonga. Only the last of these men owed their position to Lerma's influence. The others had all been elevated to their posts because of their abilities or their services. Miranda and Idiáquez had held positions of considerable influence even in the reign of Philip II.[25] It is inconceivable that such men would have bowed to the will of the first minister, especially when the survival of the monarchy was at stake. And indeed, it is quite clear from an examination of the consultas produced by the junta that the members did not always agree with one another in the way one would expect of a faction. Moreover, at times the junta requested that the full council deliberate matters rather than try to propose the best solutions to problems on its own.[26]

We are left, then, with the weakest of all arguments regarding Lerma's role in the decision-making process: that he stood over the shoulder of the king and dictated Philip's responses to the consultas.[27] For this we have no evidence whatsoever and given the nature of early modern monarchies, with their careful regard for royal prerogative, it is highly unlikely that Philip III would have readily handed over so much of his control. And when important decisions were made, Lerma was often separated from the king either by one of his or his wife's many illnesses or because of negotiations with the Cortes, the parliamentary body of which he was, on important occasions, a member.[28] Without doubt, Lerma had a tremendous influence over the king and probably had a significant role in the decision-making process, but the extent of that role cannot be known. In the end, the comments on the consultas are in the king's hand; the final strategic decisions, as supported by the evidence, were his.

The principal liaison between the Council of State and the king and Lerma were the two secretaries of state. The senior secretary was in charge of correspondence pertaining to Italy and the Mediterranean; the junior had responsibility for correspondence related to countries to the north— Germany, France, Flanders, and England—as well as to Persia and the East and West Indies. All the letters and dispatches sent by the various am- bassadors and ministers outside of Castile to the Council of State passed through the hands of these two secretaries, who opened them, put them in order, and remitted them to the king, usually via Lerma. Letters marked "To the king, our Lord, in his royal hands" were sent to the king un- opened. Once the king or Lerma had read the dispatches, the secretaries forwarded them to appropriate individuals or put them on the agenda to be discussed by the Council of State. The secretaries were also respon- sible for delivering the consultas to the king and then returning them, with the king's annotations, to the council, from which replies and in- structions were drawn up for dispatch, in conformity with what the king had ordered. But it would be a mistake to think of the secretaries as mere functionaries; they were powerful figures within the administration and had access to the information and personnel upon which policy making depended. Andrés de Prada, secretary of state for the north, often acted independently—as he had in 1603, for example, until rebuked by the king. Given his experience, it was perhaps not surprising that he also com- mented on policy. Writing in 1600 to the king's ambassador in the Low Countries, Baltasar de Zúñiga, he openly criticized the use of funding for land forces, arguing that if the money had been devoted to the war at sea, "the reduction of the rebels would have been more advanced since they would have been pressured more than they have been by the taking of a fort."[29] Finally, he was often able to set the agenda of the council meetings, much like a modern speaker of the house, doing so with the collusion of Lerma and the king at the important juncture of Diego de Ibarra's mission in 1607 to sabotage the peace negotiations with the Dutch (see Chapter 9).

In addition to these key figures within the central administration, other important ministers on the fringes of government no doubt had an impact on the determination of policy. Martín de Padilla, Adelantado of

Castile and one of Philip's most important naval commanders, often sent forward his views concerning the state of affairs in the Atlantic theater (see Chapter 4). Then, of course, there is the fairly well-known correspondence between Philip III and the duke of Medina-Sidonia, Captain-General of the ocean fleet and the coast of Andalucia, concerning the plight of Iberia's southern coastline.[30] A constant stream of such correspondence, along with proposals for military strikes and economic retaliations, requests for subsidies or military assistance, and the like, poured in from all corners of the empire, all attempting to persuade the king and council to make policies that would benefit local areas of interest.

But perhaps the most important correspondence directed toward the king and his ministers came from the ambassadors. By the beginning of the seventeenth century, Spain had developed one of the most sophisticated diplomatic corps in Europe, staffed with experienced individuals who were often capable of extraordinary achievements and initiative despite a lack of support from the center.[31] Indeed, in the years immediately after the Truce of Antwerp, Spanish diplomats would do more to preserve Spanish power in Europe than the once invincible Spanish infantry, prompting one Spanish historian to proclaim the reign of Philip III the "golden age of our diplomacy."[32] These ambassadors were given the task of establishing themselves at often hostile foreign courts, where they negotiated on behalf of the king, played advocate for Spanish nationals living in those countries, smoothed over disputes, bribed courtiers, and generally tried to keep war from breaking out. As representatives of the king they played a significant role in maintaining all aspects of their sovereign's reputation. Yet they were not merely the representatives but the eyes and ears of the monarchy. From these foreign courts they sent back to the Council of State and the king a constant stream of correspondence full of whatever information they thought might be useful for determining policy. Both of these roles made ambassadors an important component in the policy-making process. Some, like Baltasar de Zúñiga, ambassador first to the Low Countries, then to France, and finally to the Holy Roman Empire, and the count of Gondomar, ambassador to England, would parlay that importance into positions of influence on the Council of State itself. Although they were, for the most part, circumspect—"it is necessary for a man to swallow his own understanding and content himself with doing that which he is ordered in the best manner possible," wrote Zúñiga to a fellow ambassador—they could at times be openly critical of the decisions

sent to them by the Council of State.[33] Responding to orders forwarded
to him in September 1601 that he rebuke Archduke Albert for opposing
the policies of the king, Zúñiga told the council plainly that such a move
would only "make him suspect my confidentiality, which in the present
state would be very inconvenient and would not gain anything."[34] Indeed,
some ambassadors, like the count of Villamediana in London, even felt
confident enough to give their own opinions about what Philip's policies
should be.[35]

All of this input would have to be sifted, organized, and synthesized
by the ministers in the center, then debated, weighed, and considered before being sent to the king for a final decision. Invariably, by the time the
council's recommendations were ready for the king, further information
would have arrived that would necessitate changing or discarding the recommendations. Even if the king and council did decide on a particular
policy, events would many times have overtaken it. Correspondence between the ambassador in London and the court often took three months
between the initial letter and the receipt of a reply. That between the Low
Countries and the court, four to eight weeks. At any one time Philip and
his ministers had to grapple with the past, provide for the present, and
anticipate the future strategic, political, and economic needs of the monarchy. It was a fearfully complex and time-consuming process. As R. B.
Wernham has rightfully pointed out, foreign policies are the product of a
long series of day-to-day reactions and responses to the actions of all the
states with whom one's government has contact. It takes time for these
ad hoc responses to coalesce into a consistent and coherent strategy.[36]

We turn now to how Philip III and his advisers developed both short-
and long-term strategies for getting out of the wars in northwestern Europe, while simultaneously upholding the traditional strategic priorities
of the monarchy. Although it is impossible to construct a complete picture of grand strategy in the reign of Philip III, we can at least try to
understand the myriad influences, considerations, aims, and resources that
the king and his ministers had to take into account every step of the way.

CHAPTER I

The Failure of the Habsburgs' "Bid for Mastery"

✤ ✤ ✤

Every one may begin a war at his pleasure, but cannot so finish it.
—NICCOLÒ MACHIAVELLI
Discourses

The death of Philip II in September 1598, coming so soon after the signing of the Treaty of Vervins with France in May of the same year, jeopardized much of the political work of the Spanish king's last years. His aim during those years had been to salvage what he could from the wars against France, England, and the Netherlands and leave affairs so that his son "could give attention to the many necessities within the broken and spent kingdoms which he was leaving to him."[1] The burdens produced by this three-front conflict had caused the final "bankruptcy" of his reign in November 1596—and it was this bankruptcy that finally brought Spain to the bargaining table.[2] His Council of State, in a meeting in mid-November 1596, had suggested in its consulta that peace might be better than continuing the war against so many enemies at once. "Peace," the councillors wrote, "is always the final goal of wars if it is possible to achieve it with agreeable conditions; so the door should not be shut on these talks, especially since three wars are being sustained, with the French, English, and rebels as openly acknowledged enemies, not counting other concealed ones that are believed to encourage them."[3] The treaty with France had thus been necessary to reduce costs and enhance the possibilities of success on the other fronts, but this was not the only benefit Philip reaped. In May 1596 France, England, and the Dutch rebels had signed the Treaty of Greenwich, which promised mutual military support on condition that none of the parties make independent peace agreements with the Spanish. By signing with the French king, Philip had managed to drive a wedge between the French and their allies, thus weakening for a time their military effectiveness against him. The "Triple Alliance," so dangerous in its possibilities, had been effectively broken.[4]

Philip's success in this endeavor was not without its costs. however. In the same November consulta, the Council of State had advised Philip that although peace was the desired goal, it might be unwise to make peace with the French while remaining at war with the other two enemies because of the benefits that would accrue for French power. The French king, Henry IV, would consolidate his position within France and make himself powerful, while Philip, instead of recuperating, would be draining himself and his kingdoms in offensive and defensive measures against the others; afterward Henry would return to the battle and find Philip in a weaker state. The council had suggested instead that Philip try for peace across the board, but by means of individual treaties with each enemy, since this arrangement would give the Spaniards more bargaining power.[5] The following year, however, the Spanish military situation deteriorated as a result of the bankruptcy. By March 1597 the council was advising Philip that given the conditions in which his forces found themselves, they could no longer insist on individual treaties if it would mean that all the wars would continue.[6]

But the council, in its assessment of the options, failed to mention one of the chief motivating factors in Philip's policy in these wars: religion, an element that significantly changed the parameters of negotiation in Philip's eyes.[7] To his ambassador at the Vatican, the duke of Sessa, he wrote that as a Catholic prince he found it distasteful to treat with heretics but would consider it for the sake of the peace, which the pope believed would be good for Christianity. If he had to make peace, he thought individual treaties would be better, if only because separate treaties with the Protestant states would be less likely to tarnish the treaty to be made with Henry, since it would thus remain a treaty solely among "Catholic" princes.[8] But in another letter to Sessa that same day, Philip gave indications of having reservations about *any* peace with England given that his foremost aim was, and had always been, religious freedom for English Catholics.[9] And he made it clear that, although it was an aim he may have been forced to abandon for political reasons, he would like to see it secured by other means: "In the matter of England, in case it should be necessary to bring her [Elizabeth I, queen of England] into the advertised peace . . . His Holiness ought to take it upon himself to bring about as a first condition that the exercise of Catholicism be freely extended to the Catholics throughout the realm."[10]

In April, as a last ditch effort to avoid having to treat with the English, Philip, following the advice of Colonel William Semple, proposed to Cardinal-Archduke Albert, governor of the Low Countries, a third invasion of England, this time in the north. He suggested putting three thousand men from the Army of Flanders ashore north of the Humber River in Yorkshire with enough arms to rally around them ten or twelve thousand Catholics, "that part of the country being the most Catholic of England and more inclined to revolt and from which it would be possible to raise good cavalry, the people of those parts being the most skilled horsemen in England."[11] But in their review of these plans in July, the council informed Philip that, in spite of the benefits such a blow to the English would bring to Spain's reputation and to the Catholics of England, the forces at their disposal were not sufficient for the invasion and the logistical support, nor were the intelligence reports of their English Catholic informants, Father Joseph Creswell and Thomas Fitzherbert, sufficiently unbiased to be trustworthy concerning the willingness of English Catholics to support the Spanish cause. Religious issues, though always of paramount importance in policy making at the Spanish court, were not in this instance allowed to cloud the judgment of those entrusted with the maintenance of the Spanish monarchy. Thus the councillors resolved that the land invasion be left for a time when "God should be more disposed to assist."[12]

Philip, however, gambled on one last effort; in September he sent his third armada against the British Isles.[13] This fleet, almost as large as the one for the 1588 invasion, consisted of 136 ships, more than 13,000 men, and 300 horses, but once again the forces of nature intervened to disperse the fleet before it had even entered the channel, resulting in the loss of 28 ships. The commander of the armada, Martín de Padilla, Adelantado of Castile, wrote candidly to Philip in October explaining the disaster of his armada in much the same terms used to explain the 1588 defeat ("God's obvious design"), but with more pessimism: "Even though the intent that was had of reducing England and Flanders to the service of God and your majesty was so virtuous in itself, it appears that God has not wanted to accept this service, something which should give a lot of comfort, because Our Lord is not accustomed to give similar disfavors without just causes." Philip could only reply that "all possible was done. God punishes us for our sins." His final attempt to defeat the English had failed, and with its failure ended his exclusive direction of Spanish policy in the north.[14]

By the beginning of 1598, Cardinal-Archduke Albert was forcing Philip II's hand by making the decisions on the spot in the Low Countries. Despite Philip's explicit instructions to the contrary, Albert, during the Franco-Spanish peace conference in January, agreed to the restitution of Calais—Spain's only deepwater port on the English Channel and a strategic city for any successful invasion of England—to the French, explaining to Philip that "even though I have considered what your majesty has written to me of this, and the order that you have lately sent to me about it . . . things are so changed and different in the present than they were then that the ruined state of them has obliged me to resolve to concede the said restitution." In the same letter he informed Philip that he had begun separate talks with the English through the mediation of Charles Paget, an Englishman then residing in Brussels. These initial probes proved worth developing and in February Albert wrote to Philip requesting a separate commission to treat with Elizabeth; England would now be included in the talks underway with the French.[15]

A few days later, however, the French, not willing to make their peace with Spain contingent upon English demands, tilted in the same direction as Philip, telling the Spanish commissioners that they would proceed even without the English; Henry depended on himself and God alone.[16] Effectively the treaty between Albert, Philip, and Henry had been secretly assured. To maintain the appearance of propriety, however, the French had to participate in formal talks with the deputies of England and the United Provinces during March and April. In the midst of these conferences the English and Dutch tried desperately to persuade the French to continue their offensive and defensive league. But captured letters from Albert to Philip informed the English of the agreements between the French and Spanish. Despite the vehement protestations of the English deputies to Henry over this matter, he insisted on denying any collusion, and the English deputies were forced to return to England for further instructions. In the interim the Treaty of Vervins was made public.[17]

The announcement of the treaty between Philip and Henry in May 1598 no doubt stunned the leaders of the Dutch provinces and the English government. To them the Spanish "success" in securing the treaty meant that the States were simultaneously deprived of an important financial ally and presented with an enemy now able to bring more forces to bear against them. The English queen, for her part, found herself compelled to carry the whole burden of protecting the States since she had no intention of leaving them to fight Spain single-handedly.

The English and Dutch, having been abandoned by the French, scrambled to concert some effective action. On the English side there was a division between those favoring the option to join in a general peace with the Spanish (there was a six-month window within which they could do so) and those favoring continuance of the war. The queen herself and her favorite, Robert Devereaux, second earl of Essex, were of the latter persuasion, while her leading minister, William Cecil, first Baron Burghley and lord treasurer, was of a more pacific inclination.[18] The Dutch, on the other hand, seemingly had no questions about what policy to follow: their delegates at the peace talks had been instructed from the start to do what they could "to break off the conference between the King [Henry] and the Cardinal [Archduke Albert] about the peace."[19]

In June, Elizabeth sent Sir Francis Vere, commander of the English expeditionary forces in the United Provinces, to the States-General, the governing body of the rebel provinces, to determine if they wished to carry on the war and if so what they would contribute to the effort.[20] Elizabeth was determined to use the current Dutch dependence on her to secure better terms than she had received in the Anglo-Dutch treaty of 1585.[21] In the years since that treaty, the United Provinces had launched themselves on the road to world economic primacy, pitting themselves directly against English interests. An important cause for the spectacular growth that Dutch trade witnessed during this period was the ironic fact that it was the English and not the Dutch who were denied access to Spanish and Portuguese markets. In May 1585 Philip II had confiscated all English and Dutch ships in Iberian ports and implemented a full-scale trade embargo against the two powers, but his inability to come to an agreement with the Hansa, who were needed to fill the role of the Dutch merchants in securing Baltic grain and military supplies after his intervention in the French civil wars, forced him to turn once again to the Dutch and their commercial network.[22] He therefore lifted the embargo against them while leaving in place that against the English merchants, who were not in a position to help him in his war aims. Thomas Edmondes, Elizabeth's ambassador at Paris, stated the English case succinctly to the Venetian ambassador: "The people are very desirous of peace, for it is they who live on navigation and trade, and so feel the burden of these times. They

are shut out from Spain and the ports of the Empire on the ground of
their seizure of vessels carrying provisions to Spain. Longer voyages, such
as to Italy and elsewhere, are possible only for those who have capital. The
English accordingly are reduced to getting their goods through Holland
and Zealand. The Dutch, though at war, are not excluded from trading
with Spain, and so have amazingly increased their wealth."[23]

There were then certain advantages to be gained for English trade
should Elizabeth decide to join the French in peace with Spain, advantages of which the Dutch were undoubtedly aware. Yet, offsetting these
advantages was the fear that without assistance the rebellious provinces
might not manage to maintain their independence, simultaneously de-
priving Elizabeth of the hope for reimbursement for her costs and rekindling English fears of invasion from a wholly Spanish Netherlands.[24] This
consideration meant that the Netherlands could not be abandoned. But, as
part of the price for continued English assistance, the States were to cease
trade with their southern cousins in the Spanish Netherlands, thus level-
ing the playing field commercially. As one irate Englishman fumed, "If
they [the Dutch] would have wars, they should refrain [from] victualling
and providing the enemy."[25]

At the end of July the States sent delegates to the queen to settle the
terms of a new alliance, which was accordingly concluded on 16 August.
By this agreement Elizabeth pledged to furnish men to garrison Flushing,
Brill, and other forts but was no longer responsible for providing or paying for an expeditionary force; those currently serving in the Netherlands
would come under the command of the States. In addition she arranged
for yearly repayments of the States' debt to her and secured a mutual
pledge of assistance in case of Spanish invasion.

The States were clearly in a weaker position as a result of Philip's
diplomacy, but he did not stop there. Simultaneously with the peace,
he made arrangements to hand over sovereignty of the Spanish Netherlands to his daughter Isabel and her future husband, Cardinal-Archduke
Albert.[26] The States-General of the obedient provinces accepted them as
their lawful sovereigns on August 22. Transferring the sovereignty of the
Netherlands to Albert and Isabel, Philip hoped, would satisfy the rebellious provinces' demands for independence.

But it did not take long for the Dutch to realize correctly that the independence of the archdukes was only nominal and that the Spanish had
no intentions of permitting the return of Protestants to their provinces.[27]

By the terms of a secret addendum to the donation, the Spanish army was to remain in the Low Countries and be controlled by the Spanish court.[28] This element, and the third clause of the marriage contract, which enjoined the archdukes to recover the disobedient provinces and bring them back to the Catholic faith, suggest that Philip had no real intention of letting the northern provinces remain independent, and therefore no real desire for peace.[29] The policy of his latter years, therefore, seemed less pacifistic than pragmatic. It was not so much peace for its own sake that he wanted but rather peace as a means to the reintegration of the Spanish Habsburg patrimony. This was Philip II's sole instance of ideological flexibility with regard to his long-term strategic aims. He was temporarily "giving up" territory so that it would be possible eventually to get it back. But the question on everyone's lips when Philip II finally died on 13 September 1598 was, Would the new king continue his father's policies?

It was soon clear that the new king was not to be ruled by the dictates of his father, in either administrative or foreign policy. As is well known, a few hours after Philip II's death, his trusted first minister, Cristóbal de Moura, entered the new king's chambers with papers of state to be signed, only to have Philip III order him to set them aside for the marquis of Denia to handle. Philip then relieved Moura of all his household duties.[30]

Throughout October there was some fear that Moura's fate awaited the three other senior ministers, Juan de Idíaquez, the count of Chinchón, and the marquis of Velada.[31] In the end these men remained at court but were no longer given the monopoly of power they once held. After only a week in power, Philip III, in order to reduce the weight of the opinions of these senior councillors, who had so often acted in an extra-official capacity, restructured the Council of State. He added new members of higher noble standing, and ordered that henceforth he was to be consulted after every meeting. A week later the junta de noche appointed by Philip II to oversee his son's government was abolished. Thereafter the Council of State assumed greater importance in the new king's government, meeting weekly during the first months and comprising most of the major nobility by November.[32]

Even more indicative of an administrative change of direction was Philip's new emphasis on the Council of War. To this body he appointed distinguished military commanders who now sat, on average, twice as often as under his predecessor, a trend that disturbed Spain's enemies, who received word that "only such as are fit for the wars are in estimation with him [Philip]" and that "all the old martial men are sent for, and soldiers are training."[33]

This belligerence was likewise apparent in Philip's first speech to the Council of State, in which he pointed out to the councillors the two elements he thought essential for the "stability and increase of his crowns": that the government be in accordance with the divine law, that is, that it follow the dictates of the Catholic religion, and that the forces necessary to carry on the wars in defense of the Catholic faith be sufficient to obtain victory, "since God has given us power and people enough to accomplish it." He charged them also to be attentive to the swiftness of prosecuting the wars, since by this means his predecessors had obtained fame and glory.[34]

But as his father had been made frustratingly aware in his last years, policy decisions were now made at two nodes in the Habsburg circuit: Madrid . . . and Brussels. The warlike attitude emanating from Philip's court showed that the two courts were separated by more than miles. Cardinal-Archduke Albert had been sent to Flanders as governor-general in 1595; there he had been active first in the interventions in France and later in securing the peace at Vervins. Having been on the scene and having fought in the front lines, he was acutely aware of the weakness of the Habsburg position in the Low Countries. As has been shown, he had been prepared to contradict the orders of Philip if he thought it in the best interests of Flanders. After the donation of these states to the archdukes in May 1598, Albert was even less inclined to allow them to continue to be the bearers of so much expense and trouble. He wanted peace with both England and the United Provinces so that he might enjoy his new bequest. The states of the province of Hainaut had instinctively realized this shortly after hearing the news of the donation of the Low Countries to the archdukes, writing to Albert that "to find this peace which is so much desired and is even more necessary to your highness because it is the principal, nay the sole, foundation for the happiness of your future marriage, you should, under humble correction, try every means to fathom the intentions of the King of France, the Queen of England and the Dutch, so as once and for all to put an end to this long unhappy war."[35]

In August 1598 the archduke had written to Philip II from Brussels indicating his continuing desire to bring the English into the peace. He had informed the king that the English were still disposed to peace but that they feared he did not have the necessary powers to treat with them for-

mally since they believed—rightly—that he could not make decisions independently. They therefore refused to make the first open moves, asking
instead that the initial approach be from the Habsburgs. Albert suggested
that after his and Isabel's upcoming marriage, he should make advances
to the English on behalf of the infanta as the independent sovereign of
a new country, using the argument that to remain at war would in fact
be declaring a new war with a non-Spanish country. He argued that such
a move would save face for the Spanish king, since the entreaties would
not seem to be originating from the Madrid court, and that such a course
might also open the way for a settlement with the rebels.[36] In any event,
no reply reached him before his departure on 14 September for Spain to
consecrate his marriage to the infanta. And because Philip II had died the
day before, it would now be up to the new king, a king whose inclina-
tions were not demonstrably in favor of a peaceful arrangement, to decide
the direction of policy toward both the English and the Dutch.

Everyone learned soon enough that the new attitude of the Spanish
court was not to be one of peace. Within two months of taking over the
reins of power, Philip III, reversing the position his father had taken after
1590, imposed a comprehensive trade embargo on the Dutch in order to
force them into submission.[37] The Spanish had no intention of giving up
on the northern provinces. The new king's belligerence was not reserved
solely for the Dutch, however. He wasted no time in agreeing to a plan
initially proposed by Federico Spínola to Philip II in 1597, which involved
taking five thousand men and a detachment of horse and seizing a bridgehead in England, to which he would then transport the Army of Flanders.[38] Albert, however, was not about to limit his possibilities, and even
while he reluctantly gave his permission to Spínola to raise two thousand men in Flanders, his representatives were attempting to open talks
with Elizabeth.[39] Henceforth the courts of Brussels and Madrid would be
working at cross-purposes for much of the time, each trying to pressure
the other into following a foreign policy seen from its own point of view.

Upon his departure for Spain, Albert had left the administration of
the provinces in the hands of his cousin, Cardinal Andrea of Austria, who
in December decided to send an envoy to the English queen to test the
waters.[40] He instructed Jerome Coomans to go secretly to England and
procure an audience with the queen, during which he was to suggest the
possibility of a treaty between the sovereigns that might also lead to a
reconciliation with the northern provinces.[41] He was also instructed to

take care that nothing give the English the impression that the archdukes and their representatives were acting unilaterally, thus keeping the English guessing as to which of the Habsburg courts was soliciting the peace talks.[42]

If Philip had knowledge of these negotiations, he let them proceed, being more interested in the upcoming journey to the east to meet his bride, Margarita of Austria, traveling with the archduke by way of Italy. He departed from Madrid on 22 January 1599 accompanied by his sister, Isabel; the marquis of Denia; the major court officials; and the nobility, arriving in Valencia on 4 February. He would not return until the fall.[43]

During these months in the eastern kingdoms little action was taken in the realm of diplomacy. Indeed, Philip seemed almost oblivious to the need to define a foreign policy, concentrating more on winning an early victory than on setting a long-range strategic agenda. Instead the young king preferred to act the part of war leader, relying to a large extent on his restructured Council of War for advice, a group that included the members of the Council of State but was augmented by men more experienced in the military affairs that appealed to the young king.[44] The Council of War met no fewer than sixty-eight times during the progress in order to plan the defense against Elizabeth's rumored invasion fleet and to discuss the options for Philip's own ad hoc plans concerning England and Ireland.[45] In comparison, the Council of State, the body responsible for coordinating the various demands on the monarchy and for recommending a comprehensive policy, met only four times during the entire trip, and even these meetings lacked the counts of Chinchón and Miranda, two of the more influential members.[46]

This lack of a comprehensive strategic policy, and the failure to address the complex decision-making issues occasioned by the transfer of sovereignty over the Netherlands meant that during this first year the military and political situation in the Low Countries had deteriorated.[47] Francisco de Mendoza, the Admiral of Aragon, had been left in charge of the Army of Flanders while Archduke Albert was in Spain. Mendoza, heir to one of the most prestigious titles in Aragon, had been named *mayordomo mayor* to the archduke in 1595 and had accompanied him to Flanders. In the summer of 1597 Albert appointed him to the post of Captain-General of the Cavalry, the highest-ranking subordinate command in the Army of Flanders, and the following summer left him in temporary command of the army. His orders were to march his army across the Rhine and secure a

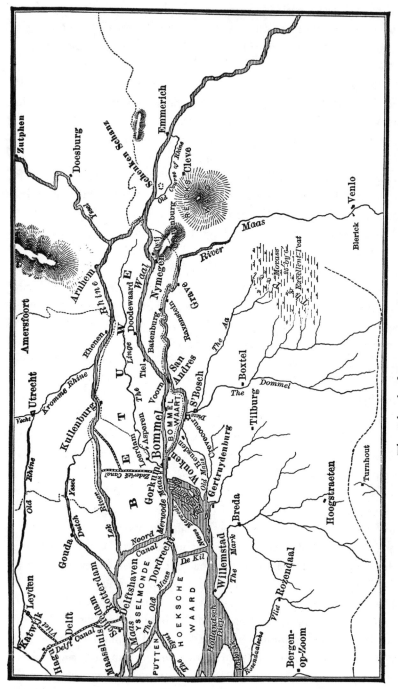

1. The Island of Bommel and Environs
(from Markham, *The Fighting Veres*)

bridgehead in the northern provinces, where he would then quarter his troops at no expense to the government in Brussels. After some early successes in October—he took the towns of Orsoy, Rheinberg, Wesel, Rees, and Emerick—the admiral was soon halted by a Dutch army under the command of Count Maurice of Nassau, second (and Protestant) son of William of Orange and new Stadholder (chief magistrate) of Holland and Zeeland. As a result of that encounter, Mendoza was forced to turn back and winter his army in the duchy of Cleves, in the process losing two of the towns he had captured.[48]

At the start of the new campaigning season in April, influenced by courtiers wishing occasion to profit by war and disrupt Spanish authority, Cardinal Andrea was persuaded to venture forth to take charge of the army.[49] Against the advice of his Spanish councillors and administrators, he attempted to seize command from the admiral and move the army against the island of Bommel, a strategic site between the Maas and Waal (fig. 1). Mendoza at first refused to relinquish command of his army, but threatened with beheading, he soon backed down and the army was ordered to Bommel. The dispute between the two leaders caused division within the army and resulted finally in the complete failure of the mission, along with high casualties. By the middle of summer, the army, low on food and ammunition and unable to take the town of Bommel, resolved to construct a fort—named San Andrés, after the cardinal—on the part of the island they controlled. In August, as the fort neared completion, the cardinal, hearing of the imminent arrival of the archdukes, departed for Brussels and left the admiral in command, "getting out of the business of the whole summer [only] the construction of the fort of San Andrés, so costly of men and money, and of so little fruit, as has been seen."[50]

Throughout the journey to and from Valencia for his wedding, Albert had been in constant communication with the Admiral of Aragon and knew of the worsening condition of the Army in Flanders.[51] At the start of the trip, in November 1598, Albert had already asked the king's favorite, the marquis of Denia, to see to the provisions for the army—especially those needed to put an end to mutinies in Antwerp, Lier, and Ghent—repeating his pleas throughout the early part of the following year while he was delayed in Italy.[52] In March 1599, Denia, already in charge of the dispensation of funds, provided Albert with two hundred thousand ducats.[53] This sum, however, was apparently not sufficient to cover the archduke's needs, and in May, after his arrival, he asked Denia that the first two

months' provisions for 1599 be sent forward to Flanders and that the rest
be given to him to carry when he departed the following month. The king
finally provided Albert with the payment for 1599 but would not commit to anything more permanent, promising only that he would provide
"the assistance that he could" in the coming years, an ambiguous phrase
that Albert, not surprisingly, immediately asked to be clarified. Four days
prior to his departure from Barcelona, Albert wrote to Denia that a fixed
sum would be better for Habsburg interests than the unclear aid promised by Philip. He suggested that if it was publicly understood that the
king was committed to providing such a specific sum on a regular basis,
then Albert's government would have fewer financial, military, or political
problems.[54]

This ambiguity on the part of Philip toward Flanders, promising complete assistance yet delaying the provision of funds, stresses the difficult
circumstances occasioned by the transfer of sovereignty. Indeed, the renunciation of the southern provinces to the archdukes was already viewed
by some—including possibly Philip himself—as a serious error, both strategically and for the reputation of Spain. Francesco Soranzo, the Venetian
ambassador in Madrid, reported that "it is certain that were the deed to
do again the alienation of the States would not take place. The grandees
openly declare that it would have been better to have given Portugal to
the infanta rather than Flanders, so important do they consider Flanders
to be, both on account of the ocean traffic and as a bridle on France."[55]

It was certainly reasonable to ask what Philip would get in return for
the payments given to Albert. Who would determine the policy of the
Low Countries if the Spanish kingdoms were paying for it? And Albert
certainly did not appear above using a subtle form of blackmail against the
king. In June he wrote to the duke implying that if Philip did not provide
sufficient funds, then the archdukes just might not be able to guarantee
their "unity and conformity with all the States of His Majesty, as [they]
ought to."[56]

It is difficult to tell at this point in his reign how Philip considered the
situation of Flanders, and the scarcity of records for the Council of State
for this year means that we lack, too, the ministers' estimates of the fact
of the newly changed relationship existing between the courts of Madrid
and Brussels. Consequently, no matter how significant a moment in the
history of the Spanish monarchy, we do not know how Philip felt when,
on 26 May 1599, he became the first Habsburg king to have to appoint

an ambassador to his former territories in the Low Countries.[57] The man chosen for the office was the infantry captain, Baltasar de Zúñiga, who, as a staff officer aboard the flagship of the Gran Armada of 1588, had been specially selected to tell Philip II of the fleet's failure and its return by way of the North Atlantic. After a most successful career in the diplomatic corps, he would become the most influential member of the Council of State and effectively prime minister during the transition to the rule of Philip IV and the count-duke Olivares.[58]

Zúñiga did not come to his new office without some qualifications. He was the second son of Gerónimo de Zúñiga y Fonseca, count of Monterrey, and Inés de Velasco, sister of the Constable of Castile, one of the most influential grandees of Castile. His father had served as Philip II's ambassador to the Council of Trent and his older brother, Gaspar, was viceroy of New Spain and later governor of Peru. In his youth Zúñiga had been sent to the court, but in 1582, having grown tired of the leisure there, he accompanied his brother-in-law Enrique de Guzman, the count of Olivares, on his embassy to Rome; there Zúñiga's talents in the arts of diplomacy "were awakened by the variety of serious business he handled and countries with which he communicated." After leaving Rome and serving some time in the armies of Spain, he had returned to the court to assume a post as Gentleman of the Table (*gentilhombre de la boca*), where he was groomed by the old king himself for "great things." We are told that it was Philip II who ordered that Zúñiga be made ambassador to the archdukes.[59] In any event he was with Philip III in Barcelona when it came time to appoint one.[60] He was provided with a senior secretary of dispatch, a secretary of languages, and a yearly salary of six thousand escudos.[61] Accompanied by the newly appointed ambassador and carrying coffers filled with monies provided by Philip and Denia, the archdukes departed Barcelona for Flanders on 7 June 1599.

In the meantime the Council of State learned that Elizabeth was seriously ill and began to consider more carefully a possible Habsburg policy toward England. Up to this point one of the main motivating factors in the Spanish monarchs' English policy was, as we have seen, to aid English Catholics in their struggle for toleration. But after three failed armadas, there was a growing feeling on the council—no doubt a residual effect of Philip II's final policy positions—that force might not be the best means of obtaining that objective. According to Joseph Creswell, some members of the council even thought that "Spain [had] been hurt by giving aid to the English Catholics" and considered it "treason to advise [his] Majesty to try on another occasion to send help there, seeing that it was impossible."[62] The councillors were therefore ready to look at other options. Shortly after the archdukes' departure, the council members, in one of their four meetings during the progress in the eastern kingdoms, considered a paper of Father Creswell concerning the English Catholics' desires for the succession of England in the event of Elizabeth's death. They discussed the hard choices facing the young king. If he did not respond to the Catholics' request for a nomination, they would become suspicious that he himself desired the crown and wished only to add England to the rest of his territories, something even his most ardent supporters there did not wish. But if he named someone else, he faced losing the rights to that crown, which he held through the house of Portugal, the person named would bleed the forces and treasury of Spain in establishing himself, and all the other pretenders to the throne would consider him as an enemy. They therefore advised Philip to thank the Catholics and tell them that he would take the matter under advisement, keeping the pope informed of his plans, and that as a minimum he would require the person named to be neither a heretic (a specific reference to James of Scotland) nor English.[63]

It was clear to the Spanish government that Philip stood a good chance of securing at least his own candidate, if not himself, on the throne of England. Logic suggested that those chances would be enhanced should England and Spain be at peace when Elizabeth left the throne vacant. It was just about then that Coomans arrived from Brussels to give the Spaniards a direct account of his negotiations with Elizabeth. They were obviously pleased to find that the queen, perhaps fearing Spain's fourth armada preparations, was willing to continue the negotiations, for a week later, while the archdukes and ambassador Zúñiga were still en route to Brussels, Philip dispatched full powers for them to treat for peace with the English.[64]

But the future succession of England was but one factor motivating the Spanish to consider peace in the north. Spanish policy always consisted of a constantly shifting set of immediate priorities. No doubt the Spanish court also thought, as the French king suspected, that freed from their commitments in the north they might aid the duke of Savoy in his growing dispute with France. In 1588 Savoy, taking advantage of French internal troubles and the distractions of the Spanish armada, had seized the marquisate of Saluzzo, in the Piedmontese Alps, from France. Henry IV had tried to demand the marquisate's restoration during the negotiations at Vervins in 1598, but to no avail; Savoy refused to be cowed by his Spanish allies, whose own interests in the affair concerned the security of the Spanish Road, that vital land corridor through which the forces in Flanders were resupplied. In the years immediately following the Treaty of Vervins, the issue began to escalate toward military confrontation.[65]

There was, however, some cause to fear the archduke's commitment to support the Spanish moves. On 25 August 1599 he wrote to the king expressing his desire to give Zúñiga complete responsibility in the talks with England in order to avoid the contortions he would face should the English deputies suggest that he had no real authority from Philip.[66] It may have been the case that Albert wanted to distance himself from the negotiations if the king insisted on pushing for his own ends. Likewise, there were indications that he did not support Spanish policy concerning Savoy, a policy that would have a direct bearing on him. In a letter the same day, Zúñiga reported to the king that there were some in the retinue of the archduke, possibly even the archduke himself, who believed that Albert should not break with the French over the issue of Saluzzo—despite the clause in the donation of the Low Countries that required the archdukes to be at war with the same enemies as Spain—since he could not afford to carry on the war against both France and England.[67]

The negotiations with England had been put on hold until the archduke arrived in Brussels with full powers to treat with Elizabeth.[68] In the meantime neither side had proved willing to stand down their naval forces. Eventually, showing the ease with which arms races escalate into confrontation, the English fleet, comprising some eighty-four ships, finally sailed and appeared off the island of Grand Canary on 26 August and took the city of Las Palmas. The attack forced the Adelantado, Martín de Padilla, once again commander of the Spanish naval forces, to take his incomplete fleet in pursuit of the enemy. As a result of the Adelantado's actions it proved impossible to complete the new armada, thus precluding any chance for a large-scale attack on either Ireland or England that year.[69] The English had once again proven that they could disrupt Spanish invasion plans. That the desire for peace on both sides was strong nonetheless is evidenced by the fact that the actions of these fleets at the end of August caused no halt to the negotiations.

On 20 September, having arrived in Brussels, Albert sent word to

Elizabeth that he was ready to appoint the commissioners for the talks. Her reply, however, was delayed a month by the sudden return of the earl of Essex from Ireland. In August 1598, Essex had been appointed to command the new royal army, some 17,300 strong, being sent to quell a major Catholic rebellion in Ireland, led by Hugh O'Neill, earl of Tyrone, and supported at times by the Spaniards.[70] Essex's army was the largest ever sent to Ireland and was three times larger than the English expeditionary force in the Netherlands. Given a task beyond his abilities and poor material support from England, Essex soon encountered difficulties. By the end of summer 1599 he and his forces were holed up in garrisons and would not attack the Irish. In September he met with Tyrone, signed a six-week truce with provision for renewal until the following May, and immediately afterward returned, without authorization, to Elizabeth's court. Because he had failed to subdue the rebellion, the English found themselves in precisely the same situation as their Spanish enemies, with a war abroad and a rebellion in their own territories.[71] Elizabeth's reply to the archduke's initiative was understandably favorable and showed a willingness on her part to treat in good faith. Still trying to protect her own interests in northwestern Europe, however, she insisted that her allies, the United Provinces, needed to be notified of her intention, and on 27 October she sent Noel Caron, the Dutch spokesman in London, to learn the decision of the States-General.[72]

While the English were waiting for the reply from the Dutch, the Spanish, not a little shaken by yet another "defeat" of their invasion plans, were proceeding with their preparations for the peace talks. In mid-October Philip had sent Zúñiga more instructions and a corresponding amplification of his powers, telling him that "as my minister you should negotiate with the most freedom and least considerations," an indication of the immense trust the king placed in this diplomat, despite its being his first appointment.[73] In December, probably in an attempt to emphasize Spanish interests over those of the archdukes, Philip appointed as one of his representatives Hernando (or Fernando) Carrillo, his legal councillor in Castile and former superintendent of military justice in Flanders. Zúñiga and Carrillo would balance Albert's two representatives, Jean Richardot, president of his council, and the Admiral of Aragon.[74]

To the Spanish the run up to the negotiations looked to be going fairly smoothly and they undoubtedly felt they would be in a strong bargaining position, if they could rein in the archduke. Had they known that

Noel Caron would return to London on 19 December with the States' resolution to carry on the fight and that Elizabeth would resolve to initiate the talks without them, the Spanish undoubtedly would have been overjoyed. But given the delays in communication between Brussels and Spain, they would have learned of the good news with the bad. For just one week after the Dutch were deserted by Elizabeth, the Army of Flanders, their arrears not paid by the archduke upon his return and winter settling upon them, erupted into the largest mutiny since 1594, seizing Hamont and soon after inspiring the revolt of garrisons in Crèvecoeur and San Andrés fort, the latter having recently been erected through the expenditure of scarce resources.[75]

CHAPTER 2

Setbacks

❦ ❦ ❦

God grants victories as he is served.

—PHILIP III
upon learning of the Spanish defeat at Nieuwpoort

Why, if the Spanish ministers had such reason for optimism about securing peace, were the troops of the Army of Flanders in open mutiny as the new century opened? For the four-year period 1596–1600, the paymaster-general of the army received in excess of sixty million florins from the Spanish treasury, more than for the four-year period of Spain's preparations for the 1588 campaign against England. And although Castilian remittances to Flanders had dropped somewhat during 1599, the more than three million ducats provided that year were certainly not dramatically lower than in other years (fig. 2).[1] Where, then, had the money gone if not to the army? The answer probably lies in a statement made by Francesco Contarini, the Venetian ambassador to France, in January 1599: "Archduke Albert is already spending on his journey the money intended for the war next year."[2]

That Albert borrowed heavily for his journey is supported by his letter of 6 December 1598 to the marquis of Denia requesting that payment be sent to cover the money he had borrowed in Milan, for, he wrote, "lacking other remedies, I had to take advantage of the credit of 200,000 escudos that the king and his late father gave me as a bonus just for my journey, saying they would send it later." Even with this, he was just able to scrape enough together to leave Brussels, although later "the need to bestow rewards and entertain himself" forced him to borrow the same sum once he reached Milan. Approximately 412,000 ducats, over 13 percent of the remittances for 1599, was therefore spent just so the archduke could travel from Brussels to Milan! It can be assumed that he spent as much, if not more, on the journey from Milan to Valencia, the wedding

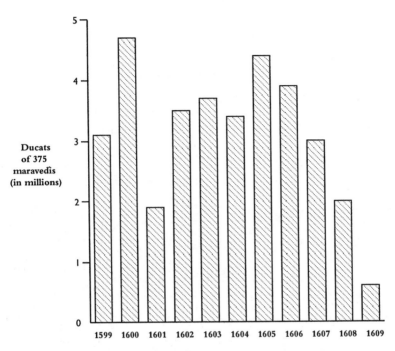

2. Remittances from the Spanish Court to Flanders,
1599 to June 1609

These figures reflect all monies sent to the archdukes, not just those
used for military purposes (from *Relacion del dinero remitido á Flándes,*
AGS Estado 626, fol. 43; printed in *CODOIN* 36, 509–44). The figures
omit money paid by the southern provinces after 1600 for the
maintenance of more than twenty thousand men in garrisons
(Gachard, *Actes des Etats Généraux de 1600,* 553–60).

ceremony, and the journey back again to Brussels, this time accompanied
by the infanta, whose jewel-studded saddle alone was estimated to have
cost 200,000 florins! In sum, perhaps a third or more of the money needed
for the army in Flanders was probably spent on this extravagant progress.[3]

The financial costs to the new king of giving up the sovereignty of
some of his territories were all too clear. And these would have repercussions not only in the military sphere but in the political as well, going
far toward undermining Spanish strategy in western Europe. As Baltasar

de Zúñiga noted to the duke of Sessa, the mutiny of Spanish forces in
Flanders came "in a very bad conjuncture" and was probably responsible
for the English delay in sending someone to discuss the preliminaries,
a delay that did not bode well for the negotiations, demonstrating the
close connection between military and foreign policy. Nevertheless, Zúñiga had been sent to Brussels with explicit instructions to open peace
talks with the English, and he would have to persevere in his efforts to get
the English to the table in spite of Spain's strategic and financial losses.[4]

Yet, these setbacks certainly put some constraint on what Zúñiga and
the Spanish could demand from the English. Zúñiga wrote to Sessa that,
concerning the issue of religion, Philip had instructed him "that in no
way should anything be concluded that does not settle the matter of freedom of religion in that kingdom." But Zúñiga himself, already showing signs of the prudence and realism that would distinguish his career,
and no doubt reflecting the worry caused by the military and political
situations, knew that such unflinching ideological stands would probably
not be possible given Spain's circumstances. "And so Your Excellency," he
wrote Sessa, "can assure His Holiness and his ministers of the care His
Majesty shows in cases touching religion. But unless it should appear differently to Your Excellency, I think it would be wise that this should be
indicated to the pope as a general rule without obligating ourselves to
anything for His Holiness, since we do not know what necessity will dictate." Zúñiga's appraisal of Spain's ability to dictate terms was therefore
not at all hopeful, and although he received word from the English that
the negotiations were to proceed, he had to point out that he feared the
English would want to shut out all discussion of religion.[5]

Sessa, in his worry-filled reply at the end of the month, agreed with
Zúñiga that the conjuncture of circumstances, whether in the north or
throughout the rest of Europe, certainly did not appear favorable to the
Habsburgs:

> I am worried to see by what you write that the negotiation of peace
> with England and the reduction of the rebels should run on so long and
> with so little hope, at least insofar as the latter, which, unless I deceive
> myself, I think is the most substantial. For the more we are friends of
> the French or that we should be of the English, the more they [France
> and England] will enjoy the fruit of the peace and they will not lack the
> means of aiding our enemies and inciting them secretly. And since our
> men begin to mutiny, it is a sure sign that we don't have the money nec-

essary to sustain the war. The humors of Germany and the carelessness and melancholies which, according to Don Guillen [de San Clemente, ambassador to the Empire], the Emperor suffers from, give cause to fear changes in the Empire, all to our harm. On top of this, if because of our failure to settle the issue of Saluzzo the peace with France has to be broken, we will not have sufficient means to cover everything. His Majesty has many very great councillors of State and so we should hope that he will know how to free us from the storm that these clouds threaten.[6]

While these storms brewed around the Spanish monarchy, the diplomats in the north proceeded to set the stage for the conference between the Habsburg and English commissioners. On 17 January Elizabeth's appointee, Thomas Edmondes, arrived in Brussels to discuss the particulars of the meeting, and two days later was presented to the archdukes, where, on behalf of Elizabeth, he expressed the English willingness to send commissioners and then suggested that the conference be held on English soil. After two weeks of haggling, both sides finally agreed to a conference at a neutral site in France: Boulogne. In addition, the archduke's ministers agreed to send Luis Verreyken, the archduke's chief secretary of state, to see the queen and discuss the terms of the treaty. Edmondes certainly thought things were going well and believed the English were clearly in the stronger bargaining position. To his chagrin, however, no one on the opposite side seemed to recognize this fact. After agreeing to Boulogne as the chosen location, Edmondes was finally able to see the archduke's commission to treat. He was upset to learn that the wording of the document suggested that the queen was in fact soliciting the peace![7]

Nevertheless, Edmondes was convinced it was the Habsburgs who were desperate for peace. In Flanders he noted that the people in general wanted peace, since they found it a great burden to sustain the war against their northern brethren. Moreover there appeared to be widespread discontent with the Spanish presence in the Low Countries and the heavy sums the southern Netherlanders yearly surrendered to pay for it. He pointed out to Sir Robert Cecil, the secretary of state, that the mutiny and disorders of the army, the lack of funds in the treasury to meet expenses, and the fears they had concerning the resurgence of French power all suggested that the Habsburgs needed and wanted the peace above all else. Puffed with patriotic pride and trusting his sources from Spain, Edmondes even declared that peace was desired "both by the king [Philip] and the whole countrie, which is wearie of the long continuance of the warres, and the afflictions they have receaved chiefly by our nation." And of Philip himself, Edmondes wrote:"It is said that he is of no stirring spyritt, wholly governed by the marquis of Denia, who also is not maliciously afflicted, but rather desiring a peace, as best serving to maintain his auctoritie."[8]

Henry IV of France, however, as an outsider to this peace, could afford to be more realistic. In a letter to his ambassador in London, Jean de Thumery, monsieur de Boissise, he expressed the opinion that although the Spanish did want peace, it was not because of either military or financial exhaustion. Instead he suggested three reasons for the Spanish moves: to be able to subdue more easily the provinces of Holland and Zeeland; to secure their coasts and fleets against the depredations of the English pirates; and to improve Spanish chances of intervention in the succession of England at a later date.[9]

Cecil himself was not unaware of such explanations for Spanish actions. He knew from his own informants that Philip's hopes for a chance at influencing the succession were an important consideration in his decision making at this time and that Spanish military activities certainly belied any concern on their part with financial difficulties. Toward the end of January a Captain Robert Ellyott, soliciting a military position from Cecil on the basis of his intimate knowledge of Spanish tactics and strategy, sent the secretary an outline of "Spanish practices and designs" for the coming year. In it he told Cecil that even though the Spanish were not going to assist the Catholic rebellion in Ireland directly, the Spanish ministers were persuaded that their military might seize certain key points in Wales and cut off all supplies to the English forces in Ireland. As an alternative to this, they were considering landing twenty thousand foot soldiers near Portsmouth or Plymouth and then marching on London. But even more suggestive of how the Spanish considered the relative strengths of the two parties to this peace was Ellyott's report that "since the peace hath been spoken of, divers have persuaded the K. of Spain that her Majesty's treasure is altogether consumed and that our nation beginneth to lose reputation and honour, presenting to him all the overthrows and losses sustained [because of] Tyrone, terming the Irish naked and savage men, not so much to their disgrace as to our dishonour." The irony, of course, is that one need only switch the subjects and substitute Maurice in Flanders for Tyrone in Ireland to have a fairly accurate statement of English beliefs about Spain. It appeared that neither side considered itself weaker than the other![10]

More important than Ellyott's reporting of possible Spanish strategic choices was his assessment of the underlying rationale for all their decisions regarding England. His assessment was strikingly close to that of Henry IV—suggesting that the Spanish considered the struggle for the throne of England to be at one and the same time a struggle for control of the sea—yet it seemed to be based on information closer to the source:

> Divers of the Spanish Council hath alleged that her Majesty is far in years and by course of nature cannot live above 7 or 8 years more. In the which time, having peace, they will bowel up their Indies, gather together what wealth they can, estimating in that time to have beforehand 70 or 80 millions. They presume they shall be able to build and furnish into the sea 200 of tall ships, besides those they have already. That they will have quiet traffic to their Indies and to all parts of Christendom, and that they will take present order for the increase of their mariners. To animate men to that profession, they will assure them particular honours and dignities. They conclude to be so beforehand in 7 or 8 years, that they will not care whether the peace hold or break, and say that when God shall call away her Majesty, they will be ready to give a great stroke for the advancing of the Infante's [Isabel Clara Eugenia] title.

He continued that the Spanish considered the archdukes' chances of securing the throne very high because of the English nobility's jealousy of one another and because of "the great commodity that would grow to the crown of England by joining the Provinces of Flanders to it." Whether or not his assessment was based on inside sources, it was close enough to the truth, as will be seen below.

Yet while the Spanish strategy seemed clear to the English and their informants, in Philip's Council of State there was considerable division about the policies to be pursued. Some of the members strongly desired the Dutch to take part in the negotiations. But, whereas this minority believed that the talks should be broken off if Elizabeth refused to use her influence to bring them to the table, "the majority were opposed to this, [saying] that an accord with the English should be reached if nothing else, since it was better to have only one enemy rather than two as we have now." But despite this majority ruling in favor of peace, the Spanish councillors, like the English, were still not sure of the opposing side's commitment, some arguing that the English did not want peace and that any agreement on their part would be the result of French persuasion. Others, however, said that the English were without sufficient forces or money to continue the war and were therefore ripe for peace. Unable to resolve the differences of opinion, they finally, as a body, recommended that the king take no chances: "Your Majesty ought to arm yourself on all sides, which is the most effective means of securing an honorable peace." Peace they wanted, but not because they were unwilling to continue the fight. These were no pacifists; it was to be peace with a decided military advantage.[11]

Meanwhile they had not given up on diplomacy to achieve their political aims. The council and Philip decided to proceed as before in establishing the groundwork for the conferences. In late February, Philip sent Hernando Carrillo to Flanders with a long set of instructions concerning the peace talks, supposedly duplicating those of Zúñiga, but with additions reflecting the then current state of affairs. Carrillo's instructions are important in any evaluation of Spanish gains and losses in the north during this period, for they detail, explicitly, Philip's aims in the negotiations.[12]

In the beginning of 1600 the Spanish court had heard that the English were demanding that any conference take place on English soil. For reasons of prestige, this stipulation was totally unacceptable to the Spanish crown, and Philip therefore made it the first order for the new delegate to refuse any such request. Philip's instructions instead suggested that Carrillo propose a site in Flanders, knowing that the English would likewise refuse and that both sides would then have to compromise by choosing a neutral location, such as Boulogne (which was in fact precisely how things turned out). Compromise, however, applied only to particular issues where both sides could accept the basic principle involved; in this case the principle was a mutually acceptable site. With regard to moral issues, where the two sides differed even in their basic principles, compromise would be more difficult. Point four of Carrillo's instructions reiterated Philip's desire concerning religious issues: "The point that I desire most in the event that the peace should come together, and which you should try by all means to get, is that they should tolerate the Catholics that are in that realm, with the exercise of Catholicism free and undisturbed, both because it suits the service of our Lord and the profession I make of amplifying our sacred Catholic faith in all regions, and also because I do not want to see the Catholics abandoned to the persecution that would happen to them if this clause were absent."

Nevertheless, Philip and his ministers were aware that strong religious convictions would not carry much weight when it came to persuading the English to sign a treaty with Spain. Indeed it was possible that they would even mistake it as a Spanish pretext to flood England with Catholic insurgents. Accordingly, the instructions informed Carrillo that Philip was willing to give the English open trade with Spain — "since what would most insure peace is free trade and unbroken commerce" — in exchange for toleration and that additionally such toleration would insure that the Spanish authorities would not molest Englishmen trading in Spain. Notwithstanding this commercial generosity, Philip expressly instructed Carrillo to secure a clause preventing English trade in both the East and West Indies (clause 10). The two issues, then, on which Philip adamantly insisted were religious toleration and prohibition of English navigation in the Indies. To secure the former he could even, as his father had done in 1597, agree to give up reparation for war damages caused by English fleets and privateers (which point, however, he instructed Carrillo to bring up as a counter to whatever demands the English might make). Finally Philip instructed Carrillo to request that the towns held by Elizabeth as security for her loans to the Dutch be handed over, suggesting that the towns' turnover would be a demonstration of good faith. In the event that such arguments had no effect, Philip permitted Carrillo to offer the English payment, although it had to be as low as possible. All these latter issues were to be discussed initially in order not to jeopardize the early negotiations by bringing up religious matters. After he understood how the English felt about these matters, Carrillo could touch on the point of religion, which Philip esteemed most; if they continued to show obstinacy, Philip ordered him to report back to the court in Madrid for further instructions.

Regarding the provinces in rebellion, Philip told Carrillo to attempt to secure assistance in reducing them to obedience, "alleging the interest that all rulers had in the cause of subduing the vassal to his lord." Philip ordered that the rebels must enter into talks with himself and his representatives directly and not by roundabout means such as treating with the obedient Estates. Furthermore, if pacification resulted, it had to consist of three principal points. The first was that those cities with a mixture of Catholics and heretics had to give the Catholic religion precedence and those cities composed solely of heretics had to accept Catholicism within their confines. As a corollary to this point, the provinces in general had to restore previously seized ecclesiastical estates. In other words: Protestantism was to be rolled back in the north. Second, the provinces had to recognize their due obedience to their natural lords. Third, and most important for the security of the provinces, the rebels could not ask for the departure of foreign troops. In addition to these three main points both the English and the Dutch were to be excluded from trade with the Indies.

Carrillo's instructions then—and presumably those of Zúñiga as well—adhered strictly to the principles of Spanish foreign policy as delineated under Philip III's predecessor: the defense of Catholicism, the preservation of the Habsburg inheritance, and the maintenance of the trade monopoly with the Indies.[13] But whereas Philip II had, since the 1560s, relied essentially on Spanish military dominance to achieve these strategic goals, circumstances were forcing Philip III and his ministers to rely more heavily on negotiation and diplomacy.

At almost the same time that Carrillo was receiving his instructions, Albert, complying with the agreement made with Edmondes, sent his *audiencier*, Louis Verreyken, to the queen to discuss the preliminary issues involved and to determine what the English wanted from the peace negotiations. His instructions were only to touch upon the reparations, to ask for the renewal of the ancient offensive and defensive alliances, to request that the English cease all aid to and trade with the Dutch, and to seek the restoration of the cautionary towns. Under no circumstances was he to do anything substantial without prior approval from the court in Brussels; the archduke was proceeding cautiously. Verreyken had to try to become familiar with Cecil, telling him that the archdukes were confident of his genuine desire for peace.[14]

But when the queen heard the "proposterous" points of Verreyken, she flatly refused to consider them, pointing out that giving up the cautionary towns would not only be dishonorable but also strategically dangerous and that it would be better for the English to do without trade to Spain than to give up the safe and profitable commerce with the Dutch. Moreover, following their preliminary meetings, it did not take long for the English to realize that Verreyken lacked the necessary authority to debate the issues or agree on the terms, and so he left after a month of rather one-sided talks. Thomas Edmondes followed him to Brussels with a letter for the archduke answering the points proposed by the audiencier and explaining that the queen thought such impossible demands reflected an unwillingness to come to terms. He was to declare to Albert that although Elizabeth desired peace, she would not submit to such conditions and that in consideration of this she wanted the main points reconciled beforehand. She wanted straight answers and less extreme proposals before committing her deputies to the bargaining table. The archduke and his representatives nevertheless refused to back down and insisted that all bargaining was to take place in Boulogne. In the end Edmondes could do nothing except leave unsatisfied, although he did finally agree to 16 May as the date for formal talks in Boulogne. The Habsburgs had won another round.[15]

But back in Spain the Council of State was not so sure that it was winning anything. It had received the archduke's letter requesting money to pay the mutineers and for other necessities of state. The council urged Philip to come up with the money or lose the strategic advantage of having the Low Countries take the blows from the forces that would, under normal circumstances, be directed against Spain. "It is advisable," the ministers emphasized, "to attend to the conservation of the States of Flanders with the same care and seriousness that was used before, it being the bit with which to bridle and hold back the power of the French, the English, and the rebels, whose forces, if that shield were lost, would charge Your Majesty and his kingdoms from all sides, resulting in even greater expenses and damages." The members of the council knew only too well that the ordinary remittances to Flanders would not be sufficient to pay for the upkeep of the army and for the eventual settlement with the mutineers. It was necessary, they told Philip, that "the latter be taken care of or [he would] not only risk losing all that was spent but in the end lose everything."[16]

Moreover, in the same consulta, the council illustrated one of the major stumbling blocks it faced in trying to guide the monarchy's grand strategy: its lack of control over finances. The councillors suggested that Philip do everything to find some extraordinary sum to send in addition to the ordinary remittances for the previous six months, even if it meant cutting expenditures in other areas. Nevertheless, they could do no more than suggest what appeared to them to be the best strategies, since, owing to the disconnected structure of the policy-making administration, they did not know whether the means were available to accomplish them, admonishing, "If the President of the [Council of] Finance had given an account of the state of treasury (as Your Majesty ordered in the first place) the Council of State would have been able to give more clearly and with more foundation its opinion about the means by which this could be provided." Meanwhile, the ministers would respond to the archduke "using sweet words without promising or assuring anything, telling him that meanwhile he should try to accommodate and cover things as best he can with the money already sent." It was the best advice the council could offer at that point, because Philip, like his father before him, was the only one with a comprehensive view of the activities of his various councils.

This last implication was not entirely true. The king's favorite, the former marquis of Denia, who in November 1599 had been elevated to duke of Lerma, was also, no doubt, aware of each council's activities, especially those of the finance council. But with regard to foreign policy, he and Philip can be viewed as a single unit, with the same coordinating functions as Philip II and his private secretaries.[17] Nevertheless, the council was right about the main point: the king and his favorite alone were able to coordinate the Council of State's advice with the realities of the treasury. And at that moment, Philip and Lerma understood one thing: the treasury was dry. This Philip expressed clearly when he instructed the council that they had better write to Albert and tell him to "make do."[18]

Two weeks later, upon the arrival of the fleet from the Indies, the Venetian ambassador in Madrid, Soranzo, confirmed Philip's miserable financial state: "The merchants here have not been able to prevent the King, who is in great difficulties, from keeping back fifty percent of the sum secured upon this fleet, and although he has done so with their assent, and they are to draw the ordinary rate of interest, still many of them are very anxious; for, as I have already told your Serenity, the credit on the future fleets is engaged to the year 1603. In this way the arrears are sure to mount up, and some fine day a royal decree may be issued, which will throw everything into confusion, as did the decrees of the late king." The financial situation was indeed shaky. In early May it was even reported that the king was reduced to holding an anonymous auction of some of his furniture, jewels, and silver, and talk of his debts was common among people on the streets because of the large number of his creditors among them. The Spanish ministry was desperate, especially because it thought the French king was "amassing money on all sides, and already [had] a considerable sum laid by."[19]

Such fears could not help but influence Spanish foreign policy, especially in the area of Savoy, where Spain might soon have to engage the
French. The conjuncture of circumstances was apparently worsening. Simultaneously with the arrival of the silver fleet in April the Spanish had
learned that the English and Dutch fleets had sailed, prompting fears of
more attacks on the coasts of the peninsula or the islands. Soranzo even
reported violent quarrels in the council over the deployment of the three
thousand troops left from the Adelantado's failed mission of the previous year. The Adelantado argued that they should remain to protect the
coasts of Portugal and Andalucia, while the count of Fuentes insisted that
they accompany him to Milan, where he was being sent as governor because of the precarious situation existing between Savoy and France.[20] At
the same time, the earl of Tyrone was pressing the Spanish to invade Ireland to support him. The Adelantado's troops were certainly the nucleus
of any potential invasionary force. But where should the Spanish commit themselves: Savoy, the Atlantic, Ireland, or Flanders? The matter was
finally solved when the English fleet sailed for Ireland instead of descend-
ing on the Spanish coasts, letting the Spanish commit the remainder of the
Adelantado's forces to the count of Fuentes. The latter finally left Madrid
for Milan by way of Barcelona on 12 June, carrying with him one million
ducats to "attend to whatever necessity that should arise in that State,"
money the archduke, for one, did not think was necessary.[21] With this decision it was clear to all concerned that the north was not to be a military
priority in 1600.[22]

As noted earlier, Philip and his ministers did not want a two-front
war. By July everyone at court was aware that the Low Countries were
not a priority. Soranzo, however, drew the conclusion that nothing could
be done about Saluzzo if the Low Countries were not also somehow strategically involved. "Seeing that no active preparations for Flanders are
going forward here [in Spain]," he wrote, "one concludes for certain that
they do not mean to come to a rupture [with France over Saluzzo]; for if
they wish to make a diversion they would certainly have to increase their
forces in that part."[23] The Spanish rulers' possible strategies were therefore constricted by the very interconnected nature of the monarchy. They
could not cut back their forces in any one area without jeopardizing their
aims in others.

So, precisely when the Habsburgs needed to go to the bargaining table
with the appearance of strength, the Spanish crown had declawed Albert

and the other negotiators both militarily and financially. The archduke, almost immediately upon receiving the news that he would have to make do with what he had, turned to the States-General of the Catholic provinces for the necessary sums. But at the end of May, when the talks in Boulogne were scheduled to get under way, he had still received no promise of assistance from them, handicapping the Habsburgs' negotiations with the English.[24]

The commissioners for the two sides finally came together on 28 May in Boulogne, exchanging their commissions the following day. Both sides had been given commissions to treat with full power to conclude a peace. After first making direct claim of precedence (superiority in rank), the English representatives were to obtain trade with all Spanish dominions, safety for English merchants from the Inquisition, and the avoidance of unjust tariffs. They were to "yield to nothing which may overthrow the state of the Low Countries" and to declare that the English would never be party to any hostilities against them. In addition they were to refuse to enter into any offensive or defensive league, to refuse any Spanish demands that they hand over the cautionary towns, and to refuse to stop trade with the States. If the Spanish demanded a cessation of English trading to the Indies, as was expected, the English were to argue that this did not show a true amity—though the deputies could, if necessary, agree to a prohibition on all trade to *inhabited* parts of the Indies. And finally, they were to prohibit all Spanish aid to the rebels in Ireland. Given that these points were completely opposite the Spanish proposals in most respects, it is no wonder that the talks foundered almost from the first. Neither side would concede a single issue to the other.[25]

The English wasted no time in complying with their instructions and immediately demanded precedence over the Habsburg representatives. The latter, not able to concede a point so detrimental to Philip's prestige, suggested that if the meetings were held in the Spanish ambassador's quarters, their side would give the English commissioners "all due honour." Neither side would back down on the issue, however, and following more bickering over minutiae concerning the form of the powers given to the Habsburg commissioners, matters were at a standstill. Both groups of diplomats were forced to send for more instructions before they could proceed.[26]

Even without these obstacles, events beyond Boulogne were soon to have a direct negative impact on the negotiations. The Dutch had not been inactive during all these months. Elizabeth's evident desire for peace during the winter of 1599–1600 had caused them to be anxious for their own future. The severe financial strain placed on the Provinces by the "blockade" fleet of the previous year and the hastily repaired defenses at Bommel had left the States-General unable to make the repayments promised in the recent treaty with England. As such they feared that Elizabeth would be less than vigilant of their interests in the treaty negotiations. If they hoped to damage the progress of the talks, the Dutch could not afford to relax their campaigns against the Spanish; the question for the campaigning season of 1600 was only where the initiative should take place.[27]

There was a strong argument in favor of an attack in Flanders. Such a move would strain relations between France and Spain, since the French would fear a possible spillover and the archduke's attention would be diverted from the peace talks. In addition, it was reported that there was widespread disaffection in Flanders, which suggested that the Dutch might even be able to liberate some of the southern provinces. The most compelling case for such an offensive, however, was the plight of the merchants of Zeeland. The Spanish blockade of 1598 had been most effective against shipping leaving the Zeeland ports; Spanish galleys under the direction of the Genoese mercenary Federico Spínola, in constant vigil off the coast, were inflicting notable losses. Privateers from Dunkirk, preying on *all* shipping in the English Channel, only served to add to the Spanish menace.[28] More threatening, though, was that most of Zeeland's garrison were stationed in Ostend, a coastal town across the Scheldt waterway from Zeeland's main territorial holdings, a vulnerable position in the event of a siege by the Spanish forces, who might easily interdict their supply lines. The Dutch had feared such a siege since at least as early as 1598.[29] With the Spanish army in mutiny and lacking the money to campaign in the coming season, it seemed, therefore, a good time to press home the advantage by capturing Dunkirk and some of the other Flemish port towns, thus freeing Ostend from the threat of siege and Zeeland from the ravages of the blockading forces.

Johan van Oldenbarnevelt, advocate of the States of Holland and effective leader of the civilian government in the northern provinces, agreed with the Zeelanders and in April went to the front lines to visit Count Maurice, who had opened the season by laying siege to the Spanish fort, San Andrés. The advocate was eager to see the siege concluded so that plans could be made for the assault on Flanders. But Maurice had sound reasons for not pressing the siege too strongly. Because the garrison was then in mutiny, he figured it was simply a matter of time before they sold the fort to the Dutch: he had only to wait them out. For once Oldenbarnevelt, who did not always see eye to eye with the Dutch military leader, agreed with Maurice and put in motion negotiations with the mutineers, personally promising to secure them 125,000 florins. The mutineers handed over the fort shortly afterward, thereby freeing Maurice's soldiers for the invasion force.[30]

While Maurice planned the attack, Oldenbarnevelt spent the next two months frantically procuring the money necessary to assemble the resources for the invasion. It was an immense undertaking, but the Dutch expected to be ready by the middle of June. Their aim was to launch an amphibious assault, take Nieuwpoort within a short time, and then capture Dunkirk afterward. Neither town had strong defenses, nor could they count on the promise of immediate aid because of the mutiny by Catholic troops. From such an attack they expected to gain relief from the pressure on the coastal sites, receive an increase in the convoy tax, free Ostend from the blockade, and carry the war to the enemy. As Jan Den Tex has pointed out, there was a certain irony in the campaign: "It was principally a campaign for financial purposes; one might almost say, in order to save money." In addition to these economic advantages, there was a foreign policy benefit to be gained: the possible rupture between France and Spain might bring Henry IV back into the war and thus keep Elizabeth fighting as well. Neither of these aims sat well with Maurice. Strategically the Dutch amphibious landing, leaving as it did strong Spanish fortresses (e.g., Sluis) between the army and its supply lines to the Dutch mainland, looked to be almost suicidal: he would either have to win all the battles or be completely crushed on foreign soil. Moreover, the element of surprise depended considerably on the winds and weather.[31]

In any event, Maurice's objections were overruled by the Hollanders, who insisted that the general's usual method of a slow land advance would be too time-consuming and costly. Instead they chose to proceed with the cheaper and quicker plan of a direct amphibious assault. On 20 June a fleet of almost one thousand transports, twelve thousand infantry, two thousand cavalry, and thirty-eight pieces of artillery rendezvoused in the evening near Flushing, intending to depart the following morning for Ostend. The weather the next day prevented the force from sailing, and after more deliberations they "resolved rather to adventure the hazard of an enemy country, than to commit the success of so royal and hopeful an enterprise unto the mercy of the wind". It was therefore decided to change the plan and land at Philippine, passing by land to Ostend, a distance of some fifty miles. They crossed the Scheldt to Philippine on 22 June, reaching Ostend four days later.[32]

Both the politicians accompanying Maurice's army and the soldiers composing it were optimistic of their chances of success. As Lord Grey, an officer with the English forces in Maurice's army, jubilantly observed with regard to the Dutch: "the enemy full of distress, of mutinies, of misery: our progress likely to be very great. To conclude, such is the preparation, such the nature of the service (being not only to besiege but to carry an army in despite of the enemy through the heart of his country), such the favour and care of the States and his Excellency [Maurice] to yield me all satisfaction, as I protest never did I with equal content enter any action, nor could I, since my Lord of Leicester's being here, have apprehended the like opportunity."[33] Oldenbarnevelt's own confidence caused him to write to all the towns and villages on the army's route, demanding that they pay for their liberation within two weeks or suffer the consequences. He sincerely believed the southerners would welcome their release from the Spanish yoke at the hands of their northern brethren. That the peoples of the Spanish Netherlands might not want to be freed—especially by heretics who had caused the southern lands such hardship since the early days of the revolt—but instead might want a peace based on compromise was unthinkable to him. In the end, his threats failed to convince the southern townspeople, who knew that the army could not afford to remain in any one area long enough to extract the money; no sums were forthcoming and the army moved on to Nieuwpoort.

Maurice arrived at Nieuwpoort on 1 July and split his forces to undertake the siege of the town, leaving his cousin, Count Ernest, with three thousand troops on the side of the bay closest to Ostend. He was completely unaware that the archduke had managed to win over the mutineers at Diest, had assembled an army of almost eight thousand infantry and a thousand cavalry, and was following rapidly on the heels of the Dutch army. Albert reached Nieuwpoort a day after Maurice, and the latter immediately sent Ernest with two regiments to defend the passage to the Dunes, the area of beach between Ostend and Nieuwpoort. Ernest's force was defeated and suffered heavy casualties, but it gave Maurice time to

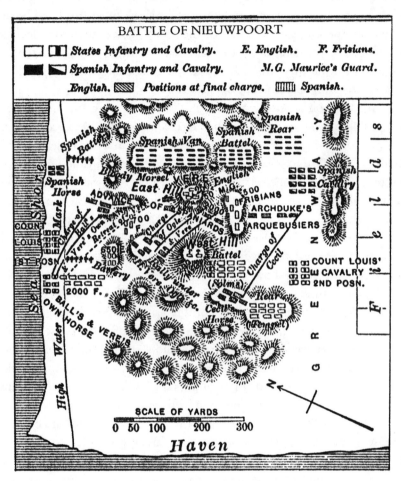

3. The Battle of Nieuwpoort, July 1600
(from Markham, *The Fighting Veres*)

assemble his remaining troops and draw them up for battle (fig. 3). Afterward, having sent away his ships in a move reminiscent of the great conquistador Cortés, Maurice urged his men on with exhortations of victory or death, since "seeing they were on everie side encompassed with the Sea and enemie, there was no meanes in the world to escape but by giving battaile."[34]

The battle was joined a mile from Nieuwpoort and two miles from Ostend at three o'clock on Sunday, 2 July, after " 'tirs' of great ordnance" had passed through the ranks of both sides. After a hotly contested battle of two and a half hours—the archduke in personal command near the thick of the fighting—the Dutch cavalry (composed partly of Spanish mutineers) was finally able to vanquish its foe (commanded by none other than the Admiral of Aragon) and round on the Spanish infantry on the dunes. The archduke's foot troops, which until then had fought bravely and successfully against the vanguard of Maurice's army, finally broke under a combination of grapeshot from the Dutch cannon and the assault from the cavalry.[35] Maurice had won the day, although it was to prove a Pyrrhic victory.

The casualties on both sides were heavy. Albert had lost almost half his force, many of them irreplaceable veterans, and he himself had been wounded. In addition, the Admiral of Aragon and many others had been captured. For the Habsburgs it was a devastating blow. Maurice, for his part, had lost some two thousand men, and some of his most able commanders, including Sir Francis Vere, had been seriously wounded. "It was a magnificent and gallant victorie," one account put it, "but obtayned with much labour and bloud."[36] Moreover, almost immediately came news that more Spanish cavalry, under the command of Luis de Velasco, was approaching; unable to capitalize on his victory, Maurice was forced to retreat back to Dutch territory.[37]

Understandably, however, the Spanish loss could not help but affect the state of the Anglo-Spanish negotiations. Francisco Soranzo wrote on 10 July that "the disaster in Flanders will cause the Spanish envoys to grant all they can to the Queen to induce her to conclude peace."[38] This, however, was precisely what the Spanish would not do. When the Council of State learned of the negotiations over precedence, they were outraged, thinking it beneath the dignity of His Majesty even to discuss the issue and declaring that no equality of any kind could be admitted "without such notable ruin to reputation (which ought to be so looked after) that it will be much less inconvenient to not make peace than to lose even one point of it."[39] On 29 July the audiencier returned the Habsburg reply to the English commissioners: no concessions on the point of precedence. The English, knowing their own position to be improved vis-à-vis the Spanish, soon replied that they would accept only equality of place. The Spaniards countered with their final offer of English precedence only if the English brought the Dutch into the negotiations and if the talks would take place in the Low Countries, a demand that effectively meant that the talks were over. At an impasse, the commissioners finally broke up and returned home. Maintaining Spanish reputation had suddenly become far more important than any peace. The English for their part were thrown into confusion over the sudden change of heart exhibited by the Spanish. On 8 September, Cecil, in a letter to Sir George Carew, the president of Munster, expressed clearly his perplexity over the current Spanish policy and its motivation: "Thus, do you see, there is yet a kynde of vegitation which we will keepe on foote; but, for my owne part, when I compare how this curiosity differeth from the former greediness that was shewed, I am iaylous [worried] least their myndes are altered since the tyme they first begann the treaty. That may be out of theise two reasons: ether that they should thinke that her Majesty is sufficiently intangled with Ireland; or that they are in hope to prevayle over the Low countryes; whoe indeed (to tell you trew) doe everie day grow worse and worse." [40]

Indeed, shortly after receiving the news concerning the Battle of the Dunes, Philip resolved to go ahead with the invasion of Ireland (following the advice brought back by Martín de la Cerda, who had been sent as an emissary to Tyrone in April), telling the Council to raise two thousand infantry to be united with another two thousand veterans then in Andalucia and "put them in Ireland." After giving more instructions concerning raising the fleets, securing commanders, and locating the money to pay for it all, Philip concluded with an almost excited flush: "I am waiting for this with the impatience that you might expect of someone who has desired so much since the death of my father, who is in heaven, to see this help for Ireland carried out." [41]

Here was a clear case of the different viewpoints of Philip, who wanted to take England by storm, and his council, which was seeking more peaceful and less expensive alternatives. The occasion for these orders was a discussion of the succession issue in England. The council, no doubt prompted by the circumstances in which Spanish forces found themselves in the Low Countries, considered the succession a means of reducing the strains on the Spanish monarchy in northern Europe. Council members suggested that Philip do everything in his power to secure the throne for the archdukes, following the policy of Philip II in not wanting to unite England and Spain but rather, England and the Low Countries. Without doubt, they argued, the unification of England and Spain would only result in worsening their situation, because "it would be the cause of a perpetual war which would cause great unease and excessive expenses, to the notable damage of Catholicism; and if, from jealousy of the grandeur of Your Majesty so many enemies and such great expenses and unease have been born [already], it is clear that if they see that Your Majesty aspires to unite that kingdom with your others, they will make the final effort to hinder it." Uniting England and the Low Countries, they argued, would instead assuage the fears of neighboring countries concerning the power of the Habsburgs, would please the citizens of the respective countries better, and would ultimately allow the reduction of the rebel provinces, all of this "saving His Majesty a very great part of the care and expense that conquest or succession of new kingdoms brings with it." Philip, however, did not seem overly impressed by their arguments and instead chose to "think about it all" while pursuing his own agenda concerning Ireland.[42]

The council diplomatically agreed with the king that such an enterprise would bring both the king and Spain much honor and reputation and that "the world, considering his strength so diminished, would see by his works the contrary." But they suggested that it would work better if there was a chance of the deed actually being accomplished. Given Philip's financial state, they argued that he should not rush the Ireland project, since a failure owing to the foul-weather season and lack of care beforehand, coming so soon after the failure in Flanders, would weaken Spain's reputation still further, doing serious damage to the Catholic cause instead of promoting it. Philip, however, taking a page from his father's book, exhorted them that God would solve all the difficulties inherent in such a cause: "This work will be so much in God's service that he will help to overcome the difficulties that you point out . . . and I will order the provision of the money, even if it should mean cutting my own personal expenses." He concluded with orders to get on with the planning and have all the necessary documents forwarded to him for consideration as soon as possible. The fleet would carry six thousand troops levied on the pretext of infantry for Italy, and the rest would be prepared as if it were intended for the Indies. This was to be Philip's own Gran Armada.[43]

Meanwhile something had to be done about the situation in Flanders. Almost immediately the archduke had used the loss at Nieuwpoort as a pretext for requesting more funds and soldiers both from the Catholic States-General and from Spain.[44] He even suggested that the troops being sent with the count of Fuentes be dispatched to Flanders. But for

the court in Spain this was a very serious matter. Already at the end of
June, using a windfall promise of three million ducats from the Cortes,
the king had sent Albert some 750,000 ducats to pay for the mutineers
and the ordinary provisions for the month of July.[45] Now he was being
called upon to make up for the archduke's disastrous loss and still provide
for the normal remittances. And, as the council pointed out to Philip on
20 July, if the archduke lacked the ordinary remittance he would be forced
to use the money that had been provided for the mutineers, thus dashing
all hope of calming them and in the process encouraging others to resort
to mutiny.[46] Necessity dictated that the money be found. An immediate levy of fifteen hundred troops was needed to reinforce the archduke's
army, and an additional six thousand men were to be raised for the invasion of Ireland. The estimated cost for amassing the troops and sending
them to Flanders and Ireland was over 630,000 ducats. Putting the best
face on a decision with which they disagreed, the council members now
argued that the enterprise of Ireland was a good strategic move, since it
would indirectly help the archduke by diverting Elizabeth's military away
from the Low Countries and to Ireland instead.[47]

So much for the strategic side of things. What frightened the Spanish
councillors more was the precarious command situation in Flanders. In
just one battle the archduke had almost managed to destroy the army's
high command. He himself had been wounded; one of his battalion commanders, Gaspar Zapena, after being wounded in the battle, had been captured and later killed in cold blood by Scottish troops in Ostend; and the
cavalry general, the Admiral of Aragon, had been captured.[48] Suddenly
the council, aware of just how tenuous was their hold on Flanders, advised
the king "to send someone of quality, valor, and prudence to assist the
archduke and when occasion demanded to command the army, because if
God had not freed His Highness, the infanta and those states would have
been so close to death that one should not think about it."[49] Philip agreed
and ordered that a search be made for someone suitable. This, however,
would prove to be harder than expected.

The councillors reported back that they were having a hard time finding a qualified general who could be sent to Flanders. "We are very sorry,"
they wrote, "that even though we have run over the list of everyone we
could remember who is in Spain and Italy, we found no one in whom
there concurred, jointly with distinction [i.e., nobility], the experience
and the ability necessary to command an army." The few nobles who did

have the requisite stature were not interested in a command without title or name, nor did they wish to leave their estates and lawsuits for long periods of time. Given their lack of success in finding an appropriate candidate, the councillors advised the king to consider sending instead two men: one to act as the infanta's mayordomo mayor and the other to be Captain-General of the Cavalry—the most prestigious, and now vacant, Spanish post in the Army of Flanders. Furthermore, they urged that since Spain lacked any qualified military commanders at court, the king should consider sending some of the younger *grandes* (upper nobility) to Flanders to learn the arts of war. They followed this advice with a list of potential military commanders, most of them experienced generals, from among whom the archduke could fill the lower command ranks; but the vacancy in the senior command was a problem that would not be solved completely for some years.[50]

In Flanders itself the archduke was busy setting his house in order and preparing for his next move. Using the fears raised by his defeat at Nieuwpoort, on 4 July he had persuaded the States-General of the loyal provinces to provide him with three hundred thousand florins per month for the provisioning of more than ten thousand men.[51] Even the normally cautious Zúñiga was prompted to think the situation was getting better, as evidenced by a letter to the duke of Sessa: "I hope to God that the enemy will continue to suffer from the expense of this business, and that, with the provisions that have now come from Spain and the 200,000 ducats [*sic*] a month conceded by the States-General, the affairs of these states will be put in much better shape than they were before."[52] In return for the concession of a subsidy, however, the archduke had to agree to let the States-General treat for peace with representatives from the north, a request that ran exactly contrary to Philip's desires as expressed to Carrillo and later to both Carrillo and Zúñiga.[53] The States-General shortly afterward dispatched a request to the northern provinces asking them to enter into talks.[54]

The Dutch for their part were prepared to accept the proposal for talks, thinking that the recent victory would allow them to dictate unilaterally the terms of peace. Oldenbarnevelt thought that Albert's defeat had made the southern provinces willing to unite with the northern provinces even without the sovereignty of Albert intact. There was, however, some debate over these terms in the Dutch camp. Maurice himself thought that a peace on these terms was "neither realistic nor desirable"; forming a state with papists could result only in continual discord. But after more argument Oldenbarnevelt prevailed against the count, and the Dutch finally agreed to the talks.[55]

On 21 July 1600 the delegates of both sides met in Bergen op Zoom, where Oldenbarnevelt immediately expressed the Dutch demands: the southern provinces would be required to take up arms or at least to allow levies of troops in their territories; they would be required to confiscate all forts from the Spanish; and finally they would be required to unify with the northern provinces without the archduke. These exorbitant demands were too much for the southern delegates. They were willing to give up a lot for peace but would not turn traitor to their sovereign; the talks broke off almost immediately, leaving the Catholic delegates even more resolved to assist the archdukes monetarily.[56]

Nevertheless, despite the failure of the negotiations at Bergen op Zoom, Philip's ministers still wished some form of negotiation with the Dutch to continue; they objected only to the southern provinces treating with their northern brethren, not to the talks themselves. As noted earlier, the Habsburg delegates had demanded that the English bring the Dutch into the talks between themselves and the Habsburgs. English refusal at the end of July had been a direct cause of the breakup of the Boulogne talks. The Council of State still thought it unwise to conclude peace with England if the United Provinces were not also involved:

> The peace with England by herself would be very dangerous for Your Majesty and their Highnesses, on the one hand because of the profit the Queen and her subjects would gain from resting and the fruit they would enjoy from trade, in which the rebels would participate, and on the other hand because they would secretly aid the rebels, troubling both Your Majesty and their Highnesses; if the peace was general then not only would these inconveniences cease, but it would also be the first means of undoing the popular government of the Islands [the Dutch Republic] and the confederation they have with the Queen.[57]

The council advised the king that he should immediately dispatch wide powers to the archduke to treat for peace with the rebel states. The king, all too aware of the problems besetting the monarchy, agreed and on 25 September Andrés de Prada, secretary of the council, drew up the *cédula* (royal order) granting that the Archduke Albert could, in the king's name, "accept peace with the said neighbors and residents in the said Islands of Holland, Zeeland, Friesland, Utrecht and in the other parts and places in-

cluded in the States and Low Countries that from the past to the present
are out of their rightful obedience to . . . their Princes and lords, rightful sovereigns of the said States . . . in the form and manner that appears
best to him and with the most agreeable conditions possible, expecting
that they will be such that the service of our lord and the well-being of
Christendom are achieved."[58]

It was an enormous grant of power by the young king. Albert, despite his noted desire for peace at any cost, was given extensive powers to
achieve just that.[59] And the reason, considering the previous clashes with
the archdukes over this issue, can only have been the precarious military
situation in which the Spanish found themselves.[60] On 13 September the
council had outlined clearly the reasoning behind their willingness to see
the Dutch engaged in talks, preferably with the English: it was not possible to continue providing the sums necessary to continue the war. Since
the final objective was to lull the rebels with an easy life of peace and trade
rather than war, the council advised Philip that the best strategy would
be to secure a long-term armistice. The armistice would have the effect of
diverting the rebels from warfare into trade. Demonstrating remarkable
insight into the factional politics of a government at war, the councillors argued that as a consequence military men would be removed from
control over the government of the provinces, thereby indirectly assisting
elements within that government more favorable to reconciliation with
Spain. But the council was not overly optimistic regarding their possibilities. Despite obviously needing peace, they were prepared to back up their
diplomatic initiatives with force and advised Philip that Albert should be
prepared to do everything possible to pressure the Dutch by cutting off
completely their trade and fishing.[61]

But the threat on this occasion was really nothing more than an elabo-
rate bluff. As the year was drawing to a close, it was clear that the Habsburg
monarchy was facing an ever-worsening crisis, and its ministers undoubtedly knew it. Compounding all the difficulties in the north was the issue
of Saluzzo, looming ever larger and diverting both Spanish attention and
Spanish resources. On 11 August Henry IV had published a declaration
of war against Philip's ally, the duke of Savoy, and the following day he
had launched a three-pronged blitzkrieg against the duke's forces, seizing
most of the disputed territory in less than a week. The Spanish ministers were unable to escape the inherent problem of their fragmented but
powerful empire: everyone wanted a piece of it, which entailed a constant

shifting of priorities and resources to those areas under attack. The ever pessimistic Sessa summed up what would be the Spanish malaise for the next century: "It seems to me that little by little we are creating a world where everyone wants to shoot their arrows, and you, sir, know that no empire, no matter how great it may have been, has been able to sustain for long many simultaneous wars in different parts. . . . I might be fooling myself but I doubt that by just defending ourselves we can sustain an empire as widespread as ours is."[62]

CHAPTER 3

Strategic Overstretch: Saluzzo, Ostend, and Kinsale

❧ ❧ ❧

Since the obstinacy of the rebels precludes the hope that they will ever be
reduced, unless constrained by pure necessity, it is advisable to
make war on them with fire and blood.

—THE COUNCIL OF STATE
3 July 1601

By the beginning of September 1600 the focus of Spanish attention had moved to the war that had broken out between Henry IV and Charles Emmanuel, duke of Savoy, over the question of Saluzzo.[1] The integrity of the Spanish monarchy depended upon the successful resolution of this issue. According to the Spanish ambassadors stationed in Italy, the semiautonomous states there showed signs of a desire for independence because of the probable resurgence of French power. They even had thoughts of a defensive league against Spain, which could easily have evolved into an offensive league led by either Florence or Venice, both jealous of Spanish power in the peninsula. The prevention of a French foothold in Italy was therefore vital to the security of Spanish power.[2] Moreover, the Spanish Road, the corridor along France's eastern border through which the Spanish moved troops to the Low Countries, was at stake. If the French succeeded in taking Saluzzo, they would then be in a position to shut off reinforcements to Flanders.[3] Additionally, both the Spanish negotiations with England and the situation in Flanders had to be considered in any assessment of options regarding Saluzzo. On the one hand, Elizabeth would not continue to treat with the Spanish until she was sure of the outcome in Savoy; on the other hand Philip could not afford to "display to the French his dread of employing his forces in many places at one and the same time" and so had to continue supporting the archduke in the north.[4] Indeed, such support was vital to the success of Spanish aims in Savoy in that it would provide something of a diversion for French intervention.[5] In this instance, supporting Albert brought certain advantages: the French would have to face not only the recently arrived army under the count of Fuentes but also the fear of an attack by the Spanish forces on their flank in the Low Countries.

The Spanish needed to support the archduke militarily, however, just as much for the situation in the Low Countries itself as for any advantages that such support might give them in Savoy. The Council of State believed that Philip had to provide for Flanders—thereby demonstrating that the monarchy was "well-prepared for war"—in order to push both the English and the Dutch toward peace with Spain.[6] But the Spanish ministers would provide only what the archduke needed to maintain himself, and not for any extra operations. At the end of November 1600 Albert wrote to report that the ordinary provisions had been exhausted and requested more money and more men for the army. In addition he suggested hitting the Dutch where they would feel it most: cutting off their attempts to secure salt in the Caribbean and attacking their fishing fleets in the North Sea. The council, given the financial state of Spain, was not as excited about these prospects as was the archduke. They pointed out that putting together a fleet was difficult in itself and that such a strategy might have limited success against the well-guarded Dutch. As for the fleet to attack Dutch fishing, they replied that given the lack of money and supplies, nothing could be done that year, though they would try to provide the archduke with all he wanted as soon as possible. To all this Philip could only peevishly add that "provisions for Flanders have not and will not be lacking." In the meantime they were going to send Albert between 150,000 and 200,000 ducats along with the reinforcements being shipped.[7]

In the face of the situation in Italy, what the Spanish wanted most in the north was some form of respite. Receiving word from Zúñiga that he believed the peace talks with England and the subsequent attempt to bring the Dutch into them had gone sour because of the situation in Savoy, the Council responded that this assessment was no doubt correct but that everything possible should be done to reopen negotiations, even if it meant leaving out the Dutch.[8] The council, though still of the opinion that peace with the rebels was ultimately the means to reduce them, was temporarily willing to set aside that ambition to settle the outstanding war with England and reduce, for the present, their commitment in the north.

The Spanish certainly faced an interesting challenge: they could not pull out of wars they no longer wanted to fight. The problem stemmed from the nature of the coalition of states ranged against them. Each of Spain's three major enemies—France, England, and the Netherlands— wanted peace on its own terms. None of the powers, however, wanted the others in their coalition to sign a unilateral peace that would weaken their own bargaining position vis-à-vis Spain. Henry IV had gained a decided advantage by signing peace first. In August 1601 the Venetian ambassador to France noted that "there is some slight rancour against the King of France, because, although thanks to her [Elizabeth's] harassing of Spain he was able to get better terms for himself, he has never yet given her that support which she looked for."[9] And with the others still engaging the might of Spain, Henry was free to proceed with his own aims in the Savoy corridor to Italy. He had only to keep the other two parties at war to pin down Philip's forces and prevent any Spanish action against himself. The English, too, wanted peace, but without French might behind them they obviously no longer appeared threatening enough to force the Spanish to accept English terms. The Dutch were doing everything in their power to prevent any conclusion of peace between England and Spain, because this would leave them isolated against the full strength of Philip's armies. They needed both English and French backing and were not foolish enough to enter into talks without it. The only option left to the Spanish, therefore, was to use force to bring their opponents into peace while preventing themselves from being fatally weakened in the process.

In light of this dilemma the news that the Dutch were in serious financial difficulties could not help but please the Spanish ministers. In December Zúñiga sent a letter reporting that the Spanish had captured a Dutch ship carrying letters to Queen Elizabeth "stressing the straits that the States are in, and how they think it almost impossible to last if the war continues, which confirms what we know from others. The problem is that here we are not in a much better state."[10] But despite Zúñiga's view of the financial situation, things were beginning to look up in Spain. For even while Zúñiga was writing that letter the third silver fleet of the year was arriving in Cádiz with an estimated eight million ducats aboard, the king's share of it raising the crown's total receipts from the Indies that year to more than four million ducats.[11] As Albert later remarked to Lerma, the *servicio de millones* (tax allocation) of eighteen million awarded earlier and recently confirmed, "together with the fleet which . . . has also arrived, will be of great assistance for taking care of things suitably."[12]

As might have been expected, this seeming improvement in the Spanish king's financial resources had at least a temporary beneficial effect on his military preparations, especially in northern Italy. Fuentes had arrived in Genoa on 24 August with four thousand Spanish veterans to protect the vital duchy of Milan from a possible spillover of French troops from Saluzzo. The control of Milan, the heart of the monarchy and the cornerstone of its unity, was, in the words of Cano de Gardoqui, "vital for sustaining hegemonic authority in Europe, constituting a military position of the first order, both for attack and defense. In a word it could be considered the key to Western Europe."[13] Everything therefore had to be done to protect it from the French army. On 29 August, Philip had forwarded to the French king his ultimatum that if Henry did not return the conquered territories, he was resolved, even at the expense of breaking the Vervins treaty (which he had not yet ratified), to defend the duke of Savoy "with all [his] might."[14] Fuentes was instructed to prepare for war. In October, Fuentes set about raising forces in Germany, Naples, and Switzerland in order to increase his army by some twelve thousand troops. Philip himself was brought to the height of martial fervor by these preparations and expressed to the Council of State his intentions: "I have resolved to use the forces that God has given me . . . not only, I trust, to insure that he [Henry] does not press on with his intentions, but also to recover that which he has occupied, and attend firmly to that which is most fitting, and you will see that I will prepare for it even to the point of going there myself if it should be necessary . . . to augment the army as if for a great campaign . . . and achieve with it the recovery of the duke's states!"[15]

Nevertheless, despite the martial rhetoric, Spain remained unwilling to see hostilities break out. Spanish military preparations in Milan had two purposes: to force the pope, seeing two armies prepared to engage, to mediate the dispute; and to show Henry that the Spanish were prepared to fight if necessary. In the end, the pope failed to intercede. But even while building up the army in Milan, Philip had continued to use diplomatic pressure against Henry, employing the ratification of the Treaty of Vervins as a bargaining chip.[16]

Henry had until this point believed that Philip and the Spanish would do anything to preserve the peace formulated at Vervins. The delay of ratification and Fuentes's military buildup suggested that he may have miscalculated.[17] Moreover, at the end of October, the duke of Savoy, at the head of an army, moved against French forces besieging Montmélian, achieving some minor successes before being forced by the approach of winter to retire to the Italian side of the Alps. Although not completely successful, the duke's campaign did help to reinforce Henry's growing disposition for peace. By the end of January 1601, Soranzo was reporting that terms for peace had been exchanged between Savoy and Henry IV. The duke was to surrender La Bresse as far as the Rhône and retain Saluzzo, leaving the Spanish Road narrowed but open for the time being, which, as Zúñiga pointed out, though a disadvantage for the Spanish Low Countries, "was less of one than if His Majesty should be burdened with such a great new war." It would be some months before the treaty was concluded, but it was clear to the Spanish that in this instance a show of strength had forced their enemies to bargain without actually coming to blows. Perhaps this tactic would work in other areas.[18]

So although northern Italy was not yet completely free of problems of state, success there allowed the Spanish ministry to turn an eye again to the north. In December the issue of the English succession had once more come before the Council of State. It had received word from Zúñiga in Brussels that the English Catholics there had been pressuring him for some resolution concerning an invasion of England. Mollifying the Catholics was of the utmost importance, whatever feelings the councillors had toward the enterprise, and so they advised Philip that because conquering England by force was out of the question, he needed instead to address the issue of the English succession as a way of restoring Catholicism to that realm.[19] A little reluctantly perhaps, Philip finally considered the succession issue in January 1601, ordering that word be spread of his support for the claims of the infanta to the throne of England. In addition he forwarded two hundred thousand ducats, to be held in reserve by Zúñiga until Elizabeth's death, at which time he could use the funds for whatever men and arms should be necessary to put the infanta on the English throne.[20]

In the meantime the Spanish ministry decided to step up the military pressure on the English. Having the previous month ordered more galleys to be sent to Flanders to Federico Spínola, so he might continue to prey on Channel shipping, in March the council finally agreed to advise

Philip to assist the Irish more directly, justifying the move as "the thing from which to get the greatest repute and most benefit." They were emboldened to this action by the outbreak in England of the Essex rebellion, which they thought would keep the queen occupied for the time being. Even in Flanders the problems of the English were sparking thoughts of new military ventures, with some proposing an attack against Ostend, since the English would be tied down by the Essex affair.[21]

Albert, however, could not begin to take any action against the Dutch until he had received reinforcements for his armies from Spain. At the end of January the archduke had written to the king requesting that more men and supplies be sent from among those raised by Fuentes. The Council of State agreed that because the king had ordered ratification of the peace between France and Savoy, thus preventing a French foothold in Italy, there was no need to keep the count's army together in Milan; it therefore suggested that four thousand infantry be sent to reinforce Albert.[22] The councillors repeated their suggestion the following month when they advised the king, in some detail, that in their opinion a final thrust in Flanders would be enough to save the archdukes, the king's treasury, and even the rest of the king's states. They pointed out that the opportunity offered was "of great moment for the making or breaking of the issue according to the amount of assistance made of men and money, because if the archduke should find the money to oppose the rebel force, putting his all into it and His Highness prevail against them (as is hoped from Our Lord), pure necessity will get them by the nose, the more so since, because of the peace with France and the English troubles, they will not have the same assistance they have had in the past." But, they stressed, if because of a lack of suitable military provisions the archduke should be unable to defend himself against the rebels, "not only those countries, but also the persons of their Highnesses would be in serious danger and the inconveniences of losing everything would be of such notable damage to the State and to our reputation that a final effort should be made to save us from them." The expenses of mere defense would be as great, they argued, as for an offensive war, and indeed, probably more so since Spain's other enemies would use the opportunity of the diversion of Spanish resources to strike against other territories of the monarchy. Moreover, "it would not be possible to defend all sides in times so tight and when not only the royal treasury but the very substance of the kingdoms and subjects of Your Majesty are so used up and finished. Adding to this that if a disaster should happen in Flanders, even those now in obedience would not be secure."[23]

It is clear that, though hopeful about the effect of military force in the short term, members of the council were alarmed at the precarious state of Philip's empire in the long term. Like a great bear baited by many dogs, the monarchy's only option was to strike out with all the force and resources at its disposal, hoping at best to get some long-term respite or at worst lose everything. This time they advised Philip to order Fuentes to send six thousand Neapolitan troops and all the Spanish infantry he had to the archduke immediately. With this one stroke they hoped to secure Flanders, be ready to strike at the moment the English succession crisis should start, aid the Catholics in Ireland in their rebellion against their English overlords, preserve the peace with France, and save their reputation. It was a tall order for such a modest army.

Even with their confidence in Spanish arms, however, the council had not completely given up on diplomacy to achieve their ends. Their projected military successes were dependent upon the rebels not receiving aid from England. It was hoped that the problems resulting from the Essex rebellion would keep English attention focused on domestic affairs and make England willing to to negotiate an end to hostilities once again. But while talks between Spain and England were again under way in April, by the end of May the English had broken them off again, this time on the grounds that the Spanish had lent a hand to the Earl of Essex in his plot.[24] Other methods would have to be employed now against the English.

In the meantime, despite Philip's orders that Fuentes send men to the archduke, they had still not arrived by May—and the infanta wrote Lerma that they were not expected for two more months. Nonetheless, the Dutch had not shown themselves in force at the opening of the new campaign season and the court at Brussels began to believe that the losses of the previous year and the suspension of English aid was taking a toll on Dutch readiness. But military force was still needed to press home the Habsburg advantage, a position the archduchess succinctly summed up in Flanders: "If they are pressured now, everyone is certain that they will come to an accord."[25]

But if the men were not forthcoming, neither was the money. In June everyone in Brussels, including Zúñiga, began to worry that Flanders was being ignored while the court's attentions were focused elsewhere. Despairingly he wrote to Sessa: "We hear that there are preparations for an

62

STRATEGIC OVERSTRETCH

enterprise to the Levant, which cannot help but be very costly, and this together with the business in Lombardy will cut the water supply of aid to Flanders. Everything should be looked after well, but *until matters here are concluded, it is important to hold off on other voluntary enterprises.*"[26] Indeed, Philip had many "voluntary enterprises" in the works. In the summer and fall of 1601 Philip and his councillors were simultaneously planning an attack on Algiers, dealing with the situation in Savoy and Milan, planning the invasion of Ireland, assisting the Archduke Ferdinand in Hungry against the Turks, planning the acquisition (by force) of the Margravate of Finale on the Mediterranean coast near Genoa, and entertaining the Persian ambassador, who arrived in August to request aid against the Turks.

As Zúñiga had anticipated, by the summer of 1601 some of these other projects would indeed receive higher priority than the Army of Flanders. Some months earlier, in February, the Council of War and the king, excited by the arrival of the fleet, and no longer concerned about the future of the Franco-Savoyan dispute, had finalized the plans for the invasion of the British Isles that Philip had wanted ever since he had assumed the throne. A two-pronged attack was envisioned, one directed at Ireland and the other, commanded by Federico Spínola, at the southern coast of England.[27] Esteban de Ibarra, the secretary of the Council of War, estimated that the cost of the expedition to Ireland would be 305,000 ducats, two-thirds of which would be taken from the sums set aside for the Indies fleet. Despite the fact that the king himself did not know where the additional money would come from, he had given his assent to the project and preparations were under way.[28]

In May the naval commander of the expedition, Diego de Brochero y Añaya, arrived in Lisbon to finish assembling his invasion fleet. It was hoped that the Spanish forces would sail by the end of July. Meanwhile, in April Philip had ordered Spínola to raise, at his own cost, another six thousand men in Italy, to be sent to Flanders under the command of Federico's brother, Ambrosio, for the coming assault on southern England. At the same time, Federico was to secure an additional eight galleys, which, combined with those he already had in Flanders, would be used to transport these troops to England and occupy a beachhead. The estimated cost of all this, which Philip had to repay by 1603, was 470,000 ducats.[29]

The trouble with these expeditions was once again the lack of coordination among various outposts of the monarchy. At the court in Spain the ministers were blaming the lack of an integrated policy on the uncoordinated independent activities of the Spanish representatives in other areas of the monarchy. This, however, was the fault partly of the central court, who would often not provide the information or the resources subordinates needed to follow centrally dictated policies. Nevertheless, it could not be doubted that the local governors were sometimes less than sympathetic to the court's policies or activities. The preparations under way in Lisbon ran into difficulties when the viceroy of Portugal, Don Cristóbal de Moura, conflicted with Diego de Brochero over direction of the arrangements.[30] In Flanders the archduke still dragged his heels over assistance to Federico Spínola and in May confiscated for his own use all the munitions Spínola had set aside for his expedition against England.[31] It was not the first time that the archduke had shown signs of an unwillingness to cooperate with the central court. In May the council was shocked to hear from Zúñiga that the archdukes would have been unwilling to side with the Spanish against the French had war broken out between them. The council's advice to the king was that Baltasar de Zúñiga remind Albert and Isabella at an appropriate time that "in conformity with the gift of those states they are explicitly obliged to be at peace or war with the same foreign powers as Your Majesty."[32] Even more serious, however, was the refusal of Fuentes, fearing the emasculation of his own army and power, to send the Spanish and Italian tercios (infantry regiments) to the archduke; nor would Fuentes provide troops to Ambrosio Spínola.[33]

The problem, of course, was that the king's councillors were looking at the big picture, whereas the archduke and those like him had to see everything within the context of what was locally possible. It was clear that Albert, given the state of his military forces, could not have risked engaging the French. At the same time that the council was thinking of admonishing Albert, the infanta was writing to tell Lerma that the army was literally falling apart and that Flanders would fall with it. "We find ourselves," she wrote, "in the worst fix that we have ever been in since coming here, having had another mutiny in the part that could cause us most harm. . . . I wanted to tell you the state we are in, and if it is not remedied, then my brother will lose these States."[34]

In June, Albert sent Rodrigo Niño y Lasso to the king to inform him of the difficult state of things in Flanders—namely, that they had not received the provisions for March, April, May, or June and that they were still owed 175,000 ducats for February.[35] Providing for the army was not only necessary but made good strategic sense, for, as Lasso told the Spanish councillors, their enemies were watching closely what Philip sent and would have renewed courage if it was seen to be little; courage would falter, however, if they saw the army in top form "since it [was] the principal cause of their having come to terms."

The council, after reviewing carefully Lasso's suggestions, certainly agreed with them and reiterated what they had told the king before, that the Dutch were just as exhausted and consequently susceptible to military pressure. Therefore doing everything possible to secure the necessary provisions for the archduke was crucial. Other means having failed, they suggested that the king try to arrange with the Fuggers, the German banking family who had already donated large sums of money for the imperial aims of the Habsburgs, to make the greatest provision possible. Philip could do nothing but reply, remorsefully, that he was sorry about the state of his treasury and was doing everything he could.[36]

Indeed, the treasury was in dire straits. In February, Philip, prompted by the urging of Lerma, had ordered that the court be moved from Madrid to Valladolid, thereby incurring great expense for which money had to be found. Despite the enormous profits coming from the Indies, this placed yet another strain on the crown's already overburdened resources, forcing the king to seek ever more inventive solutions to his monetary difficulties. As one recourse, in April Philip ordered an inventory of all the silver in the country, undoubtedly with the aim of confiscating it at some future time. Nevertheless, by June it was clear that no one was willing to comply with the order and in July the idea was abandoned.[37]

Nevertheless, despite the problems of finance, the delays, and the lack of coherence caused by Philip's undertaking so much at once, preparations for the various enterprises proceeded apace, and in mid-July Francesco Soranzo was able to report that a fleet and army had been assembled in Portugal, among other places, perceptively noting that "the ministers have embarked on this enterprise when already engaged in so many others in order to show the power of this crown. Nor do they omit to go about vaunting and exaggerating the ease with which in a short time they have put together such military and naval forces; for they calculate that at one and the same moment the King has despatched thirty thousand infantry, namely eight thousand to Flanders, six thousand to the Archduke Ferdinand, ten thousand on board the Mediterranean fleet, and six on board the Atlantic Fleet."[38]

But while preparations continued, events were occurring elsewhere that would affect the outcome of these undertakings. In Flanders, the archduke, despite the mutiny of some of his garrisons and the lack of provisions or reinforcements, was eventually forced to sally forth and engage the Dutch forces, who had started the year's offensive at last.[39] Count Maurice had assembled his army at the end of May and, after making some show of attempting assaults on Flanders or Brabant, had finally turned toward Guelders, arriving at Rheinberg on 10 June and immediately laying siege with a force of seventeen thousand men and fifty cannon. The archduke, unable to raise the siege without the reinforcements coming from Milan, took a desperate gamble and decided to try and divert Maurice from Rheinberg by himself laying siege to the seaport town of Ostend. The Dutch had staged their incursion into Brabant as part of a two-pronged strategy whose main target was once again the Flanders coast. Once the Spanish forces had been diverted toward the northeast, Dutch and English forces were to have crossed the sea to Ostend, where they would stage an assault on Flanders. Albert's moves preempted the second phase of the Dutch plan.[40]

Ostend was the last remaining Dutch citadel in Flanders and as such was a thorn in the side of the Habsburgs. In 1578 it had been extensively fortified by the Dutch and, after a failed five-day siege by the duke of Parma in the 1580s, these fortifications had been extended and enhanced. After 1596, fearing the newly arrived archduke too would lay siege to the fort, they undertook further rebuilding and strengthening of the fortifications, completing the modifications in the spring of 1601. It was now strongly garrisoned by a multinational force led by the English. Without doubt, the fortifications as they stood when the archduke's army encamped before them on 5 July 1601 were formidable and state of the art (fig. 4).[41]

Albert began by splitting his force of seven thousand men into two parts, placing about two thousand on the east and the rest on the west with a battery of cannon, and immediately started firing artillery rounds over the walls and into the town. Despite this initial bombardment, however, it was thought by some that the archduke had neither sufficient forces nor munitions to effect a full siege, one agent reporting that "they shoote not above a Shott or two in a Day."[42] Actually, the problem was not with the scantiness of ammunition used but rather with its complete ineffectiveness. For by August Albert's forces were pouring a constant hail of artillery on the town both day and night. It was estimated that he had

4. The Siege of Ostend, August 1601

used more than thirty-six thousand rounds (at a rate of six or seven hundred a day) and killed some eight hundred defenders; yet, as an English captain pointed out, replacements were coming in at the same rate via the sea, and the bastions, though battered, were holding strong and returning some three to four hundred rounds per day![43]

In fact there were many who thought the undertaking was foolhardy to begin with. As great a military leader as Parma had abandoned his siege of the fort in 1583, deeming it impossible to take. Because it was a port town with a good harbor for resupply, the only chance Albert had of capturing it was through naval superiority that would have enabled him to stop reinforcements from getting through to the garrison. Naval superiority, however, he did not have, nor, seemingly, was he possessed of the ability needed for such a difficult enterprise. The English taking part were certainly unimpressed by the archduke's showing; one, after some months of siege, even providing Cecil this withering critique:

> the Archduke by the often shifting of his ordnance, his idle attempting and unperfecting of mines and saps, doth more and more manifest the greatness of his desires and the meanness of his abilities. Indeed, I see now how it may stand with reason that a town like Ostend, with one of the ablest commanders in Europe [Sir Francis Vere, commander after July], wherein are a far greater number of hands to defend than can possibley be brought to assail the same, and so plentifully stored with whatsoever may be required for the conservation thereof, and lastly, so friendly neighboured with the sea, which yieldeth a constant opportunity for retiring the sick and wounded and restoring sound men in their places, cannot be carried by a much more potent enemy than the Archduke.[44]

Nevertheless the archduke, even admitting his strategic, tactical, and financial difficulties, could not pass on the offer that the States of the province of Flanders (the Staten van Vlaanderen) made for ridding them of the presence of the fort and its exactions: three hundred thousand florins per month during the siege and ninety thousand per month for three years thereafter should the town be taken.[45] This incentive, plus the fact that he expected to receive reinforcements in due time from Fuentes, prompted Albert to view the enterprise with optimism, even—it was rumored— promising to take the town before Saint James's day (25 July).[46]

As reinforcements from the archduke's territories made their way to Ostend, the problems of insufficient forces and munitions were slowly being mitigated, and the prospects of making progress were improving. By the middle of July, Albert's army totaled some fourteen thousand troops. It was soon clear, however, that Maurice would not be diverted by Albert's activities in Flanders. Upon learning of the siege, Maurice was reported to have said, happily, "Let us leave him there knocking at the gate for a long time, this piece here [Rheinberg] shall not escape me."[47] He refused to call off his own siege of Rheinberg and instead merely sent two regiments of reinforcements to Ostend under the command of the English general Sir Francis Vere. In a short time Vere had strengthened his own position and had begun sallying out to attack the besiegers, inflicting considerable losses in the process. Nonetheless on 25 July the first reinforcements from Italy began to arrive and were immediately thrown into the fray, thereby saving the archduke's forces from a surprise attack by Vere's troops and giving Albert hope that the operation would ultimately be successful.[48]

In the first week of August, however, when Rheinberg capitulated to count Maurice, thus freeing up the army that had besieged the city, it was apparent that Albert's siege of Ostend had failed in its primary aim. Nevertheless the archduke could not abandon the siege; prestige now demanded that he take the fort. Prestige, too, demanded that the Dutch hold it. Ostend, once no more than a localized problem for the province of Flanders, was therefore transformed into the focal symbol of the entire war. In short order this dramatic struggle attracted international attention from observers who were careful to note the issues at stake. The Venetians, ever sensitive to the political ramifications of events, pointed out that the loss of Ostend for either side would be a severely damaging blow to reputation: "Both sides put out all their strength. The Archduke has declared that he will die rather than retire. The States, assisted by the Queen of England, omit nothing for the defense of the place. If the Archduke is forced to retire, he loses in reputation, and will have wasted a vast quantity of money. The fall of Ostend would be a great blow to the States and to the Queen of England." Strategically, too, the outcome of the struggle was of the utmost import, one observer noting, with some exaggeration, that "if the Archduke faileth in this project, he must, in all likelihood, seek himself elsewhere than in Flanders; but if Ostend be lost, it is more clear than the sun that all the towns in Zealand will be transformed into villages, if they be not utterly abandoned."[49]

At the end of August even Henry IV moved to Calais, where he could better watch Spanish activity. The Habsburg side assumed that this move was designed to make the archduke worry about possible French action to save the rebels. Other observers, too, thought that Henry was eager for some direct confrontation with the Spanish; the Venetian ambassador wrote home that "if the King could find a good excuse for declaring war, he would most probably do so." In reality Henry was not yet willing to wage open war against Spain and was instead engaging in a bluff designed to put the Spanish on the defensive at a time when Habsburg forces were occupied at Ostend so that Philip would ratify the Vervins treaty. The Spanish were indeed not a little distressed at signs of a new French aggressiveness, both in the Low Countries and along the border with Navarre, where it was rumored that Henry had started amassing troops. The Council of State suggested that Philip prepare his forces for a new war with France.[50]

Albert's ill-conceived siege, while saving the Habsburg provinces from the two-pronged invasion by the Dutch and English, had certainly put the Spanish in difficult straits and threatened to unravel all the carefully woven threads in Philip's military strategy. Henry, knowing the Habsburg forces were pinned down in the north, thus freeing up his flank, could make feints toward the Spanish territories on his southern border. Moreover, the intended invasion of England could not go forward because Albert was using all the munitions stored for it on his campaign, and the English would not now feel as threatened by the diversion in Ireland since they knew the archduke would be syphoning off the needed Spanish military supplies. And in fact this was exactly how the English reacted. In March of the following year, Cecil, demonstrating a keen grasp of strategy, was to write:

> He [the Spanish king] will not be so vain to attempt England (east or west) till Ireland were fitted to his appetite, and the army of the Low Country (without which England shall never be invaded) freed from the siege of Ostend. In which consideration seeing that place comes in question, I think it not amiss to let you know that next the preserving of Ireland . . . all things consider it importeth infinitely her Majesty: for although it is true that in the defence thereof the Estate's means are much consumed, yet if the Duke's obstinate siege long continue, and conclude without success, the apprehension thereof in all the Provinces will work an infinite alienation. Besides that, whiles the army is so engaged, we are sure it hath his hands full.[51]

The Spanish ministers were soon to discover, however, that not only had Albert disrupted their military strategy, he was also threatening to upset their diplomacy. In August he had Elizabeth's envoy seized while entering Flanders, complaining that the queen had betrayed him by sending someone to negotiate while simultaneously providing upward of two thousand men for the defense of Ostend. The effect of his actions was to push the English closer to the French and Dutch. This ran directly contrary to Spanish aims, which were to divide the English and French if possible; they wanted to prevent not only a joint military action but also an English succession favorable to the French king. Henry, for his part, wasted no time in seizing the opportunity to enlist the queen in new ventures against the Spanish. In September he met with Elizabeth's ambassador, Thomas Edmondes, to discuss possible collective action, suggesting that if she launched an attack on Flanders, he would help defray the costs. As the Habsburg luck would have it, Henry refused to back up his words with an army, and it was finally judged that his intention was merely to get the English and Dutch to commit heavily while he waited on the sidelines.[52]

Also in August the court learned that Albert was engaged in secret negotiations with the Dutch. A representative of the northern provinces had approached the archduke wanting to know how he would respond to the four major points needed to reach an agreement: a religious settlement; the removal of the Spanish army; the form of government; and the security of any final agreement. The archduke responded that he would grant free exercise of Protestantism, give full satisfaction regarding the removal of troops, give the Dutch a share in the government, and provide reasonable security for the agreement. Baltasar de Zúñiga, unwilling to see these talks proceed so swiftly that the Spanish would have no input, suggested that Albert try to arrange a cease-fire while the issues were discussed, since delays were inevitable. But Albert responded that "there were only two roads open to them: the one to prosecute the war with the good assistance of Your Majesty; and the other the peace, because a cease-fire [alone] would be to remain in perpetual war." The archduke also pointed out to Zúñiga that by the terms of the donation of the states, he had only to keep garrisons in three cities, but that these could be of any nation and not just Spaniards. And in terms of how the government would be arranged, it was even suggested that Maurice unite with the Habsburgs through marriage! Clearly, the archduke was not acting within the guidelines laid out for Spanish diplomatic strategy, in either the short

or long term. Zúñiga was at a loss as to how to proceed and even requested that someone else be sent to assist him in dealing with not only
the issues but the archduke![53]

In September, a stripped-down Council of State, a new junta similar
to Philip II's junta de noche, composed of Juan de Borja, president of the
council of Portugal; Juan de Zúñiga, count of Miranda; Father Gaspar de
Córdoba, the king's confessor; and Juan de Idiáquez, Grand Commander
of León, took up the issue.[54] The junta was dismayed at the archduke's actions. Although it recommended that some measures might be discussed,
it emphasized that Carrillo already carried full instructions regarding the
religious issue (see chap. 2). But despite their agreement with elements of
the archduke's measures, the junta was still deeply disturbed at his independence, telling the king that they were concerned that Albert should
have "declared with such liberty that he does not want an armistice,"
which was the only measure the councillors considered advisable. They
felt that the archduke could not possibly have promoted only two alternatives—permanent peace or war—since neither would be beneficial to the
his maintenance of his own states. Given that, they suggested that Albert
was merely trying to prod the king into guaranteeing the subsidies he
had promised, for it was "not possible that he could live in such a fantasy
world." The junta resolved, therefore, that Rodrigo Lasso be sent back immediately with as much money as could be gathered—some five hundred
thousand ducats—and a message assuring the archdukes that everything
possible was being done to solve their problems (in that the king looked
upon them as his own) but that future provisions were not assured. The
king agreed but insisted as a condition of any assistance that no treaty be
concluded which would require the withdrawal of Spanish troops, pointing out that "it is necessary to consider the situation there and the one
here, both for present purposes and for when the day of my succession to
those states should arrive, since the passage of time keeps revealing the
inconveniences of the alienation of them that were not thought of at the
time."[55]

Worry over the future of the Low Countries had certainly grown.
There is even a hint that the Spanish were considering taking over the
sovereignty one way or another. The councillors recommended that, in
the event of the archdukes' giving up the territories and going elsewhere,
Fuentes, being a capable general, be sent to govern Flanders; they also reminded the king that Parma had won back the southern provinces with

a mere 1,800,000 ducats a year.[56] Meanwhile, as an answer to Zúñiga's plea for assistance, they again recommended that someone be sent to serve alongside the infanta as mayordomo mayor and represent the Spanish interest in the provinces, suggesting as candidates Francisco de Rojas, marquis of Poza and president of the Council of Finance, and Enrique de Guzmán, count of Olivares.[57] In any event, the king refused to make a decision about sending someone, although it was subsequently obvious that he did think long and hard about the issue of the archdukes' giving up Flanders: a couple of months later he asked the junta to look into the benefits of suggesting that they be persuaded to relinquish the states of Flanders to Spain. The members responded that such a move would better guarantee the security of the Spanish-controlled provinces, since the king had more resources at his disposal than the archdukes, but that a loss of the provinces while under his protection would severely damage his reputation. To prevent this they suggested that the transfer take place only after a cease-fire had been agreed upon, thus leaving the southern provinces temporarily free of military commitments. Finally, they urged the king to consider massive bribes to Maurice and other ministers of the northern provinces to win them to the idea of the cease-fire.[58]

Massive bribes, however, were something Philip could not, at this stage, have managed. He now had other commitments. After so many delays and hesitations, the armada against Ireland, totaling thirty-three ships, had set sail from Portugal on 3 September, carrying 4,432 men. Philip's dream of landing forces on British soil was about to happen.

That this was a late departure for an expedition to the north became readily apparent. Contrary winds and then a storm, which dispersed some of the galleons, kept the fleet from reaching the planned invasion site in northern Ireland, close to the Irish rebel forces led by Hugh O'Neill and Hugh O'Donnel, earl of Tyrconnell. Instead Juan de Aguila, the infantry commander, was forced to disembark at a secondary rendezvous site; on 2 October he landed with only seventeen hundred men at the town of Kinsale, on the southern coast of Ireland.[59]

The expedition was a failure from its inception. The forty-five hundred men were far fewer than the six thousand initially envisioned and even mandated. This force, as Martín de Padilla—who did not get command—had previously pointed out to Philip, was far too small for the invasion of Ireland, since garrisons would be needed to hold the towns and forts that were captured. Nevertheless the king and the rest of the council believed that it was more important to bolster the confidence of the Irish for the time being, and so they let the armada depart, with the expectation that reinforcements would soon follow.[60] As a result of disputes among the expedition's leaders and the wintry weather, however, Aguila now found himself situated at the point farthest away from the rebel Irish forces and therefore failed to make the necessary linkup. In addition, the army was not only ill equipped but inadequately victualed and so could not attempt to push out of Kinsale to effect the link. Kinsale itself was not a site conducive to withstanding a siege. It was poorly fortified and surrounded by high ground on which enemy cannon could be placed. The English, on the other hand, were well armed and provisioned and their recruits were of high quality. Nevertheless, despite the problems he faced, Aguila set about diligently fortifying the town and requesting resupply from Spain.[61]

On 9 October two of the ships that had been separated by the storm managed to arrive in Kinsale, which brought the total of Aguila's force to a little over three thousand men. But on the same day, Brochero, the naval commander, under orders, left with the majority of the ships to return to Spain, leaving the Spanish without a secure access to Kinsale by sea. Philip, upon hearing of Aguila's landfall, immediately ordered the raising of reinforcements and the dispatch of food and munitions, but, since he was unaware of the scale of operations being prepared in England, they were not in the amounts needed to make the operation successful. By the end of October, Aguila's force had been reduced through sickness, overwork, and desertion to only twenty-five hundred effectives. On 4 November, the English commander, Lord Mountjoy, with an army of more than seven thousand men, managed to seize one of the hills overlooking Kinsale and immediately began to bombard the Spanish within the town. The siege of Kinsale had begun.[62]

The ineffectiveness of the Spanish invasion of Ireland was not determined by material forces alone. There were also failures at the conceptual and ideological levels. Part of the problem was the Spanish inability to choose one course of action, because of the need to address strategic as well as ideological needs. The invasion of Ireland was meant to push the English into signing a peace treaty with Spain and at the same time to secure the Spanish a foothold in the British Isles from which they could enforce their claims to the throne in the event of Elizabeth's death. But there was also the real desire on the part of Philip to assist the Catholics against their Protestant overlords. The Spanish force was to provide the backbone for a countrywide Catholic uprising, complete with papal sanction. In the end it was the failure to secure widespread Catholic support that prevented the Spanish from realizing either of their other aims.

Papal support for the Hispano-Irish project was inextricably bound up with the issue of the English succession. To achieve a general uprising of the Catholic Irish in support of the Spanish troops, O'Neill and Philip's ministers had to convince Pope Clement VIII to do as Sixtus V had done for Philip II's proposed invasion of England: make it a matter of conscience for the Catholics to support the Spaniards.[63] To secure this, however, the Papacy had to be convinced that Spanish intentions were in its own best interest and in that of Catholicism in general. This was indeed difficult. There was no love lost between the Spanish and Clement VIII, who had successfully freed the Papacy from the dominance of Spain by supporting Henry IV in the latter's conversion to Catholicism. Once again the Papacy stood in the position of broker between the two most powerful Catholic kingdoms. Giving too much support to Spanish aims might have jeopardized that position.

The duke of Sessa had been engaged in negotiations concerning the succession of England throughout 1601 and discussed these at length with Baltasar de Zúñiga. In August Zúñiga suggested that the Spaniards should not try for the throne, since not even the pope would be convinced that such ambitions were based on religious zeal; rather, they might be interpreted as "the Spaniards trying to make themselves lords of everything." Zúñiga pointed out that the infanta's claims would face many difficulties from the kings of France, Scotland, and Denmark, as well as from the "heretics" of Germany, Holland, and England. Given this, he thought it best to enlist the Jesuit priests in England to gain the support of the nobility with bribes and use them to give a reasonable assent to the succession. The French, too, were interested in the issue of the succession and wished to see their own candidate put forward, favoring in this respect King James of Scotland because of the long association of the French and the Scots. In the interests of their own position in Europe, the French clearly could not allow the Spanish to succeed. One thing was soon apparent, however: the pope would not throw his weight behind the Spanish claims. The court at Rome ultimately leaned heavily toward the candidacy of James because of his apparent Catholic tendencies and their hopes of his eventual conversion, though an even more important motive, as

Sessa perceptively noted, was to prevent the kingdom from falling "into our hands or into those of someone favorable to us, envy of our greatness permitting such behavior." As a result of an untimely triumph of *raison d'état* over ideology, Juan de Aguila carried no order for the Irish Catholics to rise up and defend the faith, leaving him to face the English forces virtually alone.[64]

Not surprisingly, in the face of its lack of either ideological or material strength, the Spanish landing in Kinsale failed in its intended aim of pressuring the English into peace. In October, Albert had once again sent Jerome Coomans to the queen to arrange for a meeting of deputies to discuss peace. The latter listened willingly enough to his proposals but, given the concurrent negotiations with the French for assistance against the Habsburg forces, would not commit herself to more. Soon afterward, indignant at hearing of the Spanish landing in Ireland while simultaneously being sued for peace, Elizabeth abruptly dismissed the archduke's envoy. So as 1601 was drawing to a close, the English and the Habsburgs were once again not on speaking terms. Although the situation did not look favorable for the Spanish, on the English side there was a certain amount of optimism, allowing Cecil, a trifle gleefully, to sum up their respective situations thus:

> In the meantime you see we are not asleep, nor all the conditions agreed on for the peace, between the King of Spain and the Queen, nor we that are pensioners to the infanta (according to the excellent Scottish intelligence) so faithful to him yet, but that we keep him from Ostend and mean to pull him by the ears out of Ireland. . . . So as when I consider who is there [in Ostend] with such a garrison, and how gallant a Deputy and a President we have in Munster, with a good army, I hope this year will not prove [Philip's] jubilee, if it prosper no better than it beginneth; for he hath lost Berke [Rheinberg], he hath failed of Ostend, his army failed before Algier, and I hope the like shall follow in sequence in Ireland.[65]

The Spanish were indeed in a difficult period. All Philip's enterprises had suffered disaster. Despite the extensive mobilization of Spanish forces in the Mediterranean "on a scale unknown for years," the eventual expedition lead by Gian Andrea Doria had resulted in no substantial gains for the monarchy. Striking out for Algiers on 5 August, Doria had been struck by severe weather and strong winds, which prevented any landing. To make matters worse, on the return journey the storms had dispersed the ships and all the men. Philip's attempt to settle things once and for all in North Africa had failed.[66] At Ostend, just when it seemed that the archduke, buoyed by a constant stream of fresh troops, was on the verge of taking the beleaguered and starving town, a fleet of five ships from Zeeland arrived filled with some six hundred reinforcements and a store of ammunition. The garrison immediately resolved to cease all talk of surrender and continue their defense of the town, much to the dismay of the archduke, who had been on the point of winning it so easily.[67]

In Ireland much the same turnabout of Spanish fortunes had occurred. At the beginning of December a fleet of ten ships under the command of Pedro de Zubiaur set sail from La Coruña with more than eight hundred reinforcements and provisions for Aguila's forces in Kinsale. Unfortunately, once again the forces failed to land where they had intended. Six of the ships, carrying 621 infantry, managed to make port in Castlehaven, thirty miles to the southwest, and a seventh, with eighty men, landed at Kinsale. Nevertheless Zubiaur's decisiveness in the face of having missed Kinsale impressed the local clans, who at last declared for the Catholic cause. At the same time O'Neill and O'Donnell, in an incredible feat of generalship, brought their forces south through miles of hostile terrain and inclement weather and arrived on the flank of Mountjoy's besieging forces.[68] All of southwestern Munster was in arms, and the Spanish situation had apparently taken a turn for the better. Then suddenly the Spanish position fell apart. On 31 December O'Neill made to attack the English rear but then withdrew and decided to try again. His assault was supposed to coincide with a simultaneous sortie by Aguila's forces, but something went wrong. When O'Neill again attacked on 3 January 1602, Aguila's forces still failed to sally forth and O'Neill once more withdrew. This time, however, Mountjoy's forces pursued the rebel army and inflicted terrible losses. O'Neill's army was finished. A week later, an exhausted Aguila, recognizing that he was seriously outnumbered and without hopes of immediate reinforcement, surrendered the town. With his defeat went all hopes for both Irish independence and a Spanish beachhead for the invasion of England.

CHAPTER 4

"Driblets like Sips of Broth": In Search of the Elusive Cure-All

❖ ❖ ❖

You see here, sir, how the enemy always has the advantage against us
in strength and forces in campaign. And thus those who flatter His Majesty
and let him think that the enemy has no power, are doing much wrong.
For this is the way to lose everything and put the very
states of His Majesty at risk.

—Anonymous advice paper sent to the count of Solre

The year 1602 was a critical juncture in Philip's conduct of the
northern wars. The failures in Algiers, Flanders, and Ireland demonstrated that it was time to reassess Spanish strategy. Already in
late December 1601, though still unaware of Aguila's surrender, the Council of State had begun such an analysis. The occasion was the discussion of
Martín de Padilla's letter to Philip written earlier that month. In a blister-
ing criticism of Spanish policy to date, the Adelantado told Philip: "The
reinforcement needed [for Kinsale] is one that will end the business for
once and for all, and not driblets like sips of broth, that will only prolong
the agony, and allow the invalid to die after all. . . . I have been grieved
for some years past to see that, from motives of economy, expeditions are
undertaken with such small forces that they principally serve to irritate
our enemies, rather than to punish them. The worst of it is that wars thus
become chronic, and the expense and trouble resulting from long continued warfare are endless."[1] The council could not, of course, fault the
Adelantado's analysis, even if it did come from someone many considered
partially culpable for past Spanish failures. So the members gave immediate orders for the preparation of a new fleet that would sail in the spring,
as soon as weather permitted.[2]

In addition to this cutting criticism of policy, however, the Adelantado also offered some constructive suggestions. In the face of recurring French and English threats, he recommended that a fleet of galleys, continuously manned with infantry, be stationed in Spain to be rapidly deployed wherever needed. This, he pointed out, would cut the costs and problems of sending armies to every location where the Spanish apprehended danger. "Otherwise," he stated, "it will not be necessary for our enemies to make war on us; they need only threaten to do so, and our expenditure itself will crush us without their drawing a sword."[3] Again, the council wisely chose to heed the Adelantado's advice and agreed to the development of such a "rapid deployment force."

The exigencies of these situations notwithstanding, however, the council ran headlong into the same problem that always confronted them: the inability to find the money for the operations. The king's confessor, now handling matters of finance, attempted to temper their excitement by pointing out to members that the treasury was dry; instead of preparing new fleets they would have to trust in God to watch over the Spanish forces in Kinsale. At any rate the Spanish soon learned that all hope for success in Ireland was lost, even had they had time to get fleets ready for deployment. On 29 January the council heard of the defeat and retreat of the earls (O'Neill and O'Donnell) and realized that there was little they could do. "The worst of it," the councillors apprehensively told the king, "is that your Majesty's prestige is at stake, and there is no means of sending effective and prompt aid for want of ships, men, arms, etc.; everything here being very scarce and short." Nevertheless, refusing to give up without a struggle, they suggested the immediate dispatch of the militia from Estremadura to Portugal to man the defenses there so that the Portuguese garrisons could be sent to Ireland "without an hour's delay." And they even promised Zubiaur (since returned to Spain) a knighthood if he could get them all to Aguila before the latter's defeat. "But," they said, in a clear demonstration of pessimism, "all these are only palliatives, and not cures for the disease, nor will they prevent any attempt on Spain itself; it is advisable that everything should be put in order of defence here."[4] With regard to England, they knew that they had lost the initiative and could now only wait out events. Their pessimism was substantiated when within less than a month, on 25 February, while the preparations for a new fleet were still in the planning stages, the Spanish received word at La Coruña of Aguila's surrender. As a final humiliation, although perhaps one unknown to the Spanish, in September the English used captured

Spanish silver to mint new coinage for Ireland! Spain's Irish strategy was a clear failure and so too, by implication, was its overall English strategy. The ministers would have much to reconsider in the following months.[5]

Meanwhile the councillors were busy examining their policy toward Flanders. Toward the end of January a junta, composed of the count of Miranda and the king's confessor, Father Gaspar de Córdoba, advised the king that the best way to promote Habsburg interests in the north and secure the sea lanes to Spain and the Indies would be by "attending very deliberately to the conservation of the states of Flanders, putting naval matters there in order and preparing those here, at the same time spurring on Federico Spínola in the execution of his project."[6] The naval preparations spoken of may have been those suggested to one of Albert's advisers, Philippe de Croy, count of Solre, at about this time. In an advice paper addressed to him that was later seen in the Council of State in Spain, it was suggested that three things were necessary to defeat the Dutch: the Habsburgs would have to put things in good order in Flanders; arm ships to be used against the Dutch trade (at an estimated cost of 300,000 to 400,000 ducats, which would give them all the time necessary to prosecute the land war); and send an army to stop shipping on the Rhine.[7]

But while the ministers in Valladolid were considering naval preparations and their effects on the security of Spanish interests, the archduke continued to act unilaterally to protect his own. On 7 January Albert had launched an assault against Ostend. By then, however, the forces inside were up to strength and well provisioned. The result for the archduke's forces was an unmitigated disaster, "for some dayes after there was nothing to bee seene, but wagons full of maimed souldiers, which they carried to Bruges, and other places: and among others, there were seventeene Spaniards, which had but two legs among them all, the canon having carried away the rest."[8] Sources estimated that he lost over seven hundred men in that one assault. And it was the Spanish troops who bore the brunt of the military action: on 20 January the archduke wrote Philip that his army had few crack Spanish troops left since these had been used in the vanguard of his assaults. As was becoming usual, however, the Spanish were to make up for his military incompetence; on 19 January Albert received from Castile letters of credit for five hundred thousand ducats and within a week, on the strength of that bonus, he had begun raising reinforcements.[9]

It was increasingly evident that with the archduke in command it would take more than military activity to conserve the states of Flanders.

For the long term it would be up to diplomacy to resolve the issue. In late January, Baltasar de Zúñiga wrote to the king that Albert had finally swung around to the idea of an armistice and had set in motion a series of measures to bring it about. By means of the nobility, who had family and financial ties on both sides, he hoped to achieve some sort of understanding that the war was damaging to their interests. Through the intercession of an intimate friend of Oldenbarnevelt, Albert hoped to persuade the Dutch leader that the Habsburgs were seriously interested in a suspension of hostilities. Finally, he ordered Felipe de Ayala, his agent in Paris, to let Thomas Edmondes know that Elizabeth's positive intercession with the Dutch in the matter of an armistice would redound to her benefit in the Anglo-Habsburg negotiations. To sweeten his various offers Albert was to revoke the prohibitions on trade to the Catholic provinces.[10]

The council and Philip were elated to hear that the archduke would now follow their lead in treating for an armistice and ordered their representatives to get the talks going, though they urged Zúñiga to ensure that "great account be had of his Highness's authority and reputation" in that these were already endangered by the failures at Ostend. At the insistence of Zúñiga and Carrillo, the king and his advisers would not hear of allowing trade between the northern and southern provinces, for the continuance of such restrictions was, in their opinion, the sure way to make the Dutch need the peace.[11]

But what of the English? On 6 March Zúñiga reported that they showed renewed interest in the peace talks now that they were free of the Spanish menace in Ireland. To ferret out the truth of this, Zúñiga suggested that he, as opposed to Coomans, go to England this time. He advised, however, that the enemy's naval preparations suggested anything but a desire for peace and that the Spanish would therefore do well to continue to try to divert the English via continued support of the rebels in Ireland.[12]

But the advanced state of English naval preparations precluded any effective Spanish countermeasures. Cecil had persuaded the queen to send a fleet to the coast of the Iberian peninsula because he feared that Philip would unite Aguila's returning army with the reinforcements that had been intended for it and thus create another invasion force. A fleet of twelve English and twelve Dutch ships was ready to depart at the end of February with orders to "intercept and attack the Spanish fleet intended for Ireland . . . [;] to repair to the Spanish coast, between North Cape

and Lisbon, to discover what preparations are making; and . . . to intercept such provisions as are sent thither."[13] The fleet would certainly arrive before the Spanish could prepare anything to send north. Indeed,
the chronicler, Cabrera de Córdoba, reported that not only Spanish fleet
preparations but also defensive capabilities in general were so poor that
the residents of the Portuguese coast were leaving their homes in fear of
their lives. On 21 March the Venetian ambassadors reported that the king
had called off his projected trip to Portugal, giving the excuse that "it is
not fitting for the King to be so close to his enemy unless he is better
provided than he is at present to repel their forces."[14]

It certainly appeared that the council's distrust of supposed English
"longing for peace" was well founded. The English wanted peace only
because they now held the decided advantage, not only in the Atlantic
but in Flanders as well. As noted earlier, the English were not about to
give up their support of Ostend, "for," opined Cecil, "if we can still engage and waste that army which is the garland of Spain before that place,
[Philip] will be at little ease to think of other enterprises; it being sufficient reason for us to value that port at a high price, seeing he could be
contented to purchase it at so dear a rate." And if the English were willing to stand toe to toe with the Spaniards in military matters, they were
even more willing to stand firm when it came to diplomatic negotiations,
especially given their favorable bargaining position. At the end of March,
Edmondes, when confronted with the archduke's newest proposal for reopening talks, replied in no uncertain terms that the queen would not be
duped and would enter negotiations only when she saw "on the part of
Spain, equally with the Archduke, a real disposition towards a lasting and
honourable truce." He also reiterated that the queen would not consider
abandoning the cautionary towns to the Spanish, nor would she agree to
formal negotiations until all the details were hammered out in advance. In
other words, her stand remained as it had at Boulogne: no compromise.[15]

This unyielding approach to negotiations was clearly the result of the
deterioration of the Spanish military situation in the north. The English
knew that the failures of the past year had demoralized the Spanish and
threatened to jeopardize their military readiness. Moreover, their allies,
the Dutch, showed no inclination to give the Army of Flanders a respite.
Toward the end of March the States began gathering together a large army
near Nijmegen for another strike into the heart of the southern provinces.
The archduke, aware that it would be impossible for him to counteract

this new threat while simultaneously carrying on the siege of Ostend, continued to request reinforcements from Italy. By the end of April, when the main body of troops from Milan had still not arrived in Flanders, he was getting desperate.[16]

The States' army was reportedly ready to move by the beginning of May. Although there had as usual been some question between Maurice and Oldenbarnevelt as to whether the Dutch offensive would take the form of another expedition or a siege, the advocate's view prevailed: it would be an expedition into east Brabant to free their Protestant brethren.[17] So sure were the Dutch that theirs was a war of liberation that before moving they published and distributed a declaration inviting the people of the southern provinces to rise up and join them in expelling the Spaniards.

At the Spanish court the ministers were still unaware of this latest Dutch military initiative. They continued with their reexamination of foreign policy and on 18 May produced two consultas touching on a variety of issues affecting their position in the north. The occasion was the receipt of letters from Baltasar de Zúñiga. Present were the Constable of Castile, the count of Alba, the marquis of Poza, the count of Chinchón, and the count of Miranda. From Zúñiga the councillors learned that Albert was once again taking matters into his own hands. While the archduke had set things in motion for the armistice, he had also told Zúñiga that he saw no other way to pacify the States than by assuring them they would never return to the Spanish crown. He therefore suggested naming the duke of Savoy as the successor of the archdukes! In the meantime Albert thought it best to call a halt to talks and suggested instead that he continue to try to obtain Dutch neutrality by utilizing a plan of reincorporating the Low Countries into the Holy Roman Empire, from which they had been separated by Charles V in 1548–49.

Not surprisingly, council members were displeased at this latest scheme of the archduke but placed the blame less on Albert himself than on those who were advising him, believing that "some of the natives in whom the archduke trusts and others interested in the war because of the benefit that accrues to them from it, have cooled the archduke [toward the armistice] and that this might be the cause of the laxity with which he has treated this business."[18] In other words, there were some members of the archduke's court who stood to lose much in the event of a cessation of hostilities. By the logic of the council members, those with an interest in the war held sway over the archduke's court and were using their influence to get Albert to promote peace measures that were bound to be unsuccessful. Juxtaposed to these warmongers were advisers whose ultimate aim, according to Carrillo, was the expulsion of the Spanish from the Low Countries: "Some people of those States, of better position than intention, try as much as possible to negate the talks of truce, sweetening their venom through flattery of his Highness and counseling him that permanent peace is better, it seeming to them that with permanent peace the Spanish and their forts would end, but that with the truce everything would have to remain in the same state as now."[19] From the perspective of Madrid, then, neither of the main factions at the archdukes' court had Spanish interests at heart. At a loss as to how to proceed, the council's only advice on this matter—perhaps showing an understanding of its limits in influencing policy making in Brussels—was to win over such people with the promise of rewards for those who endeavored to implement a truce.[20]

Even if the councillors could get the archduke and his advisers to support an armistice, however, they knew they still faced the problem of getting the Dutch to agree to it. They fully realized that their diplomatic position was directly linked to their military position (or at least to its appearance). While pointing this out to Philip, the council nevertheless recommended continued efforts to seek a truce, "even though getting a truce with the rebels is a great difficulty, because what will move them to it is seeing Your Majesty superior or at least equal in the forces necessary to wage the war against them, and it is clear that they have to consider that if Your Majesty craves the truce it is because it is good for him and for the same reason it is not agreeable to them."[21]

The council's other main concern was the situation regarding England. The failure of the Ireland campaign was a setback to Spanish plans to have a military force ready should Queen Elizabeth die. Moreover, the councillors had as yet been unable to find the two hundred thousand ducats for Baltasar de Zúñiga to use in that event to aid the Catholics and support the claims of the infanta. As such they feared that Elizabeth would die before anything could be done to prepare for the infanta's assuming the throne and that James of Scotland would therefore be able to realize his own claims. And, as they told Philip, "it is clear enough that he will be a more powerful enemy than the Queen of England is now and things will be in a worse state than ever."[22] They suggested, therefore, that if the money for Zúñiga could not be found, then someone—perhaps Colonel

William Semple—should be sent to Scotland to win over the king and the Scottish Catholics. Although Philip agreed with this measure, he had not yet given up hope of seeing his own claimant on the throne and ordered that the money for Zúñiga be found immediately. Additionally it was soon clear that he still harbored plans for an invasion of England.[23]

In June, Philip sent word to Zúñiga and the archduke that the troops going to the Low Countries under the command of Ambrosio Spínola were for the express use of his brother, Federico. They were to pass directly to the port where Federico had his galleys, and this force, together with another five thousand Walloons and Germans, would, it was hoped, strike such fear into their Dutch enemies that they would not "dare to leave their houses," thus forestalling Maurice's invasion. By no means, Philip wrote, was the archduke to detain these forces, since, "upon this army is founded a design that he [Spínola] is taking care of; and if Your Highness detains him you will undo it all."[24]

Philip's instructions, however, arrived in Flanders too late to stop Albert (even had they been able) from deploying Spínola's troops to reinforce his own. On 20 June, Maurice and his army, consisting of more than twenty thousand infantry and five thousand cavalry, had crossed the river Waal and, proceeding with excellent discipline and order, had moved down the Maas (Meuse) to Maastricht, deep in the heart of Habsburg territory. There they suddenly halted for five days while the English troops, misinformed as to how many days victuals they would need, had to be reprovisioned. Upon hearing that Maurice's army had begun its invasion, Albert immediately dispatched the newly released Admiral of Aragon to block the Dutch advance. For this the archduke had gathered together from the garrisons along the French frontier and from levies of old men an army of almost ten thousand soldiers. Just then Ambrosio Spínola arrived from Italy with his contigent of 8759 men; without hesitation Albert sent him along to reinforce the admiral. Spínola, of course, protested against this diversion of his forces but could not wholly refuse them when their necessity was so apparent. Mendoza certainly welcomed Spínola's reinforcements but, no doubt remembering his own ill success at Nieuwpoort, hesitated to engage Maurice in the field. Instead he entrenched near Thienen (Tirlemont) and awaited the Dutch forces.[25]

Maurice's army arrived in the neighborhood of Thienen—only a day's march from Brussels—on 2 July. After a few failed attempts to get Mendoza to engage him, Maurice finally called a halt to his march; it was obvious to him that he could do nothing about such a large force situated behind adequate defenses and that advancing further would only leave it on his flank—and himself deep in enemy territory. Consequently, on 10 July he turned his army about and began to retrace his steps. He was unwilling, however, to write off the campaign as a whole and so decided to proceed with what had been his original intention before being diverted by Oldenbarnevelt and the States: to invest the town of Grave on the River Maas. On 19 July he began to fortify his position, eventually encircling the town with a ring of fifty masterfully designed forts "rather [more] worthy of the grand Emperor of the Turks than of a little commonwealth."[26]

Meanwhile the Admiral of Aragon had called his officers together to decide on the Spanish army's course of action. They decided that the best plan would be to follow Maurice's army and hope that it would fall into disorder during its retreat. But the admiral was still wary of an engagement, fearing that his few forces were no match for the Dutch. To remedy this he suggested an immediate levy of every man with soldiering experience in the country, which would give him an additional eighteen to twenty thousand men, enough to engage Count Maurice. But even the troops he had were ill equipped; the artillery, for instance, needed carpenters and drivers. Indeed, his best-supplied troops were those that had come with Spínola, but these were still untried recruits who lacked combat experience. Instead of following on the heels of Maurice, he therefore decided to move his army to the vicinity of Diest and wait to see what the latter would do, hoping in the meantime that Maurice would expend his provisions on the march. In the end, this hesitancy to engage the enemy was a serious tactical error, for it gave Maurice plenty of time to secure his position around Grave. Mendoza did not leave Diest until 20 July, by which time the Dutch army had already arrived at Grave. He held up his army at Hornen until 1 August, awaiting resupply and reinforcements, then proceeded to move between various camps, trying unsuccessfully to entice Maurice from his positions. When the admiral finally went directly to aid the fort at Grave on 10 August, it was in vain, "because he [Maurice] already had fortifications up to the sky and had taken all the most significant passes and high ground in the area."[27] Mendoza could do nothing but take up positions around Maurice's siege lines and try to make it as hard for him as possible.

By this time, despite being much weakened by sickness, Spínola's tercio had become an integral part of the admiral's offensive against Maurice's positions and could not possibly proceed to the rendezvous with Federico's galleys. When Philip learned of this, he could, of course, do nothing but acquiesce in what Albert had already done, telling Spínola that he was to "assist the Archduke, my uncle, wherever and however he orders you." These orders, however, ostensibly pertained only to the summer campaign, and even as late as September Philip had not given up hope that the enterprise of England might be brought off in the future. On 4 September he wrote Zúñiga of having received word from Spínola that his men were in a terrible state and much weakened by illness, "so that," he explained, "as I understand it little can be done with them *this summer.*" The plans for an invasion of England in 1602 were finished, the Spanish strategy seemingly defeated by the exigencies of the moment and by the independent activities of policy makers on the scene.[28]

Indeed, the Spanish seemed once again capable only of reaction in the face of their enemy's action. They could not plan strategy, since all their available resources had to be diverted to where they were most urgently needed. They had lost the buffers (of men, resources, time, and money) necessary to absorb even tactical errors, and hence their every failure affected the military and political situations elsewhere. Ironically enough, even their attempts to extricate themselves from their defensive posture brought them additional problems. A perfect example of this occurred in May when the French monarchy, taking advantage of Spanish preoccupation with the English fleet and the Dutch military activity in Brabant and seizing upon the unfolding Biron conspiracy as a pretext, decided to begin new levies of troops. Upon hearing the complaints of the Spanish ambassador in Paris, the French king could only reply that "he was really desirous for peace and that he wished to observe the terms of the treaty [of Vervins]; but seeing that others were arming he could not help doing the same." It was clear that Philip, if not careful, might be in danger, through weakness, of uniting his enemies against him once again. Spanish resources were being further drained by the fact that the monarchy did not have sufficient funds to finish off its enemies with one stroke. Spain was strong enough for any one of her enemies but too weak to face them all.[29]

This is not to say that Spain's enemies were always successful in their own tactical aims. On 10 April, Leveson and the English fleet had sighted the Spanish silver fleet returning from the West Indies but found themselves too outnumbered to attempt to capture any of the galleons. The

Spanish fleet arrived safely in San Lúcar on 16 April with a cargo of eleven million ducats, three million for the king. The English continued to have poor luck and were unsuccessful at stopping Spanish shipping along the coast of Portugal until 13 June, when they encountered a lone carrack from the Portuguese Indies. This ship, lost at sea for nearly two years, was limping home under the guard of eleven galleys, including eight commanded by Federico Spínola and destined for Flanders. After a short fight in which two of the galleys were sunk and the rest driven off, the carrack surrendered to Leveson's squadron. Unwilling to lose such a rich prize, Leveson chose to escort the carrack to Plymouth, putting an early end to English plans for a permanent blockading fleet.[30]

This lack of a fleet to espy Spanish preparations in their Portuguese ports was the cause of some distress to the English, who thought it might just be possible for the Spaniards to launch another autumn invasion of Ireland. On 19 July, Sir William Monson was ordered to take the English fleet out once again to monitor Spanish military activity, to destroy any Spanish shipping, and to buy up military provisions going to Spain on allied ships. However, contrary winds prevented his fleet from sailing for the entire month of August, and he did not depart until 10 September.[31] Even this did nothing to alleviate English fears, since in Cecil's estimation invading Ireland was a useful strategy that the Spanish would not forgo: "And truly (my Lorde) when it is considered how great a benefitt it is to the King of Spayn to consume the Queen with charge in Ireland, by bestowing only once a yeare some such forlorn Companyes—besides that he keepeth upp some kind of reputation abroad in followinge on his first deseigne by sending a feawe, which (being added to that which fame spreadeth of greater nombers) filleth the world with contynuall rumours of his undertakinge humor—I cannot be secured but that he will still feed that fyer with fuell."[32] Clearly the English were not as confident as they might have been given the Spanish setbacks. They could molest the Spanish empire, but they could not defeat it.

Likewise, Elizabeth and her advisers were not completely satisfied with the turn of events in Flanders. The queen had wanted another offensive somewhere near Ostend in order to divert the archduke's forces from the siege where her own forces and money were significantly engaged. To this end she had offered three thousand English troops and half their pay for the enterprise. According to Sir William Browne's account of an interview on this matter, she was not pleased at the truth: " 'When I heard,' continued the queen, 'that they were at first with their army as high as Nemighem [Nijmegen], I knew no good would be done; but Maurice would serve his own turn, and would in the end, turn to the Grave. I looked that they should have come down nearer to Ostend or Flanders. That might have startled the enemy, and that they promised me, or else I would not have let them have so many men.'"[33] Even the English soldiers were disappointed with the outcome of Maurice's campaign. In a perceptive commentary on the little that came out of the expedition, one of them also managed to highlight some of the main problems of the wars in Flanders: "So strange must it needs seem that our invincible army, which should have marched clean through the enemy's country, now lies entrenched at the siege of a little town, and suffer their [the Spanish] army to lie in open fields within three leagues of us. . . . Of the condition of this army, *the head and great General discovers it plainly that he will never make other war but by sieges, except such great advantages of an army as he shall never have but by the absolute decay of the Spanish power.*"[34]

Unfortunately Maurice's inability either to make any substantial gains or to decide the issue militarily was of little help to the Spanish, since his ineffectualness did nothing to alleviate the heavy monetary charges placed on the Army of Flanders or to help their bargaining position. Toward the end of July, Baltasar de Zúñiga wrote to the king that the States were unwilling to discuss any cease-fire; given their military successes, they felt such talks were prejudicial to their interests. Albert, assailed on both the military and diplomatic fronts, had reached the point where he was willing to concede everything in the latter to alleviate the former. He suggested that he would "embrace whatever measure, either this one [of cease-fire] or of neutrality or whatever other is offered," which Zúñiga interpreted to mean that he would favor the measure of neutrality — whereby he would withdraw from the war — over any other; effectively it would mean peace, with all that a full peace entailed. In other words, Albert was ready once again to go his own way and secure his interests ahead of those of the Spaniards.[35]

The king and his ministers received word of these new diplomatic initiatives and the military situation at the end of July. Despite the critical situation, however, it was not until 17 August that the members of the Council of State sat down to consider the matter. Exceedingly alarmed at the military situation, they reminded the king that their position had never before been so extreme and that the security of not only the Low

Countries but of the archdukes themselves depended on the conservation of the army, which would be impossible to effect unless a significant sum of money was sent with the shortest possible delay. Evidently jolted by all this, Philip, with tremendous effort and at high interest, managed to raise letters of credit for nine hundred thousand escudos, which he immediately dispatched to Flanders.[36]

Turning next to the field of diplomacy, Philip decided once and for all to put a stop to the archduke's independent activities. He told the council that "not only should my uncle be told that the deal must commence with a cease-fire, but also that he should open his eyes to the fact that he is not to consider anything else." The council, with Philip's consent, decided that in light of the problems with the archduke the powers to treat with the rebels should be sent to Zúñiga instead of Albert, even though some members believed that sending any powers before the Dutch showed signs of willingness to engage in talks would be detrimental to Philip's reputation. On 10 September the king sent the powers with a letter to Baltasar de Zúñiga. They represented the trust placed in Zúñiga not only by the Council but also by the king, for they gave him "power and faculty as ample, complete, and sufficient as such a case requires, that for me and in my name, he might treat, capitulate, and assent to the said cease-fire . . . in the form and manner that should appear good to him and with the most advantageous conditions that can be hoped."[37]

It was soon clear, however, that this extensive grant of authority to negotiate would do little to alleviate the problems in Flanders. The Spanish military situation there had gone from bad to worse; the rebels would be unwilling to discuss any peace. The admiral's soldiers, disgusted at his indecisive command and for the most part unpaid and without food and provisions, launched yet another mutiny, this time taking the town of Helmont (Hamont), south of Grave, before eventually moving to seize Hoogstraten, below Breda. By mid-September the number of mutineers stood at more than three thousand, including fifteen hundred cavalry— usually men of social standing and independent wealth. This disruption within his army made it all but impossible for the admiral to effect any relief of the besieged garrison in Grave. On 19 September the garrison of some eight hundred men capitulated. The Dutch army had suffered much in the two-month siege—the English companies being reduced to between forty and eighty men, mostly through sickness caused by the swampy conditions in Maurice's trenches—but the success meant that any consideration of a truce was out. As Zúñiga pointed out when he received his powers, "Our situation having worsened so much, in no way will the enemy come to the table, especially now that Grave has surrendered."[38]

In any event the archduke's administration was too preoccupied with the latest mutiny to concern itself with peace negotiations. Luckily the receipt of the extraordinary subsidy from Spain arrived in time for the archduke to pay three months of the army's arrears and thus prevent a wholesale disaster.[39] With the rest of his force assured, the admiral moved against the mutineers in Hoogstraten in order to force their capitulation. On 15 September the archduke published a decree banishing all those who did not return to their colors within three days and "giving leave unto all persons, of what estate and condition soever, freely, and without any danger of punishment, to kill the said mutineers, or any of them, after what sort and manner he may most conveniently do it." For every man killed, the person responsible would receive between ten and five hundred crowns. It was an extraordinary recourse that caused even the Dutch and their allies to offer some show of sympathy when the mutineers proffered their services to them in return for protection. While deciding not to accept the mutineers in his service, Maurice did offer them the protection of the guns of Bergen op Zoom should the admiral's forces prove strong enough to dislodge them. In the meantime the archduke took advantage of an offer from the papal nuncio, Ottavio Frangipani, to mediate the dispute. The mutineers demanded a retraction of the edict of banishment and proscription, which Albert promptly refused to grant; matters drew to a standstill.[40]

Back in Valladolid the latest mutinies forced the Council of State once again to consider the method of financial provisions for the provinces. In a long statement about the damages that the mutinies had caused to Spanish interests in the previous few years and the necessity of insuring against more, they recommended finding a means to make prompt and regular payments to the soldiers of the Army of Flanders. Under the system then in effect, they were forced to get letters of credit for large sums at high interest in Castile and then send them on the long journey to Flanders. By the time the letters reached the soldiers, much of the money had already gone toward repayment of interest. The councillors did not, however, know how to remedy the situation. Philip, in his reply, was more open. He told the council in no uncertain terms that everything possible had been done but that "the ministers of the treasury cannot do any more."[41]

The king's finances were indeed in a terrible state. In June he had issued a new supply of *vellón*, the copper money used in daily transactions, with less weight but the same face value, thereby inflating the money supply and earning himself a return of 100 percent. By the fall this measure had already begun to work its pernicious effect on the Spanish economy. Combined with other economic factors, it meant that the Cortes was unable to meet its obligation to provide the three million ducats of the millones for that year. The tax of an eighth part of the sale of wine and vinegar had brought in only half of what the kingdoms owed the king, and by October the procurators of the towns were in a serious dispute over whether they would have to make up the shortfall, given that the king had also not complied with the conditions of the grant to which he had agreed. Most of the representatives adhered faithfully to the government line that they would have to meet their obligations so that the king could faithfully execute his duty to protect the kingdoms. Using the domino argument by now all too prevalent in the discussion of the war in Flanders, they reminded the others that if Flanders should be lost, then so too would be the trade with the Indies and the peace of the peninsula, "since lacking the war in Flanders, they [the enemies] would come to wage it in Spain."[42]

The big question the Cortes, like the council, wanted to tackle, however, was how to provide sums on a continuous basis at low rates of interest, because, as one representative put it, echoing the words of the Adelantado in December of the previous year, "the plans that we are setting in motion serve only to refresh with a pitcher of water this kingdom which is seriously ill with fever, cutting its thirst while not removing the threat of death that awaits it."[43] Nonetheless, the immediate need to find money meant that they could do nothing to address these long-term needs. Just like their counterparts who were entrusted with the country's foreign policy making, these domestic leaders had lost the buffers necessary to engage in effective long-range financial strategy. Like the king they could only react to situations as they arose, applying the patches necessary to keep the leaky vessel of state afloat but unable to repair the structure enough to make it truly seaworthy.[44]

With money not forthcoming, little could be done about the precarious military situation engendered by the mutinies in Flanders. But as if this was not enough to wreck all of Philip's plans for the year, the destruction of half of Federico Spínola's fleet of galleys in the first week of

October assuredly ended any hope of an effective invasion of England. Already Spínola had lost two of his galleys in Portugal. Now, proceeding north with the other six, he encountered a fleet of English and Dutch ships patrolling the Channel off Dunkirk and Sluis. Caught in a pincer movement, Spínola lost two more galleys to gunfire; of the four remaining ships, two were forced to run aground where they were made ineffective by the desertion of their slaves. Federico managed to save a good portion of the treasure he carried—rumored at two hundred thousand ducats—but lost many of his soldiers and slaves, including those needed to bring back into service the seven galleys he already had at Sluis.[45]

But even before this latest disaster, it had been painfully clear to all concerned that a thorough reassessment of Spanish grand strategy, especially as it concerned the northern theater, was overdue.[46] Every new bit of information served only to confirm that impression. At the end of October the king and his council had letters from Baltasar de Zúñiga and the archduke on the sorry state of affairs. From them they learned that the Dutch would probably not be willing to hear talk of cease-fire at this stage and of Albert's proclamation and activities against the mutineers, two more indications that Albert could not satisfactorily carry out Spanish plans. Moreover, informants in London reminded them of the situation regarding the Catholic rebels in Ireland, the importance of which the council well understood. Nevertheless, the councillors had to inform the king that "for now we cannot see how we can assist them with the abundance of men and other things that such an enterprise requires."[47]

Under the circumstances the council argued that no treatment of a cease-fire should go forward at that time since it would be too damaging to the king's reputation; some military balance was necessary to make such a discussion feasible. It advised delaying consideration of the person to be sent to assist the archduke until a "cure-all" (remedio general) be found for the matter of Flanders, which was to be discussed in the near future; in the meantime, it was suggested, something might be done to entice Jorge Basta, a veteran of Alexander Farnese's wars in the Low Countries, to take the position, perhaps by awarding him the title of count.[48] Regarding the mutinies, the council argued that the archduke's drastic actions, while warranted, may have made the situation worse and suggested that something be done to mitigate the effect of the proclamation in order to prevent more widespread desertions to the enemy. With regard to Ireland, it suggested sending at present thirty thousand ducats to keep the

Irish rebels fighting and then ten thousand a month beginning in January 1603.

The most sweeping recommendations, however, came from the Constable of Castile. He distrusted the king of France, who while feigning a desire for peace, made military preparations and schemed with Spain's enemies on the side. He thought that Henry might join with England and the Dutch once again, especially since the latter two powers had received such a monetary bonus from the seizure of ships from the Indies, and make some effort against Philip's forces in the Low Countries. Or perhaps, since the English and Dutch had "fattened themselves" on what they had gained by sea that year, they would want to continue that course with greater force, this time going directly for the fleets or individual galleons returning from the East or West Indies. Given all this, he suggested—and the rest of the council agreed—that the king should consider what might be done "to oppose on all sides whatever they might intend, without focusing on one enterprise in particular, since according to the state of things it will not be a little thing to be able to attend to the defense with reputation." He promised that with all the Spanish forces in position and ready, they would not hesitate to seize whatever chance was offered them against Spain's enemies. It was just the right touch of martial rhetoric to win over the young king and, though overruling the council's recommendation that the talks proceed, he nevertheless agreed that the military situation should be looked into. The stage was set for the remedio general.

On 22 November, Albert wrote to the duke of Lerma that the government of Spain had to take a prompt resolution regarding the situation. He was obviously getting tired of constantly having to request a remedy to the problems in Flanders for, as he pointed out to Lerma with some exasperation, "the material in itself is so clear, and the importance of it so easy to comprehend, that I am spared spending time and reasons to persuade Your Lordship of it, and thus it remains for me only to beg you that since what is requested is so important to His Majesty, it is getting to be inexcusable so notably to hazard the loss of everything here."[49]

After all the failures that had occurred in the previous year as a result of the incompetant administration of Spain's military and financial resources—the loss in Ireland, the failure to stop Maurice's invasion of Brabant, the inability to take Ostend, the loss of Grave, the mutiny at Hamont, and the failure of the attack on Algiers—the Spanish themselves had come to the same conclusion; on 20 November, just two days before the archduke wrote this letter, the ministers sat down at a conference in Valladolid to arrive at just such a remedy. The consulta "concerning the general remedy for Flanders" that resulted from this conference runs to no less than fifty-two folio pages; writing perhaps the longest set of comments of his reign on any consulta, Philip annotated thirteen pages with his decisions. Without doubt this was a serious effort on the part of the policy makers in Spain.[50]

The councillors saw only four options open to them with regard to Flanders: to make a great effort in the war; to come to terms in either a truce or peace; to continue as they were; or to desist from the enterprise altogether. None of them believed the fourth option viable. First, Philip had an obligation to protect the Catholics who remained in those provinces. Second, to leave the northern provinces existing as a political entity, they argued, would be to create a more powerful enemy, one who, freed from the expenses of a hot war, would become an economic giant capable of carrying on three simultaneous wars and still coming out on top. "Such a power," they said, using the familiar argument of the diversionary war, "would be a direct threat to the Spanish monarchy throughout the world. They would be able to bring together great ocean fleets; the Indies would not be secure. Neither would the peace in Italy last, which has been conserved for 40 years because Flanders has been the battlefield of Europe. . . . And, it is to be believed, that by means of this war we have been without one in Spain . . . which is how the charges, tributes, and expenses which the treasuries of these kingdoms have incurred for Flanders have been justified." And third, giving up the war and therefore the provinces would be a severe blow to the king's reputation, an important component in the monarchy's power. For, they argued, "without reputation kingdoms cannot be maintained and it would surely be lost by cutting off such states, and even more so since they are a patrimony inherited in the male line; . . . if they were abandoned, with the whole world thinking it was because of a lack of the force necessary to sustain them, it would open the possibility that others would lose respect, and the evil intentions which are not carried out [by them] now for fear of being punished might then be discovered."

Likewise, continuing the struggle as they had done to that point seemed useless. Only the marquis of Velada urged a great effort against the Dutch, using a combination of two armies to invade the northern provinces, a fleet of galleys to prey on Dutch shipping, and the rupture of the dikes holding back the North Sea to force the rebels into submission.[51] Clearly these men knew that the monarchy could not at that time win the war, nor prolong it indefinitely.

So the real question was, as it had been, whether to strive for a permanent peace or a temporary armistice. The remaining councillors unanimously opted for the latter, since, as they had repeated countless times before, a peace would mean the withdrawal of all Spanish forces in Flanders and the endangering of the archdukes and their territories. "With the truce," they argued, "we would be assured against this danger, give ourselves time to rest from such excessive expenses and labors, and weaken the rebels militarily while they attended to the profit from trade and commerce, which, along with the peace they would enjoy, would show them how they have been fooled by those who govern them."

Having decided on an armistice, the councillors then had to contemplate how best to achieve that. None believed that the Dutch would readily agree to such a measure unless they were constrained to do so by military necessity. In other words, the Habsburgs would have to force the Dutch to the table. To do that Philip would have to order a thorough reform of the Army of Flanders in the hope of retrieving its once formidable reputation. This could be done by reducing its size, increasing the percentage of Castilian soldiers, improving its command structure, and insuring prompt payment of wages for the soldiers by keeping strict accountability and by separating such sums from those designated for the archduke.[52] But all this was not enough by itself; something still had to be done about the archduke's military incompetence. Their advice was a reiteration of that given by the council before: to send someone to Flanders "in whom should concur the parts and qualities that are needed [to command the army in the archduke's absence]; and it would be even better if he was even more qualified, so that not only would he serve on like occasions of the archduke's incapacitation, but would counsel and execute diverse things at the same time, like the siege of Ostend and the setting forth of the army offered this year." And to give the reformed army a chance to work its intended effect on the Dutch, the councillors urged Philip to back down in his dispute with Henry IV over the matter of the Biron conspiracy, since it was imperative that Spain maintain the peace with France; he could not afford to open another front.

Finally, Philip could do one thing more to bring the Dutch to the negotiating table: put a stop to the trade upon which they so depended by waging unrelenting economic warfare against them. This he could accomplish by strict enforcement of the trade embargo; by imposing a blockade on Dutch trade to the southern provinces; by attacking Dutch and English shipping; by putting a stop to the Dutch fishing fleets; by the formation of a fleet to patrol the Gibralter straits in order to shut down all Dutch trade to the Levant; by denying Dutch access to salt in Caboverde, Margarita, and Araya (in northern Brazil); and by allying himself with the king of Denmark in order to block the straits into the Baltic, thereby cutting off the Dutch grain supply.

Every one of these recommendations would have to be undertaken if the Spanish were to have any hope of success. Yet even this would not be enough, as Chinchón pointed out; Philip would have to take back sovereign control of the Low Countries from the archdukes, "with which would cease many of the inconveniences that have resulted from [their] going about in a different and less powerful proprietorship." Next, Philip would have to make a great effort, spending four or six years' budget in one. The Councils of State, War, and Finance would have to work day and night on the particular areas pertaining to them, trying to find ways to increase the military forces while cutting down and reforming their expenses. With all the planning done, Philip would then have to go in person to the Low Countries to win those in the loyal provinces to his cause. This would be achieved not only by his presence but also by publication of his orders that from a certain date forward only the Roman Catholic religion would be permitted in the provinces and by spreading throughout the provinces a paper detailing how the rebel peoples had been duped by their leaders. Finally, he would have to promise rewards and honors to those powerful people who would do what they could to win the northern provinces back to the Habsburgs.

It was a lot for the king to weigh and consider, and it took him some weeks to respond.[53] Undoubtedly he sought additional advice, perhaps even from Lerma, but since the response to the consulta is written in his hand, we must accept it and the decisions taken as his own. He was clearly overawed by the immensity of it all, for his first decision was to turn to his father's expedient when things did not seem well; he appealed to a higher authority to solve the problems: "I want you to understand that for the defense of my siblings and in order that those states are wholly reduced to the Catholic religion and do not leave their dominion nor my

Crown, I will venture both those [states] which God has entrusted to me and my own person if the other measures do not work and the Council thinks I should. And I trust in Him who will protect this cause as His own and help me if we do not force Him." To that end he called for prayers and sacrifices throughout the kingdom to extirpate sin and placate God's anger. And he rejected, as being contrary to his stated aim of reducing all the provinces to Catholicism, the idea of desisting from the struggle to get the rebel provinces back.

Having dealt with this spiritual aspect of policy, the king was willing to turn to more concrete proposals. In fact he had been completely persuaded by the more martial aspects of the council's opinions. His first order following the call for prayers was to cease all discussion of peace or a cease-fire immediately, even if it should proceed from the States-General themselves. Next he proceeded to overrule the more moderate council members and stated that although it might be better not to reopen the war with France, he would not tolerate French assistance to the rebels and their interference with the passage of tercios over the Spanish Road. As he saw it, "We experience [now] the same or just a little fewer of the damages and expenses of war as we would in open war while that king enjoys the comforts of peace [and] quiet at home, [all the while] fomenting the rebels who, with his assistance, have made and are making their well-known progress in those States, in these seas, and in the Indies, forcing on me such expenses. And I doubt not that if he should suffer part of these damages and expenses he would come much more quickly to terms for a good peace."

Passing on to the financial provisions for Flanders, he ordered that a monthly provision of two hundred thousand escudos be made to the archduke to be used solely for the army's expenses.[54] With this measure it was hoped to put things on a more stable footing and reduce the costs of raising great sums on short notice. To find the resources that would make possible such a drastic overhaul of the financial system, he ordered that every individual involved in finance, from the veedor general down to the the lowest official, be changed; the ministers would begin to treat fiscal matters with the attention they deserved, reforming past excesses and looking for anyone with the necessary experience, understanding, and legal training to assist in this task.[55]

Next Philip tackled the military situation, making it understood that he, and not Albert, was in charge: "That army is mine and needs reforming to such an extent that we should begin there, reducing it to a competent number made up of all nations, with at least six thousand Spanish effectives, not including the garrisons, and in time the nine thousand in Savoy will go from Milan, embarking in the galleys that should return to Italy." That done, he was finally willing to make a decision on the post of *maestre de campo general* (Captain-General of the Army). Since the only other distinguished candidate, Pedro Ernesto, count of Mansfelt, was thought to be too old (he was eighty-five), Philip ordered that the post be given to Jorge Basta, who was to return immediately from Austrian territory.[56] To command the cavalry, he appointed Luis de Velasco over the head of the more senior Agustín de Mejía.[57] He realized that these appointments were not, however, the answer to the problem of having someone to work alongside or, should it be necessary, in place of the archduke. Philip well understood that such a person was vital for the smooth control of the Low Countries, but he was hoping that the reformation of the army and the appointment of commanders would mitigate somewhat the immediacy of the problem. To ensure, however, that the reformation of the army not be corrupted by Albert's interference, he ordered that none of the archduke's "creatures" were to serve in it and even suggested sending some well-respected soldiers to act as overseers. Effectively Albert was to be stripped of his influence in military matters.

With the necessary military and financial reforms in place, Philip had no doubt that he could succeed against the rebels. Indeed, the rhetoric of his closing instructions indicates that the euphoria generated by this attempt to take a firm grip on the reins of policy in the north temporarily allowed the young king to believe that he might not even have to make peace: "Since the obstinacy and malevolence of the rebels and of those that foment them have gone so far, as you can see, the occasion has arrived to make war on them with blood and fire, carrying it by sea and land into the most vital of their homes, burning and drowning them and laying waste to their fields." Strong words indeed; yet, as will be seen, like those of 1574 or of 1599, they did not reflect the realities of Spanish power.[58]

CHAPTER 5

The English Succession and the Hope for a Settlement

❧ ❧ ❧

Already you will have heard of the death of the queen of England
and also that the king of Scotland has been proclaimed monarch of that
kingdom afterward. And although my right to that throne is well-known,
for now my intention is not to pursue it but rather to insure that
he who is most suitable to God and the augmentation
of the Catholic faith should get that crown.

—PHILIP III
instructions to Don Juan de Tassis

It was one thing to propose a cure-all and quite another to carry out its provisions. Almost immediately Philip and the council learned of some of the problems involved in reforming the Army of Flanders by increasing the number of Spanish troops: they could not get Spanish troops to Flanders. The French still threatened Savoy and were keeping the Spanish Road closed. Until the Spaniards could find another route north, no troops would be able to pass on to Flanders. Nevertheless, Philip ordered Spanish troops to Milan to be near Savoy in case an opening occurred through which they might move north.[1]

But the overriding problem was, as always, that of monetary provisions for the army. The councillors of state did their best to persuade Philip to order the provision of the remaining three hundred thousand ducats from the budget for 1602, plus an additional four hundred thousand to allow the archduke to raise more troops and put together an artillery train well ahead of the time when they should be needed. This, they suggested, would allow things to be completed faster and at less cost than if they waited until necessity forced their hand. Philip, however, had already made up his mind concerning the provisions for Flanders and was not about to change it before the new year had even begun. He would send two hundred thousand ducats for December, and then in January the provision of two hundred thousand ducats per month would begin. This, he thought, would be adequate once the council took into consideration the reduction of the army in line with the decisions taken in the remedio general.[2]

Monetary difficulties were also wreaking havoc with Spanish policy in Ireland. On 13 January 1603 the ministers read a memorandum concerning the state of the Irish rebellion and the plight of the Catholics now that they had no support from Spain. In a frank report to the king, the council wrote that the thirty thousand ducats promised to the Irish in March of 1602 should be provided immediately by any possible means; otherwise, the Catholics would go down in ignominious defeat and the English would be spared the expense of the war in Ireland. The councillors felt that the Catholics who had fought on after the defeat at Kinsale had done so because they had confidence in the promises of Philip III. By delaying assistance to them, Philip had already persuaded many that he must have changed his mind; they would not believe that his lack of support was caused by a lack of money. If he would not provide the promised sums, the council suggested, then "these people should be undeceived, so that they may be enabled to make the best terms they can, bad as the consequences might be, and such as his Majesty should never allow." Without money, policy was useless — and the councillors were not above telling the king so.[3]

Indeed, after having urged the king to decide on the cure-all, the council seemed intent on having him take more practical policy stands. In February it brought before him once again the issue of the succession to the crown of England. Elizabeth was by now showing definite signs of a final illness, and her demise was expected at any moment. Clearly, the king had to resolve once and for all what course he would take at the hour of her death. The issue loomed as the central policy question of the new year. The English Catholics were pressing the king to let them know his plans so that they could make their own accordingly. Waiting until the event had occurred would destroy their hopes of having a suitable candidate ready to contest the Scottish king's party, and their reliance upon Philip's help would "thus have only brought about their final ruin, to the irreparable injury of your Majesty and your dominions."[4]

The council, after careful review of correspondence from the English Catholics and Ambassador Zúñiga, gave a brief summary of its earlier recommendations of 11 July 1600. At that time it had been in favor of putting the infanta on the throne of England, as the most advantageous plan for Spanish aims, but emphasized that such a recommendation had been made "always on condition that we had the resources at our disposal necessary to carry the enterprise to a successful issue." Now those resources did not appear to be at hand, nor were the Catholics so favorably disposed toward the archdukes as they had once been, since the archdukes showed no willingness to carry out the enterprise, nor, more important, did the couple appear, four years after their marriage, to be able to provide an heir. Clearly it was unwise for the Catholics to support the candidacy of claimants who would put them in precisely the same situation just a few years on. Given all this, the councillors had to point out that there appeared no way to put the archdukes on the throne, especially given the opposition such a move would engender from France and the Protestant countries. To prevent the formation of a Franco-Protestant league against the Spanish king, the ministers therefore suggested that another candidate be put forward who would depend upon the support of Spain and would therefore be bound to Philip by patronage ties. They ruled out the duke of Savoy and the duke of Parma because of the opposition their candidacies would engender. Instead they recommended that Philip set aside concern for his own interests and consider as his most important objective the winning of England back to Catholicism; to accomplish this, he could accept a candidate from among the English Catholics themselves. This would satisfy the English desire to have an English king and would placate the French king, who would not want to see Scotland united with England and would therefore support an English candidate who had only indirect ties to Spain.

To insure against any contingency, the council recommended that current plans concerning the invasion of England go forward, since even if they proved to be unnecessary, they would still be of use in Flanders. The proposal was happily summed up thus: "The knot of the succession question will thereby be cut, and by one expenditure your Majesty will provide against two eventualities of the highest importance, without the risk of the expenditure being wasted." Finally, they suggested that if nothing positive could be done, then Philip should figure out a way to avoid offending James while not actually helping him either. This would at least insure his neutrality after becoming king. At any rate the decision had to be taken promptly and done in such a way that Philip would not appear to be backing down on his own candidate out of weakness but rather out of generosity and piety. Moreover, something would have to be done to secure the tacit support of the Henry IV for whatever candidate might be advanced. And if all of this was not done before Elizabeth's death, the Catholics would be "handed over to the executioner and religion would be finished off, and Flanders too, because of its vicinity." Faced with all this advice, Philip, in his characteristic manner, firmly and quickly resolved to deliberate further! Even the reportedly imminent death of the great queen could not move him to swift action.[5]

But, to be fair, the king had more immediate problems. On 13 February the council had presented him with their conclusions regarding the budgeted provisions for Flanders. According to their estimates, two hundred thousand ducats per month was just enough to support 22,763 infantry troops and 3,033 cavalry, of which 3,885 would be needed for garrison duty. This left an effective fighting force of only 21,911 men, certainly not enough to engage Maurice's army, for unless the Habsburg forces outnumbered the Dutch, the Habsburgs always suffered the worst of it. Moreover, these figures did not include the costs for artillery, weapons, munitions, or equipment, which fluctuated from month to month but normally amounted to a third of the cost of the army.[6]

Over a three-year period, the provisions certainly appeared large, but such guaranteed sums presupposed that Philip's army would be in a position to dictate whether it went on the offensive or remained on the defensive. This, of course, was clearly not true, for the Army of Flanders always had to "follow the road down which the enemy will travel."[7] If the Spanish army was unable to match the forces put into the field by the States, then Maurice would end up capturing all the towns on the Maas River and therefore be in position to cut off reinforcements coming through Luxembourg. The result would be that those loyal to the archdukes would see no hope of winning and would make accords with the States, to the detriment of Philip's monarchy, reputation, and treasury.

The council advised that Philip's forces must be ready to send Maurice reeling back, his head in his hands, which would in turn cause all the States' protectors to reconsider their support. To this end the ministers suggested increasing the provision to three hundred thousand ducats per month and shortening the time span over which it would be given. In addition they urged Philip to remit the remaining one hundred thousand ducats due from the previous year, plus the four hundred thousand requested by the archduke. That done, it would be necessary to order the four thousand Spanish troops in Savoy to march immediately to Flanders, since it was easy to see "how little fruit there would be if by guarding Savoy they should lose Flanders."[8]

Philip, in his reply, reminded the council that the archduke was expected to make up the difference in the sums required to support the whole Army of Flanders from the money provided by the obedient provinces. It amounted to at least one hundred thousand ducats per month. This, and the two hundred thousand sent from Spain, would have to be enough. Indeed, Philip also pointed out that even the two hundred thousand was conditional upon nothing extraordinary happening in his other kingdoms that might necessitate the diversion of resources.[9] Nevertheless, overturning his previous decisions, he did make immediate provision to send letters of credit for eight hundred thousand escudos to help the archduke proceed with the siege of Ostend; it was the best he could do.[10]

But military activity was not the monarchy's only effective means of waging the war; it could also take economic and diplomatic recourses. On 27 February, in an outright attempt to cripple Dutch trade, the crown published a proclamation permitting members of any nation that was either an ally of Spain or a neutral party free trade to Spanish territories (except the Indies), so long as the Dutch had received no benefit from the goods being traded. In other words, the Dutch were to be cut out of any role as middlemen in trade to the peninsula. The import of some goods was restricted unless they bore a seal certifying that they had been made in the Spanish Low Countries. In addition the Spanish imposed an export tax of 30 percent on all goods being taken out of the peninsula. To minimize the damage to Mediterranean and Hispano-Flemish trade, merchants engaged in commerce in either of these areas were exempted from the impost. And in an article the ministers would later regret, the proclamation permitted the archdukes to grant passports exempting some Dutch traders from the 30 percent duty, provided they could show themselves to be loyal to Spanish sovereignty, despite the official attitudes of their governors.[11] To ensure that the proclamation had the greatest possible psychological effect on the Dutch, on the same day as the proclamation Philip sent an order to Baltasar de Zúñiga and the archduke to cease all peace and truce talks immediately. The Spanish clearly intended to make the Dutch sweat.[12]

Discussions with England regarding some rapprochement were not included in this injunction, however, and even if they had been, it does not appear that the archduke would have listened. There was an ongoing attempt to persuade the English to continue the discussions begun in 1600. Indeed, the archdukes seemed genuinely desirous of peace despite all the hesitations on the part of the Spanish. In March, the archdukes were using one Señor Hurtado of Portugal to communicate with the English court. Jean Richardot, writing a brief history of the earlier negotiations for Hurtado's information, expressed perplexity that the prior communication had been broken off. Through the queen's ambassador in France, Thomas Edmondes, the archdukes had informed Elizabeth that they were willing to negotiate and that someone should come to discuss terms, but, Richardot told Hurtado, "to this letter there was no answer, and holding, as we do, to our intention of procuring a stable peace we do not know what reason there can be for this silence; for had the person come, it would have been easy to go on from that point to the peace which all desire."[13] Richardot went on to explain to Hurtado the two main conditions upon which the negotiations depended: the state of religion in England and the cautionary towns. With regard to both these points, the archdukes were willing to accommodate Elizabeth so that the arrangements would be "found to the Queen's liking." With the Dutch, he suggested, if no peace could be had, at least terms for an extended truce might be reached which would include free trade for the duration.[14]

Meanwhile, back at the court in Valladolid, the Council of State was still advising the king how to proceed on the succession issue. Clearly at this point—unlike the thinking at the archdukes' court—notions of concluding peace with Elizabeth were far from the Spanish ministers' minds. The council had considered some suggestions offered by Olivares in his vote on the succession and now had formulated revised proposals. Before proceeding to give the view of the rest of the members, the council requested a summary of Olivares's own solutions. Olivares replied that the foremost consideration was to preserve Philip's reputation and that this should take precedence over making a quick decision; the best means to resolve all the problems, he believed, was to come to an arrangement with the French. This, however, would have to be done carefully to ensure that the Spanish would not lose prestige by suddenly appearing to change their mind by withdrawing their backing from one of their own candidates. To this effect, he recalled an earlier, offhand remark by the pope that the French and Spanish should agree to a candidate; Olivares would reply in such a way to make it seem to have been an actual proposal and then heartily agree to the idea on behalf of the king. The Spanish ambassador in Rome would assure the pope that neither Philip nor his father had ever had any intention of uniting the crowns but had desired only to convert England to the Catholic faith. Although originally—the ambassador was to relate—Philip had thought this might be better accomplished by having one of his own relatives on the throne, now, seeing that the pope had another solution in mind, the king, it was to be hinted, "would be greatly influenced by the opinion of his Holiness, whom [he] respect[s] as a father." Lest it seem that Philip was freely giving up all his rights in the matter (which would appear as weakness), the Spanish ambassador was to remind his Holiness that Philip would naturally expect to exercise some influence over the choice of candidate and would expect also some gratitude on the part of the pope for renouncing his legal claims to the English throne.[15]

These diplomatic maneuverings would have to take place as swiftly as possible, requiring not only the duke of Sessa but also Father Persons to convince the pope of the actions he would have to take. The pope would have to persuade the French king to accept a candidate proposed from among the English Catholics, but great care would have to be taken to avoid divulging the whole plan to Henry, since he might let Elizabeth know, in order to "embroil matters." Furthermore, the pope would have to understand that only Spanish troops should be used to back their claims, since problems always arose from joint Franco-Spanish operations, which in this case would allow James of Scotland to slip into the rift. On the military side, troops in Flanders would have to be ready to make the landing in the south of England. The number required would not be as great as for an invasion, because "the forces which would be insufficient for an undertaking on our own account, will be more than enough to help a native ruler, particularly if France can be prevented from interfering."[16]

Finally, Olivares thought that the Spanish should not attempt to make the new king a puppet of Spain. The better strategic move would be to allow the English Catholics to repay the king for all these actions over a period of years and in addition request the cession of the Isle of Wight to Philip. Although Olivares did not see as much advantage in such possession as some others did, he did think there would be "a very good pretext for demanding it from the first for the purpose of harboring the fleet, and subsequently as a convenient point from which to relieve Flanders, and to keep England (and even France) in subjection; though in both cases this must be done with dissimulation." Possession of the island would, he thought, be less threatening to the English than possession of one of their ports, because it would "not appear so evident that we want to keep our foot on the neck of the king and his country." In the face of this, Ireland, which appeared to him "a noisy business, and more trouble than advantage for your Majesty," should be abandoned.[17]

Both the council in general and the king agreed with the proposals of Olivares, with the exception that they thought it better not to force the issue of drawing the candidate from among the English Catholics, leaving the decision instead to the pope. Furthermore the ministers preferred to wait to consider the military preparations and the cessions of strategic places until such time as the diplomatic negotiations had proven fruitful, although they unanimously agreed that the king should be fully prepared and armed. Although military preparations did, in fact, proceed, time was already running out.[18] As late as 18 March, Philip had still not given an answer to the English Catholics, even though Father Creswell, at the Spanish court and already aware that Elizabeth was not expected to recover from her latest illness, was writing urgently to both Lerma and the king requesting a decision before her death.[19]

As it turned out there was virtually nothing short of war the Spanish could have done to put their own candidate on the throne, for Sir Robert Cecil had already secretly arranged to have James of Scotland declared king. Simultaneously with the news of her death on 3 April (24 March o.s.), the English heard the proclamation of the Scottish king as her successor. By the time the Spanish ministers in Valladolid heard the news from Juan Baptista de Tassis, the ambassador in France, it was a fait accompli. Nevertheless, this did not stop them from sitting down to decide what course to take. On 21 April they presented their opinions to Philip.[20]

The count of Chinchón thought that the proclamation may have been meant to dissuade Philip from taking any action, in that he would believe it impossible to effect anything. Even given this, however, Chinchón felt that Philip had two options in response. One was to use force to prevent James from assuming the throne. This would mean assessing how many forces Philip had available and how much time it would take to get them into position. Furthermore, he would be forcing James into the position of an enemy, thereby ensuring that the Scottish king would unite with the Dutch rebels and possibly even with the French. On the other hand, Philip could "take the route normally used by prudent men in business," which was to show pleasure at James's achievement, congratulate him, and remind him of past alliances and friendship that existed between the Scottish and Spanish kingdoms. Such an advance, however, could not be made through official channels, lest it demonstrate weakness; rather such praise should come from one of the Scottish king's confidants, who would at the same time remind James how bad it might be to have Spain as an enemy, given the greatness of Spanish power. Indeed, the threat of force and the great power of Philip might even move James to declare himself Catholic, or at least to extend liberty of conscience to the Catholics in his kingdom. In any case, Chinchón suggested, military preparations had to go forward.[21]

This advice was approved, for the most part, by the rest of the council. The count of Miranda thought that prayers should be raised to ensure that the Lord favor Spanish plans. The constable thought that any discussion of getting involved was ridiculous since Philip had no one in mind as a rival candidate, nor did he have the forces to stop James's succession. Instead he thought there was even more reason to proceed with the peace talks since the war was with Elizabeth and James had been a neutral party in it. Otherwise the ministers were in agreement that the options were limited.

Philip, for the second time in a major decision—perhaps a reflection of feelings of Spanish inability to free themselves from their ill luck without divine assistance-ordered that before anything else prayers be said throughout the realm. Following that, he blusteringly ordered his forces to be put in readiness so that "the King of Scotland or any other pretender to the English throne might see how much help such forces might be if they were with him, and if not, how much threat." Furthermore, he wishfully ordered that monetary provisions totaling 1.3 million ducats be sent to the four corners of the monarchy to cover any contingency. In the meantime he thought it would be beneficial to foment the Catholics of Scotland and Ireland against the new king in an effort to wrest concessions from him regarding the practice of Catholicism. All of this was, however, to be done in such a way that the Spanish would not be shutting the door on a rapprochement should their activities not produce the intended results.

Given the worsening situation in Flanders, there was really little the king could do to intervene in the affairs of England. On 19 March the archduke had written pleadingly to Lerma to send money with which to carry on the war, thanking him for his previous efforts but pointing out that when money arrived after the time it was needed, it was useless.[22] Two days later he wrote again to complain that the letters of credit for the promised eight hundred thousand ducats had still not arrived, even though he had understood they were sent by express courier. The Dutch were already beginning their campaign, and Albert did "not have a single *real* nor the credit to get any" and was "forced to look for it in exchange for whatever interest he could get just to maintain the ordinary expenses of the army."[23] The problem was that the letters of credit had in fact never been sent. Now, even if they were sent immediately, the short-term interest rates the archduke had been forced to accept would take a significant chunk out of the money.[24]

Besides these financial difficulties, the archduke faced matters of more immediate military significance. As it turned out, the king's appointments of the past year to the posts of general of the cavalry and general of the artillery had set off disputes among the other commanders.[25] Don Luis de Velasco, former general of artillery, had replaced the Admiral of Aragón as commander of the cavalry; Charles Bonaventure de Longueval, count of Bucquoy, had given up his command of a tercio of Walloon infantry to take charge of the artillery; and Count Théodore de Trivulcio, commanding general of the Italian troops, had assumed the post of lieutenant-general of the cavalry. None of this sat well with some of the more place-conscious noble commanders. Indeed, the recently arrived Pedro Téllez Girón, duke of Osuna, refused to serve under Velasco and Trivulcio and instead disbanded the two cavalry companies he had raised.[26] This move seriously compromised the archduke's command structure and threatened to cripple his military effectiveness at a time when it appeared vitally necessary. Albert wrote to Lerma expressing his outrage at such an affront to his prestige and the lack of consideration shown him by the king, but there was really little he could do at that point.[27]

It was no doubt these considerations that prompted the infanta to recommend settling the dispute, now that England had a new monarch. "It is necessary," she wrote Lerma, "to lose no time in cultivating him. . . . For, by joining together England and Scotland, and joined to Denmark through his father-in-law, he will be lord of the Ocean; and for this reason and others his friendship will always be a good thing to have, and particularly the Indies would remain secure with it, since the Dutch without his assistance would be able to do little and would have to agree to peace terms, even if they did not want to, with which my brother would be relieved of such a heavy burden of cost to him."[28] Nonetheless, despite these fears of James's power, the death of the queen was not without its benefits to the archdukes. Probably as a result of the uncertainty caused by her death, the Dutch had delayed their campaign for that year. Moreover, according to the Venetian representative in Paris, Elizabeth's death had meant that the forces raised in England and Scotland were prevented from crossing to the Low Countries to reinforce the Dutch.[29] The Dutch were forced to change their plans swiftly and focus on winning over the new king by means of a delegation composed of prominent figures, among them Oldenbarnevelt. One of the express purposes of this embassy, besides securing James's general favor, was to request substantial help for Ostend.[30]

The momentary hesitation of his Dutch opponents in the prosecution of the war accounts in large part for the archduke's temporary success against that town. On the night of 14 April, following a terrific storm the day before that had toppled some walls within the town and even the church steeple, the Habsburg forces assaulted both the east and west sides of the fort. After initially being repulsed, they succeeded in seizing the three outworks on the west side, which they successfully held against a Dutch counterattack. Habsburg losses were heavy, but it was their first substantial victory in the siege. Although it did little to alleviate the overall military situation for the archduke, it did strengthen his (and by extension, Philip's) diplomatic position in the short term. For the first time the English and Dutch began to fear the loss of the town.[31]

The news of the archduke's successes spurred the Lords of the Council in England to write to James requesting instructions whether to proceed with their previous orders to aid the Dutch and if so to what extent. In other words, they wanted to know just what James's policy was going to be toward both the Provinces and Spain. "We dare not presume," they wrote, "in any other sort to make levies; because we know not upon what terms your Majesty meaneth to stand with those princes . . . ; your Majesty hath in right of your crown of Scotland amity with Spain and the Archduke; but in the succession to the throne of England a descent cast upon you of confederacy with these provinces, and an interest of great sums of money due from them."[32]

Indeed, there was a real fear on the part of some of the English that James was willing to abandon the Dutch cause and seek some sort of rap-

prochement with the Spanish.[33] Almost from the moment of his accession, critics were pointing out the errors of such a policy. In mid-May,
shortly after James's arrival in London, Sir Walter Ralegh presented him
with the trenchant and prescient "Discourse Touching a War with Spain
and of the Protecting of the Netherlands," which argued that the Dutch
could not defend themselves and would therefore have to turn to France
or, once again, to Spain if the English were to abandon them.[34] Either way
he thought this would be putting England in the dangerous position of
having their major trade routes to the East spied upon by enemies. Moreover, he pointed out, the Netherlands would be a perfect launching pad
for an invasion of England.

But the main reason Ralegh gave for not making peace with the Spanish is that they wanted peace merely to recover their forces so as to prosecute war in the future:

> The Spanish empire hath been greatly shaken, and hath begun of late
> years to decline; . . . But if now the king of Spain can obtain peace
> upon any condition reasonable, so as he may fortify his weakness, both
> in Europe and the Indies, and gather again sufficient riches, putting the
> English from the exercise of war in those parts, and so make us to forget
> his Indies . . . ; he will soon grow to his former greatness and pride:
> and then, if your majesty shall leave the Low Countries, and he find us
> by ourselves, it will not be long ere he remembers his old practices and
> attempts.[35]

This showed a remarkable understanding of the Spanish mind, since, as
we have seen earlier, this was precisely the thrust of Spanish reasoning
behind the peace talks. Despite this understanding, however, James did
not find Ralegh's arguments persuasive. This had less to do with the argument than the person making it. For James, Ralegh was the epitome of
the old Elizabethan "war party," and as such he was to have no place in the
new regime. Instead, for his boldness in criticizing James's policies, Ralegh
was soon afterward falsely accused, convicted, and sent to the Tower on
charges of plotting against the king.

Ralegh was not the only one to argue against peace with the Spanish,
however, nor was he in any sense representative of a war party at the court.
Around the same time that Ralegh presented his argument, another manuscript was put into circulation, entitled "Advertisment of a Loyall Subiect
to his Gratious Soveraigne." The "Advertisment" opens with a criticism of
James's proposed peace with the Spanish and abandonment of the Dutch

cause. The argument closely follows Ralegh's, pointing out that in peace Spain would gain and so would the French:

> If the *Spaniard* prevaile against those poore forsaken men, his forces by sea are more then trebled. Peace will quicklie inriche him, wealth will add to his pride, his pride will increase his hatered to your religion and people. . . . Yt is saide that if your Majestie discontinew the league with the States, the French are readie to interteyne the bargaine. There is a certaine antipathie between them and us, and it is harde to iudge whether the *Frenche* or the *Spanierd* will prove worse neighboures unto you. Your true subiectes therefore praye you to keep them boathe at the staves end.

The authorship of this piece has been ascribed to none other than the Lord Henry Howard, member of a long line of crypto-Catholics, some of whom would within little more than a year be receiving a Spanish pension. Clearly then, antipeace sentiments were not derived from membership of any supposed Protestant war party.[36]

Nevertheless, despite the reasonable arguments advanced in favor of war, James would not be persuaded. In May he let it be known by public edict that all hostilities with the Spanish at sea were to cease effective 24 April (o.s.). Even before that act, the Spanish, despite their official stance concerning the succession, were showing signs of demonstrable relief at the queen's death and James's evident desire for peace. But, while willing to entertain the idea of peace between the two countries, they were not above using James's weakening of the English bargaining position to secure some advantages for themselves, such as requesting a return of the "cautionary towns" in Flanders.[37]

As usual, however, the archduke had moved rapidly to undercut the Spanish position by too readily showing his own willingness to treat. On 15 April Albert had sent word to Valladolid that he had already taken the liberty of sending an envoy to James to congratulate him on his accession and to sound him on ideas for peace. Indeed, at the time of Elizabeth's death, one envoy, Nicholas Scorza, was already in Scotland discussing the recruitment of Scottish soldiers to fight in the Low Countries. Hearing from him that James was inclined to peace, Albert had immediately ordered all the coastal towns to permit free passage of British ships and men and to set English prisoners free. Shortly thereafter he dispatched the count of Aremberg to give his congratulations to the new king. To support this move and avoid offending James, Albert also removed references to English and Irish Catholics from the edict regarding trade that Philip had promulgated in February (but which Albert had published only on 30 March) and suggested that Philip do the same. All this, he thought, would allow Philip to see what reaction James would have and thereby enable him "with more authority and reputation" to order things as he saw fit.[38]

Upon receiving word of the archduke's actions, Philip realized there was little he could do under the circumstances to pressure James; at any rate, it appeared he had become convinced that peace might, after all, be the right route to take. In his response to a consulta about the issue, he resolved that James's messages by way of the pope and his public professions of friendship had opened the door to a resolution with him and that the archduke's actions had been correct. He therefore agreed to cut out from the trade ban the references to the English Catholics and decided to send his own representative to London to congratulate James and assure him of Spanish friendship.[39]

The man Philip chose as his representative was his *correo-mayor* (postmaster general), Juan de Tassis. Tassis had had a distinguished career in the military, having seen action in Oran and in Flanders with Philip II's brother, Juan de Austria, and had been one of the latter's pallbearers when his body was laid to rest in the Escorial. He was reputedly Spain's best swordsman and because of this had been banned from sword fighting by Philip II. His father, Raymond de Tassis, of ancient Milanese stock, had come to Spain by way of Germany and Flanders in the reign of Philip II and had been made his postmaster general; undoubtedly Juan learned much about diplomacy from him.[40] Essentially the postmaster general had a contract with the king to deliver official mail—comprising everything that passed between the monarch and his ministers in foreign countries—for certain rates and within a specific amount of time. Couriers' duties often included the receipt and delivery of verbal messages from and to the king and his council. Clearly couriers numbered discretion and trustworthiness among their virtues. Courier duty, then, and certainly the management of it, was considered excellent training for the diplomatic service.[41] It was this experience that presumably influenced Philip III in his selection of Tassis to be the first Spanish agent in England since the expulsion of Bernardino de Mendoza in 1584.[42]

On 29 April, Tassis received his instructions from the king. Among them, as was almost always the case, was a set of secret orders, an important window on Spanish policy toward the north in 1603. He was dispatching the count, Philip told him, because the current state of affairs would take much tactful negotiation and would need someone on hand to assess the situation. But Tassis had another function that Philip considered just as important as his journey to the English court. He had no doubt learned from Baltasar de Zúñiga, recently returned from Flanders to give his report on the situation there, that Henry IV, Count Maurice, and various Protestant Electors within the Holy Roman Empire were endeavoring to prevent the election of a member of the House of Habsburg as the king of the Romans, normally the successor to the emperor.[43] This would effectively depose the Habsburgs from the imperial throne and thus constituted a significant threat to the very foundations of Habsburg prestige (and therefore power) in Europe. Tassis was instructed to assure the archdukes that Philip would hazard all the forces at his disposal, military and diplomatic, to insure that the election remain in the family. That done, Tassis was to send word by express courier what the archdukes wanted from Philip and then proceed with his mission to England.[44]

These instructions concerning Tassis's assignment in England were replete with the bluster for which Philip was noted—"The purpose for which you are sent is to insure that whoever should be King of England understands how important it will be for his survival to be allied with me"—but at the same time the Spanish could not help but be realistic. In the event that Tassis found James to be secure in his power, he was to congratulate him and remind him of the ancient friendship that had existed between the two crowns and that the queen having died, so had the reason for the war. After that he was to sound out James on the issue that had been discussed in Rome with the duke of Sessa and on James's conversion to the Catholic faith, for "religion will open the road to alliances and marriages, which can be built on this foundation and no other."[45]

Moving then to more political (as opposed to dynastic) issues, Tassis was instructed to look for occasions to undermine the Anglo-French relationship by pointing out all that France had done to prevent a unification of the crowns. Not above using every ploy possible, even that of betraying former diplomatic allies, Tassis was told that he could even go so far as to tell James of the proposed Franco-Spanish agreement to put an English candidate on the throne to show how far the French were willing to go to prevent James's accession. Additionally Philip even pledged his assistance in helping James recover lost English territory in France if he should so wish.

If James did not appear to be secure in his power against the other claimants, Tassis was to try, while alienating none of the parties, to determine who would have the best chance of success so that Philip might decide where to throw his weight. Above all, however, Philip would require of any candidate that received his assistance that he or she give up the cautionary towns in the Low Countries. Second, he wanted the security of English Catholics assured, preferably by having a Catholic on the throne. In the event that Tassis discovered such a chaotic situation, he carried with him blank letters for each of the main factions, to be filled in with particulars as the occasion warranted. Finally, to facilitate everything, he carried with him letters of credit for one hundred thousand ducats. These he could use to "win over the people and ministers by whose hand the things you intend can be assured."[46]

Instructions and letters in hand, on 3 May Tassis departed from Aranjuez and the king. After a short stop in Valladolid to finish arranging matters, he headed north on 20 May, thus ushering in a new era in Spanish foreign policy.[47] From this point onward, for almost twenty years, Spanish diplomacy would be geared toward keeping England out of continental affairs. Moreover, this activity would now be undertaken on the scene in England rather than by means of various agents and intermediaries. Spanish diplomacy in general was to win successes that could not be had on the battlefield, preserving, at least for a time, Spanish influence in Europe despite increasing military weakness. There would still be much to do, both militarily and diplomatically, before a semblance of peace would fall over the Spanish monarchy, but James's accession and Philip's consequent dispatch of a permanent representative to his court were the first positive diplomatic steps on the road to Spain's Pax Hispanica.

CHAPTER 6

The Policy of Rapprochement

✤ ✤ ✤

At war with all the world but at peace with England.
—maxim attributed to Fernando Alvarez de Toledo, third duke of Alba

Although the rulers of Spain and England perhaps needed the peace, opposition to it still existed on both sides. In Spain, Philip himself was not completely won over to the idea, nor, if the chronicler Jerónimo de Sepúlveda is correct, were many of the intellectuals, who instead saw it as a betrayal of Catholicism to the dictates of *raison d'état:* "The councillors of our king advised him that he should make peace with the English, with such infamy to ourselves, even going to the extreme of begging for it in their house. Thus all men who have understanding and knowledge of negotiations feel that to make peace with such a great heretic and the greatest enemy of the Catholic Church was very badly done and ill-considered, from which a thousand prudent men have it that it is not possible that God will favor us, having made peace with his ene- mies the heretics."[1] In England, James himself had demonstrated his clear desire for peace, but some of his councillors, "deeply impressed by the lofty aims of the late Queen" and "convinced that the best way to pre- serve oneself is to harass one's neighbors," advised him to continue the war. Indeed, even those English councillors who favored peace with Spain wanted James to continue aiding the Dutch.[2]

The question of English aid to the Dutch was of critical importance to the peace negotiations that would soon ensue. Since the Spanish wanted peace with James primarily to improve their situation in Flanders, the cur- tailment of England's assistance to the Dutch rebels would be their prin- cipal aim. The possibility of success in this seemed assured from the first. When presented with a report stating the danger of Ostend's fall with- out continued English support, James was reported to have said, "What of it? Was not Ostend originally the King of Spain's and therefore, now, the Archduke's?"[3] To Cecil, to whom this reply had been given, James must have appeared woefully naive in matters of diplomacy: here he was giving away at a rapid pace all his bargaining chips without receiving any concessions from the Spanish in return. This served only to weaken the English position in the negotiations.

The Dutch for their part were doing their best to persuade James to continue his support. Noel Caron, the Dutch representative in London, put it about that in the event that the United Provinces were left to themselves, they would have no other recourse but to seek a settlement with Spain. Such an action would give Philip two advantages: he would be relieved of the enormous expense of the war in the Low Countries and would have at his disposal the naval might of the States-General with which to achieve dominance on the high seas—a clear threat to English interests. To lend weight to their not so subtle threats, the Dutch agreed to open preliminary peace discussions with the archduke.[4]

Perhaps the strongest urging for James to continue the war with Spain came from the French, however. It was they who had the most to gain from the continued engagement of England and Spain in war. From 1598, French policy had been to keep Elizabeth and Philip from the treaty table, and the French ministers were no less active now that James had assumed the throne. "You know how much interest I have in this," Henry told his ambassador; "it is the most important affair of my reign. You must never forget what my interest requires, that these two kings shall never come to an agreement. I don't wish the States to enter into the treaty or to lay down their arms on any pretext. Nevertheless, I ought not to appear to have any wish to prevent a peace between the two kingdoms, nor the reconciliation of the provinces."[5] These instructions in hand, the French ambassador set about to persuade the English that the Spanish would achieve European hegemony once they were free from war with England.[6] Meanwhile, Henry IV, spared the expenses of active war, was free to pursue his own aims along his borders and to recoup his strength. French power was on the rise.

On the other hand, to Sir Anthony Shirley, the English-Scottish-Spanish triple agent, this growth of French power was precisely the reason why James should come to terms with the Spanish. The French, he said, received all the benefits from the war with Spain, while England suffered all the charges. Besides steadily strengthening themselves through alliances with the German princes, the pope, the Venetians, various Italian rulers, and the Turks, the French were indirectly benefiting from the damage being done to Spanish power. The Spanish, for their part, could never be trusted and would use "all sorts of treachery which may serve their own interest." Nevertheless, Shirley emphasized, Philip III "has none but himself to maintain him, his allies being so distracted that they can do no more than maintain themselves. If you [James] oppose yourself also unto him he is ruined, and so it is as much as confessed by his frequent seeking of you." And then summing up his reasons for supporting Spain rather than France, Shirley enunciated the balance-of-power concept that was to become the mainstay of British foreign policy in the eighteenth and nineteenth centuries: "If you please to make any amity with him [Philip] you counterbalance the world."[7] Shirley's balance-of-power arguments found a receptive mind in Robert Cecil. In October, Cecil explained to the Venetian ambassador, Scaramelli, why it was necessary for England to do everything in its power to maintain an independent Netherlands: "At the present time the Christian powers in Europe are three, England, France and Spain . . . [which] balance one another, and remain in equilibrium, but if the weight of the States were added to any one of them, especially to Spain, the other two would be tottery and off balance."[8]

None of these arguments really mattered as much as James's own views of the situation. Quite frankly, he abhorred the Dutch and their revolt against their sovereign, and this hatred was only strengthened by political considerations. He had reportedly told Nicolas Scorza in March: "I have no love for the Dutch nor for their cause, but do not tell anyone I said so." Indeed, it was the Dutch themselves who ended up pushing James into the Spanish camp. On 14 May, eight days after the king's arrival, the Dutch delegation reached London; it was composed of Count Frederick Henry of Nassau, the youngest son of William of Orange; Walrave van Brederode, the principal nobleman of Holland; Jacob Valck, the treasurer of Zeeland; Johan van Oldenbarnevelt; and a number of other notables and gentlemen. The delegation wanted an immediate audience with the king but, ominously, were snubbed until 27 May. In the eventual audience they congratulated James on his accession and then pointed out the precarious military situation they faced in the Low Countries. James, claiming ignorance of the state of affairs but in fact wanting to wait and see what offers the French and Habsburgs would make, brushed them off with assurances of continued friendship.[9]

If the Dutch were disappointed in their preliminary audience with the king, however, they could not but be pleased at the turn of events in the English Channel two days earlier. Early on the morning of 25 May, Federico Spínola and his fleet of eight galleys and four frigates had been caught by a fleet of five Dutch warships. After two hours of intense fighting, the Dutch were able to bring their heavy guns to bear, whereupon "the slaughter was very great, especially in the Spanish gallies; neither partie shewing any base cowardise, they were so eager one against another with cannon, musket, and harguebuse [sic] shot; and they came to the half pike, two hand sword, coutelas, and other armes, that it was a fearefull sight to behold; so as in the end the Spaniards fainting, seeing such great abundance of blood runne out of the skupper holes of their gallies, they fled in great disorder to Scluse [Sluis]." With them went all hope for both an invasion of England and a naval defeat of the Dutch in the north.[10]

Luckily for the Spaniards and the archdukes, this loss of their alternative to peace (i.e., invading to secure the throne for their own candidate) did not affect James's negotiating stance. Instead, as the Venetian secretary reported, James "heard with disgust" that the Dutch had sent out warships to prevent, as he saw it, the archduke's ambassadors from crossing the Channel to congratulate him, and thereafter he showed even more willingness to side with the Spanish. Moreover, the English expressed a growing concern over the increasing power of the Dutch, who seemingly experienced no trouble inflicting damage on the Spanish while simultaneously reaping huge profits from the war. Nor did the lavish sums spent by the Dutch delegation while in London help win members of the court to their cause; one report commented that "the Ambassadors of the States are spending upwards of three hundred crowns a day, which the world thinks monstrous and the King ridiculous, for while here to beg for aid it is they who are ruining themselves, and they are no longer visited and favoured by the Court as they were at their first coming."[11]

In the face of James's eagerness for peace, however, the Spanish were cautious; they did not want to demonstrate too much willingness to negotiate since this would prejudice their cause. The count of Miranda, showing remarkable understanding of how Spanish diplomacy was perceived to work and how to use that perception to further Philip III's aims, told the king that "since the whole world thinks that everything here moves slowly, if they now see that your Majesty pushes things, it could cause them to think less of you." Instead the council decided to do what the Spanish did best, use delay and waiting to their advantage while mean-

while putting on a show of force by going ahead with military preparations.[12]

The situation appeared even more favorable to Habsburg aims when
Karel van Aremberg, the archduke's envoy, arrived in London on 17 June.
An ardent opponent of Oldenbarnevelt, his presence could only worsen
the Dutch position. That position had deteriorated steadily since their arrival. Five days earlier, on 12 June, the English Privy Council had discussed
proposals concerning the peace with Spain that were themselves unfavor-
able to the Dutch. It was proposed to call a cease-fire in the Netherlands
once peace was made between England and Spain. After that, a deal would
be worked out whereby the archduke would retain nominal sovereignty
of all the provinces and handle foreign policy while the internal administration of the northern provinces would remain as it was, with full freedom of conscience and free elections to military and civil posts. In addition the provinces would be allowed a certain limited right of navigation
to the Indies. James would be the guarantor of the peace and as such would
receive the cautionary towns as a pledge. Peace there would be, but at the
price of Dutch independence. Nevertheless, James received the support
of only seven members of the twenty-four-man council: the rest favored
continuing the policies of Elizabeth with regard to Spain and the Netherlands. Their only hope lay in the imminent arrival of the French ambassador, Maximilen de Béthune, marquis of Rosny (later duke of Sully).[13]
They hoped that Béthune and the Dutch delegation would together be
able to bring the king around to their view that Spain had to be prevented
from getting possession of the Dutch naval forces at all costs.

Aremberg assisted the Dutch cause when, claiming an attack of gout,
he refused for some weeks to request an audience with James. Béthune,
however, arriving two days after Aremberg, on 19 June, wasted no time
in winning allies at the court and requesting an audience.[14] The first public audience was granted on 22 June, and after a shaky start owing to
Béthune's having first outfitted his retinue in mourning black (for Elizabeth), thus risking upsetting the king, the French ambassador and his
sumptuously attired retainers proceeded to dazzle James. In the private
audiences that followed Béthune seemingly won James over completely
to the Franco-Dutch side. James agreed to write off the French debt to
England in return for Henry's raising his subsidy to the Dutch. England
would then recoup the money from the Dutch after the termination of
the war. In addition James advanced the Dutch a large sum as a direct sub-

sidy payment, thus demonstrating his goodwill toward the Dutch cause.[15] A month later, on 30 July, the secret Hampton Court Treaty was signed by James, Henry, and the United Provinces, and a new Triple Alliance was seemingly born.[16]

Despite his willingness to sign this treaty, however, James had still not ruled out peace with the Spanish, even while he assured Oldenbarnevelt that any such peace would not put the Dutch in jeopardy. On 3 July, James reissued his proclamation ordering a cessation of all hostilities against the Spanish at sea, a sure indication of his willingness to reach an agreement. Aremberg, finally pushed by events to seek an audience with James, urged him to conclude a peace treaty. Everything now seemed to await the arrival of the Spanish ambassador; even James was somewhat perplexed and annoyed at the delay, since he had done nothing but express his inclination to peace.[17]

Juan de Tassis, however, had only just arrived in Flanders after a brief sojourn at the French court to consult with his kinsman Juan Baptista (or Bautista) de Tassis.[18] He was waiting to see how well Aremberg got on at the English court and also for revised instructions from Philip based on more recent appraisals of the situation. On 24 June the Council of State, with Lerma making one of his rare appearances, considered Tassis's first dispatches, along with various other letters. From these it learned that James was putting a great deal of pressure on English Catholics. The councillors recommended that because their forces were deemed insufficient to effect an invasion, they should do all they could to alleviate the plight of the Catholics through diplomacy. Lerma, however, belying his reputed pacifism, added that Philip should step up the production of ships and the embarkation of armadas in order to pressure the English to come to favorable terms. Two days later Philip asked the council to meet in his presence to discuss these issues further.[19]

If the Spanish appeared to be in some confusion over the policy to follow, so too were the English. The Spanish councillors were receiving mixed signals out of England, whose proper interpretation would be vital to the success of the negotiation. James still appeared to be interested in coming to terms, seemingly as a result of fears about Philip's military preparations. Even the English Catholics considered these fairly substantial, reporting that they had thirty thousand men ready to rise up in the event of outside help. But at the same time, some at the English court did not appear to be swayed by the threat of force. Robert Taylor, a doctor of theology in the employ of the archduke and later secretary to the Spanish ambassadors in London, reported that Cecil was letting it be known (through an intermediary) that *money* would help smooth the way for negotiations, implying thereby that its lack could force things the opposite way. So the question for Philip's ministers would be whether to proceed via threats or bribes. But once again the archduke acted unilaterally, sending Taylor to London to assure the English of his willingness to negotiate and even to concede some English demands.[20]

The councillors' reaction to these notices were mixed. Idiáquez advised negotiation, for he felt the English Catholics could be trusted neither in their estimates nor in their judgment. And he argued that the use of bribery to open the English ministers to negotiation would not be disreputable in that "disrepute comes from selling and not buying" and would in any case save money over the costs of war. His overriding concern was that all the men on the scene were demonstrating too strong a willingness to negotiate, since "too much eagerness either makes success impossible or makes the end result worse." He likewise considered it ill advised to send further powers to negotiate until Tassis's efforts had played themselves out, since this too would demonstrate eagerness. Lerma disagreed. Instead he thought that powers should be sent secretly to the archduke, which could then be forwarded when the occasion called for them. He commended the efforts of Tassis thus far and felt that the negotiations would be greatly facilitated by having someone on the scene in London, since they would no longer have to dispute the location of the talks as they had in 1600. Finally, he proposed sending Tassis six hundred thousand ducats to bribe the English ministers and to buy the cautionary towns.

Turning to the method of negotiation, the constable expressed his opinion that Tassis was far from qualified to engage with the more experienced representatives of the English. "The English being such astute negotiators," he pointed out, "it is to be feared that Don Juan de Tassis will be thwarted [in his diplomacy] like a man who, despite his other good qualities, has never engaged in such matters, in which the Catholic King [Philip II] always employed 3 or 4 or 5 of his best negotiators."[21] In this view he concurred with the archduke, who had written to Lerma to express the same misgivings. Instead Albert recommended that the king should send Juan de Idiáquez, the constable himself, or the count of Olivares to handle the talks.[22] Finally, the constable thought that Richardot and any others who had shown a desire to expel the Spaniards should not be allowed to participate in the negotiations.

While it is impossible to know what Philip may have said in council, his remarks on the consulta were—no doubt to the frustration of the councillors—remarkably short. He wanted everything done to secure the Catholics' freedom of worship ("which is what I most want"), for which Tassis was to spend whatever he deemed necessary, and he wanted the rebels brought into the peace by means of a preliminary cease-fire. Rejecting Lerma's advice, however, he refused to discuss or send any further powers to negotiate a settlement.[23]

On the same day that the council members presented Philip with their consulta regarding England, they also took stock of the situation in the Low Countries. Albert had expressed his hope that the mutiny that had been going on since September of the previous year would soon be over, given that the enemy appeared too weak to assist the mutineers and was having problems moving its forces about. The mutineers had retired to the neighborhood of Breda and were terrorizing the area bounded by Breda and 's Hertogenbosch in the north and Hoogstraeten in the south, sometimes even going as far afield as Trier, Aachen, Luxemburg, and Lorraine in search of contributions. Albert's forces, some eighteen thousand strong, had moved to the region of Eindhoven, thereby preventing the mutineers from crossing the Maas. The archduke requested that Spain double the monetary provision for the summer months so that he could adequately carry out his designs. These included engaging the mutineers' forces and/or invading across "the rivers" (the river barrier composed of the conjunction of the Maas and Rhine). The Council of State thought that the conjunction was extremely favorable—"the best in years"—and advised that Philip provide an immediate extraordinary provision of seven hundred thousand ducats to ensure the success of the issue. Council members felt the rebels were in dire straits without the assistance of the English and that this was their opportunity to carry the war to the Dutch side of the rivers. Moreover, they felt it would be very bad for their negotiations with the English if James should see such a force raised and then dissipated immediately afterward because the king of Spain could not afford to keep it under arms. To all this Philip tersely replied: "Everything that can be is being done just to carry out the provision of 200,000 escudos per month." In other words, Albert would not be able to engage in an offensive.[24]

Throughout the summer the archduke continued his efforts to reduce the rebel forces with the resources he had available. At Ostend the Spanish forces were making great progress. They had worked their siege gun platforms in very close to both the east and west inlets from the sea, a position that threatened to close off the town from all succor. Plague was raging within the fort, and the Dutch and English defenders had barely enough men to occupy their defensive posts. In Brabant, Frederic Vandenberg and Luis de Velasco were besieging a garrison left behind by the mutineers in Hoogstraeten, and half of the mutineers had reportedly returned to the archduke's fold. Maurice seemed to be playing the waiting game and had still not moved his army from Geertruidenburg. Everything appeared to be going Albert's way.[25]

The favorable tide turned, however, toward the end of July. The beleaguered garrison in Ostend managed to set afire the Spanish siege engines and fortifications, hindering the progress of the attacking force by an estimated four to five months. On 3 August, Maurice, having finally signed an agreement to protect the mutineers until they should be reconciled with Albert, began marching his army toward Hoogstraeten to relieve them. Three days later Maurice's vanguard caught the rear guard of Vandenberg's retreating forces and inflicted some minor losses. The Habsburg army fled in disarray as far as Herenthals, but Maurice refused to pursue it, much to the dismay and irritation of his compatriots. Soon afterward, twenty-five hundred reinforcements for the archduke's army arrived from Italy, in time to shore up its determination. The two armies then faced off while Maurice looked about for a town in which to house the mutineers. For the time being there was a stalemate: neither side was willing to risk losing the advantage by moving.[26]

Meanwhile, back in Valladolid the Council of State on 21 August read letters from the ambassador in France, Juan Baptista de Tassis, regarding Béthune's successful embassy to James. Understandably, they were not pleased by what they heard. They deeply regretted the fact that their own ambassador was not present to mitigate the effects of Béthune's machinations and urged that Juan de Tassis be sped on his way. Moreover, they learned that certain English Catholic priests had been captured after the discovery of their plans to kidnap James, an episode known as the "Bye Plot" and linked to the "Main Plot," which involved an attempt to put Arabella Stuart on the throne. The issue of the conspiracy was regrettable, since it threatened to damage the pending Anglo-Spanish détente.[27]

But James's attitude toward peace was apparently not swayed by the plot or by Béthune's designs. On 10 August the king wrote to the United Provinces informing them of his intention to negotiate a peace settlement and requesting that they summon their States-General to discuss their demands. But despite this demonstration of good faith, James was not about to give in easily to Spanish demands. On 28 August Cecil wrote to Aremberg that the latter's belief that James had promised to restrain his subjects from serving in the Low Countries was a mistake. James, Cecil informed Aremberg, could not without shame abandon all consideration of the States-General in this way but, rather, would wait for the States' reply before taking any such negative action. And in a further move designed to check the desires of the Spanish, James sent a representative to see the pope and inform him that under no circumstances could he allow liberty of conscience within his kingdoms "for fear of tumults." Clearly the Spanish quest for toleration would face an uphill battle. Meanwhile the English commissioners informed Aremberg that both he and Tassis would be required to have the necessary powers to treat for peace before they could go further. With the ball now in the Spanish court and plague raging in London, James departed with his retinue on a combined six-week hunting trip and official progress through his new kingdom.[28]

On 24 August, Tassis sent word to England that he had arrived in Dunkirk and was awaiting English ships to pick him up and transport him across the Channel.[29] At last he was coming. With his suite of fifteen gentlemen and their retainers, he arrived in Dover on the final day of August and was greeted enthusiastically by its citizens. His arrival, however, so long anticipated, was overshadowed by investigations of the Bye and Main plots, and because his landing occurred during the court's progress, he had to wait some time before his first audience with James. From Dover he set out immediately in search of the king, and on 12 September, "after many slow and tedious journeys" through the southeast, he finally arrived in Oxford, just seven miles from the palace at Woodstock where James was expected shortly. His audience was set for 27 September.

In the meantime Tassis was lodged in Christ Church and immediately began decorating his rooms with his hangings and furniture in order to dazzle his hosts. The English were indeed impressed by his plate and furniture but were disappointed that "the rest of his expenses and liberalities [i.e., tips and bribes] . . . [were] very mean, and no way answerable to that which was expected and bruited by his forerunners." Despite wishing to display no usage inferior to that of Béthune, he lost the first round in the comparison with the French and Dutch embassies. Even worse, however, was the fact that from the moment of his landing, recusant Catholics began flocking to him, and his company began visiting detained priests. Clearly he meant to be a visible ally of the Catholic minority in England. Cecil was as yet unsure what the motive might be for his visit apart, from congratulating James, but assumed that he would not wish to broach the topic of a peace, instead pretending that Spain and England needed no truce since they were not at war, lest there be "a diminution of his master's greatness to be the first sender where there were no friendship." Nevertheless, Cecil was almost certain that, owing to James's disposition, peace would result if other leaders were similarly disposed.[30]

Cecil's reference to other leaders no doubt included the States-General. They replied to James's letter of 10 August that they viewed "with the greatest reluctance his inclination to treat with the King of Spain and the Archdukes in regard they have the deepest apprehension that the evasive treaties and ambitious designs of the Spaniards and their followers tend alike to the destruction of the true religion, and the setting up of an universal tyranny over all Christendom, to the great prejudice of his Majesty and the United Provinces." While they requested more time to consider the matter, Cecil sardonically noted that there was "small distinction between their delay and a refusal." Nonetheless the leaders of the provinces did have a legitimate excuse for delay: once again they were experiencing a measure of success against the Habsburg forces. On 8 September, Maurice, with members of the States-General in attendance, had finally driven off the archduke's army and had begun the siege of s' Hertogenbosch. On the same day word came from Ostend that Albert's new floating cannon platform, for which the Spanish had such high hopes, had been utterly destroyed by the tides. Such events would render the Dutch anything but disposed to discussing peace with the archduke.[31]

But the archduke soon had reason to be more optimistic regarding the military situation. On 28 September he wrote to the Spanish court that he had concluded an agreement with Ambrosio Spínola in which Spínola, in return for being given sole charge of the siege of Ostend, guaranteed to end it within a year.[32] It was a move forced upon Albert by his pitiful financial circumstances and one that involved a great risk: Spínola was virtually untried as a commander, having been involved in only one previous engagement (see Chapter 4), and his experience consisted mostly of high finance and trade. Within two weeks, however, Spínola managed to make great strides. On 8 October he arrived before Ostend to inspect the trenches, bringing with him two months of arrears of the soldiers' pay, for which he was triumphantly saluted by all the guns. Immediately thereafter he set about restructuring the thrust of the siege; he would concentrate his firepower upon the western side of the town rather than the eastern and would blockade the harbor of the town with frigates. The Dutch would now find resupply of the besieged town seriously hampered.[33]

Meanwhile, in England, Tassis's stature, already weakened by his dilatory arrival, his early parsimony, and his associations with the recusants, was damaged even further when one of his servants died immediately before his audience with the king. The servant having died after only a few hours' illness, rumor quickly spread that the ambassador's household was afflicted with the plague. James, fearing for his life, not only postponed the audience but also ordered Tassis and all the other ambassadors to depart at once for Southampton, ten miles from Winchester, where the court had decided to winter, removed from the plague. All audiences would be postponed until the king's arrival there.[34]

It was not until 4 October, having determined that the envoy's servant had not, in fact, died of the plague, that the king and queen granted Tassis the long-delayed audience. As a first audience it was merely for purposes of congratulation and compliment. The exchanges took place in Spanish and Italian and involved mutual pledges of a desire to "renew, but enhance with greater significance" the ancient friendship and alliance between the two crowns.[35] The serious audience took place four days later, on 8 October, the same day that Spínola arrived to take charge of the archduke's forces at Ostend. In this second, private audience Tassis told James that Philip fully intended to secure a good and lasting peace with England so that he could more effectively reduce the rebel provinces. He asked that James join with Spain in this endeavor and "show the world that he looked unkindly upon rebels, thus standing as an example to his own vassals." In other words, rebels were to be feared by every good king, and they were all in the fight together. James, having himself ruled a fractious Scotland for so long, could not help but be persuaded by such arguments and agreed in principle to aid the Spanish, if only by withdrawing aid from the Dutch rebels. Tassis then asked James to demonstrate his good faith by putting a stop to the levies then being made in Scotland on behalf of the rebels, but to this James replied that he had no control over the levies since they were not done under his auspices. As for the peace talks, Tassis said, James had only to propose where, when, and with whom they would take place.[36]

The following day a delegation of Privy Councillors, including Cecil, visited Tassis to discuss the issues further. The English ministers let it be known that they were interested in discussing three points: free trade to the Indies, freedom of worship for the Dutch, and an Anglo-Spanish marriage alliance. Tassis, playing coy, replied that he had no further business to conduct unless the points he had already raised worked out well. But when the English ministers asked if he carried full powers to treat of the peace, he could only admit that he did not—but expected no difficulty in getting his king to agree to anything he should arrange. While expressing their satisfaction with the person of Tassis, the ministers regretted this lack of legal powers and declared they would have to delay any conference until he should receive them.[37]

This last point finally convinced the members of the Council of State and Philip that the Constable of Castile, appointed by Philip in the spring to go to Flanders to "have a hand in the reduction to obedience of the Islands [Low Countries] and the mutineers and in settling other issues," should also carry full powers to conclude a peace treaty with the English.[38] Since using a representative already on the scene to negotiate a peace treaty would be damaging to his reputation—it would be, in Sepúlveda's phrase, like "begging for it in their own house"—Philip would not give Tassis, by now the count of Villamediana, the full powers but instead ordered him to maintain a close correspondence with the constable once the latter arrived in Flanders. The Spanish court was not willing to lose another point of reputation by making Villamediana Philip's plenipotentiary until such time as the English had made some firm moves down the road to peace. When the time came, Philip would appoint Villamediana to the team of negotiators for the final treaty so that the count might better advise the constable at the actual conference table.[39] Further diplomacy, therefore, would await the arrival of the constable in Flanders.

In the Low Countries, things were daily looking better. Toward the end of October, Albert, now in personal command of the forces in Brabant, managed to slip a garrison of a few thousand soldiers into 's Hertogenbosch. Maurice could not now hope to take the town. Therefore, despite the dangers of retreating with Albert's army encamped nearby, on 5 November Maurice broke off the siege and marched away during the

night without incident. A week later Albert himself marched off, leaving
behind a garrison of twenty-eight companies. His pinched finances notwithstanding, Albert had proven the stronger in his own territories and
had managed once again to drive Maurice from the Spanish provinces.[40]

In the midst of these successes, the more mundane affairs of diplomacy
continued. Throughout November and December, while everyone waited
for the imminent arrival of the constable, both the archduke and Villamediana were busy working out the details for the upcoming peace conference. The archduke was putting together his own team of negotiators,
with Aremberg, Richardot, and Luis Verreycken heading the list. There
were, however, some doubts about Aremberg's acceptability at the English court following his involvement in the Bye plot. These were finally
resolved toward the end of December: Aremberg would stay in the Low
Countries and would leave the negotiating to the constable.[41]

Meanwhile Villamediana continued to learn more from confidantes
about what the English would look for at the negotiating table.[42] But
perhaps more important, because of his presence on the scene he could
now observe those things that might influence James at a personal level.
At the beginning of November the Council of State received word from
Villamediana that James and his courtiers all demonstrated a keen desire
to have Spanish horses for their hunting. He requested that Philip send
him two dozen to give as gifts. Philip, himself appreciative of the joys of
hunting, willingly agreed. While seemingly a trivial matter to the modern
reader, such personal details had extraordinary importance at a time when
diplomacy was primarily a matter between rulers acting as individuals and
not between abstract entities like modern state governments.[43]

Because of such attention, Villamediana was succeeding wonderfully
at winning the respect and admiration of the English king. Despite problems between Villamediana and James's English subjects, on 5 January
(26 December o.s.) James decided to honor him with the first of the cus-
tomary Christmas banquets for ambassadors, giving him precedence over
the French representative.[44] Even more astounding to observers was that
in the course of this impressive display of ritual James rose and, removing
his hat (an unprecedented sign of respect), proposed a toast to the health
of the Spanish king, the first toast he had ever given to a Spanish ambassador. And, as if this was not enough to show his liking for the ambassador,
he and his son remained standing with their hats off while Villamediana
responded in kind. Queen Anne even went so far as to kiss the foot of the

cup with which she toasted her counterpart; this was a supreme honor. Such an extraordinary display of courtesy and approval toward the new count boded well for the negotiations. Nonetheless, without full powers to negotiate there was little Villamediana could do beyond banqueting. Everything, as an English informant advised, now depended on the constable. On the last day of 1603, that worthy finally arrived in Brussels, enabling serious negotiation to begin.[45]

The constable had to set the agenda early in order to win significant concessions from the English. The initial talks hinged on two issues: the location of the conference and the position of the English Catholics, neither of which would be easily resolved. Immediately upon arriving he sent word to James's court that talks could get under way in short order. Questions of precedence and reputation immediately surfaced, however, when the constable suggested that the talks take place in the Low Countries rather than in England, since the Low Countries could be considered neutral territories not under the sovereign control of either power.[46] The reasons behind this were that the constable did not wish the Spanish to appear too eager for peace (with the attendant loss of reputation that such a stance entailed) or the English to dominate talks that took place on their own soil. It was an issue over which the Spanish could expect only trouble: the English were adamant that the talks take place in England, claiming that they could not afford to absent their principal ministers during the upcoming Parliament. The constable solved the problem by giving constant excuses for not wanting to leave Brussels while simultaneously allowing Villamediana to conduct behind-the-scenes negotiations without full authorization from Spain. This path had the advantage of not displaying too much eagerness to negotiate and at the same time provided the Spanish with a good excuse for vetoing any settlement reached by Villamediana that they felt would be damaging to their interests. It was a poor attempt at salvaging the damage to Spanish reputation engendered by treating in England, but one which, as the constable pointed out to the council, allowed the talks to go forward.[47]

The constable raised another point in his reports to the Spanish court. The English Catholics, it now appeared, were insufficiently strong to effect any significant action if called upon to support Spanish moves. Nonetheless the constable suggested that the Spanish needed to continue giving the Catholics just enough support to keep them in the Spanish camp while at the same time preventing them from trying to make any drastic changes in

England that might affect the new spirit of detente. The constable promised them, however, that their interests would be looked after in the event of peace.[48]

Yet it should not be assumed that Philip and his ministers had entirely given up on the Catholics. The king did not see himself as abandoning the Catholics to their fate. Instead he justified his short-term actions by appealing to a more distant end: the eventual reduction of England to the Catholic faith. As he pointed out in a reply to suggestions that he offer his daughter in marriage to the English prince, he would hold this card until last, "since it will facilitate the other conditions and at least everything possible will have been done by us to reduce that crown to the Catholic religion, which is my principal aim in this negotiation as God knows, and thus I hope He will guide it as He sees fit."[49] He and his advisers were attempting to effect a far-reaching change in the ranking of Spanish foreign-policy aims. Short-term gains were now to be sacrificed (if the need arose) to the higher long-term goals of grand strategy rather than the reverse. With the Spanish adoption of such a pragmatic approach to policy, negotiation of disputes, particularly those involving religious issues, was finally a viable option; diplomacy—the ongoing dialogue with one's opponents to effect one's long-term aims in the international arena—could be reborn.

The constable decided to refrain from discussing one further issue that was on everyone's mind until such time as the military situation in Flanders guaranteed that the English would accept it: their total exclusion from navigation to the Indies. At the start of the year it looked as if that time might never come; the situation in the Netherlands certainly did not warrant any English timidity toward the Spanish negotiators. The constable, now on the scene, and able to see for himself the true military situation in Flanders, urged Philip to make a great effort to prevent the Dutch from gaining the upper hand that year. Albert, too, insisted that more assistance had to be forthcoming from Spain if he was even to maintain what he had. He once again urged the king to provide 150,000 ducats a month, in addition to the 200,000 already allotted for the army, and to send more crack Spanish troops from Italy. His requests met with a mixed response from the Council of State and the king. The council itself was not willing to jeopardize the security of Spain's Italian possessions, especially Milan—"the key to Italy"—by withdrawing any more troops from there to send to the Low Countries. Instead it suggested that

more troops be raised in Spain, which could then release those in Italy
for other purposes. Albert would get no reinforcements at the expense of
areas deemed more vital to Spanish interests. The members of the Council were more sympathetic however when it came to Albert's requests for
funds. But while the council agreed that "reinforcing the army of Flanders and ensuring that it is put in order as soon as possible, will be of great
importance, not only for the conservation of the obedient provinces and
the reduction of the rebels, but also for the good direction and conclusion of the peace with England," the king nevertheless reiterated that he
could do nothing given the state of the crown's finances, claiming that it
was hard enough trying to provide the ordinary provisions punctually.[50]

Yet as Albert and others had already pointed out to the king, 200,000
ducats per month was insufficient in the face of the army's commitments.
And now the constable was lending his weight to Albert's arguments. On
5 March he forwarded a breakdown of the army's expenses that clearly indicated they were in the red. The king had budgeted 2,000,000 ducats for
the period from January to October. Out of this he had consigned 600,000
to be used for the siege at Ostend, leaving 1,400,000 for the operation
of the remainder of the army. But repayments of debt, interest expenses,
food, and pensions alone amounted to almost 1,600,000 ducats. Nothing
whatsoever remained for the actual routine functioning of the army, so
that immediate provision of an additional 2,202,800 escudos was necessary to avert disaster, prompting Albert to remark when accused of mis-
handling the funds: "Even if I could perform miracles, I would not be
able to come out better than I have done."[51]

In mid-spring the constable's worst fears were realized. As they had
done in 1600, the Dutch now decided to launch an invasion of the province of Flanders to secure a military advantage before the English and
Spanish should effect a permanent alliance. The States-General were
heavily influenced in this decision by Henry IV who promised them extensive military aid in the event that they could take some of the ports on
the Flemish coast to give him as collateral.[52] Although this alone would
not have been enough to force the Dutch hand, other pressing military
needs motivated such an action. In the middle of March, Spínola, taking
advantage of the damage inflicted on Ostend's fortifications by a storm
earlier in the month, unfurled the ensigns with his new motto "Now or
Never" and began pounding the defenders with upward of fifty cannon.[53]
Within days he had managed to take the outworks of the town despite

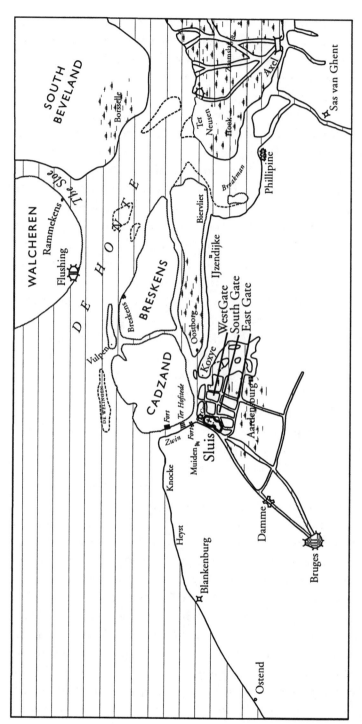

5. The Siege of Sluis, April–August 1604
(from Markham, *The Fighting Veres*)

the arrival of ten companies of reinforcements for the besieged. The defense was now reduced to the confines of the town proper and one redoubt. Something had to be done to relieve the soldiers there and prevent a blow to the Dutch reputation abroad. The States-General decided to make a feint toward Sluis, the Spanish-held port near the mouth of the Scheldt, opposite Flushing. It was hoped that such an attempt would draw the Catholic army away from its siege of Ostend to confront the Dutch forces. Maurice (as the more experienced commander) could then defeat the army in open battle. It was an ambitious plan and one that Maurice adopted with much hesitation: he preferred to lay siege to Sluis itself rather than risk all on another open engagement. By mid-April Maurice had collected a force of more than ten thousand infantry and twenty companies of cavalry—and the fate of Ostend hung in the balance. As Sir William Browne reported from Flushing, if Maurice failed, "the town would hastily make her last will and testament"[54] (fig. 5).

On 25 April, Maurice crossed the Scheldt from Zeeland and within two days had succeeded in seizing the island of Cadzand. In less than two weeks, by dint of sheer good luck, he was able to seize control of most of the forts surrounding Sluis.[55] Albert and Spínola, unwilling to risk disengaging from Ostend, did nothing other than send cursory probes against Maurice's forces, in the hopes that he would be driven off. By the end of May, Maurice had completed his encirclement of the town; the siege of Sluis had begun. Almost by accident Maurice had been given the opportunity to do what he had wanted to do from the beginning: conduct a siege campaign and avoid open battle.[56]

The archduke, in desperate straits, was incapable of continuing the siege at Ostend and launching a counteroffensive against Maurice's invasion force without more troops, especially experienced ones; but the only such forces were the mutineers at Hoogstraten and Grave. Moreover, Maurice had recently given the mutineers cavalry troops, which made them a threat to the whole of northern Brabant, a threat against which the archduke was powerless. Motivated by these considerations, on 19 May Albert ratified a treaty that granted them complete pardon, awarded them a *sustento* (monthly living allowance) of thirty-two thousand escudos per month, and promised them full payment of their arrears—in one stroke adding three thousand veterans to his forces.[57] The Council of State and Philip, however, were outraged at Albert's actions. Not only did treating with such troops in itself set a bad example, but they felt these mutineers in particular deserved reprobation, having been previously declared traitors by the archduke himself. Nonetheless the news had once again arrived too late for the council to countermand Albert's actions, and it could do little but adjust its strategy accordingly. The adjustment proved expensive, however: the settlement would finally cost the Spanish treasury more than three-quarters of a million escudos.[58]

The English wasted no time in using the situation in Flanders to put pressure on Villamediana in the negotiations, although without notable success. Even before Maurice's invasion they were demanding to know when the constable would come from Brussels to take part in the negotiations. The constable, in order to mitigate some of the English suspicion, decided to leave Brussels and make his way to the coast, ostensibly to depart. Once there, however, he feigned illness as an excuse to cancel his journey across the Channel. This ploy was enough to placate the English for the time being, and despite the setbacks in the Low Countries, the Spaniards continued successfully to set the agenda and timing of the peace talks. Villamediana used the time to advantage, winning over more and more of the English court. He took part in all the court festivals and in general tried to charm the English with his participation in their activities. But his methods went beyond mere personality. By the middle of summer, in bribes and pensions alone he had promised some 33,200 escudos, more than making up for his previous parsimony. At the same time he was taking advantage of the intercession of a female confidant—the countess of Suffolk—to win Secretary Cecil over to the peace and prepare the ground for liberty of conscience for the Catholics.[59]

In the middle of May the rest of the Habsburg deputation (both those representing Spain and those representing the archduke), excepting the constable, left Gravelines for London, arriving on the nineteenth. The representatives assembled almost daily for two months to work out the details of the peace treaty.[60] The first items brought up for discussion by the Spanish were the restoration of the cautionary towns and reparation for damages. This was a tactical move on the Spaniards' part: neither the deputies nor the members of Philip's court expected that the English would give up the towns or pay for damages inflicted on Spain during the war.[61] The Spanish merely wished to make exorbitant demands at the outset so that they would have something to give up in return for securing freedom of conscience for the Catholics and the exclusion of the English from the Indies. These latter two issues, the deputies decided, they would leave

for the constable to discuss when he arrived.[62] Given the delays in getting mail to and from the Spanish court (Philip III was in Valencia during
the spring to hold a meeting of the Valencian parliament, the Cortes),
Villamediana was allowed extraordinary freedom to proceed and negotiate as he saw fit, so long as he remained within the parameters of his
initial instructions. Philip himself was certainly pleased with Tassis's actions, writing that "since they have instructions there about everything
they have to discuss and we can see that they understand it so well and
that they govern it all with the prudence and authority that is suitable, it
seems to me that we should do nothing other than praise them for their
proceedings and charge them to carry on as they see fit."[63] Villamediana
and his colleagues were way ahead of him. By the third week of July the
main outlines of the treaty had been agreed. On 28 July one of Albert's
retainers, Luis de Guzmán, was dispatched to Valladolid with the clauses
of the treaty that had been agreed upon, causing Albert to comment, a
little prematurely, on the "good conclusion of the peace with England."[64]

Nonetheless, toward the end of July the Spanish decided to increase
the pressure on the English regarding the question of navigation to the
Indies. In hopes of persuading them that such trade would no longer be
lucrative, they posted a squadron of ships off Cape Finisterre, the west-
ernmost point of the Spanish mainland, to intercept any ships intent on
voyaging across the Atlantic.[65] At the same time Philip instructed the constable to proceed in the negotiations using the same formula previously
employed in the Treaty of Vervins to exclude trade to the Indies. This
would turn out to be a major tactical error on Philip's part; the Treaty of
Vervins contained no clause expressly forbidding trade to that region. He
had unwittingly left the constable without guidance in one of the most
important matters to be discussed in the negotiations.[66]

The constable, at a loss, could find no precedent in any of the Spanish
treaties of the sixteenth century that excluded trade to the Indies. Even
more worrisome was the fact that the English themselves insisted that the
treaty should contain the same clauses regarding trade as previous Spanish
treaties had done; effectively this would mean that the English would not
be excluded since no mention of the Indies had ever been made. Once
again (as in 1600), Cecil's historical approach to negotiations appeared to
have paid off, this time catching the Spanish off guard, leaving the constable to remark, "It has much surprised me that the English have used
this example against us as strongly as we thought we would use it against

them." The Spanish were left in the uncomfortable and surprising position
of insisting on a clause in the Anglo-Spanish accord that had not appeared
in any previous treaty, most notably that with France. If Philip did not
wish to offend the English, he would have to back down on the point of
an explicit clause.[67] In the meantime, on 16 July the Habsburg deputies,
led by Villamediana, finally found wording that both sides could agree
upon: "There ought to be free commerce *in those places where it existed before the war, in conformity with the use and observance of the ancient alliances and
treaties.*"[68] The Spaniards clearly believed that such wording excluded the
English from the Indies without offending them, even annotating in the
margin of the document, "These words exclude both the Indies." And according to Villamediana the English themselves suggested that they had
been cut out of the trade with the Indies and now feared the same for
their trade with the rest of the Spanish territories.[69]

The negotiations had now gone as far as they could possibly go without the constable. The most important matter—religion—remained to be
resolved, though nothing could be done until he had assessed the situation
firsthand. Accordingly, he decided that he could no longer avoid passing
across the Channel to England, despite being legitimately ill at that moment. Moreover, he had to carry with him the money that was to smooth
the final negotiations. For it was clear that the Spaniards now felt that the
best way to secure toleration in the British kingdoms was not by openly
demanding it, and thus risking a break, but by winning over influential
members of the court with bribes and pensions. Hints were given, via the
countess of Suffolk, Tassis's "Catholic" confidant, that the Spanish might
be able to relieve the suffering of the Catholics for twenty-one years by
paying off, or getting the Catholics to pay, the "Recusant fines"—192,000
escudos worth—that they would owe for not attending church.[70]

Meanwhile the military situation was precarious enough for the constable to worry about its possible effect on James's attitude. Therefore at
the end of July, after realizing that Ostend would not fall in time to relieve Sluis, he recommended that the archduke pull his men away from
the siege to assist the beleaguered Spanish port. The archduke, previously
counseled against sending troops to save Sluis, even by Spínola himself,
now wasted no time in using both Spínola's troops and the now reconciled mutineers to make an effort at counterattack against the Dutch.
He decided upon a two-pronged attack, ordering the mutineers across
the Rhine and Spínola's troops against Maurice's forces around Sluis. The

effort was in vain. Spínola, even while regaining two of the forts about
Sluis on 16 August, was unable to break through the Dutch lines to effect
a linkup with the defenders in the town itself. On 17 August he met face-
to-face with Maurice in an engagement that would decide the issue. After
a fierce struggle, the Dutch managed at last to repulse the Catholic army,
forcing Spínola to retire once again to Ostend. On the following day the
beleaguered garrison at Sluis, starving and without hope of relief, surrendered.[71]

But the disaster in the end had little effect on the Anglo-Spanish peace
talks. On 17 August the constable finally arrived in Dover and was greeted
by James's two representatives, John Holles, Lord Houghton and earl of
Clare, and Henry Howard, earl of Northampton. From there they trav-
eled by land to Gravesend (the constable in a litter owing to his infirmity)
and then barged the final twenty miles up the Thames, disembarking at
Somerset House on 20 August, only to find the king away on a hunting trip. Following four days of feasting and entertaining, both sides met
to hammer out the final form of the treaty. In these sessions the English
ministers convinced the constable that Parliament would never relax the
recusancy laws; indeed, they had expressly said as much. Prudence suggested that the Spanish not appear to be forcing James's hand in the matter, a move that might possibly jeopardize the position of the Catholics
even further. The constable decided, therefore, not to pay the English
the 192,000 escudos to win toleration and finally accepted that the treaty
would make no mention of it.[72] This business completed, the constable
had his public audience with the king. Four days later, on 29 August, after
more audiences and banqueting in which the constable lavished jewels on
the courtiers, James publicly swore to uphold the now finalized Treaty
of London. The Spaniards had secured peace with England.[73]

People questioned the success of the treaty almost from the beginning.
Most modern scholars affirm that the Spanish had lost in the exchange. At
the time, both sides felt that they had got the better of the other, but that
is the nature of negotiation: neither side will agree unless it feels that it has
gained more than it lost. The English had secured free trade to the Spanish
possessions in Europe but failed to get an express clause permitting trade
to the Indies; they had managed to reject any clause that secured freedom of conscience for the Catholics in England; and they had refused to
prevent English citizens from fighting in the Low Countries. The Spanish, on the other hand, had achieved many of their strategic goals. They

had got the English government to agree to cease all direct military and financial aid to the Dutch,[74] had secured a renunciation of the English treaty of alliance with the French and Dutch signed the year before, had stopped licensed English corsair attacks, had got the English to withdraw the cautionary towns from Dutch service (i.e., the ports could no longer be used by either the Dutch navy or by Dutch corsairs), and had secured permission to harbor fleets of up to eight warships in English ports. Although they failed to get an explicit clause forbidding English trade to the Indies, they felt that they had won a victory in this area.

One can say, then, that the Spanish benefited more than the English in the treaty in terms of military strategy, while the English gained in commercial matters, each of which merely reflects the particular interests of the respective countries.[75] The Spanish had needed peace with England to free up badly needed resources for their other areas of engagement. In achieving this, they had really given up nothing that they had not already tacitly conceded. Yet they had achieved their main strategic objective. The English, on the other hand, won for themselves nothing they did not already have. And certainly toward the end of James's reign, some of the English felt they were the ones who had lost by the peace, for the peace had given Spain the opportunity to pursue its aims in Europe. As Anthony Weldon, a courtier at James's court, later put it, "The Constable of *Castile* so plyed his Masters business (in which he spared for no cost) that he procured a peace so advantagious for *Spaine,* and so disadvantagious for *England,* that it and all Christendom have since both seen and felt the lamentable effect thereof." Indeed, as Weldon went on to note, doubtless with some exaggeration, the peace led to the growth of a Spanish faction in James's court, whose freely flowing gold lubricated the wheels of corruption in the court and made its members mere pawns in the hands of the Spanish: "There was not one Courtier of note, that tasted not of *Spains* bounty, either in Gold, or Jewels, and among them, not any in so large a proportion as the Countess of *Suffolke,* who shared in her Lords interest [i.e., she received a portion of the proceeds of her husband, Thomas Howard, Earl of Suffolk] . . . and in that interest which she had, in being Mistris to that little great Secretary [Cecil] (little in body and stature, but great in wit and policy) the sole manager of State affairs."[76]

But at the end of August 1604 it remained to be seen if the Spanish could capitalize on the success of their strategy and effect a positive change in their power in the north. The first test would be Ostend. Having suffered a tremendous loss of prestige as a result of the fall of Sluis, the archduke resolved to press the siege of Ostend harder than ever. At the same time the States-General ordered Maurice to finish refortifying Sluis and move to the relief of the besieged garrison. Flushed with their success, the Dutch hoped to find the Catholics unable or unwilling to fend off Maurice. Maurice, however, had his usual doubts about the effectiveness of engaging the enemy deep in the heart of the Spanish territories, especially now that the Dutch were receiving no reinforcements and no aid from the English. Nevertheless he agreed to the enterprise and set about preparing his forces. It was now a race to see which side would finish its preparations first. On 13 September Spínola launched a fierce attack on Sand Hill, the last important redoubt still in Dutch hands. His experienced German regiments took the hill by storm, slaughtering the remaining defenders. The rest in the garrison in Ostend were now reduced to the protection of a few wood and sand bunkers that were incapable of sustaining further major assaults. A week later, on 20 September, the governor, Colonel Daniel de Hartaing, lord of Marquette, having dispatched his cannon to Flushing, finally agreed to surrender what was left of the town.[77]

The siege had lasted three years and seventy-seven days. It was estimated that over sixty thousand Habsburg troops died and that the Dutch and English lost as many, if not more.[78] The scene that greeted Albert and Isabel when they came to celebrate their victory rivaled the devastation of the no-man's-land between the trenches in World War I. It was almost an alien world, devoid of all signs that humans had once inhabited the area, so harrowingly depicted by Motley:

> There were no churches, no houses, no redoubts, no bastions, no walls, nothing but a vague and confused mass of ruin. Spinola conducted his imperial guests along the edge of extinct volcanoes, amid upturned cemeteries, through quagmires which once were moats, over huge mounds of sand, and vast shapeless masses of bricks and masonry, which had been forts. He endeavored to point out places where mines had been exploded, where ravelins had been stormed, where the assailants had been successful, and where they had been bloodily repulsed. But it was all loathsome, hideous rubbish. There were no human habitations, no hovels, no casemates. The inhabitants had burrowed at last in the earth, like the dumb creatures of the swamps and forests. . . . At every

step the unburied skulls of brave soldiers who had died in the cause of freedom grinned their welcome to the conquerors. Isabella wept at the sight.[79]

Yet, if it was not exactly a conquest worth boasting of, the final thorn in the archdukes' side had been removed, and the Habsburgs were at last free to pursue other aims.[80] This fact, combined with the elimination of one of their enemies, meant the Spanish now had the opportunity to devise an effective strategy against the rebellious northern provinces. At long last it appeared that Philip would get his wish of pushing the war in Flanders across the Rhine and into the heart of Dutch territory. The final struggle was about to begin.

"Blood and Fire": Spinola's Invasion of the Dutch Provinces

❧ ❧ ❧

Because of how important it is, and also because I desire rest for Your
Highness and my sister, I have made every possible effort since I succeeded
to these kingdoms to save those states, as Your Highness well knows, and
now, with the same end and desire, I have taken the resolution you see
here, trusting in God and Your Highness's valor that the time is come to
improve our situation in the war and put everything in better state.

—PHILIP III TO ARCHDUKE ALBERT
6 February 1605

Even before the ink was dry on the Anglo-Spanish treaty, the constable made clear the central motive behind the Spanish agreement to the peace. In an audience with James before his departure
from England he asked for permission to raise three thousand English soldiers for use in Flanders against the Dutch: the Habsburgs were going on
the offensive.[1] Neither the English nor the Dutch were pleased to hear that
James would now allow such levies. According to Noel Caron, the agent
of the States-General in London, "No promulgation was ever received
in London with more coolness, yes—with more sadness. No mortal has
shown the least satisfaction in words or deeds, but, on the contrary, people
have cried out openly, 'God save our good neighbours the States of Holland and Zeeland, and grant them victory!'"[2] The Dutch, as the Venetian
ambassador noted, were themselves extremely worried about their new
situation and the ease with which the Spanish had strengthened their own
hand: "They say that though it is true that the English hate the Spanish
and like the Dutch, yet gold works miracles everywhere, and nowhere
greater than in England. They will be left alone to face Spain, and cannot

hold out long. The Spanish ambassador, who will now reside in England, will soon corrupt the whole kingdom by the ordinary means and artifices; and this is the real object for which Spain has accepted the peace."[3]

But not everything went Spain's way. Although the Spanish were free to attempt to raise English troops, the English crown would do nothing to assist them openly. Moreover James refused to prevent his subjects from serving in the Dutch army, and levies of men were crossing to the northern provinces even as the constable prepared to depart.[4] Worse still was the fact that English corsairs, whom the Spanish thought had been eliminated by virtue of the treaty, now took service directly with the Dutch and would continue to prey on Spanish shipping.[5]

Nevertheless the Spanish pushed ahead with their plans to bring the Dutch to their knees. Even before they had secured the situations in London and Ostend, the Spanish leaders decided to bring all their financial resources to bear against the rebels. Toward the end of September, the council and the king, expecting successes in both areas, finally gave the order to raise an extraordinary provision of half a million escudos to send to the archduke to quell the outbreak of a minor mutiny and to pay the besieging forces their due. They wanted the army in full readiness for the campaigns of the coming year.[6] Not content, however, with merely squaring their own finances, the Spanish decided simultaneously to put pressure on those of the Dutch. They began urging James to enter into a new agreement with the States-General over the cautionary towns, in accordance with a provision in the original treaty of 1585, which stipulated such a renegotiation in the event of an Anglo-Spanish peace. The effect of a renegotiation would be to force the Dutch to make immediate repayment of their debt to England or risk losing the towns to the English permanently. In the latter event the Spanish hinted that they would be willing to pay even more than the Dutch owed in order to get the towns back. This was indeed a succulent morsel to put before the financially strapped English crown. If it succeeded, the plan would mean the Dutch could not carry on the war successfully, either because they would lack the finances or because those vital deepwater ports would now be in Spanish hands.[7]

Yet success against the Dutch would require more than financial preparation. As has been shown, the other major problem the Spanish faced was the degeneration in the military leadership of the Army of Flanders (see Chapter 3). The Council of State and the king had tried, through the ordinances of 1603, to remedy this situation but had not yet succeeded in getting their reforms past the archduke. Albert was zealously and jealously guarding his rights in this area, rightly judging that to give in would mean a serious loss of independence and perhaps of sovereignty. As late as August 1604 a junta of the Council of State had examined the complaints of the archduke on this score, which he sent by way of Rodrigo Lasso. The ministers, however, had been unwilling to risk upsetting the situation at a time when the negotiations in England and the enterprise at Ostend were so close to termination. They decided, therefore, to postpone answering the archduke until they had received further news.[8] Nonetheless it was not a situation that could go unresolved for much longer. As the archduke's own letters made clear, the problems in the high command of the army had seriously jeopardized the Habsburg position around Sluis and had possibly been responsible for the loss of the fort.[9] Yet Albert was still hesitant that Philip appoint a second in command. But if the king insisted on doing so, Albert agreed that it would have to be the governor of Antwerp, Agustín de Mejía, the senior Spanish general in Flanders.

After receiving confirmation of the precarious state of the command situation from the constable, Philip decided to take advantage of Albert's concession and appoint Mejía to the position of maestre de campo general. At the same time he ordered everything to be made ready for a spring offensive in the Low Countries. Money was to be found, troops raised, and the infantry in Italy to be put on alert. Discussion of further plans for Flanders, such as what to do with the archduke, would await the constable's return.[10] Not only was the big thrust in Flanders about to begin—a thrust that many of the councillors had wanted almost since the beginning of the reign—but the Spanish ministers were also clearly using the new developments in northern Europe to attempt to seize greater control in Flanders.[11]

But by the time Philip resolved to do something about restructuring the military command, Albert had selected his own candidate for the position of maestre de campo general: the victorious Spínola. On 5 October he wrote to Lerma with his recommendation for the Genoese upstart:

Seeing the present state of things here, it seems necessary, for many reasons, that this position should be given to the marquis Spínola. Even though one could desire that he were a more experienced soldier than he really is, he has such ability that with a little help he will do well all that is necessary; moreover, he has so won the affections of the soldiers, and even of everyone else, that he will do more with the little he knows than others who know more could do. And, with the advantages of credit and wealth that he has, he can assist and serve His Majesty in important moments, as he did just now by providing the double wages to the army. . . . I have let him understand that he would serve as maestre de campo general.[12]

Albert thought he had finally found someone whom he trusted to be his second in command—and someone who was not a Spanish lackey. The archduke let it be known that if anyone else were to get the position, the situation of the Army in Flanders would become untenable. By telling Spínola he would get the position even before suggesting it to the king, Albert was forcing Philip's hand. Philip owed a tremendous debt to Spínola, both for his victory against Ostend and for his continual efforts to keep the Army of Flanders from total mutiny.[13] If he refused to grant the position of commander to Spínola, he risked not only offending the general but also losing the valuable financial resources that Spínola commanded.

The junta that discussed the appointment strongly opposed Spínola's candidacy. While granting that the general deserved extensive rewards, the ministers understandably balked at putting the fate of the whole of the Low Countries in the hands of an inexperienced general selected by Archduke Albert, the least qualified of all to pass judgment on Spínola's military potential.[14] The archduke was not about to let the matter rest on his recommendation, however. Despite having misgivings about Spínola's absence at such a critical juncture, Albert gave the general leave to go to Spain to plead for his reward in person. Spínola left Brussels in the middle of November, carrying with him letters of recommendation from the archdukes for the king and Lerma and requests for more money and men. More important, however, the marquis took with him plans for an ambitious offensive campaign into the heart of Dutch territory. His future depended on the Spanish ministers' and the king's deciding that only he could carry out the plan.

Spínola arrived in Valladolid on 12 December, one day after the constable, who had detoured through Paris to sign a bilateral agreement with Henry IV revoking the 30 percent tariffs and embargo that were so damaging to the trade of the southern Netherlands.[15] Both were preceded by another representative of the archduke, the count of Solre, who was to represent to the court the precarious state of the military in Flanders and beg for adequate funds. On 4 December Solre presented Andrés de Prada with a statement of costs for an army of 25,000 infantry, 4,500 cavalry, and garrisons totaling another 10,485 men for the upcoming year. In all, including victualing, it was estimated that 522,004 escudos per month would be required, of which the provinces themselves were to pay 118,704 escudos. These sums, however, did not take into account the extra munitions, transportation, food, and other supplies that would be needed to launch a serious offensive into Dutch territory. It was clear from this that Philip's provision of only 200,000 escudos per month was woefully inadequate. Moreover, the provinces themselves were not providing the archduke with enough to pay for the garrisons for which he was responsible. He had a monthly shortfall of 12,612 escudos. It was a lot for the councillors to consider.[16]

On Christmas eve the junta composed of Idiáquez and Miranda drew up an outline of the proposals for the king. They had three strategies open to them, as proposed by the constable, Agustín de Mejía, and Spínola. The constable suggested putting a force of up to 22,500 men across the Rhine into Frisia and leaving another force of 4,000 to 5,000 around Sluis to prevent Maurice from pushing south of the Scheldt. Mejía urged the king to send only 16,500 troops across the Rhine and leave 8,500 in Brabant to act as a rapid-deployment force that could meet any threat Maurice might make. It was Spínola who proposed the most ambitious plan: an offensive against Maurice around Sluis *and* an offensive across the Rhine. If, he argued, the Spanish treasury could not support such a bold plan, then they could not succeed in any offensive. The alternative was to go completely on the defensive. As he pointed out, however, the dual offensive would cost only 3,717,976 escudos for the period April–October, whereas a defensive strategy against Maurice's assuredly powerful army would cost almost two million escudos a month. Despite such persuasive arguments it should come as no surprise that the councillors could not condone Spínola's all-or-nothing plan and that they instead chose to follow the constable's more conservative strategy, thus closing the door on their last chance to win back Sluis and its surrounding territory. The king agreed with the junta's recommendations and ordered Mejía to prepare for his charge as maestre de campo general.[17]

Spínola could not help but be disappointed in the results of the junta's meeting. Not only would he be deprived of the highest command, but he would be forced to watch while only half of his plan was put into action by a cautious old man fresh out of garrison duty. His only reward was to have command of that small portion of the army remaining about Sluis to prevent Maurice's movement.[18] It was a humiliating appointment and one that Spínola would not tolerate. On 3 February he met with Lerma's right hand, Pedro de Franqueza, count of Villalonga, to deliver his ultimatum: either he receive total command of the army or he would retire to his estates, taking his vast personal wealth and credit out of Spanish service. It is impossible to state with any surety what finally convinced Philip and Lerma to appoint the persistent hero. It may have been his threat to withdraw his resources or the Spanish custom of never appointing a man to a position less prestigious than the one held before; or perhaps Spínola's argument that an army with two heads, one of which was the archduke's, would never accomplish anything, convinced them that he was the right person to place in power alongside the wayward archduke.[19] In any event, on 26 February Philip not only appointed Spínola to the supreme command (ordering Agustín de Mejía back to the court) but also made him superintendent general of finance for the Army of Flanders, thereby removing financial control from the archduke. As the envious in the court snidely remarked, Spínola had been made a general before even being a soldier.[20]

In spite of these vast preparations, which were set under way during the early months of 1605, the Spanish ministers had not completely rejected peace and remained steadfast in their goal of bringing the Dutch to the bargaining table. In February, just three days before he sent word of his military plans to Albert, Philip outlined Spain's diplomatic strategy in instructions to Villamediana. He pointed out that a lengthy armistice was the goal of any talks but could not be requested openly without ruining its chances. Therefore, Villamediana would strive for a permanent peace but make such exhorbitant demands that the Dutch would grow frustrated with this plan. At this juncture James would step in and propose an amistice instead.[21]

Spanish military strategy apparently also had a peace conference as its goal. The Council of State made this patently clear when in the middle of March it once again considered the issue of a cease-fire with the rebels. The councillors affirmed that in the event the rebels were brought to such an agreement by the invasion in Frisia, it would have to be for a long period in order to insure that the Spanish would not have to maintain an offensive force. Their aim was still to force the Dutch into a situation where they would welcome a long-term armistice. That achieved, the council hoped, the people of the rebellious provinces would recognize the exorbitant taxes they had been paying during the war, realize that their governors had led them astray for personal gain, and eventually welcome reunification rather than begin such a costly war anew.[22]

This was not such a naive plan as it may seem to the modern reader. The Dutch war machine existed solely because of the war with Spain. The taxes that the States-General imposed to maintain that machine were far greater than those that Spain had imposed initially and against which the Dutch had fought so hard.[23] If the war should cease, even for a few years, it was reasonable to assume that the tax burden would be drastically cut and the military's influence in state affairs would be reduced. The people would see that what they ended up with as a result of the war was far worse that what they had endured under Spanish rule. And, should they at the end of the armistice decide that they wished to continue the war, they would lack the military capacity to do so. But the Spanish assessment failed to take into consideration two important factors: the role of ideology in the struggle and the improving economic status of the Dutch. The ministers in Spain seemingly could not understand that the Dutch had serious ideological differences that would prevent them from ever being reconciled with the Spanish. Moreover, the Dutch people, in spite of their tax burden and the difficulties occasioned by the war, continued to improve their standard of living. Indeed, after 1590 the northern provinces were the only part of Europe in which wages rose faster than prices. In short, the thirty-plus years of fighting had made the Dutch a different people from their brethren to the south. The Spanish, by refusing to adapt their grand strategy to the changed ideological and economic circumstances of their conflict with the Dutch, were unable to grasp the fact that they could probably never win back the northern provinces by any means, peaceful or otherwise.[24]

So the preparations on both sides for the upcoming confrontation continued unabated. On 24 March Spínola left Valladolid with his new commission and the first installment of what Philip claimed would be some six million ducats, "which would leave things here so hard up that we will be able to take up other things only with great difficulty."[25] Given such a late start, the ministers were fearful that the general would not be able to get his forces together in time for the new campaign season. Meanwhile, the Dutch had set about recruiting their forces during the

winter months and had raised over one hundred new companies of infantry and thirty-six squadrons of cavalry. They planned to sally forth in the
early spring, before Spínola was ready.[26] Worried over the lack of Spanish
troops in Flanders for the summer offensive, Philip decided to take the
opportunity provided by the peace with England to ship troops via the
English Channel.[27] It was a move fraught with risks.

Now that England had settled matters with the Spanish, its marin-
ers were intent on developing their trade with Flanders and Iberia. The
Dutch, however, restricted from such trade either directly or by the imposition of prohibitory tariffs, were trying everything in their power to
cut off such commerce. The Dutch blockade against the ports of Flanders
was applied even more vigilantly, and pirates, carrying letters of marque
from Maurice, were increasing their depredations on Atlantic and Channel shipping.[28] To pass troops up the Channel, the Spanish would have
to run the gauntlet of these Dutch blockading forces. To deal with this
problem the constable had proposed stationing another fleet in Channel
waters to replace Federico Spínola's and in addition had suggested enlist-
ing the aid of Christian IV, the king of Denmark, against Dutch shipping
in the North Sea and the Baltic as a countermeasure that would draw
Dutch squadrons away from Flemish ports.[29] Philip, however, knew that
his treasury could not fund both a land campaign and the outfitting of a
new fleet. Trusting in his new agreement with James, he suggested that
Villamediana enlist the aid of the English against Dutch pirates.[30] It would
be a costly error and one which demonstrated that an England that was
merely neutral, and not an ally, was an England of only limited strategic
value for Spain.

Nevertheless, the cultivation of the entente with England went on.
Toward the end of April, news arrived at the court in Valladolid that
Charles Howard, lord high admiral of England, had arrived in La Coruña
on Spain's north coast.[31] He came—accompanied by more than six hundred retainers—as England's special ambassador to the Spanish court to
procure Philip's ratification of the recent treaty. Howard had been the
commander of the English fleets sent against the Spanish in 1588 and 1596,
and he was therefore an assertive choice for the position of English representative. Moreover his arrival was unexpected and threw the Spanish
into confusion. On 18 February the court had received word from Villamediana that the admiral would depart England in mid-March.[32] Philip
had wanted Villamediana to delay the admiral's departure until the late

spring and to change his landing site to one more suitable for such a large retinue of followers, but the orders arrived in London too late.[33] Now the English envoy had arrived before preparations had been finalized. As a result, the English were forced to find food and lodging where they could — an inauspicious beginning for Anglo-Spanish relations. The Spanish, however, working diligently, soon rectified the situation, and on 26 May the admiral arrived outside the walls of Valladolid and, despite a sudden spring deluge, was escorted with notable pomp into the city. After five days of ceremonial audiences with various courtiers, on 31 May he officially presented the new resident English ambassador, Sir Charles Cornwallis, to the king. Although the presence of an English ambassador on Spanish soil was itself an important step in fostering peaceful relations between the two crowns, Cornwallis was unfortunately a man who would prove to have little willingness to understand the Spanish.[34]

The admiral's arrival meant that the departure of Philip's own ambassador to England would be delayed. In January, refusing the slate of candidates recommended by the Council of State, he had selected Pedro de Zúñiga, his chief huntsman and son of a former ambassador to France, as the man who would represent him. He could not have made a better choice as his first resident ambassador. Since diplomacy during this period still relied heavily on the personal feelings of one monarch for another, Philip had chosen to represent himself as one lover of the hunt to another.[35] On 20 April, Philip's secretaries, unaware of the imminent arrival of the English admiral, drew up a set of public and secret instructions for Zúñiga.[36] Clause 4 of Zúñiga's secret instructions contained Philip's diplomatic policy with regard to England and the Dutch. Zúñiga, like Villamediana before him, was to use his abilities to enlist the English in persuading the Dutch to come to terms, striving for a long-term armistice. With this, Philip, expanding on his aims, hoped "to open the door on matters of religion in the rebel states, since with the communication that will result, we would be able to send priests and establish seminaries and use other subtle means to convert them." But, the instructions emphasized, Zúñiga was to try to achieve such an armistice by first asking for permanent peace and then making such a peace impossible. Instructions in hand, Zúñiga was prepared to depart, when word came of the admiral's arrival. Philip and his ministers therefore decided to delay the ambassador's departure so that he might accompany the admiral back to England.

After the initial audiences there followed weeks of feasting and exchanging of presents while the representatives from both sides debated the location where the peace would be sworn. Philip refused all English demands to swear to the treaty in church. He would not make political concessions where they might affect his personal religious salvation.[37] Finally, on the afternoon of Corpus Christi, 9 June, in a room of his palace, he swore to uphold the terms of the treaty. Just over a week later, on 18 June, the admiral departed Valladolid for La Coruña, accompanied by Pedro de Zúñiga and six beautifully outfitted horses for James's hunt.[38] The Anglo-Spanish relationship was running smoothly, and on the basis of this the Spanish still held out the strong hope that the English would assist their war efforts in Flanders by providing ships and troops against the Dutch. Events of late summer and autumn would demonstrate the naïveté of the Spanish hope.

As noted earlier, logistical and financial difficulties plagued the Spanish preparations for the offensive throughout the spring. These problems afflicted Dutch efforts no less. Owing to the delay of the grants from the provincial estates and problems with recruiting in the German territories, Maurice was unable to lead his forces out until 15 May, a full two months after the States-General had intended, giving Spínola plenty of time to build up his army. Dividing his forces in two, Maurice launched a strong attack against Antwerp with the intention of taking it by surprise. Much to the consternation of the Dutch, however, the garrison at Antwerp was ready and waiting, having somehow been warned of the impending attack.[39] Maurice was forced to content himself with the taking of a small fort at Wouw near Bergen op Zoom before he was ordered across the Scheldt to Cadzand on 2 June. Once on the island, he took up station at Biervliet, near Ijzendijke (Ysendyke) and began to fortify his position. The States-General were clearly worried about the possessions they had gained the previous year and wanted Maurice to do everything to preserve them. Spínola, finally at the head of his army, moved to follow Maurice, setting up camp within sight of the Dutch forces. Knowing himself to be outnumbered, Maurice could do nothing but await Spínola's first move. Spínola, however, contented himself with waiting for the reinforcements that were daily expected by sea from Spain.[40]

The Dutch had learned of Spanish intentions to ship troops via the Channel in early spring. They immediately sent out a fleet to patrol the waters and prevent the passage of any Spanish ships. On 14 June 'eight ships, carrying some twelve hundred Spanish soldiers, were espied by the

Dutch fleet near Dover. The Dutch descended upon the Spanish squadron with great fury, sinking or burning four of the ships. The Dutch admiral, Haultain, tied the surviving Spaniards together by twos and mercilessly pushed them overboard. The four remaining ships sought shelter in the harbor at Dover, whereupon the Dutch fleet pursued them, giving battle even at the harbor mouth, their cannon fire causing injuries in the town itself. Finally, the governor of the English castle, outraged at this violation of neutral English waters, gave orders to fire upon the Dutch fleet, saving the Spanish ships from sure destruction.

The situation put James in a difficult position. Because his men had fired on the Dutch, it was naturally claimed that he was, in fact, not a neutral party in the dispute between Spain and the rebels. Moreover, Noel Caron hinted, if James should comply with the terms of the treaty (which stipulated that free intercourse with Flanders was to be assured) and provide escort for the remaining Spanish troops across the Channel, it would be tantamount to a declaration of war against the Dutch. Unwilling to risk offending the Dutch he declined to allow his vessels to be used to transport the remaining eight hundred soldiers but did offer to mediate between the two sides. In the meantime the Dutch fleet remained stationed off the coast near Dover, effectively barring the passage not only of these soldiers but also of those who had been raised in England for Spínola's forces. Spanish hopes for an effective new supply route to Flanders were thus dashed.[41]

The Dutch naturally assumed that these setbacks, combined with the rumored deterioration of Spínola's new recruits in Flanders, would forestall any Spanish offensive that year, especially with the campaign season so well advanced. They complacently believed that Maurice had disrupted Spanish plans by maintaining and strengthening his camp at Biervliet. But this was precisely what Spínola wished them to think. In the middle weeks of August, Spínola accomplished a classic sweeping action, keeping Maurice pinned down in Flanders while he swung wide around the Dutch flank to attack them in their rear, taking forts at Oldenzaal and Lingen.[42]

Maurice had been caught completely off guard by the swift actions of the new general and was unable to reach the front until 19 August. Unable to save Lingen, Maurice rushed to reinforce Coevorden, another significant fort guarding the passages into the German territories. Spínola, however, content with his accomplishments in the area and short of reinforcements, on 14 September departed for the Rhine, pausing to regroup at the Ruhr. Maurice, reinforced with troops under the command of his cousin Lewis William of Nassau, followed closely at Spínola's heels and eventually set up camp near the Catholic position. Spínola's forces laid siege to Wachtendonk, a little to the east of Venlo. It had been a tremendously successful campaign for the virtually untried general.[43]

To prevent more Habsburg successes, on 8 October Maurice launched a surprise attack on Spínola's forces on the Ruhr. The Catholic army, however, received advance word from their scouts of the impending attack and were ready for Maurice's forces. After a battle that swayed back and forth for some time, Maurice eventually lost the day and was forced to retire; Spínola went on to cap his victory by taking Wachtendonk on 27 October and Cracau on 5 November.[44] With the fall of these strongholds the Habsburg forces controlled a string of forts along the entire length of the Dutch eastern flank.

The English were quick to realize the significance of Spínola's campaign. On 14 September John Throckmorton, the English sergeant-major at Flushing, delivered his opinion to the town's governor: "By their thus working they take away all passages both by land and by the Rhine into those parts of Germany, a matter of great dispropriety to these people. . . . The enemy hathe not only tacken us out a newe lesson of warr but allsoe an unaccustomed bouldness."[45] Spínola's advance seemed to have had the desired effect. It showed the Dutch just how vulnerable they were on their own in the face of a concerted effort by the Spanish. Moreover it demonstrated that Maurice was not invulnerable and that henceforth the Dutch might perhaps have to rely on something other than military prowess in their struggle against Spain. As a result the war party in the republic began to waver, allowing the more reasoned judgment of Oldenbarnevelt and his supporters to begin to make headway in the States-General.

Despite Spínola's successes in Gelderland, the Spanish ministers were not optimistic about Spain's ability to improve its military position relative to the Dutch. On 3 September, even before hearing of the Catholic army's gains, the Council of State sat down to consider the immediate future. Although the councillors expressed the hope that Spínola would be successful with the enormous resources at his disposal, they reminded the king that even this vast sum would not be enough. As they pointed out, complete success demanded dominance not only on land but in the

Channel. If Philip could not or would not build a permanent fleet for those waters, they suggested he not even try to go on the offensive but instead cut his forces to the minimum necessary to defend the frontiers and garrisons.[46] Prompted by these arguments, Philip agreed that it was high time to form a navy that would patrol the waters of the Channel and gave orders that the Armada del Almirantazgo be disbanded, having failed to demonstrate its usefulness in the past. From the money saved by this measure the Spanish could provide a new fleet for the northern waters and develop Ostend into a good deepwater port.[47]

The council, however, was still in doubt about the efficacy of any military measures. Returning to these issues two weeks later, it argued that forming a navy such as Philip had requested would be far too difficult and expensive an enterprise. Instead it suggested that Albert, or Spínola, try to locate Dutch insiders who might be able to facilitate peace talks.[48] Philip, however, by now having heard of Spínola's initial successes, insisted that peace talks were not the best route to take at that time: "What is fitting right now is to pressure the rebels. If as a result of this they should give some reason why we should listen to them, well and good. To do otherwise is to lose time and reputation and allow them to pluck up their courage." Having said this he proceeded to point out to the council just how they might conceivably establish the new armada, reiterating his instructions that the old armada be disbanded immediately.[49] All these additional military preparations, of course, rested on the assumption that Spínola could duplicate his achievements the following year.

Unfortunately for the Spanish, Spínola's successes even in 1605 were offset both by his inability to accomplish as much as was hoped because of his late departure and by events in England. At eleven o'clock in the evening of 4 November (o.s.) Sir Thomas Knyvett, justice of the peace for Westminster, discovered a man named "John Johnson" standing watch over thirty-six barrels of gunpowder hidden beneath the Parliament House. This man, as it turned out, was in fact Guido (Guy) Fawkes, an erstwhile mercenary from the Army of Flanders who had been hired to explode the gunpowder on the following day when King James and his family sat down to open the second session of the Parliament first convened in 1604. Fawkes had been brought over to London by Robert Winter, cousin to Robert Catesby, who in 1602 had proposed to the Spanish that he stage a Catholic uprising in England with the support of Spanish arms and money. This uprising having failed to leave the planning stage, Catesby had, in 1604, fixed his hopes on blowing up Parliament and the king in an effort to force the government to grant toleration to the Catholics. Although Winter at first recoiled from the plot, he was reconciled to it by the failure of his own mission to persuade the constable to make toleration a condition of the Anglo-Spanish peace. Now the conspiracy had failed and Fawkes, tortured on the rack, wasted no time in divulging all the details of this "Catholic" Gunpowder Plot to the English ministers.[50]

While the English, led by James, hastened to assure everyone that they did not believe the Spanish were behind the plot, it was natural that most people should believe otherwise. The new Spanish ambassador in London, Pedro de Zúñiga, did all he could to mitigate the anti-Catholic and anti-Spanish backlash. Even in Valladolid, Philip sent Lerma to meet with Sir Charles Cornwallis in order to express Philip's elation at the deliverance of the English royal family from destruction. Moreover, he resolved to send one of his gentlemen of the chamber, Juan de Mendoza, marquis of San Germán, on a special embassy to London to convey the same message to James personally.[51] James himself was terrified by the incident, which exacerbated his long-standing fear of assassination, and he blamed Catholics in general. In a letter to his brother-in-law, Christian IV of Denmark, he called the conspiracy "the most horrid and detestable of all treasons either undertaken anywhere in the world within the memory of man or conceived in thought and mind. It is all the more atrocious since it was to be undertaken by men professing themselves to be adherents and avengers of the Roman and papist religion (or rather of a most impure superstition)."[52] The whole episode struck a heavy blow against the growing Anglo-Spanish entente and destroyed all hope that the Spanish would ever secure toleration for the Catholics in England. In the session of Parliament held immediately after the incident, King, Lords, and Commons united to pass onerous new anti-Catholic laws. By early December the Catholics were being openly hounded and persecuted. It remained to be seen how the events would affect the Spanish situation in the north, although by December there were already indications that neither the English nor the Spanish wanted an open break over the affair. Indeed the English courtiers who were receiving pensions from Philip visited Zúñiga to remind him that they were expecting their Christmas installments![53]

So things stood when, as the new year opened, the Spanish court heard with some trepidation that Spínola was on his way there to celebrate his triumph and seek new provisions for his victorious army. As Philip well knew, supplying the general with the funds and supplies needed for his expensive siege campaigns would not be a simple task, and he could only hope that once again God would provide.[54]

CHAPTER 8

Exhaustion

❖ ❖ ❖

This mutiny has come at a bad time . . . and what is most distressing is
that it was started by men from companies formed this summer, to whom
it is not possible that we owe anything noteworthy. . . . In order to
prevent greater problems, it has seemed necessary to begin putting the
army into garrison, in which there is also much difficulty because of the
lack of means we have to be able to give them what is necessary there.

—ARCHDUKE ALBERT TO THE DUKE OF LERMA
18 October 1606

Spínola's 1605 campaign had put a severe strain on the financial resources of both Spain and the United Provinces, and during the
winter interruption in fighting both sides scrambled frantically to
find more funds for the following year. Since the Peace of Vervins in 1598,
a number of circumstances had combined to raise the cost of the war for
the Dutch. The five admiralties—responsible for administering the navy,
building warships, and recruiting seamen—had seen their convoy taxes
and licensing fees reduced at the same time that they were increasing the
number of vessels engaged, and they now required heavy subsidies from
the States-General.[1] The failed expedition to Nieuwpoort and the three-
year defense of Ostend had cost an extraordinary amount. Moreover, even
Dutch successes, like the capture of territory in the east and around Sluis,
had entailed additional costs for the defense of lengthened frontiers. And
finally the Spanish fielding of two armies in 1605 had meant that the
Dutch were forced to expend higher sums on the military, both to field
their own armies (now numbering some sixty thousand troops) and to
defend against the Spanish on two fronts. Indeed, even after Spínola's departure at the end of 1605, the Dutch worked frantically at building their
defenses. Throughout the winter they spent great sums to build an earthen
rampart connecting a chain of forts from the Zuider Zee to the Waal.[2]
Because of all this, from an average cost of five million florins annually
during the 1590s, the Dutch military budget had risen to well over ten

million florins in the years 1604–6; yet the inland provinces were seven million florins in arrears on their contributions (in 1604 and 1605 troops had even been sent to force Drenthe and Gronigen to pay up!). By 1606 the debt of the States-General alone stood at more than ten million florins, and because the provinces too carried considerable debts, both individual provinces and the States-General had to increase taxes significantly to avoid bankruptcy.[3]

Spain's situation was no better, despite its far greater resources. Besides the increased costs for the war effort in the Low Countries, they were spending increasing amounts on defense in the Caribbean and Atlantic. In 1603 Philip had ordered an entire section of northwestern Española depopulated to prevent Dutch trading there, an edict carried out in August 1605. In addition, in 1605 the king finally took action against Dutch salt smuggling, which was on the rise. In July the naval escort of the treasure fleet encountered Dutch smugglers off Cartagena, sinking two ships and capturing two others. Then in August, Luis Fajardo, as part of a major operation meant to drive the Dutch from the salt pans and the Caribbean, was ordered to the Caribbean with fourteen galleons and twenty-five hundred men. On 6 November, Admiral Fajardo's fleet had arrived at Araya, where it succeeded in capturing nine vessels. Fajardo spent the next month patrolling the area, racking up an impressive number of seized vessels (including three English ships) before heading off to escort the treasure fleet to Lisbon. It was an expensive operation, but well worth the effort; in the following three years only one Dutch vessel sailed to Araya. Nevertheless, the very success of Fajardo's mission was bound to provoke Dutch retaliation, which would mean even greater expenditures for defense in the coming year.[4]

Added to all these expenses were the subsidies that Philip had granted to Emperor Rudolf for his war against the Turkish-supported Stephen Bocskay in Transylvania and to pacify the growing antipathy toward the emperor himself, which was in part responsible for Turkish military gains.[5] Other subsidies went to Archduke Ferdinand for his war against Venice in the Adriatic.[6] There were also payments to preserve peace between Venice and the papacy and the enormous cost of returning the court to Madrid, a decision that Philip and Lerma took at least as early as January 1606, although they may have planned it much earlier.[7] More critical to Spain's financial situation in Flanders, however, was the sleight of hand that Philip had used to pay for the 1605 campaign. He had secretly ordered Spínola to postpone payment of the arrears promised to the army so that the money would come due out of the 1606 revenues.[8] Now 1606 had arrived and the expected revenues (in the form of the Indies treasure) had not.

This was the situation that awaited Spínola when he arrived in Spain toward the end of January, carrying with him boldly conceived plans for the season's campaign, plans that paid little heed to the plight of the Spanish treasury. His strategy for the upcoming thrust was to divide his army once again into two components: one was to pass over the Rhine as before to carry the war to the Provinces' weak eastern flank, and the other was to cross the river barriers and invade the "island" of Betuwe, a fertile area bounded on the south by the Waal and on the north by the Rhine. In other words, the inland provinces were to be crushed between two mighty Spanish pincers. All Spínola needed from Spain was a complete commitment of men and money to the effort.[9]

Upon Spínola's arrival in Madrid, the whole city turned out to greet him. After giving orders that Spínola be housed in grand style and delivering the appropriate praises to the general for his accomplishments, the king asked for a detailed summary of the situation in Flanders. In the subsequent interview the general's eloquence and command of the material stunned the king and his council; he apparently immediately won them over not only to his assessment but also to his plan for remedying the Spanish position. But there remained the problem of money. The silver fleet had still not returned from the West Indies and was now worrisomely late. Philip promised the marquis a million ducats from the crown's receipts if and when the fleet arrived but could do little else for the moment in response to Spínola's requests.[10]

Meanwhile the general continued to propound the various elements of his military strategy. These were both comprehensive and costly. On 18 February the Council of State considered Spínola's plans for the formation of an armada to patrol the waters of the Channel. Lacking the time to construct the optimum force of twenty to twenty-five ships, the general suggested instead that seven ships could be constructed by September of that year at a cost of some fifty thousand ducats. Maintenance for the fleet would come to another eighty-five hundred escudos per month. With such a fleet Spínola hoped to be able to hunt down and destroy Dutch merchants using the Channel to ply their trade. Once again, however, the councillors remained indecisive. Arguing that they were unsure of the archduke's support or of the efficacy of such a small number of ships, they suggested that Spínola discuss the issue further with Albert once he returned to Brussels. In reality, the councillors knew that the crown did not have the additional 150,000 escudos needed to embark upon the project.[11]

In fact the council and Lerma began to resent the expensive propositions of the upstart general and wished him back in the field so they could once again exercise a measure of control over the king's spending. A few days after considering Spínola's armada plans, the council advised Philip to give the general whatever he desired so long as it had the effect of removing him from the court. The councillors recognized that Spínola's presence not only threatened their own positions but also weakened the Spanish army in Flanders. Only Spínola had the financial resources to smooth the problems of payment to the army caused by the Spaniards' unsound fiscal system.[12]

The council had another reason, however, for wanting to curb spending on new projects: they were attempting to open negotiations with the Dutch. At the beginning of February, Sir Charles Cornwallis's secretary arrived in the Low Countries and was rumored to carry with him proposals from the Spanish crown for a cease-fire with the Dutch.[13] The truth of the matter was that Walter Hawkesworth carried a proposal, on behalf of Philip, for an offensive and defensive alliance with England, on the condition that James mediate a settlement between Spain and the States. The original suggestion, first broached to Cornwallis in July 1605, had been to cement the treaty with the marriage of the infanta, Ana, to Henry, the Prince of Wales, with the dowry being nothing less than part of the Low Countries (Philip would retain those sections necessary to maintain his naval forces). In the intervening half year Spínola had won his stunning victories and Spanish confidence had increased. Now Philip was only offering to hand over certain Dutch towns and a yearly sum of money for the expense of their garrisons. In the end nothing came of the whole affair, for the English stood firm in their insistence on the marriage alliance and donation of the sovereignty of the Low Countries; and so an early chance to bring the Dutch to the negotiating table was lost.[14]

The English stance was not so surprising in the face of the debacle of the Gunpowder Plot. Throughout the preceding negotiations, both the archduke and the Spanish court grappled with the problem of preserving peace with England with only limited success. In November, James ordered the English ambassador to the archdukes, Sir Thomas Edmondes, to ask Albert to hand over Hugh Owen and Richard Bayle, two Englishmen suspected of involvement in the plot. Owen had worked for the Habsburgs in Brussels for some twenty-five years, plotting against the English for the Catholic cause; Bayle was his personal secretary, a man privy not only to secret plots but also to the ciphers used by the Spanish spy system in England.[15] Both men denied their involvement in the assassination attempt, but the plot gave the English ministers a good excuse to shut down this spy operation and they spared no effort to do so. In December they extended their demands even further, requesting that the archduke hand over the Jesuit William Baldwin, vice-president of the English mission in Brussels, and Sir William Stanley, a veteran of the wars in the Low Countries who, in 1587, in order to pay his troops, had sold Deventer to the Spanish.[16] Albert could not, in all conscience, hand over these men without approval from the Spanish court. Philip and his councillors, however, were united in their appraisal: the men could not be turned over to the English for trial without grave damage to Spanish reputation and honor. They were prepared to break the peace if necessary.[17]

This was indeed a delicate matter of diplomacy. The marquis of San Germán, Philip's special ambassador sent to wish James well after the November incident, still had not arrived and the atmosphere remained tense; the Habsburgs hoped he could smooth the dispute over Owen and Bayle. Technically the treaty among the three powers did not provide for settling such a dispute. Although James tried to claim that the treaty did, in fact, cover such a matter, his actions were clearly arbitrary and designed as retaliation; in March he gave orders that no officers would be allowed to raise levies for service with the Spanish in the Low Countries. At the same time he permitted the Dutch to continue their levies. Such moves aimed to threaten the success of the archduke's efforts to raise an effective fighting force for the upcoming campaign. Lest he precipitate more drastic action, however, Albert did little more than make feeble complaints.[18]

Already, as a result of the archduke's refusal to hand over the "traitors" followed by the news that Admiral Fajardo had captured three English ships in the Caribbean, anti-Habsburg sentiment ran high in England. In February the Parliament passed stringent new anti-Catholic laws and readily granted James a new subsidy. Of more long-term significance, however, was the resolution to send an expedition to found a colony in Virginia. These antagonistic sentiments nearly boiled over into widespread violence when, on 1 April, London received word that King James had been killed while hunting. The queen and her son were immediately locked up in the Tower of London for protection, and the Tower's defenders were put on alert against a possible backlash by the populace. Things simmered down only after new information arrived with the news that it was not the king but one of his men who had been killed. Although Pedro de Zúñiga remained optimistic that all would be resolved peacefully, a light step on the Habsburgs' part seemed prudent in the circumstances—a posture that proved effective. Toward the end of March Zúñiga wrote the king that James had made public demonstrations that all Spanish complaints concerning the levies would be satisfied and in private assured Zúñiga of his keen desire to maintain peaceful relations. As Zúñiga cynically remarked, "While they speak insolently enough, what matters is what one does with them in private. There is a clear difference when they are showing you their teeth." [19]

Unfortunately for the Dutch, Zúñiga's appraisal of the English was all too correct; they had little real desire to break the peace with Spain and merely salved their consciences by interfering with Spanish plans as much as possible. This was the extent of their assistance to the States-General. As a result, the Dutch were forced to turn increasingly to the French for support. This support, too, was now problematic; by the provisions of the Franco-English treaty of 1603, one-third of Henry's subsidy to the Dutch was to be regarded as payment on his English debt. Late the previous year the French king had calculated that his debt to England was nearly paid off and that, once done, he could reduce his subsidies to the States by one-third. Henry seemingly had the Dutch by the throat. Oldenbarnevelt, however, hinted that any reduction in the subsidy would mean a Dutch capitulation, something that Henry surely did not want. Henry decided to try to bargain: in return for maintaining the subsidy, he demanded that the Dutch hear his proposals for sovereignty of the United Provinces and for freedom of worship for Catholics—the same two issues on which their dispute with Spain centered. On 6 March, Oldenbarnevelt, Maurice, and two other deputies from the States-General read the memorandum that Henry had drafted concerning the matter and returned their unequivocal answer: Dutch sovereignty was no longer open to debate and internal religious affairs were a matter of that sovereignty. Henry could do nothing. Preoccupied with a conspiracy led by Marshal Bouillon, he could not risk a breach with the Dutch. nor could he risk a Dutch defeat at the hands of Spínola's army; the subsidy therefore remained at two million florins. Nonetheless, as a result of the expenses incurred to suppress Bouillon's revolt, Henry would have to delay its provision.[20]

Meanwhile, on 18 March, the silver fleet arrived in Seville from the Caribbean, escorted by the triumphant Admiral Fajardo. Spínola wasted no time in putting his affairs in order and preparing to depart. He immediately arranged to have six hundred thousand escudos sent to Albert to forestall the negative effects of these delays on the army's preparation and then, to secure the remainder of the necessary funds, pledged his own fortune as collateral for loans to the king. With this he was able to raise an additional 1,600,000 escudos, which he would carry to Flanders himself. Thus, once again the zealous Genoese servant of the king had come to the rescue of Spanish arms with his whole fortune in tow. The arrival of the fleet put everyone in a more tractable mood regarding provisions for Flanders. On 1 April, Juan Carrillo, special assistant to Louis Verreycken on his mission to resolve certain problems regarding Spanish policy toward the Low Countries, reported to Albert that he had finally resolved the issue of monthly provisions. The Spanish had promised to pay three hundred thousand escudos per month to maintain the army. With provisions in hand and honorary memberships in the Councils of State and of War as final tokens of the king's esteem, on 8 April Spínola took his leave of the court and headed for Barcelona, where three galleys waited to take him to Italy and the Spanish Road. A week after his departure the king sent the general a detailed set of secret instructions that illustrate how deep was the trust Philip placed in him. Philip gave contingency orders concerning what Spínola was to do in the event of the death of either archduke: if Albert died, the marquis was to take over complete control of the government of the Spanish Provinces himself; if Isabel died, he was to use force to ensure that Albert swore allegiance to the king. Finally Spínola was to do everything in his power to procure the long-term armistice with the Dutch, which, as Philip pointed out, was the best way to achieve the long-range goal of winning the northern provinces back to the Spanish fold. Philip, like Albert, thought he had found the right man to watch over his interests in Flanders.[21]

Spínola's absence, despite its length, had little real effect on Spanish preparations in Flanders. Although the weather for campaigning had indeed been excellent, the levies from Italy and Germany had not yet arrived and the army lacked the forces necessary for grand designs.[22] Indeed, the

Dutch almost hoped to avoid conflict that year; Spínola's long absence and their knowledge that the silver fleet from the Indies had not yet arrived led them to believe that they just might be spared. When offered the use of three thousand men from the duke of Brunswick's army—which had until then been engaged against the Hansa in a siege of the town of Brunswick—the States were hard put to raise the money to hire them, resolving to do so only out of fear that the forces would otherwise be employed by the Spanish.[23] Delays in the French subsidy had seriously pinched Dutch financial resources. Finally, however, Maurice received certain news that Spínola was on his way with provisions and realized he could no longer remain idle. Accordingly, in early May he sent thirty companies of infantry to reinforce Rheinberg, fearing a Spanish attempt there, and gathered his remaining forces so that he could employ them wherever the Catholic army might strike.[24]

Finally, on 30 May Spínola arrived in Brussels and delivered to a relieved Archduke Albert the monetary provisions for the year's campaign.[25] It was late in the year to begin such a grandiose strategy, but the now-experienced general devoted the full measure of his organizational abilities to setting the army in shape; by the end of June all was ready. On 12 June, the Catholic forces mounted a surprise attack against Sluis but were repulsed by the defenders. Had the Catholic troops succeeded in taking the town, Spínola's plans for the campaign might have been dramatically altered. As it was he proceeded with the strategy that he had determined over the winter: on 28 June he dispatched the count of Bucquoy with eleven thousand troops to the Maas and began moving his own army of thirteen thousand men toward the crossing on the Rhine at Ruhrort. It soon became evident that the weather was not going to cooperate with the Catholic forces. Powerful and torrential storms had been hitting the Low Countries since April, wreaking havoc throughout the provinces, destroying fortifications, causing streams and rivers to overflow, and extensively damaging man-made structures everywhere. By the end of June these storms had made streams and rivers unfordable and roads virtually impassable.

Thus it was 18 July before Bucquoy's forces could cross the Maas at Mook, southeast of Grave, and strike for Nijmegen directly to the north. On the same day, Spínola's army, which had crossed the Rhine on the tenth, reached Goor in Overijssel and turned west in an attempt to cross the IJssel and proceed into the heart of Dutch territory. Maurice, meanwhile, had gathered an army fifteen thousand strong at Arnhem with which to oppose the Habsburg forces, dispatching Warner Du Bois to the Waal with seven thousand men to stop Bucquoy, and himself taking up a position behind the defensive wall constructed at such expense that winter along the IJssel. His only advantage was that his interior lines meant he did not have to stretch his forces very far. On 21 July Bucquoy's forces failed in their attempt, and the fate of the United Provinces now rested on Maurice's ability to stop Spínola.

It had not taken long for Spínola to realize that crossing the IJssel would not be easy. Hoping to divert Maurice's forces long enough to effect a crossing of his main army, he ordered Philippe de Croy, the count of Solre, now commanding the Catholic forces in Friesland, to attempt a crossing of the river at Zwolle and sent his maestre de campo, Inigo de Borgia, to attack the town of Lochem just to the east of Zutphen.[26] Maurice would not be drawn out of his lines. His forces easily prevented Solre's crossing and, instead of going to the aid of Lochem, stood by while Borgia took the town on 23 July after three days of siege. Meanwhile Solre had moved north to attempt to turn Maurice's flank by crossing the IJssel at Zwolle. Here the fortifications were possibly less well constructed, but once again the weather came to the aid of the Dutch. Because of Solre's difficulties on the march, Maurice had plenty of time to send men and artillery to strengthen his northern defenses, and, in an ironic twist of fate, the Catholic forces found that the ammunition they had was too large for the caliber of their cannon; they could not fire a shot. Thus Maurice's defensive wall held, and the Dutch Republic was saved.

Disappointed in his aim of effecting a crossing into the Dutch heartland, Spínola turned about and settled down on 5 August to lay siege to Grol, a strong outpost that would guarantee the Spanish conquests of the previous year. Despite its strength, Grol was no match for Spínola's large army. The defenders' only hope was relief by Maurice. When Spínola heard that this would arrive within a few days, he drove his men extremely hard; nine days after the siege had begun the town surrendered. His army intact and the weather abating, it seemed that the general could still achieve something worthwhile from this campaign. But the financial situation was already tightening. On 24 August a messenger arrived in Brussels: Spínola needed more money as soon as possible. Indeed, many observers plainly realized that the Habsburgs had overextended themselves to make one last effort to force the Dutch into submission: "The enemy's credit is not so good as it was, both through lack of money and otherwise. . . . Their daily expenditure is incredible. Jacques Gelle's son, who for his business has been everywhere in their quarters in Brabant, says that if Spínola and his army do not accomplish something worthy, the people will be miscontented, and he will lose his credit completely."[27] As events in the late fall would make clear, this was a fairly accurate prediction. But that was still some months away. In the meantime Spínola, unable to procure enough provisions deep in the heart of an enemy territory that presented nothing but flooded land on every side, decided to return south and launch an attack against Rheinberg.

The Dutch had considerably strengthened the fortifications at Rheinberg since their seizure of it in 1600. They had erected earthworks around the old stone defenses and throughout the summer had been putting reinforcements and artillery into the town to prevent the Spanish from retaking it. More than four thousand soldiers now manned the defenses. On 22 August Spínola arrived before the city to begin setting up the siege lines. The beginning of this siege finally induced Maurice to move out from behind his defenses along the IJssel to follow Spínola's army. On 31 August he set up camp near Wesel with an army of some eighteen thousand men. Spínola's army, now joined by Bucquoy's forces, numbered over twenty thousand. Despite the nearly equal strength of the two armies. Maurice refused to force an engagement in order to relieve Rheinberg. Instead he preferred to leave his army between Spínola and the heart of the provinces. Without hindrance from the outside, Spínola could methodically begin moving his siege lines closer to the town. Without hope of relief from the States's forces, the garrison either could not or did not wish to hold out long. And so, on 2 October the town fell, having held out for only forty days.

The fall of Rheinberg after such a short siege was a sharp blow to Dutch pride. The Spanish defense in 1600 had lasted far longer with fewer men and poorer fortifications. Moreover, the Spanish had not had an army of eighteen thousand nearby that might have saved them. But if the Dutch were disappointed with the results of the siege, Spínola himself would not have long to enjoy them. Two weeks after Rheinberg's fall, the Catholic army began to fall apart. Ever since the summer, soldiers had been deserting in groups of twenty to fifty and crossing over to the Dutch side, where they immediately sought passage for their homelands.[28] Now, after months of hard campaigning in foul weather, the newly raised—and therefore inexperienced—troops erupted into mutiny. Six hundred men marched to Breda, where they promptly offered their services to Justin of Nassau, who understandably accepted. The archduke and Spínola tried desperately to raise funds from the merchants to prevent further troops from mutinying, but to no avail. Worried by the delayed arrival of the autumn treasure fleet from the Indies, and knowing that a Dutch fleet had been sent out the month before to capture it when it arrived, the merchants were unwilling to risk loans to the Habsburgs. Spínola's own credit was severely compromised by the pledges he had made in the spring. He could do nothing except begin putting the rest of his forces into garrison in the hopes of alleviating some of the pent-up tensions. Despite this, by the end of November almost twenty-five hundred men were in mutiny.[29]

Maurice, watching the erstwhile invincible opposing army melt away before his eyes, wasted no time in taking advantage of the situation. On 24 October he attacked the Spanish garrison at Lochem, retaking the town in five days. Immediately afterward, he moved on Grol with his whole army. It seemed for a moment as if he would easily succeed in winning back all the Dutch towns lost that year. Spínola's vast efforts would have been for nought. The tempestuous weather, however, which had so plagued the Genoese general's efforts, returned now to hamper Maurice's designs. Unable to move his artillery over the flooded land as quickly as he had hoped, the Dutch leader was forced to delay entrenching his forces around the town. This piece of luck was all that Spínola needed. In the first week of November he received word that the treasure fleet had finally arrived safely in Spain; the Dutch fleet sent to intercept it had failed. Spanish credit, and by extension Spínola's, was saved. Spínola immediately raised enough money on the exchange to pull together some eighty-two hundred men and sped off to the relief of Grol. By dint of the extraordinary skill he showed in moving over broken and flooded terrain, Spínola arrived in the area even before the rumors of his departure had been confirmed and managed to surprise Maurice's forces before they had begun to entrench. Again unwilling to risk open battle with the Spanish, Maurice retired with his forces from the field, leaving Grol in Habsburg hands. With this retreat of Maurice's superior forces, it became clear that the year's campaigns were at an end.[30]

But if the campaign had ended, so too, for all intents and purposes, had the war. Spínola's failure to penetrate the Dutch defenses and effect a major transformation in the character of the struggle meant the Spanish had gambled heavily and failed. As early as September the Spanish leaders had resolved to reduce their expenses in the Low Countries beginning at the end of the year, finding it impossible to continue spending such enormous sums on the army when the crown's treasury was in such a crippled state.[31] In a statement tantamount to admitting defeat, the junta of the Council of State was forced to conclude that the only option available to Philip was a reduction in Spain's commitment to Flanders:

> In order to prosecute the war against those in Flanders with the valor and might that we have both this year and last year, we would need no less money than we used in those years, but since Your Majesty's treasury is in such a state that it will not suffer that kind of a drain—even though Your Majesty might like to forget about it—from the point of view of the benefit and conservation of those kingdoms and of the rest that God has given you it was resolved that, in order not to adventure everything, and informed of the state of Your Royal Treasury, the war in Flanders would be reduced to a defensive war only, and only 1,200,000 ducats would be provided this coming year.[32]

Nevertheless, the junta did not want to alert their enemies to the plight of their treasury. Instead they suggested that the king send word to Albert and Spínola that they were not to raise more troops during the coming year and that instead Philip would be sending part of a thirty-thousand-man army from Milan. These orders would have the effect of cutting down the expenses of the Army of Flanders and might delude the Dutch into thinking that the Spanish could resume the offensive in 1607 and restrain them from raising more troops. Philip, however, thought that it was far too late to dissemble in such a fashion. Although he agreed to go along with the make-believe army of Milan, he thought it best to tell the archduke and his general that the army's provisions were being cut, since they would have to implement the reforms necessary to bring the army's expenses under control. Despite this seemingly cooperative attitude on Philip's part, however, he merely saw this as another opportunity in which he might gain absolute control of the southern provinces once and for all. "It might be," he argued hopefully, "that disillusioned by the fact that the provisions will not be as generous as they have been in the past, he [the archduke] will realize that [his departure] will be more advantageous to him." The archduke, he suggested, could finally be given the compensation that had been suggested so many times and removed from his obstructive position of power in the Low Countries. Philip, in his

endless naïveté, could still not help but believe that all the problems presented by the Netherlands could be easily solved should he regain control
of that part of his patrimony.[33]

Unbeknownst to the Spanish councillors, the Dutch leaders also faced
an extremely grave financial situation toward the end of the campaigns,
which in short order would prompt them to engage in a similar protracted
debate about whether to continue the war or seek some avenue whereby
their military expenses might be reduced. Sir William Browne, writing to
the governor of Flushing, understood only too well that the Dutch could
not continue their war, in that "their necessities in this land are so great,
their government so unsolide, and their meanes att so low an ebb, and
they so barren of inventions to fynd out new impositions for defraying
of the great charges the warr putts them unto, as thay without meanes
from our King and other princes they will not be able to subsist against
Spinola." Indeed there existed such a mood of intense despair among the
Dutch that they were led to condemn vocally both their French and English allies for abandoning them. On 10 November the Dutch Council
of State had presented a projected war budget that likewise reflected this
mood of despair. The treasury, they reported, was empty, and the provinces had to be warned to pay their arrears or the country faced certain
bankruptcy.[34]

To the English it appeared that the Dutch had lost all heart for the
war. At the end of December, Sir William Browne noted that no new
levies of troops were being conducted—news that could only bode ill for
the coming campaign. Added to this, Browne had received word that the
emperor had made peace with the Ottomans (11 November 1606), meaning that Spínola would have more money and forces at his disposal the
following year. As Nicholas de Blocq, a secret informant of the governor of Flushing, wrote feelingly, nothing less than the Dutch way of life
seemed at stake:

> You will understand that the affairs of the United Provinces, after fight
> ing so long for liberty, were never in greater perplexity, in view of the
> debatable resolution which must be taken presently to save them. For
> it has come to the point that the State cannot further delay a decision
> either to stay as they are or to try another form of government leaning
> entirely on France, but with a regret. Knowing the incompatible nature
> of the nation, both in their lives and in their policy, God grant the rulers
> may be well inspired. All here are heavy with pain that after forty years

struggle for liberty, they should now be made a butt or at least have to trust to bad guardians of their own. I cannot say what will happen (for I think they themselves know not) but a great change is apparently coming in this part.[35]

This mood of desperation played right into Oldenbarnevelt's hands. In May, Albert had sent the Gueldres nobleman Walrave van Wittenhorst on a secret mission to The Hague to test the mood for peace in the republic. Wittenhorst had arrived in August and presented Albert's terms for opening negotiations: some nominal recognition of the archdukes' sovereignty. Oldenbarnevelt revealed these propositions to a secret committee on foreign affairs at the end of August.[36] After pointing out the desperate plight of Dutch finances and the republic's inability to continue the war without major increases in provincial taxes—something the provinces were unwillingly to consider—Oldenbarnevelt presented the committee members with two alternatives: either place the northern provinces under the protection of the French king or make peace with Spain. Since Henry had shown little willingness to undertake the protection of the Netherlands without complete sovereignty, the advocate urged the leaders to begin thinking about peace negotiations. The time was favorable, he argued, since the military situation was not yet weak, and they could bargain from a position of strength. But the committee members were not yet convinced. They appointed another committee to investigate the exact state of Dutch finances. Meanwhile, Albert, believing that Wittenhorst had failed to find a favorable audience, and in any case unwilling to give the impression that he needed peace, recalled Wittenhorst to Brussels.[37]

On 31 October the secret committee met again to hear the findings of the committee on finances. Oldenbarnevelt's summation of the poor state of affairs had been accurate; the continuation of the war was impossible. Yet Oldenbarnevelt and the committee could not afford to give the Habsburgs reason to believe that they had been forced by circumstances to negotiate. They had to preserve the illusion of being in a strong bargaining position, which meant that the normal preparations for continuing the war would have to proceed. To ensure this, the full membership of the States-General would have to remain in the dark concerning the committee's recent negotiations so that they would continue to approve funding for the war effort. Accordingly, the States-General were still unaware that the war was as good as ended when they commissioned a new fleet of twenty-six vessels under the command of Admiral Jacob van Heemskerck to be ready in the spring to revenge the defeat suffered by Admiral Haultain and wreak havoc upon Spanish Atlantic shipping.[38]

With this military activity as leverage, the secret-committee members felt confident that they could now proceed with their plan to open negotiations with the archduke. In early December, Wittenhorst received word that the States-General would soon hold a plenary session and that he should return at once to present his peace proposals openly before all the representatives. Because of illness, however, Wittenhorst could not depart, immediately prompting Oldenbarnevelt to worry that the archduke might not wish to negotiate. Accordingly, he made use of a lawyer from Turnhout, Doctor Johan Gevaerts, who had previously acted on behalf of the States-General of the southern provinces in peace matters, to convey a message to Albert that the Dutch leaders were willing to consider a cease-fire for a period of three or four years. Albert wasted no time in seizing upon this Dutch initiative and ordered both Wittenhorst and Gevaerts to The Hague to propose the matter to the States-General, with instructions that if the Dutch appeared to be willing to discuss a cease-fire, they could agree to negotiate in Albert's name.

In spite of the seeming confidence that Albert showed in taking charge of the situation concerning the negotiations, he still had doubts about whether he had sufficient authority. Throughout this report to Lerma he insisted on qualifying his remarks with cautious statements about the viability of the talks and even suggested that Lerma keep the matter from the king unless the duke should feel it necessary to advise Philip of the matter. There was nothing wrong, Albert hastened to add, with what he was doing, for he had "power from His Majesty to be able to treat of and conclude treaties or peaces"; nevertheless, these powers were old (having been given in 1599), and it would be better to clarify his position. To that end he requested that Philip, once he learned of the negotiations, should send new powers "so that in his name I might conclude and promise whatever should be necessary or whatever should appear to me suitable." These should be sent as soon as possible, he pointed out, to avoid any inconvenient delays during negotiations. It was a wily request on the archduke's part, and one that, had it been granted, would have allowed him to dictate the Habsburg terms independently. But neither Philip nor the others at court who distrusted the archduke would be so easily taken in. Proving that the king's faith in him to report the archduke's activities was indeed justified, on the day following Albert's dispatch Spínola sent word of Albert's intentions directly to the king. Neither Lerma nor Albert could now withhold the status of the negotiations from Philip, and the king would insure that everything possible was done to preserve his authority in Flanders. Thus, the stage was set when in the first week of January 1607 Wittenhorst arrived in The Hague at the head of the official mission from the archdukes, signaling that the negotiations could get under way.[39]

CHAPTER 9

Warrior Diplomacy

❖ ❖ ❖

As the saying goes in Spain that Zamora was not won in an hour, I will
say here that neither can a war of forty-one years be ended in a day.
—AMBROSIO SPÍNOLA TO JUAN VIVES
5 June 1607

Wittenhorst's mission at the end of 1606 was a clear sign that
a significant transformation had taken place in the attitudes
of the Habsburg and Dutch leaders; for the first time it was
clear to *both* sides that the war was a stalemate.[1] Neither side, however,
was completely sure that the other had come to the same conclusion.
To the participants in the decision-making process, diplomatic maneu-
vers during wartime seemed merely another means by which opponents
sought to gain advantage over one another. For these countries, used to
settling disputes by armed struggle, diplomacy was war by other means,
the conference table an extension of the battlefield. "Fundamental to such
a conception of diplomacy," as Sir Harold Nicolsen has pointed out,

> is the belief that the purpose of negotiation is victory, and that the
> denial of complete victory means defeat. . . . The strategy of negotia-
> tion thus becomes an endeavor to out-flank your opponent, to occupy
> strategical positions which are at once consolidated before any further
> advance is made; to weaken the enemy by all manner of attacks behind
> the lines; to seek for every occasion to drive a wedge between your
> main enemy and his allies; and to hold your opponents on one position
> while planning an attack elsewhere. . . .
>
> It is obvious that under such a system conciliation, confidence and
> fair-dealing are not very apparent. A concession made, a treaty con-
> cluded, is apt to be regarded, not as the final settlement of an isolated
> dispute, but as evidences of weakness and retreat, as an advantage which
> must immediately be exploited in preparation for further triumphs.

It was therefore no surprise that both the Habsburgs and their Dutch
counterparts remained wary of the motives of their opponents during

the ensuing negotiations. Before serious discussions about how to end the fighting could take place, the participants had to overcome this initial distrust of each other. Even Archduke Albert, the man most anxious for peace at any price, worried that the preliminary talks might be nothing more than a Dutch trick, because, as some of his confidentes advised, "Everything is a trick, and is hatched by them to better their affairs."[2]

Into this tense atmosphere stepped the Habsburg agents, Wittenhorst and Gevaerts, who arrived at The Hague in the first week of January charged with presenting the archduke's proposals to the States-General. After meeting with Maurice on 10 January they were at last, on 13 January, brought before an open session of the States-General where they presented their charge. They spoke at length on the tragedies of the war and then urged the States to consider the beneficial effects of a truce or a peace. The archdukes, they said, were ready to appoint commissioners and to give the States-General all reasonable contentment in order to reduce the countries to "quietness and to their ancient prosperitie." The members of the States-General listened attentively enough but decided that they could make no reply until they had received further instructions from the individual provinces they represented.[3]

On 27 January the deputies of the States returned with their reply. They seized upon the wording of Wittenhorst's original commission of 6 May and admonished the archduke for maintaining the pretence of his sovereignty over them. The United Provinces, they pointed out, had proven themselves to be free states, and this had been confirmed by the other European powers through their manner of treating with them; their sovereignty, they reiterated, was not open to question, and they would not entertain discussions with anyone who thought it was. In the diplomatic poker game that the contestants were playing, the Dutch had upped the ante.[4]

Even though the Dutch understood that they could not continue the war, their failure to compromise on this issue was understandable in the current international circumstances. In his reply to the king's instructions to proceed with the truce talks, Spínola pointed out that this new coldness on their part was no doubt "because of the war in Italy; they found their hopes on the fact that because of it Your Majesty will not be able to assist us as accustomed." The war in Italy to which he referred was the dispute between Venice and the papacy, a conflict that threatened to ignite the whole of Catholic Europe. In April 1606 Pope Paul V had carried out his threat, excommunicating the rulers and placing the city under inderdict, prompting the two sides and their allies to prepare for war. By September 1606 the count of Fuentes had amassed an army of twenty-four thousand infantry and four thousand cavalry, and Henry IV had begun to make promises to the Venetian ambassador in Paris that he would provide military aid in the event the Spanish forces moved against Venice. The dispute seriously compromised Spain's commitment to Flanders. And, as Spínola told the king with exasperation, if Spanish forces and financial resources should be diverted to Italy by the papal-Venetian conflict, "it is fitting that Your Majesty understand that not only would we not achieve anything worthwhile, but would be forced to give up ground, not to mention the great disorders that can be expected among the whole army. For my part I will do what I can, to the point of expending my last drop of blood in Your Majesty's service, but without money we cannot make war." Spínola could not work miracles. If the Spanish would not support his efforts with every possible commitment, then, he advised, it was better for them to agree to Dutch demands to achieve a truce.[5]

The archduke, without waiting for a decision from the court in Madrid, decided to send a Brussels merchant, Werner Cruwel, on a secret mission to visit his relatives in the northern provinces. While there he would let it be known that the archdukes were, in fact, willing to concede the question of sovereignty. Cruwel arrived at The Hague on 6 February and made his way to the house of his kinsman, Cornelis van Aerssens, father of the Dutch agent in France and the States-General's *griffier* (recorder). During dinner Cruwel revealed that he carried a confidential message from Richardot for Oldenbarnevelt. On 8 February he had a secret meeting with the advocate, Prince Maurice, and the griffier in which he revealed the object of his mission: to secure permission for Father Jan Neyen, commissioner-general of the Franciscans in the Spanish provinces and son of a friend of William of Orange, to treat for a truce of ten or twelve years on the sole condition that the Dutch refrain from navigating to the Indies.[6]

The Dutch leaders still distrusted the Habsburgs, however. Accordingly, the leaders told Cruwel that Neyen himself had to present a written statement of his commission from the archdukes, conceding the point of independence, before they would consider the matter.[7]

This seeming intransigence on the part of the Dutch along with the plight of Habsburg finances gave Albert the opportunity he had been seeking since taking over the reins of government. Without consulting Philip, he resolved to send word to the Dutch that he would indeed concede their independence as a precondition for negotiations for peace. In the circumstances Spínola reluctantly agreed to the move: "If Your Majesty would be able to order provision, for a specified period, of three hundred thousand escudos per month, punctually [delivered], the war could be continued with the hope of reaching a much better agreement; but if not, I am forced to assent to this agreement."[8] For Spínola the decision was the clear one between a well-funded war or none at all; a middle way would serve no logical purpose. And so, on 16 February, a week after his first meeting with the Dutch leaders, Cruwel returned with a declaration from Neyen saying that he had been authorized by the archdukes to treat with the States-General as independent representatives, the archdukes renouncing all right to the "so-called United Provinces."[9]

On 25 February Father Neyen arrived in the village of Rijswijk, a mile and a half from The Hague, to begin his mission. That night he was ushered into the first of a series of secret meetings with Maurice and Oldenbarnevelt where it was soon apparent that the archdukes' concession was less than they had expected. The commission said only that the archdukes were willing to engage in negotiations but did not indicate specifically enough that they considered the northern provinces as free states. Although such a willingness to negotiate with Dutch representatives could, in itself, be construed as a concession of sovereignty by the archdukes, Oldenbarnevelt and Maurice wanted a more explicit statement. After referring the matter to the secret committee on foreign affairs, the Dutch leaders presented Neyen with a draft of another document giving explicit recognition of the independence of the United Provinces. Neyen was to return to Brussels with this document and persuade the archdukes to draw up an official statement in exact conformity with it.

On 9 March Neyen returned to Brussels with the Dutch draft in hand. It was unfortunate for Philip and his aims that Albert was still unaware that Madrid had received news the day before of the Spanish seizure of Ternate from the Dutch.[10] Such news might have caused him to rethink his concession. As it was, however, on 13 March, having been convinced by Neyen that it was a gesture for the sake of appearances only, the archduke signed three versions of the Dutch document, each one adding slightly different provisions for the extent of the cease-fire between the two powers, something that was to be a point of contention in the immediate future.[11]

By a remarkable twist of fate, on the same day the Council of State in Madrid considered the news from Albert and Spínola that they were going to grant the status of independent states to the northern provinces and delivered their opinion to the king. Albert's grant was prejudicial to the rights of sovereignty, the councillors told Philip, and therefore should not be permitted unless the States-General gave recognition to those rights on a yearly basis. Otherwise, such a concession could take place only if "they should grant freedom of conscience to the Catholics, in which case it seems that for the good that would result to Our Lord's service, and the benefit to those souls, we could pass over the alienation of those provinces, it seeming that [doing it] for such a cause would be less a blot on our reputation than that of not having enough money to carry on the war. If there was enough money, the Council would be of a different opinion, but one must choose the lesser of two evils, and that is to cut off an arm to free the body." Having decided to grant the point of independence for the sake of religion, the council, demonstrating the utter weakness of the Spanish financial position, went on to advise the king not to bring up the point of freedom of conscience until full negotiations should be under way; they did not want to risk stalling the talks almost before they had begun.[12]

On 17 March Father Neyen presented the archduke's new document to the full session of the States-General. Hoping to gain as much as possible from the Dutch, he first showed them the draft that called for a complete cessation of hostilities on land and sea in all of the realms of the Spanish monarchy. When they rejected this, he produced the second draft, which called for such a cessation only within the Low Countries; likewise the states refused to consider it. Neyen decided to wait a week before presenting the third draft, as if he needed further instructions from Brussels. If the Habsburgs hoped to win any concessions from the Dutch, they could not afford to appear overeager.[13]

But it was not entirely the archduke's eagerness that prompted the Dutch to reject his proposals out of hand; there was also the implacable hostility of Maurice to any peace. His was a house founded upon war, and he stood to lose much of his power and prestige in the event of a cessation of hostilities. Maurice had some support for his position among the leaders of Holland and Zeeland, but the leaders and populace of the remainder of the provinces were for the most part ready to make peace. Against this kind of opposition, led by Oldenbarnevelt, he could make

little headway. Nonetheless, he could slow down the pace of the negotiations—and did so. Arguing that it was not good to proceed headlong into
either the peace or the long-term truce that the archdukes and the Spanish seemingly wanted, he convinced the States-General that it would be
better to aim for a limited cease-fire to give their ground forces a breathing space while they held further consultation on their possible courses
of action. It was only on land that the Dutch faced a challenge from the
Habsburg forces; it was only on land that the cease-fire would benefit
them.[14]

A week after his first meeting, Neyen once again went before the
States-General and presented the third version of the archduke's concession, this time written in complete conformity to the draft originally
given the friar by Oldenbarnevelt. A tentative conclusion was reached on
29 March for an eight-month cease-fire, during the first three months
of which the States-General must receive notice that Philip had ratified
the terms. Now, however, the provincial representatives had to secure
permission from the provinces before they could proceed. Accordingly,
the States-General adjourned and messengers hurried back to the provincial states. By 10 April the last intransigents, the States of Zeeland,
had consented to the accord, and the recorder van Aerssens and Father
Neyen drew up the declaration for a cease-fire. The matter was still not
settled, however; the declaration was purposely dated 24 April to give
both the archduke and the States-General time to ratify the treaty with
letters signed under their respective great seals. By 18 April the archdukes
had put the finishing touches to their ratification of the cease-fire. Albert,
Isabel, and Spínola all wrote to the court with the news: "Thanks to God
a cease-fire is concluded."[15]

The news of the cease-fire caught everyone by surprise; in short order
letters to this effect sped in all directions. Some of the correspondents,
like Rodrigo Niño y Lasso and the count of Bruay, feared that only ill
might come of it, especially since the cessation of hostilities was on land
only.[16] But others appeared more hopeful: "The disputes of Flanders and
Venice being ended," wrote Juan Vivas, the Spanish ambassador in Genoa,
"we rest in the peace of Octavian."[17]

The Dutch elite had mixed reactions to the cessation of hostilities.
While many felt great joy, "every man hoping, wishing and praying, to bee
once released from these long and bloddy warres," they were nevertheless
suspicious of a truce that had been made so suddenly and so secretly. The

nobility complained that they should not have been excluded from such a momentous decision. Many, including Maurice, clearly faced worse prospects with the coming of peace. The Zeelanders, for their part, did not refrain from demonstrating their opposition, proving recalcitrant at every step of the ratification process. The preachers either harangued against the treachery of the Spaniards or discoursed at length on the horrors of war. Pamphlet production increased dramatically after 1606 because of the opposition to Oldenbarnevelt's peace policy. "The minute talk of a truce is heard the blue books spread throughout the land in droves, each bringing forward new ideas, hammering out every fantasy that comes into his head," wrote one exasperated theologian. Only 9 percent of those "blue books" argued in favor of a truce. It was one of the first times outside of civil war that a pamphlet campaign was launched within a European country against official policies and personalities.[18]

When the English received the news at the end of April, they were dismayed and angry, incapable of believing that their "dependent" allies had taken such a step without consulting them. But while they threatened to prevent the talks going forward as planned—hinting that peace would mean the Dutch would have to repay their debt immediately—the Spanish ambassador in London, Pedro de Zúñiga, understood well enough that they were in no position now to prevent the Dutch independent actions: "Even though they say the peace talks will not continue without the license and accord of this king [James], I know they fear them and that they have taken this disobedience to heart, especially the Earl of Salisbury [Cecil]."[19] Cecil thought that the cease-fire, quite apart from its possible detrimental effects on Anglo-Dutch relations, was a bad political move on the Dutch part. Demonstrating his remarkable political acumen once again, he explained to the Venetian ambassador that the Spanish either would find a pretext for breaking off the discussions once the dispute in Italy was settled or would use the truce to win over the Dutch populace by peaceful means. When the Venetian responded that he thought the Netherlands to have been made independent by the terms of the cease-fire, Cecil rightly recognized that the wording of that clause was ambiguous at best, signifying that they were independent only with regard to treating for peace and not in perpetuity. To this remarkable politician, it was clear that further struggles lay ahead.[20]

The news of the archduke's agreement with the rebels was the cause of some embarrassment at the Spanish court. Philip had secretly given Albert and Spínola permission to open negotiations for a cease-fire, but only on the conditions that the Dutch cease their activities in the Indies and that the cease-fire comprehend both land and sea. The archduke's failure to achieve these concessions, particularly the latter, "was taken very badly" by the king's ministers, especially coming as it did just five days after the Dutch fleet, under Heemskerk, had destroyed the Spanish fleet at Gibraltar.[21] This news, coupled with the notion that the disaster might have been avoided, jeopardized Spanish ratification of the agreement. But this was not the only problem; Albert had also agreed that the commissioners for the peace talks would be natives of the Low Countries, effectively shutting out the Spanish. This was a clear affront not only to Spanish power in the Low Countries but to Spanish dignity as well. Philip hastily returned to Madrid from his palace at Aranjuez to get the advice of his ministers.[22]

Philip and Lerma resolved to send an outspoken opponent of peace and member of the Council of War, Don Diego de Ibarra, to Flanders in an effort to reassert Spanish control over the negotiations.[23] At this point, however, they faced a problem. As Andrés de Prada pointed out to Lerma on 6 May, protocol required that Philip get advice on Ibarra's instructions from the Council of State. The council, however, was unaware that Philip had given Albert tacit permission to grant free status to the provinces; there was a chance that their recommendations would contradict Philip's secret instructions to the archduke, that is, that they would rebuke Albert for his concession on the sovereignty question. The matter would have to be handled delicately:

> At this point I might put to Your Excellency's consideration whether it would be better not to tell the Council what has been written to the Archduke, but instead [tell them] that, considering the state of things and that there is no money to continue the war and that one must choose the lesser of two evils, His Majesty is making up his mind whether, in order to assent to peace or an armistice, it should be necessary to answer that each side should keep what he has, that the treaty made should be universal, and whether, in conformity with this, should go a power which safeguards the protocol required by His Majesty's greatness and the reputation of his siblings. I believe the Council will for the most part agree to this. Already the grand commander of León [Juan de Idiáquez] and the count of Miranda have agreed.

Lerma wrote back the same day with the king's orders: Prada was to call a meeting of the council immediately, and before it sat he was to talk privately with Idiáquez and Miranda and let them know how Philip viewed the matter—namely, that the powers were to be sent only if the treaty met the stipulated requirements concerning trade and hostilities at sea, these being "the two points of greatest substance, since with them everything looked good, but without them as bad as it might appear to the council." In other words, the States-General would have to agree explicitly to withdraw from the Indies and to cease hostilities at sea. This, it was hoped, would eliminate some of the public disapproval of the treaty.[24]

The council's consulta indicates that its members were confused about what was expected from them. Someone—either the councillors themselves, Prada, Lerma, or the king—caused the council to emend its recommendations.[25] Originally Juan de Idiáquez pointed out that while the archduke had contravened the king's orders by not having insured that the cease-fire covered hostilities on the seas, it was not possible now for the Spanish to reject his efforts without doing serious damage to the view that they were willing to negotiate in good faith. To salvage the matter, he suggested that the archduke should have sole power to treat with the rebels, but that Ibarra should carry a revocation from Philip in case the treaty should not be made according to the wishes of the Spanish. Thus, only the Spanish would be blamed if the talks were broken up, and the archduke's reputation as a mediator would remain intact. All the councillors present—Idiáquez, Velada, Miranda, Chinchón, and the Constable of Castile—were united in their fear of leaving Albert with too free a hand in the matter—his granting the Dutch independent status served as a warning of what they could expect from him—but they disagreed initially over the best method to avoid it. Finally they decided that Diego de Ibarra would carry two powers, one for the archduke, which could be revoked by the king if necessary, and the other a secret set for Ibarra alone, which would come into play only if the archduke began to exceed his authority. While Albert was left free to negotiate as he saw fit, Philip would also send with Ibarra a set of instructions that contained the outside parameters of the archduke's powers and orders to extend the cease-fire to cover hostilities at sea.

The emended version of the consulta drastically revised the council's recommendation. Now it was recommended that the archduke be given ample powers to complete the negotiations only if the final cease-fire should comprehend both sea and land and result in the recall of the Dutch fleet now blockading the Spanish coast. There was no mention of separate powers for Ibarra, who, by the terms of the archdukes' agreement with the Dutch, was not permitted to negotiate; instead the council clearly recommended that "if the Dutch representatives [los de las Islas] agree to Don Diego de Ibarra assisting in the negotiations, His Highness will be able to transfer the powers to him." In other words, to avoid anything that might compromise getting negotiations under way, the Spanish ministers ratified the archduke's actions while imposing only the lightest condition: that the Spanish coast and fleet be spared further depredation and injury. Contrary to what Cabrera de Córdoba believed, Ibarra was not to "undo" the treaty, nor was he to take over Spínola's functions regarding the distribution of money sent from Spain (Spínola's job as superintendent of the treasury). Instead he would be in charge of carrying six hundred thousand ducats to the marquis to forestall a general mutiny.[26]

While the debate continued in Spain over how to treat the news of the archduke's concessions, Jan Neyen, on his own initiative, busied himself with securing just such additional conditions that the Spanish wished. According to his letter to Albert, on 24 April he had returned to Lillo where he and the States-General's representative were to exchange the ratifications of the agreement. Immediately he requested permission to travel once again to The Hague, this time to explain the discrepancies between the archduke's ratification and that of the States-General. Finally after a week of arguing the matter, the States-General granted Neyen permission to make his pitch. On 7 May, three days after the cease-fire was proclaimed throughout the northern provinces and one day before prayers for peace were ordered in all the churches, the full session of the States-General heard Neyen's additional requests: that the Dutch fleet be recalled immediately and that the representatives explain what was meant by the clause forbidding "invasions of provinces or quarters." Expanding on the first of these demands, Neyen proved himself a more sophisticated negotiator than the archduke (who would have willingly given anything for peace). He informed the States that he had no doubt that Philip would ratify the terms of the cease-fire, but only if it was extended to encompass hostilities at sea. This was all a bluff; he had no inkling of the Spanish decisions in the matter and was merely trying to win as many concessions from the Dutch as possible. Finally, in an effort to deflect growing criticism directed against the "peacemongers" in the States-General (chiefly Oldenbarnevelt), he declared to the assembled representatives that neither he nor the archdukes had used bribery or promises to persuade anyone from the provinces to agree to the truce talks. "Such actions" he said, "were unnecessary in this business when the Archdukes had proven themselves so liberal by declaring the provinces free, etc." The States-General could not, of course, make a decision in the matter without consulting the States of the individual provinces, and they ordered Neyen to wait at Delft for their reply.[27]

Neyen wrote to the archduke again on 17 May, informing him of the negotiations. He had been assured that the Dutch would recall their fleet before his departure, that the cease-fire would be extended to cover the sea, that piracy would stop, and that the trade of the southern provinces would be allowed to resume. Although the provinces of Gueldres and Zeeland had so far refused to send their representatives to a general meeting of the States-General with their reply, he was confident that the matter would be resolved in the Habsburgs' favor. To insure this, Neyen urged Albert that, in the event Philip's consent to the cease-fire should arrive while he was still at The Hague, the matter would be kept secret. He did not want to jeopardize his bargaining position by consenting too early to Dutch demands.[28]

He need not have worried that the Spanish would agree so readily. On 19 May the court at Brussels received the first word of the Spanish reaction to the cease-fire and understood that it had not been favorable. Both Spínola and the archduke wrote hastily to Madrid to defend their actions. Spínola felt the king's reprobation all the more since he had thought himself to be negotiating well. He pointed out, rather disingenuously, that, aside from the question of freedom of conscience for Catholics, which would be taken up in the talks for an armistice, the cease-fire had given away nothing that lack of provisions had not already forced from them. He argued that it was ill considered to refrain from making short-term concessions while they waited to get the king's permission first and that they should instead proceed, keeping the long-range goal of a full peace or armistice in mind. As for the hostilities at sea, these, he argued, were the same as before and had not been intensified just because of the cease-fire. The king was therefore not losing anything by leaving the sea out of the cease-fire terms.[29]

Although Albert complained in a similar vein in his letter to Lerma of the nineteenth, he waited until 31 May, when he found out that Lerma too was displeased with the manner of bargaining, to give a detailed justification for his actions. As he tried to point out, he had done nothing other than what the king had ordered in his letter of February 28 and believed he had been complying with Madrid's wishes in the matter. Indeed, he pointed out, both Philip and Lerma had sent him letters patting him on the back for his endeavors. With this support in mind, he and Spínola had proceeded with the talks, arranging everything so that full negotiations could get under way by September. It was the States-General, Albert pointed out, who had requested that a cease-fire be agreed upon for the interval. When Albert had countered that such a cease-fire extend to the disputes in Spanish waters, the States-General had refused until such time as they knew that Philip would agree. Surely this was logical on their part. To do otherwise would have meant a unilateral declaration of a cease-fire with no guarantee that the Spaniards would reciprocate. Lastly, he insisted that if the States-General decided not to honor their agreement to withdraw from the Indies, then the king was not obligated to honor his concerning their freedom. Clearly, in the archduke's view, the Spaniards were being unreasonable. These were his explanations; if the king found them unsatisfactory, he could break off the truce talks. But, Albert stressed, to do so would inflict serious damage to his reputation and would suggest that a lack of understanding existed between the two courts. Moreover, if Philip chose to stop the negotiations, he would have to decide immediately to send the enormous provisions needed to return to arms and defend the country against the enemy.[30]

New worries for the archduke arose toward the end of May when a French delegation led by Pierre Jeannin arrived at The Hague to lodge Henry's complaints against the agreement of a cease-fire without his knowledge and to determine what course of action the Dutch planned to take. Henry still wanted to secure sovereignty of the territories and instructed Jeannin to press for the elevation of Maurice to sole leadership of the provinces, thinking that such a position would make French overlordship much more easily achieved. Henry's chief aim, however, was to prevent the Dutch from flinging themselves headlong into the peace negotiations. To that end Henry would hold out the carrot of an increased French subsidy if the Dutch would consider resumption of the war—and, conversely, a reduction in the event of peace.[31] Oldenbarnevelt, however, steadfastly refused to commit himself to breaking off the peace talks. Without a definite promise of more support from the French, the Dutch could not continue the war. They had estimated that they would need a subsidy of more than three million florins annually, far more than Henry was accustomed to give them. Without that subsidy the Dutch were bankrupt. On 8 June the receiver-general even offered his resignation, since he no longer had anything to receive.[32] These Franco-Dutch problems over financing any future war effort were unknown to the Spanish, however; thus Neyen must have viewed with some trepidation the meeting of the French representatives with the States-General on 28 May—the same day he was summoned before them yet again. Would they persuade the Dutch to withdraw from the talks?[33]

He need not have worried, however. In the interval between his last appearance and this one, the States-General had learned that Philip did not intend to approve the talks in the form desired by the Dutch; they feared that war would be resumed unless they made some concessions. Therefore, in reply to Neyen's request, they agreed to the extension of the cease-fire to cover sea hostilities, although they restricted this cessation to the waters of the North Sea and the English Channel. The recall of the fleet still waging hit-and-run attacks on Spanish coastal shipping, they told him, would be conditional upon their receipt of the king's approval to the agreement dated 24 April. In response to his second request for clarification of the point concerning invasions, they drew up a list of the territories covered. The final details were embodied in an act dated 1 June, which Neyen carried to Brussels on the fifth.[34]

Spínola immediately wrote to the king with the news: no more naval forces would sally forth from Dutch ports; the fleets would be recalled six weeks after receipt of Philip's confirmation of the terms. This last point was a jab at the king's dilatoriness. If Philip had sent ratification of the cease-fire immediately upon receiving it, the Dutch fleets would already be headed home. As it was, the Spanish could expect no relief until August. Even worse than this delay, in Spínola's mind, were the conflicting signals the king was sending. On the one hand, he appeared willing to open a dialogue with the Dutch; on the other, Spínola now heard, Philip had ordered Fuentes to send more troops to the Low Countries. Such a move, combined with the knowledge of Ibarra's mission, would arouse intense suspicion among the Dutch that Philip was merely toying with them and was not negotiating in good faith. Spínola pleaded with the king: "Your Majesty can believe me as your faithful creature that these people cannot be gained solely by rigor, and it is not advisable to arouse such a people as this to more suspicion than they already have."[35]

Philip's councillors saw the matter in another light, however. They believed that to win concessions they had to maintain as much pressure on the Dutch as possible. One of the councillors of state, probably Juan de Idiáquez, had advised Philip that "the Army of Flanders should not be dismissed all at once, rather just some foreigners that cost a lot and serve little. . . . [and] that in Milan the least effective of the army should be dismissed if the accord with Venice worked out, and the effective troops should be sent then to Flanders to have the same effect on this cease-fire that they had on Venice. For these two matters we should shake off weakness and provide money, even if we have to stop eating here." The king had evidently agreed; he gave instructions to Ibarra that the troops in Milan stand ready to depart at his order.[36]

But Ibarra still felt that Philip should reconsider his policy. The continuation of the war in Flanders, he argued, was far better than the loss of prestige that would be occasioned by a peace that was so advantageous for the enemy. As for the cost, it would be no greater than in peacetime, since Spain's many enemies and the rebels themselves would stop at nothing to persuade the loyal provinces to join their brethren, entailing for the Spanish crown defensive outlays and counterbribes. The only way the king could spend less on Flanders, he argued, would be if he considered it cheaper to lose the provinces than sustain them. Ibarra urged the king to pursue the opposite policy, pointing out that since the king "for now, has no other war, and there are few times that a monarch so great is seen without one, the cost of [the war in Flanders] is nowhere better employed."[37]

There were also issues of reputation, ideology, and tactics to be considered. The material factors were easily reconciled: the Spanish crown had no money to continue the war and therefore would have to make peace. The problem was that the ministers had to think in more than material terms. Ending the war by freeing the rebel provinces from their obligations as the king's vassal states jeopardized the crown's connection with its other territories, most notably the other provinces of the Low Countries, as Ibarra had pointed out, but also those in Italy. At stake was nothing less than the crown's reputation. After more than forty years of warfare and 180 million ducats (according to the count of Chinchón) spent to force Dutch submission, to declare suddenly that Castile's war against the rebels had been unjust threatened to undermine the stability of the entire monarchy.[38]

Far more serious, however, would be the damage done to the Catholic religion. If it was decided, as now appeared likely, that Philip would grant independence to the northern provinces without winning freedom of conscience for the Catholics in return, their religious counterparts in England would only become worse off. While the war continued, the Calvinist and other Protestant minorities could not afford to persecute the Catholic majority in their territories. Once the Spanish had pulled out of Flanders, the Dutch leaders would without doubt do as the English had done after the 1604 peace: launch a full-scale persecution of the Catholics within their realms, not ending until they had effected a complete eradication of Catholicism there.[39]

This, at least, was how the Constable of Castile viewed the ideological situation. And if this did not worry Philip, then the constable had more political realities for him to consider, ones that demonstrated the old minister's superior understanding of the politics of diplomacy and its effect on power:

> Apart from what I have said, I am much afraid that we proceed in this business under some great deception and slyness on the part of our enemies. I want it to be understood that there are two treaties under consideration. The first is the cease-fire, which is the means and provision for the second, a peace, or long truce. If in the former, before anything else, we free them from the direct dominion of Your Majesty, what matter is left for them or us to discuss? That [independence], which is everything, once given, I do not know what we should be able to request of them in exchange, unless we should be reduced, as forsaken and subdued men, to begging them out of courtesy that they not overrun and infest our seas and coasts.

Demanding such a condition at the outset indicated to the constable that they would demand some more outrageous condition (*alguna insolente condicion*) in the final negotiation, "like trade and free navigation to one or another of the Indies or some similar demand." And if that was the case, knowing that the Spanish would never agree to such a condition, would it not be better to break off the talks now, before they had conceded the Dutch their liberty? Summing up his position, the constable argued that if, because of a lack of money to carry on the war, Philip should choose the path of concession, then he would not be able to turn back when it came time to concede more. Instead he would be forced to accept any onerous conditions that the Dutch placed upon him, or as he humiliatingly put it, "to subject ourselves always to whatever the Dutch should fancy."

On the same day that the constable delivered his opinion, Diego de Ibarra arrived in Brussels with letters for Spínola and Albert from the king. Spínola learned from the king's own pen of his displeasure at the general's proceedings, and his exchange with Ibarra was apparently heated. The two argued at length over the king's intentions and his earlier instructions until Ibarra told him it was a waste of time to continue speaking of the past; the king's present intentions were clear from the dispatches he carried: although Philip desired peace, it would not be of the sort that would create more wars for him through a resultant loss of reputation.[40] Such obstinacy appeared ridiculous to Spínola in the face of the realities of the situation. As he could not help reminding Philip in his letter of 25 June, the Spanish military position was not strong enough for them to be using force as a threat. If war broke out again, he said, it would cost no less than three hundred thousand escudos monthly to prosecute effectively. And a defensive war was unfeasible: the Spanish lines were too long to protect. After further consideration of the displeasure expressed by the king in the matter of the cease-fire, and no doubt stung by Ibarra's obstinate defense of sterner policy measures in the Low Countries, Spínola wrote Philip the following day with a thinly veiled demand that the king restore his damaged reputation and proceed with the talks: "And since I have engaged in and advanced so far in the negotiation on Your Majesty's order, it is not just that Your Majesty allow my reputation to suffer for it; . . . and thus I implore Your Majesty to order that this inconvenience be rectified, sending me as soon as possible the ratified agreements that Your Majesty has there, so that my reputation might be salvaged."[41]

Spínola's letters, however, did not arrive in time to affect Philip's decision in the matter. On 30 June he signed two versions of the ratification of the armistice; neither repudiated the negotiation entirely nor delivered the full approval that Albert and Spínola had requested. Instead one version confirmed and ratified the cease-fire "in all its points," an ambiguous phrase that could be taken to cover even the point of freedom, even while it did not specifically agree to it. This version likewise specified at more length the purely military terms of the cease-fire. The second text was even more ambiguous. In it Philip approved and ratified "all that was contained in [the cease-fire] insofar as it was able to touch him," a phrase that would have allowed the Spanish to argue that the grant of liberty was not included. Both versions were signed with the characteristic *Yo el rey* (I, the king), the form used by the Spanish kings when signing any document in their capacity as the king and indicating in this instance Philip's ultimate sovereignty over the signatories.[42]

Still unaware that Philip had signed the ratification, and unsure of his standing at the Spanish court, Albert dispatched Father Neyen to Madrid to give a detailed account of his negotiations and the rationale behind them. Ibarra did his best to stop Neyen's departure, advising Philip that his journey was fraught with "many inconveniences, above all because of the lack of prudence and great cupidity of the friar, of which everyone speaks." At the same time, Spínola decided to send his own representative, Aurelio Spínola, to the court with copies of all his negotiations to date, complete with the instructions that Philip had given him, all in an effort to support his contention that he had acted completely within the guidelines of Philip's desires. Philip's failure to ratify the agreement in the terms desired by the two leaders in Brussels shows that their worries were perhaps warranted.[43]

Yet although the ratifications did not demonstrate a complete acceptance of Albert's and Spínola's position, they were enough to suggest to Ibarra that his mission was over. When the news of the king's decision arrived with Spínola's secretary on 16 July, Ibarra immediately gave word that he would depart Brussels and return to Spain; he had failed to put an end to the ignominious concessions of the archduke.[44]

Spínola wasted no time in dispatching a courier to the States-General with the news of the ratification and requesting permission for a passport for the audiencier Verreyken to carry the documents to the States-General and to "declare something to you from his Highness [the archduke] for the furtherance of the said negotiation." This letter, with what might appear to be a mysterious hint of further concessions, sparked a heated debate in the States-General over whether to allow Verreyken's passage. Maurice protested that the ratification should be seen before they consented to further negotiations with yet another of Albert's ministers, but in the end he could not prevail against the stronger party in favor of peace and the passport was sent.[45]

Verreyken arrived at The Hague in the middle of the night on 23 July, accompanied by the erstwhile messenger Werner Cruwel and was immediately slipped quietly into the White Unicorn inn by the States-General's

commissioner in order to avoid "a great concourse of people"; on the following day he was ushered into the presence of Maurice and fifty of the
States' deputies. He began his statement by asking that before he read
the ratification, the deputies should agree to continue the negotiations,
a move that did not put the deputies at ease with regard to what might
follow. Afterward he delivered the ratification and asked the representatives to fulfill their promise to recall the fleet that was still stationed
off the coast of Spain. But it was now clear to the Dutch deputies why
Verreyken had wanted to bring the ratification personally: the document
was in Spanish and did not contain the clause regarding the independence
of the United Provinces. The delegates told Verreyken they would need
some time to look over the documents, since none of them had fluency
in Spanish.

Two days later a deputy from each province went to Verreyken's inn
with their reply. Oldenbarnevelt declared the instrument inadequate and
the Habsburgs' proceedings in the matter suspect. Unless the king declared
the United Provinces to be free states, the Dutch feared that he might
later repudiate the treaty, since it would have been made with "rebels
and people without honor." Furthermore the document bore none of the
marks of a legally binding treaty with another sovereign state; it was presented on paper, not parchment; was written in Spanish, not Latin; was
not signed with the king's name and titles but instead merely "I, the king"
(which implied that he was the sovereign); and was not stamped with
the king's great seal. Verreyken tried to excuse the omissions and errors
of protocol, arguing, according to one report, that it was a mistake by
the Spanish Council of State, "who having of late none that handle the
busines of the Low Cuntryes, the termes myght be mistaken or not so
fully sett down as shold have been, there being now none there who took
care or were employed for the busines of these partes, seeing they so little
concerned Spayne." Since the terms of the ratification were general, the
archdukes had thought it better to send it forward to show that they, at
least, were doing their best to achieve peace. Despite these protestations,
the deputies returned on 28 July with the answer of the whole assembly:
the ratification was "imperfect and defective in every way, as much in the
form as in the substance." They gave the audiencier six days to write to
the archduke for further instructions.[46]

Albert and Spínola decided this time to play it safe by stalling for time;
they did not respond directly to Verreyken's letter but instead sent word

via Richardot that they were writing to the king for his instructions. This move allowed them to dissuade the States-General from breaking off the talks since no reply had yet come from the archduke himself. In the meantime the two leaders sent word to Philip of the States-General's reply to the ratification.[47] On 2 August Verreyken promised the deputies that the ratification would be reworded in accordance with the Dutch formula but argued that in the meantime the Dutch should recall their fleet as a sign of their good faith in the talks.

This last request once again sparked a heated debate among the deputies that lasted more than a week. Maurice was steadfastly opposed to recalling the fleet before the king had made any concessions, preferring to send out more ships to keep up the pressure on the Spanish. He was seconded in this feeling by the deputies from Zeeland. Oldenbarnevelt, however, urged the deputies to make a gesture of compromise. It was all the better to do so now, he argued, since they would not really be giving up anything to the Spaniards and, moreover, the ports in Holland needed a truce at sea to protect their own large merchant fleet returning from the Mediterranean. Without a cessation of hostilities, it was almost certain that the Spanish would capture this fleet. Besides, he continued, if the states did not recall the fleet and in the event Philip refused to ratify the cease-fire, the inland provinces would be able to argue that it was Holland and Zeeland who had scuttled the chances for peace. These arguments were enough to convince President Jeannin, who was closely advising Maurice; reversing French policy of the previous months, he persuaded the prince to abandon his opposition.[48]

Finally, on 9 August, the States-General summoned Verreyken before them once again. They started by declaring the just causes whereby they had taken up arms but finally affirmed that they sincerely desired peace. Given that desire, they urged the king to ratify the cease-fire in the proper form, one that would insure the agreement of all parties. So that the ratification might be corrected in a manner acceptable to the States-General, the deputies presented Verreyken with drafts in French and Latin, with which the king was to comply within six weeks before the peace talks could continue.[49] As a token of their esteem for the archdukes, the deputies agreed to recall their fleet from Spain and to return all prizes captured since 24 July. This concession, however, was conditional upon the receipt of the king's ratification in the form delivered to him and could, therefore, be reversed.[50] Satisfied for the time being that the negotiations had

not been completely terminated, Verreyken returned to Brussels, carrying
the draft documents with him. Everything now lay in Philip's hands, and
one question lay on everyone's lips: would the king give up sovereignty
for peace?

The choice was indeed a difficult one for the king and his ministers.
The Spanish monarchy had suffered greatly during the forty years of war;
it was financially and materially exhausted. By 1607 the crown's debt had
reached almost 23 million ducats, and revenues were anticipated up to
1611.[51] The continuance of war would only aggravate the many problems
confronting the monarchy. In Flanders alone the government found itself
increasingly powerless in the face of constantly rising costs. In July Spínola
had written to Philip that he had only enough money to give one escudo
to each soldier for his sustenance and warned the king of the grave dangers
involved should he not be able to pay the mutineers of Diest their *sustento*
(a monthly installment given them until final settlement was made). Not
only Spínola, but the new Spanish ambassador in Brussels, the marquis
of Guadaleste, insisted that without more funds from Spain, the troops
that had not already mutinied would soon do so.[52] Indeed, even the archduke rose to new heights of eloquence to plead that without much greater
resources from Spain, not even a defensive war was possible:

> I know that there are many who argue that [the war] can be fought
> with less [than three hundred thousand ducats per month], and that it
> is enough for defense, but they speak without grounds and are fooling
> themselves; I think the example of what has passed in the 41 years that
> this war has lasted is sufficient proof, since as many millions, and as
> many governors and as many famous captains general and soldiers as
> have been wasted in it have not been enough to finish it, nor to reduce
> the Dutch to their rightful obedience. Therefore, how can it be hoped
> to do it now, we with fewer provisions, and the enemy with greater
> forces and assistance than they had before? Your lordship should laugh
> at availing yourself of a defensive war, as some argue; because to do it
> well, and with assurance of not losing, as much will have to be spent as
> in an offensive war.[53]

Yet while the monarchy was undoubtedly faced with myriad problems operating in favor of conceding sovereignty to achieve peace, other
circumstances gave the Spaniards incentive to continue applying more
pressure to the Dutch during the negotiations. In the middle of August,
Philip received word from Pedro de Zúñiga that Dutch delegates were in
London to smooth relations with their allies following the independent

decision to open talks with the archduke. After mutual complaints from both sides, the discussions between the delegates and the English ministers turned to the question of the war. The delegates, Zúñiga related, had insisted that they could not continue the war without further, and more extensive, aid from the English than they had received heretofore. Nevertheless, they insisted that the Dutch leaders were resolved not to negotiate in any way until they had been granted the status of free states. Given the first admission—that they could not continue the war without aid—and the high hopes Zúñiga had that Salisbury would "handle it so that the matters in Holland would go smoothly for [Philip's] service if there should be peace," it was conceivable that just a little more pressure by the Spanish would gain them better ground in the negotiations.[54]

The council, still unaware of these considerations, nevertheless advised the king that instead of merely conceding sovereignty, he should trade it for freedom of conscience for the Catholics in the northern provinces.[55] This Philip promptly agreed to do and in the last week of September dispatched Father Neyen and Aurelio Spínola with instructions for Spínola to arrange the terms. To sweeten the pill for Albert and Spínola, he finally sent along the letters of credit for some six hundred thousand ducats—fruits of the recent grant by the Cortes and of the new optimism regarding the arrival of the silver fleet—to forestall any additional problems of mutiny among the ranks of the army; he also granted them permission to begin allowing the Dutch to send ships to Spanish ports.[56]

In spite of the sweeteners, the new instructions appeared to stun the two leaders in Brussels. Two days passed after Neyen's arrival before Spínola finally drafted his reply to the king. He and Albert would comply with everything his majesty had ordered regarding freedom of Catholic worship in the northern provinces, without alteration, when and if the delegates from both sides met again. This they could not do, however, until Philip sent the appropriate ratification document. In other words, the general and the archduke were going to undercut completely the force of the king's demand by insisting that he give up the sovereignty before receiving a guarantee from the Dutch on the point of religious freedom. Spínola swore that he would show the ratification to the Dutch delegates only to satisfy them of Philip's intentions and would not hand it over to them until they had agreed to meet for further discussions concerning the peace and freedom of worship. As if to persuade Philip that they had his best interests at heart and were not giving up everything without receiving anything in return, both Albert and Spínola decided not to allow the Dutch to begin trading to Spain unless the Dutch leaders specifically asked for permission to do so. It was a move that had all the appearance of shrewd negotiating.[57]

Philip, however, had not waited for Spínola's reply. On 10 October Spínola's secretary, Birago, once again arrived in Brussels carrying two versions of a new ratification, one of which contained a clause obligating the Dutch to permit worship of the Catholic faith; it was up to Spínola to use them properly. Philip's move forced Albert's hand. On 11 October Spínola wrote the king that Albert had decided, for all the reasons given before, not to send the ratification that demanded freedom of worship, since "something out of the blue, such as telling [the Dutch] that we would like to arrange something before the meeting starts, would run the risk of angering them." In other words, Albert did not want to risk the cease-fire and the peace talks as well by making demands that he knew the Dutch would never meet; neither he nor his army could afford a return to war.[58]

This latter consideration made itself abundantly clear in the first weeks of October. Encouraged by the news of Albert's receipt of six hundred thousand ducats, the mutineers in Diest sent word to the archduke that if they were not given satisfaction within a certain period, they would open the gates of their city to all disaffected soldiers in northern Brabant and join together in a general mutiny. Hearing this, certain cavalry troops within Herenthals began to ready themselves, only to be caught by loyal troops before they could complete their designs. Nonetheless, it was clear to Albert and Spínola that their military situation was indeed precarious; Albert even turned to the states of the southern provinces for seven hundred thousand florins to pay off the mutineers, eventually receiving almost half that amount. Meanwhile Spínola did what he could with the money from Spain, giving the army a portion of the pay owed them for the months of September and October and the mutineers their sustento plus an additional sixty thousand ducats. With that, he wrote the king, he had no more than one *maravedí* of credit left him, and more money was desperately needed to avert disaster. Spínola, better perhaps than anyone, knew that the war was over.[59]

On 14 October the States-General received the request from Spínola and Albert for permission to dispatch Father Neyen and the audiencier Verreyken with the new ratification, and with the permission granted, on 25 October the two delegates appeared before the assembled representatives. After delivering a speech detailing the negotiations of Neyen in Spain, their effect on the king's decision to concede the ratification in the appropriate form, and the promises made by the states themselves, the two men brought out the document; once again, it was written in Spanish, on paper, stamped with an ordinary proclamation seal, and signed "I, the King." Even before they had time to fully react to this outrage, Verreyken went to work to mollify the Dutch. He delivered to them copies of the document in Dutch and French and proceeded to explain why the king could not have been expected to change his style, either of language or of signature, especially when he himself had accepted without complaint the style adopted by the states. This, he argued, would have been "contrary to all reason and equity."[60]

Yet while the document once again departed from the officially accepted form, more disturbing from the deputies' point of view still was the difference in substance.[61] The ratification did indeed contain the crucial phrase desired by the Dutch leaders—"We principally declare that we are content that in our name, and on our part, the said States shall be treated in the quality of, and as held by us for, free countries, provinces, and States, over which we make no pretensions"—but other words were either left out entirely or put in the wrong places, and one entire passage was added that had not been in the draft version given to Verreyken by the Dutch. This last passage, it turned out, was the point of most contention. It declared that "if the treaty for a peace or a truce of many years, by which the pretensions of both parties are to be arranged—as well in the matter of religion as in all the rest—shall not be concluded, then this ratification shall be of no effect and as if it never had been made, and in virtue of it, we are not to lose a single point of our right, nor the United Provinces to acquire one."[62] The passage may not have been as explicit regarding trading sovereignty for freedom of religion as in the withheld second version of the ratification, but it was enough to move the states' representatives to angry hesitation.

On 29 October Oldenbarnevelt and the other members of the secret committee on foreign affairs again met with Neyen and Verreyken and told them of their complaints regarding the document. Asked if they had another form of the ratification to deliver in place of it, the Habsburg representatives could only reply in the negative, adding that all doubts and difficulties could be resolved during fuller negotiations. Under these circumstances the Dutch leaders decided to deliberate at more length and return their reply in writing at a later date. In the meantime they would turn to their allies for advice.[63]

The French delegation, led by Jeannin, had been dispensing advice to the Dutch leaders in the Netherlands since April, but it was not until 10 August that James had commissioned Sir Ralph Winwood and Sir Richard Spencer as his representatives at the talks. They had finally arrived at The Hague on 1 September and had immediately begun to take stock of the situation. The Dutch wasted no time in inquiring where England stood in the matter: could the Dutch expect more assistance from them in the event of war? A negative reply meant that James intended to pursue a peace policy. After conferring with their French colleagues, the English deputies decided to hedge on the issue. At the time, they replied, they saw no reason for not proceeding in the matter until peace talks should be agreed upon. At that point, once terms were announced by the Habsburgs they would advise the Dutch whether to agree to the peace or resume the war.[64] Now that the ratification of the cease-fire had arrived and Philip was apparently willing to make concessions, both the English and the French deputies were less inclined to promote an expensive war; they advised the Dutch to accept the ratification as it stood, arguing that in substance it met the States-General's demands. But, they suggested, the Dutch leaders should do three things: decide their terms for the upcoming peace and stick to them; bring about good internal government; and arrange alliances with foreign powers in order to guarantee the peace that might be made.[65] The Dutch, in other words, would be allied in peace—the proposal for the reform of internal government, coming as it did from the French, even suggesting something closer than alliance—but they would be alone in war.

These suggestions had their intended effect on the Dutch negotiating stance. On 3 November, Oldenbarnevelt went alone to visit Neyen and Verreyken. He began his discussion by pointing out once again all the complaints the States-General had against the ratification in the form in which it stood, arguing that the last clause in particular would cause difficulty when submitted to the provincial states for approval. He pointed out that those in the profession of arms and those supported by it stood in intense opposition to the peace and were joined in that effort by all those who made their living from the West Indies trade—which, he reminded them, he had terminated to promote the peace talks.[66] Nevertheless, he continued, since the French and English representatives had advised the

States-General to accept the ratification and proceed with the negotiations, they would submit the ratification to the provincial assemblies as it stood. If their approval was not forthcoming, then all the blame was on the king's shoulders "for not having sent his simple ratification" and on the archduke "for not having procured it as he had promised."[67]

Yet the Dutch leaders had not surrendered completely. That same afternoon the committee of the States-General carried their written reply to the quarters of the archduke's representatives. Having handed over the document and requested Neyen's and Verreyken's signatures, the deputies suddenly demanded the original copy of the ratification in return. The archduke's men were "stunned by such an unexpected demand" and tried feverishly to deliver their reasons for not handing over the document, arguing that the Dutch had never given any indication that they would want it and that it could wait until further negotiations had been agreed upon. The Dutch deputies would have none of it, however; they had come prepared. They rounded on the two men, pointing out that those actions were the quickest way to undo the whole business, since they were merely asking for what the archduke had promised. If he could not keep even such a small promise, they argued, how could the Dutch people be expected to trust his word in the matter of peace and their freedom? Neyen's summary of Oldenbarnevelt's arguments put the matter clearly: "Everyone will say that we lie, and the provinces, without doubt, will believe it to be so, and they will never consent to the principal conference. And moreover, the States-General will not be able to induce them to do so unless they have this ratification, because the first thing the rest of the provinces will ask is if they have the ratification; and hearing no, the opinion they have conceived of His Majesty and of Your Highnesses, that with so many cunning moves you want nothing more than to deceive them, will be absolutely confirmed." The Dutch refused to slacken the pressure and demanded a yes or no answer immediately. The archduke's men in turn refused to budge. Finally the Dutch accepted their proposal for Father Neyen to return to Brussels for further instructions while Verreyken remained at The Hague with the ratification. As they pointed out, however, this meant the deputies could not return to the provinces until Neyen's return, entailing still more delays.[68]

Delays at this point could only bring further difficulties for the Habsburgs. Despite occasional disputes over trade issues, Pedro de Zúñiga had succeeded remarkably in preserving and even extending good relations with the English after the Gunpowder Plot two years earlier. James I had consistently demonstrated a certain reserve toward the Dutch, and throughout the autumn his representatives at The Hague did all they could to promote a peaceful resolution in the Netherlands. Even Cecil had begun to come under the Spaniard's influence, going so far as to show him confidential letters from Cornwallis, the English ambassador in Spain. Then suddenly, on 14 September, an event occurred that blackened the cooperative mood of the English court: fearing for his life, Hugh O'Neill, earl of Tyrone and former leader of the Irish rebellion against English rule, fled Irish shores for the sanctuary of Spain.

The drama of the Irish rebellion and Spain's relationship with it had not ended with the debacle at Kinsale.[69] Philip III continued to entertain proposals to send another expedition to Ireland in support of Tyrone up until the death of Elizabeth, in April 1603. Following Elizabeth's death, however, the irenic sentiments in both the English and Spanish courts had motivated a cooling of Spanish support for the Irish earls. Philip had decided that the best course to follow would be to use the new Anglo-Spanish entente to further the aims of the Irish Catholics.[70] Tyrone, ever the political survivor, managed to secure letters patent from James that guaranteed him the restoration of his estates and in the meantime waited patiently for an opportunity to continue his struggle in the event of the expected breakdown of the Anglo-Spanish peace. Nonetheless, the plight of Irish leaders in Ireland continued to worsen in the face of the determined efforts of the local English government. In 1606 the struggle between England and Tyrone was compounded by a dispute over territorial claims between the earl and his son-in-law, Donal O'Cahan, a subchief who had supported the English against Tyrone. Eventually, in July 1607, the ministers of King James, who had been using the dispute to "divide and conquer" the Irish leadership, decided that the case would have to be heard in London; James issued a warrant for Tyrone to appear at the court during Michaelmas, toward the end of September.

There would be no resolution of the dispute, however; Tyrone had been set up by his enemies. On his arrival in London he was to be arrested on charges of treason, confined to the Tower of London, and executed. It was only Tyrone's receipt of a warning from someone on the Privy Council that saved him and prompted his headlong flight, along with the earl of Tyrconnel, their families, and their supporters, toward the shores of his former supporters. The earls had initially struck out for La Coruña,

but storms had forced them to land in France, near Le Havre. They immediately sent a request to Henry IV for permission to continue to Spain,
but the French king, though refusing the English ambassador's request to
arrest the men, had no desire to jeopardize seriously his relations with
the English. So instead of honoring the refugees' request for free passage
to Spain, where they would forever be out of the reach of the English
crown, Henry allowed them to cross northern France to the archduke's
territories. The Irish fugitives finally arrived there on 18 October.[71]

The "flight of the earls" struck fear into the English leaders and people,
a fear that intensified when the rumor arrived that Tyrone and his group
had landed safely in Spain. Since the English knew that Philip had been
amassing a fleet in the ports of Spain, they could only conclude that it
was intended for a new strike at Ireland, led by Tyrone himself. Thus the
mood in England had already turned ugly by the time James learned that
the archdukes in fact had custody of the earls, whereupon he demanded
their immediate extradition. Albert, however, as he had done before with
similar requests, refused to comply. As a result of this response, English
desires to assist in promoting a Hispano-Dutch peace took a notable turn.
The Dutch, for their part, hoped that the dispute might be the origins
of a new Anglo-Spanish war, one that would surely strengthen their own
hand against the Spanish, and accordingly they wasted no time in putting
even more pressure on the Habsburgs.[72]

On 11 November, Oldenbarnevelt went to see Verreyken with the
news that a dispatch had arrived from the emperor. In the letter dated
9 October, Rudolf expressed his extreme surprise that the States-General
had even begun and then advanced so far into the peace talks with the
Spanish; the Spanish, he insisted, were not their overlords! In Oldenbarnevelt's mind, this letter raised the question of what right the Spanish had
to grant the northern provinces the status of free states. If the northern
provinces were not in fact under the sovereignty of the Spanish, then all
grants by them of independence were moot. Verreyken was in a difficult position. Quickly he assured the advocate that the feudal dues still
owed the emperor by the provinces were minimal and of "little substance"
and should therefore not disrupt the smooth advance of the negotiations.
Moreover, the audiencier reminded Oldenbarnevelt, the Dutch had asked
His Imperial Majesty for assistance in their dispute in the past and had
been rejected; since their independence therefore had been achieved by
their own blood, without the assistance of the emperor, they owed him no

consideration. In the circumstances it was a good answer on Verreyken's part, though it openly conceded that independent sovereignty was not something granted but something won. Oldenbarnevelt withdrew satisfied that he had tightened the screws yet another turn.[73]

Three days later, on 14 November, Father Neyen returned from Flanders carrying the archduke's permission to give the States-General the original of the ratification, on one condition: that, in accordance with the deputies' promise, they sign a document promising to return it if the principal treaty fell through. Oldenbarnevelt and the six other deputies who visited the Habsburg agents the following day were outraged; they had never promised any such thing. To have done so would have been contrary to all they had fought for. Instead, they reminded Neyen, they had promised to return the ratification if the archduke did not agree ex post facto to Neyen's giving it to them. Since Neyen and Verreyken had refused ever to give up the original, this promise was not an issue. To the Dutch deputies it appeared that the Habsburgs wanted nothing more than to while away time during the cease-fire to keep the Dutch off balance and that they had never intended to follow through and arrive at a true peace. This had to be why the archduke had demanded that everything revert to its previous state if the peace talks fell apart. All their suspicions of the Habsburgs would be proven true if the two agents insisted on the written promise to return the ratification. Neyen and Verreyken were dumbstruck by the speech and asked for time to think of some expedient that would satisfy both parties. The following day the States-General's representatives granted Neyen permission to dash off yet again to discuss the matter with Albert.[74]

Neyen returned to The Hague on 29 November, and the Dutch deputies ordered both the Habsburg agents to appear before the general assembly at eight A.M. to deliver their answer. Neyen began by explaining the archduke's initial reasons for balking at handing over the king's ratification: that he had not wanted such an important document to pass through the hands of "the masses" (el vulgo). However, given that the individual assemblies' agreement to the talks depended on their having the original in hand and given his sincere desire for his people to be relieved of "such a cruel and bloody war," Albert had decided finally to give the States-General what they had asked for. With a flourish Neyen presented the ratification to them.[75] As one Jesuit historian acidly remarked of this final act of resignation: "Nobody can decide which was greater—the obstinacy

of the federal Government in screwing out the opposite party everything
it deemed necessary, or the indulgence of the archdukes in making every
possible concession."[76]

The major concession granted, it was left to the archduke's agents
merely to agree on the number of deputies to be sent to the peace talks
and where they would be held. The States-General agreed that Albert be
allowed to appoint up to eight delegates and that the peace talks should
be held in The Hague. That decided, the two agents departed for Brussels
the following day, 1 December, carrying with them nothing more than
the reply given them on 2 November and the States-General's promise to
send further word regarding the arrangements by 20 December.

Everything now depended upon how the individual provinces would
receive the idea of negotiations; leaders on either side could not predict
how the matter would be resolved. The situation was made even more
tense by the arrival of news from the court at Madrid of Philip's declaration of bankruptcy. In October, Philip, worried over state debt, had convened a special junta of theologians, jurists, and members of the treasury
to discuss how to remedy the crown's financial situation. They decided
that the current short-term debts of some 12 million ducats would have
to be converted to a long-term debt with lower interest rates. Accordingly, on 5 November the king signed a decree that disencumbered the
royal revenues from the Indies and instead made those debts payable over
a period of nineteen years, at 5 percent interest, from the remittances of
the Cortes.[77]

Although the decree was potentially disastrous, in reality it was a cordial solution agreed upon by the Genoese bankers who held the king's
debt. The major debt holders, including the Fuggers, Spínola, and Octavio
Centurion, were either exempted from the decree or provided with large
lump payments to offset its effects. It was a necessary step if the crown
wished to have liquid revenues to dispose of during periods of need. But
as had been the case with previous bankruptcies, it meant that the Spanish
now found it extremely difficult to transfer funds to the Low Countries.
Such difficulties might have a profound effect on how the northern provinces viewed their bargaining situation, "since with the experience that
the enemy has that on the occasion of such decrees order and provisions
are lacking, it might fall out that they will not want to make peace." Philip,
however, hoped that Spínola could temporarily offset the crown's lack of
credit by bringing funds directly from Milan.[78]

But if the financial situation of the southern provinces was still less than stable, the military situation was improving. On 27 November the archduke settled with the mutineers at Diest, immediately dividing them into smaller companies and sending them to separate garrisons throughout his territories. Then, on 4 December, without their having committed any other offense, he published a decree that gave them twenty-four hours to leave his provinces, under penalty of death. The last great mutiny in the Army of Flanders was at an end, and the army was finally under control; paradoxically it was the peace initiative that finally gave Albert the firm hand he had desired from the start.[79] This could only improve the long-term stability of the archduke's rule.

And although bankruptcy certainly threatened to cause short-term problems for the monarchy, in the end it had no negative effects on the negotiations. On 20 December the deputies of the States-General returned to The Hague with their commissions from the provinces. After a few days of dispute over the wording, they finally agreed on 23 December to send their reply to the archdukes. In sum, notwithstanding the defects of the king's ratification of the cease-fire, the deputies agreed to enter into full-scale peace negotiations, appointing seven or eight delegates for that purpose, and agreed to prolong the cease-fire for six weeks. They gave the archduke ten days after receipt of their letter to appoint an equal or lesser number of delegates for the same purpose according to the terms previously proposed. Although theoretically this latter caveat meant that the Habsburg delegates were limited to natives of the Low Countries, in a private note to Neyen and Verreyken, Oldenbarnevelt hinted that one or two foreigners might be permitted, provided they were not members of the Spanish high command. Albert, however, took this to mean that one of the Spaniards could not be both Spanish and a commander, but that there were no restrictions regarding the other. Accordingly, he promptly appointed a reluctant Spínola to the position, a move that the Dutch, unwilling to brook further delays, accepted the following month. Meanwhile, the archdukes' reply, written on 31 December, contained no surprises. Compromise had finally been reached, and to all appearances it was the Dutch who, at the end of nearly a year of stubborn resistance to Spanish demands, finally stood triumphant and unyielding. It would be a good position for them when the negotiations opened the following month.[80]

The Spanish ministers approached the matter cautiously. The plight of

Spanish finances and the international situation forced them to advise the king to seize the chance to open talks, but they suggested that Philip refrain from delivering the news of the military cutbacks that were to take place that year, since if the Dutch had an inkling of this, the Spanish bargaining position would be seriously weakened. Instead, they urged Philip to order Spínola to arrange a truce before the Dutch realized that the Spaniards could not afford to maintain their military. Only one member of the junta, Pedro Franqueza, count of Villalonga and erstwhile creature of the duke of Lerma, opposed the talks, primarily because he distrusted both Spínola and the archduke. He suggested that the whole notion of peace talks was a ploy on their part to insure that Philip continue to provide provisions and "by merely persuading Your Majesty that they are engaged in talks, they insure that Your Majesty cannot refrain from continuing the provisions in the same amount as last year."[81]

But the opinion of Villalonga, soon to be arrested on charges of corruption, no longer carried much weight with Philip; the king's reply to the junta can be seen as a direct repudiation of both the minister and his view: "Although I can understand the reasons that are here set forth for proceeding with caution, one cannot help but admit that the truce talks are most convenient, and thus I have signed the letters for Flanders and Genoa. You, the count of Villalonga, are to dispatch them today with the utmost diligence. . . . Of the marquis Spínola, I expect that he will serve in this business as well as he is accustomed to do in everything."[82] Philip had no choice but to place his trust in Spínola; he badly needed a respite from the war in the north. Yet if Philip seemingly had to trust that the talks were legitimate, the Dutch leaders had no reason to look upon them so favorably. The Spanish had made overtures before, but only when they thought they would gain the advantage. Perhaps the current feelers had the same motivation.

And so, as the chronicler Grimeston would summarize, "With these accidents, deliberations, difficulties & resolutions touching the affaires of the Netherlands, this yeare of 1607, ended; leaving to the beginning of the next yeare, an universal expectation in a manner of all the worlde, for the pacefiing of the troubles of the Netherlandes, and the ceasing of the long continued bitter warres; Wherein either partie pollitickly seemed to seeke his owne advantage."[83]

CHAPTER 10

The Search for the Advantage: Negotiation of the Twelve Years' Truce

❀ ❀ ❀

All parties desire the peace greedily, but every one with great advantages.

—SAMUAL CALVERT TO WILLIAM TRUMBULL

25 February 1608

Everything looked hopeful as the new year opened. On the same day that the States-General received Albert's agreement to open negotiations (7 January), the Council of State in Spain looked over a draft of the powers requested by Spínola and added only minor changes before sending it out on 10 January. On 11 January the Dutch sent word that they agreed to Spínola's appointment as one of the delegates and were dispatching the appropriate passports. By the third week of the month the Habsburg delegates—Spínola, Verreyken, Neyen, Richardot, and Juan de Mancicidor, the secretary of state and war originally appointed by Philip II—were ready to depart.[1]

On 26 January, having received the powers from Philip, Archduke Albert drafted his instructions. After admonishing his deputies to cooperate with those of the allied powers, especially President Jeannin, he turned to the three most important points. First, they were to remember that the free exercise of the Catholic religion was the most important issue and had priority in any treaty. If the Dutch refused to consider this question, they were to be reminded that the archdukes had already gone to great lengths to satisfy the Dutch demands for sovereignty, and this gesture warranted reciprocity on their part. Moreover, Albert warned, the Catholics of the northern provinces, if they failed to secure freedom of worship, would no doubt begin migrating to the southern provinces, enriching the

latter and impoverishing the former. The delegates were to try to secure
Jeannin's assistance with this point in particular, since it was something
as desirable to Henry IV as it was to Philip III. Turning to commerce,
the second issue, Albert instructed the delegates that they could concede
trade to the Iberian peninsula on an equal footing with the English and
French, on the condition that the Dutch renounce absolutely all navigation to the Indies and agree to punish those who transgressed. They could
allow mutual trade with the southern provinces, subject to the obligations
and taxes that had existed before the war. Last, Albert turned once again
to questions of religion. The delegates were to do all in their power, with
the aid of Jeannin, to secure restitution of at least part of the benefices
and estates of the Catholic ecclesiastics who had been dispossessed by the
war.[2]

Once they had addressed these main points, the delegates could tackle
issues of lesser or more local importance. Of primary concern was how
the archdukes would be compensated for the loss of territory entailed
by the grant of sovereignty. If they could not get compensation, then
they wanted at least to receive the proper rents from their estates in the
northern provinces. Boundaries between the provinces would have to
be determined, preferably at the Rhine and Waal, with the exchange of
Rheine, Lingen, Oldenzaal, and Grol for Bergen op Zoom, Geertruidenberg, Breda, Heusden, Grave, and Nijmegen. If these should strike the
Dutch as unequal trades, the delegates were to remind them once again
that they were getting their sovereignty in return. Albert would, however, give up Geertruidenberg and Heusden if necessary, since they had
always belonged to the province of Holland, and would forget about Nijmegen if he could get Grave. Moreover, to sweeten the whole deal, he
would give up the fort at Rheinberg to the Elector of Cologne, thereby
forfeiting the Habsburgs' only Rhine crossing. Finally he asked that the
monetary systems of the two countries be brought into conformity to
facilitate trade.

Having delivered these instructions regarding specific issues, the archduke presented a radical and secret plan to prevent either of the countries
from being dominated by outsiders. Suggesting that neither could survive
without the other, he proposed that the northern provinces place themselves not under his sovereignty but under his "protection" for the good
of the common "fatherland." If this plan proved impossible to consecrate,
then he wanted at least some form of mutual defensive treaty to protect

both countries from invasions by foreigners and to prevent either of them from aiding and abetting the enemies of the other. This latter point made, he refused to budge on the crucial issue of the withdrawal of the Spanish soldiers, arguing that he had more right to entertain them than the Dutch did the French, English, Scottish, and others in their service. Finally, the delegates were to insure that they would do everything possible to benefit their allies: the count of Emden, the duke of Cleves, and the Elector of Cologne.

Given the money spent, the lives lost, and the infrastructure destroyed during the forty years of warfare, this was not a particularly impressive list of demands. Indeed, the sovereignty alone, as the archduke now realized, had been the most valuable thing the Dutch could have demanded and was worth more than all that he could ask for in exchange; and even then he was willing to surrender most of his demands. Only two points had any substance: the freedom of conscience for the Catholics and the prohibition of trade to the Indies, neither of which had been an issue at the start of the war. The Spanish had fought for so long to prevent the alienation of their territories and to destroy the heretics; now they had failed in both aims. The negotiation that would settle it all would seem little more than an anticlimax, an almost embarrassing "pop" after so much thunder.

Nevertheless, the delegates had to play out their roles in this sorry affair. Spínola put on his best face, though painfully aware of "the risks to which [he] put his reputation by taking part in something so uncertain." And so, with their instructions in hand, on 27 January the five men—each representing a different part of the Habsburg inheritance—accompanied by a retinue of 180 gentlemen along with their retainers and secretaries, servants and cooks, departed Brussels for The Hague. After traveling at a leisurely pace by land to Breda and then by sledges across the frozen rivers, they were at last greeted at Rijswijk on 1 February by a reluctant Maurice, his cousin William Lewis, and a host of other distinguished gentlemen. Spínola dismounted from his coach, and the erstwhile adversaries greeted each other with cordial but epigrammatic phrases; the two then embarked in Maurice's coach for the short trip into The Hague, accompanied by hordes of onlookers and the blare of trumpets.[3]

The next few days were used up with the obligatory greetings among the various representatives, ambassadors, agents, and deputies, and it was not until 5 February that the States-General decided to proceed. They began by appointing nine deputies to treat with the Habsburg delegates: William Lewis and Walrave van Brederode for the whole United Provinces; Cornelis van Gent for Gelderland; the advocate Oldenbarnevelt for Holland and West Friesland; Jaques de Malderee for Zeeland; Nicolas van Berke for Utrecht; Doctor Gellius Hillama for Friesland; Johan Sloet for Overijssel; and Abel Coenders for Groningen. The principal negotiator would, of course, be Oldenbarnevelt.

On 7 February the delegates from both sides met for the first time in a special chamber set aside for the purpose near the council room of the States-General. The negotiators sat at one table while the commissioners of France, England, Denmark, and nine German principalities sat looking on and giving guidance from another. After the usual disputes and protestations over the extent of the powers granted to each of the parties, the delegates finally settled in for business on 8 February. By the thirteenth the Habsburg delegates had already consented (in theory) to the grant of sovereignty to the northern provinces as specified in the terms given them by the Dutch (see Chapter 9). In return for this magnanimous gesture, Spínola and the others asked the Dutch to accede to their terms regarding the trade to the East and West Indies. The Dutch, they said, would be allowed to trade with all the peninsular kingdoms of the Spanish crown but would have to refrain from their interloping in the territories of the Indies.[4]

At this point things began to look a little less hopeful than they had a month earlier. The Dutch delegation "made a lot of noise and protests" over this issue, telling their counterparts that they would concede a prohibition on trade to those parts controlled by the Spanish but that they could not consent to a prohibition on free trade to territories not subject to the Spanish crown. This desire of the Spanish to lay down the law regarding their trade and livelihood, they argued, was incompatible with their newly won independence.

It is perhaps difficult to understand their intransigence in this matter. They had already won their independence; everything else they could get from the Spanish would be just so much gravy. The trade to the Indies was a recent development that had nothing to do with the initial central issues of the struggle against Spain. Most of the provinces had no stake in the Indies trade, and many citizens believed it was the private interest of only a handful of merchants in Holland and Zeeland. Profits had not, up to this point, been very considerable. Yet in spite of these factors seemingly favoring a conciliatory attitude, other factors mitigated against it. Recent financial returns from voyages to the Indies showed a bright future regarding profits, especially after news arrived of the Dutch victory at Malacca in the East Indies. This information emboldened parties involved in the trade, many of whom began to assemble at The Hague to begin a massive propaganda campaign aimed at convincing the rest of the nation that the livelihood of not just the merchants but of the provinces themselves was at stake, for they were a people who lived by the sea. In the wake of such developments, Oldenbarnevelt believed that if he conceded the Spanish their Indies monopoly he would lose the tenuous coalition that was backing the peace plans.[5]

Therefore, on 27 February, following three fruitless meetings on the sixteenth, nineteenth, and twenty-third, the Dutch deputation tabled three new proposals regarding the Indies trade: that they would not trade with areas subject to the Spanish; that beyond the Cape of Good Hope there should be a truce for some years during which the question could be discussed and resolved; and that the same rule that was used in the treaty with the English should be applied in this case, namely, that merchants traded to those parts at their own risk and any hostilities would not endanger the peace in Europe. Such proposals were, of course, unacceptable to the Habsburg deputies. At this point, however, recognizing their inability to drag any concessions from the Dutch on the issue, they decided to shift their tack and leave the Indies trade to one side while they pursued other questions.[6]

Over strong objections from the Dutch, the archduke's deputies further decided not to broach the volatile issue of religion until other points had been covered. Spínola was aware, as he pointed out to the king, that the Dutch were resolved never to allow interference in the internal affairs of their provinces such as the Spanish demand for freedom of worship entailed. In December the individual provinces had signed an agreement to support one another to the fullest extent possible in this matter and had agreed that all talks be broken off should the Spanish insist on such a concession. It was for this reason that the Dutch deputies wanted the Habsburgs to declare, at the earliest opportunity, what their position would be on the issue; there was no point in proceeding if, as they suspected, the Spanish would prove intransigent.

Spínola, knowing that such a declaration would mean a breakdown of the talks, decided to write the king for further instructions. Now that

he was among the Dutch, he told Philip, he could see for himself that
the people were united in their opposition to open worship for Catholics, even those who agreed to the peace in principle. Indeed, he pointed
out, things were looking worse and worse for the Habsburg position. He
could sense the strength and influence of the war party in the provinces,
as well as their renewed enthusiasm for war, now that they had the full
backing of the French. If Philip would not accept peace without freedom
of conscience for the Catholics, then he would have to order the necessary
provisions for war. Meanwhile Spínola and the others would try to divert
the Dutch by discussing the issue of the borders between the provinces.[7]

The marquis could not have been more out of touch with the feelings
at the Spanish court. On 28 February the Council of State had advised
Philip, and he had agreed, that he ought to reiterate his instructions regarding the point of religion, in case the archduke's commissioners had
forgotten:

> The instruction that the archduke gave to the marquis and the rest be-
> gins well, since the question of religion is put in the first place, although
> without the force that Your Majesty has ordered and that is necessary
> so that the rebels understand that the free and public exercise of it has
> to come before everything else, since for this reason alone Your Maj-
> esty agreed to cede them the sovereignty. . . . And thus, it would be
> well to write to His Highness and to the marquis that, although Your
> Majesty believes they remember what you have ordered concerning this
> point, still, in order to comply with the obligation you have of making
> everything redound to the honor and glory of God, you have wanted
> to remind them that for no reason should they agree to anything that
> would be contrary to this end.[8]

Meanwhile, try as they might, the Habsburg delegation was finding
it impossible to ignore the two central issues of trade to the Indies and
freedom of worship. The States-General's deputies continued to insist that
both sides table their propositions all at once, arguing that this would in no
way prevent them from proposing other articles at a later date. Richardot
and Spínola, however, without further instructions from the king, and
not wanting to show their whole hand, hesitated to commit themselves
to debating all the issues at the beginning. Nonetheless they realized that
by their refusal they risked the entire peace process. On 4 March, after
a particularly hard day at the table, Richardot wrote to Albert that there
was probably little they could do about the Indies trade question with-

out jeopardizing the whole discussion of peace. He advised the king and archduke to accept the Dutch proposal to discuss the problem in separate talks and await a time when "they might find their affairs better disposed for making war."[9] Indeed, both Richardot and Spínola began to propose nothing less than a revision of the peace strategy that the Spanish had followed up to this point. Now the Spanish would sign a peace with the Dutch while setting the question of trade to one side. Once the peace was in place, they would be able to discuss the issue of the Indies at leisure. Eventually the Dutch, immersed fully in the lucrative peninsular trade, would not be willing to risk a reversion to war over the trade to the Indies; they would be forced to give in to Spanish demands. It was a plan certainly in keeping with the whole Spanish notion of peace as a weapon of strategy used to undermine the enemy's willingness to engage in military conflict. This time, however, the policy was based upon a major unproven premise: the idea that the peninsular trade would be worth more to the Dutch than their Indies trade.[10]

Finally, on 7 March, after further arguments and assurances from the Dutch that such action would not prejudice their negotiating position, the Habsburg delegates agreed to exchange mutual propositions. The Dutch immediately brought forth a list of twenty-eight points they wanted considered in the negotiations. They were detailed, specific, and written in plain language. In contrast, the seven propositions tabled by Spínola and the others were short, general, and obscure, making it all but impossible to determine what was meant by them. Where the Dutch sought (point 4) a "declaration of the respective borders and what depends on them," the Habsburgs wanted to discuss only (point 1) "the borders." Where the States-General requested (point 8) "restitution of the lordships, properties, foundations, and activities of the other lords and individuals lost by confiscation or warrant (*anotación*) for the said cause, both in the Low Countries and in the Duchy of Luxembourg and the Counties of Burgundy [Franche-Comté] and Charolais and their dependencies, and also the ships that have gone to trade and have been embargoed," Spínola and Richardot proposed to talk only of (point 2) "the matter of the restitution of property."

Naturally enough, neither side was pleased at what the other had presented. Richardot complained that such a list of proposals would be tedious work, entailing lengthy negotiations, while the Dutch deputies considered the Spanish proposals to be so general as to be unintelligible and requested an immediate explication. They were very worried about the Habsburgs' sixth point, "Concerning religion," a clear indication that they had not given up their pursuit of this issue, despite the Dutch deputies' earlier indications that there could be no compromise.[11] The archduke's representatives, however, refused to clarify their position on this point until it should come up for a full discussion. Meanwhile they would turn to the other proposals in order, beginning with the question of trade between the parties.

On 12 March the Habsburg delegates decided to offer a compromise on the issue of trade. They asked the States-General's representatives to draw up separate proposals concerning European trade on the one hand and the Indies trade on the other. This latter, they said, they would send to Spain for approval. Accordingly, on 17 March the deputies of the States-General delivered their terms to their counterparts: intra-European trade guaranteed by a security of 1.5 million ducats and a continuation of trade to the Indies for nine years, during which time the matter could be discussed further. To the Habsburg delegates these were, of course, unacceptable demands and demonstrated a singular unwillingness to compromise. Three days later, after having already laid out their position concerning intra-European trade — the obligatory opening of the Scheldt — the Habsburg deputies countered with a draft version of the second article. In their version, the Indies trade was to gradually taper off during the nine years and come to a complete halt at the end of that period.[12]

By now, as one observer noted, everyone was becoming wearied by the lack of progress toward peace: "To-day we speak as if it would be certainly concluded tomorrow, but the next day they blot again, and every hour as it were resolve to do something, and yet nothing is done. The point of commerce is remitted to the last place. All is confusion and our poor Ambassadors so harassed that they have scarce time to breathe."[13] The Dutch, under pressure from even the English and French delegates, realized that they would have to reduce their demands if they ever hoped for agreement from the archduke and king.[14] Therefore, on 29 March, after having presented successive drafts of their demands in an attempt to find a version that would be more agreeable to Spínola and the others, the States-General's deputies finally submitted an acceptable version. They proposed a separate cease-fire of nine years in the Indies, during which time the Dutch would continue to trade with all the places they had up until that time and which were not expressly held by the Spanish or Portuguese. To ensure that both sides had time to notify their forces, the cease-fire was to take effect on 1 September 1608 in the Atlantic and on 1 September 1609 in the Far East. Two years before the treaty was to expire, delegates would be sent by the respective parties to open negotiations concerning the continuance of the trade. If, however, no settlement was reached at the termination of the nine years, the peace between the two countries in Europe would not be affected. Richardot and Spínola had achieved everything they had thought possible regarding the question of trade; now they would have to convince the Spanish court.[15]

The duty of convincing Philip and his advisers that they would have to accept Dutch trade to the Indies fell to the man who had earlier proven himself capable in this regard: Father Jan Neyen. Given forty days to return with Philip's reply, he set out immediately on his task.

But if some thought the talks to be moving too slowly, the Spanish thought everything was happening too fast. Many were of the opinion that the negotiations had been a bad move from the start, and the frequent concessions by the archduke's delegates only strengthened that opinion. On the occasion of the friar's departure for Spain, both Hurtuño de Urizar and the marquis of Guadaleste took the opportunity to protest the terms of the treaty, especially the concession of the Indies trade, which, as the ambassador told Philip, could lead only to "a diminution of Your Majesty's greatness and an augmentation of that of the rebels."[16] Even in Spain, feelings against the treaty ran high. Before the Spaniards had yet heard the latest rounds of compromises, Francis Cottington, the English ambassador's secretary, could report from Madrid: "So much is your treaty of peace misliked here as many stick not publicly to rail at Lerma (who hath engrossed the government) saying that had not he been base and traitorous, these propositions could not have proceeded from a King of Spain. If I should endeavor to make you understand this man's greatness, you would think I wrote monstrous lies."[17]

Others, too, reported on the unrest directed toward what many perceived to be the duke's foreign policy. Cabrera de Córdoba wrote that in July various pasquinades appeared throughout Madrid "urging the people to wake themselves up because a tyrannical governing privado was holding the king and kingdom at gunpoint [el último punto]." Not all the opposition to Lerma was caused by a dislike of his foreign policy, however. In August some of the eleven towns whose jurisdictions Lerma had bought from the crown demonstrated their opposition to the move by tearing down or dirtying the arms of the duke that had been placed over their gates and by posting their own pasquinades. And in October Francis Cottington reported that many had begun to accuse Lerma of skimming off the wealth of the country, one friar even cursing the duke with the words "vox populi, vox Dei [est]," implying that God would seek restitution for his crimes against the people of Castile. Indeed, so shaky was Lerma's control of the situation at this time that he had even begun regularly attending council sessions, something Cottington had never seen before; he also announced that he would be leaving the court.[18]

In late March, given the overwhelming public rejection of the negotiations, the councillors of state unanimously advised the king that to accept the Dutch terms regarding the Indies and their uncompromising stance on the religious question would be extremely unwise. Although they recognized that war would be disastrous, they now agreed that it would be far worse to go to war after the Dutch had established themselves in the Indies. They advised, therefore, that Philip try to buy time by dragging out the negotiations—preferably by means of a three- or four-year armistice—making sure in the meantime that the archduke and Spínola fully understood that Spain was prepared to go to war rather than give in to Dutch demands.[19]

Into this strained atmosphere Father Neyen arrived on 25 April, just after Easter. Because the king and queen had already begun their progress throughout old Castile, coordinating Neyen's visit would prove difficult. After handing over his advice papers concerning the points of religion and trade, Neyen made his official visit to the king at Aranjuez. This was all mere formality, however; the friar would receive no swift answers. As the Council of State had already advised delay, this appeared to be a perfect opportunity to engage in it. Besides, by all reports no one was happy with the news Neyen had brought. Even before Neyen's arrival, Cottington had been reporting that "all begin to condemn the friar for a flatterer and a liar, and the choice of Spínola for one of the Commissioners." Given this attitude and the fact that the ministers, especially Lerma, were busy with negotiations for the millones, it was not at all surprising that the Council of State did not even begin to discuss the reports brought by Neyen until 6 May. By then the forty days the Dutch had granted him had almost expired and everyone in the Low Countries was becoming restless. Dutch suspicions reached the point where they were rightly guessing the real Spanish strategy in the matter, as Spínola pointed out: "Your Highness knows very well that . . . the principal complaint which those contrary to the peace allege against it, is that the goal of His Majesty and of Your Highness is nothing less than to make them lay down their arms and take time to put their affairs in good order and then return to make war on them with greater force and convenience than could be done now."[20]

On 6 May, Lerma, still recovering from having been bled twice to cure one of his frequent illnesses, passed Neyen's opinion papers to the Council of State for consideration.[21] The council, having already finished its discussion of the letters sent by Albert and Spínola at the end of March, had to draw up a separate consulta concerning these additional documents. Nonetheless the council's opinion, it pointed out, had not changed, "because not one of the measures that are proposed in either the one or the other article contents us, since Your Majesty, in compliance with your duty to God and yourself, cannot cede the sovereignty except in return for the free and public exercise of the Catholic religion, as Your Majesty has resolved." Once again, it advised the king, both in this addendum and in the earlier consulta, to delay. They needed time, the councillors argued, to weigh carefully the list of twenty-eight articles presented by the States-General, preferably after having received detailed advice from Brussels, which they would send for immediately.[22]

Even more important, they needed time to see how their strategy regarding France worked out. The tactic was to send Don Pedro de Toledo, newly created the marquis of Villafranca for the purpose, to the French court, where he would attempt to dissuade Henry IV from his support of the rebels or at least get him to push for the free exercise of Catholicism in the United Provinces. The carrot that Villafranca, uncle of the queen, was to offer the French was nothing less than a triple marriage alliance, uniting the infanta, Ana, with the dauphin; Henry IV's eldest daughter, Isabel, with Prince Philip; and his other daughter, Cristina, with the infante, Don Carlos, third son of Philip III. The Spanish were—incredibly—willing to sacrifice their future dynastic interests if it meant securing a peace that would benefit Catholicism and their trading interests.[23]

Unbeknownst to the court, however, Albert was at that very moment writing to inform Lerma that neither the Spanish nor the French could ever pressure the Dutch into granting freedom of worship. Oldenbarnevelt and the griffier, Cornelis van Aerssens, had spoken with one of the archduke's agents about the issue and had informed him in no uncertain terms that they would never consider doing anything affecting the reli-

gious state of the country just to secure the peace. "They would do," the
Dutch representatives told him, "what they saw would be convenient for
them, so that whatever they did the Catholics would thank *them* for it,
and not anyone else." Albert, realizing that such staunch resistance did
not bode well for the negotiations, tried to smooth over this rejection of
Spanish demands by arguing that the Dutch had implied that they would
do something, but not because they had felt pressure. Albert's implication was clear, therefore: the best thing the Habsburgs could do would be
to back down from their demands. And to juxtapose the alternative, the
archduke slyly requested that the provisions for war be sent, knowing full
well that none were available.[24]

Meanwhile, the time for Father Neyen's return came and went, and
with its passing both sides confronted the possibility of an expiration of
the cease-fire. Spínola and the others had stayed at The Hague precisely
because they wanted to keep up the appearance of ongoing negotiations.
There had been some fear that the States-General's delegates, having once
been allowed to leave for their home provinces, might not be allowed
to return. Now it appeared that they might have prolonged the talks for
nothing. They need not have worried, however; Oldenbarnevelt was just
as unwilling to jeopardize the peace talks at this point. He was well aware
that the States-General could not resume war that year; their credit was
in a shambles as a result of the uncertainty concerning the peace. Only
Maurice opposed the idea of continuing the cease-fire on principle, arguing, quite rightly, that discipline in the army would slacken and that the
people would not want to resume the war after so long a period of tran-
quility. After much argument the Stadholder reluctantly agreed to a two-
month continuation. Still this was insufficient; Oldenbarnevelt insisted
that they would need the rest of the year just to recover and reorganize.
In the end only the mediation of Pierre Jeannin brought about a compromise settlement: an extension of the cease-fire until the end of the year,
but with the proviso that the States-General would within two months
take a final resolution concerning peace or rupture.[25]

The agreement, as Spínola was quick to point out to Philip, meant that
the Dutch would not yet disband their troops. Consequently, the Army
of Flanders would have to remain in arms in order to present a matching
appearance of strength. For this Philip would have to send an additional
two hundred thousand ducats to pay the wages of the German soldiers

still serving and recruit more if necessary. Once again everything seemed to turn on the question of which side could hold out longer financially.[26]

It certainly looked as if the Spanish situation in this regard was improving. By the middle of May the crown had won the concession of a new grant of millones from nine of the eighteen cities represented in the Cortes; only one more was needed to make it a majority vote. Even more promising, however, was the compromise struck between the crown and the newly formed syndicate of Genoese bankers, the Diputación del Medio General, on 14 May 1608. By this agreement the king granted the victims of his November decree *juros,* or bonds, worth 6.5 million ducats in return for the immediate availability of liquid capital.[27]

Philip once again failed to use the opportunity wisely. Instead of devoting all his resources to resolving the situation in Flanders, he began new preparations for a major attack against North Africa, by September amassing an armada of sixty-eight galleys carrying some eight thousand men. Cottington believed that its sole aim was to strike at Dutch trade in the Mediterranean, cynically remarking, "This makes us believe that their only end in the Treaty was to gain time." Cottington, whose complete lack of objectivity tended to cloud his analyses of situations, was, as usual, wrong in his assessment of Spanish aims. Not only was the attack on Larache part of a larger and traditional Spanish strategy in the western Mediterranean, but it also reflected a growing appreciation of the need to strengthen Spain's sea defenses. For, in addition to the attack on North Africa, Philip finally assented to the creation of an Armada de Barlovento to protect the Atlantic shipping, providing forty thousand ducats up front to begin construction and pledging part of the silver remittances to pay for the remainder. With all this new military activity, it remained to be seen how Spain's improved financial situation would help Spínola and the archduke in the Low Countries.[28]

Toward the middle of June the archduke received the latest set of instructions from the king: delay the negotiations and reject any compromise on trade or religion. Spínola, when he received the news, responded tactfully. He was sending back the twenty-eight points tabled by the States-General with the Habsburg delegates' annotations, but he urged the king to take action on them as soon as possible before the close of the two-month window for the continuation of the cease-fire. Neyen, he insisted, would have to return by the end of July or the talks would be finished. Albert, however, was not so circumspect; he wrote angrily to Lerma of his outrage over the king's orders:

> All I can tell Your Lordship is to beg him [the king] earnestly to observe how this negotiation is going: that if His Majesty wants to and can continue the war, there is little to do but pressure them [the Dutch] to agree to what His Majesty might want; but if His Majesty is obliged (for whatever reason) to desire the peace, he should not allow himself to be beguiled by the displays and rhetoric of the French and others that are known to do whatever they can to block it. Your Lordship should think about it for the love of God and represent it to His Majesty, and he should believe that it is necessary to decide immediately for one or the other course of action; because thinking about improving the business with delays and new proposals, I fear, will find us deceived and left behind in the one course and unable to gain in the other, as I do not doubt that Your Lordship understands better than I can say.[29]

Delays and new proposals were, indeed, creating new problems for the Habsburgs to face. On 6 July, just two weeks after Albert forwarded his complaints to Madrid, the English and Dutch finally agreed to enter into a defensive alliance. Up until this point Pedro de Zúñiga had thought he had been very successful at dissuading the English from entering into any league with the rebels, despite the fact that they were extremely distraught over the Franco-Dutch treaty. As late as 21 April Philip had written to thank James for remaining aloof and only ten days before the treaty was signed, Zúñiga was writing to reply that everything still looked undecided on the issue. It was now clear that he had been led on. The surprise was, though, less a result of Zúñiga's inability to read the situation than of James I's desire to help England's traditional ally while keeping on good terms with the Spanish. In the end the English king had decided that he could have it both ways.[30]

By the terms of the Anglo-Dutch treaty, the Dutch agreed to pay off a debt of £818,408 in yearly installments of £60,000, beginning two years after the conclusion of peace. They also agreed to assist James with troops, ships, or money in the event of an attack on England (to include English territories in Ireland), and confirmed English trading privileges in the Netherlands. In return the English promised to provide the Dutch with six thousand infantry, four hundred cavalry, and twenty ships if they were attacked. Both sides agreed to pay back whatever costs were incurred. For the English it was little short of a win/win situation; they would be repaid in the event of peace or would have now self-supporting allies in the event of war. Yet, while it was all that the English had hoped for by the treaty, it was no less beneficial for the Dutch. The two treaties of guarantee together (i.e., the Franco-Dutch and Anglo-Dutch treaties) meant that the Dutch hand appeared to have been strengthened in the event of a return to war. Whatever willingness to compromise that had existed among the Dutch ranks was now all but negated.[31]

Philip was probably still unaware of these developments when he dispatched his new instructions for the Archduke on 15 July. He graciously gave the Archduke and his deputies permission to do as they saw fit regarding the twenty-eight points tabled by the States. The two principal points "of the religion and Indies navigation" were a different matter entirely:

> Being of such great importance, especially the one of religion, I have thought very carefully about them and commended the answer to Our Lord; and I consider that I would not be complying with what I owe to His Service . . . if I should cede the sovereignty of the United Provinces for any other price than that of the free and public exercise of the Catholic religion within them. Therefore, desiring, as an obedient son of the Church and defender of the faith, to comply with this primary duty, free from all human considerations and interests, including matters of state that might compel me towards the opposite [course of action], I tell you that, as I have written to Your Highness before, my determined desire and last, immutable resolution *is that if those of the United Provinces agree that there should be free and public exercise of our holy Catholic Apostolic and Roman faith in each and every one of them . . . I will agree to cede them sovereignty . . . for however long the free and public worship lasts.*[32]

Philip took this decision without benefit of the advice of his council. At the time he was in the town of Lerma, attended only by Juan de Idiáquez, Rodrigo Calderón, and Lerma. From the sequence of events it is clear that Philip made his decision after finalizing the instructions for Pedro de Toledo and that the ministers and king placed great hopes on the success of his mission. These instructions were drafted independently of the Council of State, which, still in Madrid, did not hear of them until four days later. Despite accusations to the contrary made by historians as varied as Motley and Israel, it seems clear that the king was moved in the talks primarily by his zeal for the Catholic faith. While such beliefs have been unfashionable among historians for at least the past 150 years (if not longer—we must remember that Philip's contemporaries did not believe his motives either), ultimately one must decide the issue on the basis of the available evidence. None of the evidence suggests that either Philip or any other minister was merely paying lip service to the religious issue. If they were lying, then they were also lying to themselves, and doing so with amazing consistency over a period of more than a decade.[33]

To the suggestion that the Spanish allow the Dutch to continue trading in the Indies for a period of six or eight years while they dismantled their infrastructure and recovered their investments, Philip replied that he would not grant them the right to trade for a single day, let alone such an inordinate and unnecessary amount of time. To do so would mean leaving them free to establish alliances and put down roots, making it all the more difficult to expel them at the termination of the truce. What it all boiled down to was that there would be no compromise on the two issues deemed most important by the Spanish court.

Philip was under no illusions about what the Dutch reaction would be to these demands. Such "arrogant," "hard," and "obstinate" people could have but one response: complete rejection of the terms. Nevertheless, the king did not want to rule out completely some sort of settlement in the Low Countries. Therefore he suggested that Albert try to get Jeannin to resurrect the idea he had earlier proposed to Richardot: a temporary armistice for five or six years. This, as we have seen, had been the long-range goal of the Spanish negotiating strategy from the beginning (originally with the hope that the English would be the ones to table the idea). Such a truce would not, of course, contain the possibility of sovereignty for the Dutch Republic. Finally, Philip closed his instructions on a note of audacity. No matter what the Dutch and their allies had agreed to in secret, the cease-fire would remain in force for the duration of 1608; no secret agreement would be allowed to undermine the original cease-fire agreement (which had mentioned no necessary conditions). At the same time, in case the two sides should return to war, Philip agreed to provide Brussels with the provisions requested earlier by Spínola. This time, however, on the advice of the Council of State, he decided to send someone (as yet undecided) to oversee the distribution of the money to ensure that it was used for its intended purpose: the recruitment and upkeep of field forces.[34]

Although the Spanish administration generally welcomed delays, Philip deemed these instructions too important to await the departure of Father Neyen. He therefore sent them by express courier directly to Brussels, where they arrived two weeks later and were forwarded to the delegates at The Hague.[35] There was really no rush, however. Since Jeannin had not yet returned from France (where he had gone to take part in the reception for Pedro de Toledo), Spínola and the others decided that it was best not to announce the king's new resolutions. They wanted to ask for the French minister's assistance with a long-term truce. The Dutch deputies, themselves waiting for word from the French king regarding the extent to which he would aid them in the event of war, did not press the issue. In their replies to the king, both the delegates and the archduke expressed full approval of the resolutions, although Albert, upset at learning that Philip did not trust him to disburse military funds, rather ambiguously concluded that "thus we all remain supremely confident that if the Dutch do not want to agree to reason, then Our Lord has to give us very great sucesses against them."[36]

At length, on 14 August, Jeannin arrived back at The Hague. The following day he was visited by all the major players, including Maurice, the deputies from the States-General and England, and finally Spínola and Richardot. Jeannin assured the Dutch right away that his master in no way intended to abandon his assistance to them, despite their fears concerning Pedro de Toledo's embassy. That embassy, he reported, was already a failure. Fortified with this knowledge, five days later the Dutch deputies demanded the king's resolution. Once it had been delivered—over the objections of some of the Habsburg delegates, the deputies replied that they would present it to the full assembly of the States-General.[37]

Spínola had no illusions about prospects for acceptance of the resolutions nor for the successful agreement of a long-term truce, believing even Jeannin to be "very much against it." Oldenbarnevelt, too, knew that a breakdown of the talks was imminent. Although he himself suggested a willingness to open up certain churches in predominantly Catholic areas to Catholic worship (more as a gesture of goodwill toward his French allies than out of a desire to mollify the Spanish), there was considerable doubt about how the States-General would view such a concession. In any case the Spanish had made it clear they wanted complete freedom of worship and would sign peace for nothing less than this.[38]

On the twenty-fifth the States-General's deputies returned with their reply. It was a lengthy document, containing a detailed account of all that they had done over the past two years to procure a good peace; it concluded, however, that they could no longer continue to treat with the Habsburgs since they had been unable to come to an agreement on any of the points in contention. As a concession to their French associates, they put the religious question in last place; Jeannin had expressed concern that breaking off the talks over Catholicism would prevent Henry from assisting them. They concluded by stressing that the blame for whatever wars would result lay squarely on the shoulders of their opponents. The peace talks were ended.[39]

Yet almost immediately Jeannin moved to reopen negotiations, this time with the aim of an extended truce. On 27 August, he, along with representatives from England and the German states, presented their proposal for a long truce conditional upon Spain's grant of sovereignty and free trade for the duration of the treaty. At the same time they hinted that they would be unable to assist the Dutch in their struggle if they chose not to follow this advice and instead resorted to war; Jeannin had finally convinced Henry that his support of the Dutch would be far too expensive for the French treasury to bear. The English had no wish to honor their recent treaty with the Dutch if they would have to do so only because their allies actively sought war.[40]

Three days later the States-General agreed to open discussion of a truce. They demanded, as the foreign representatives had (perhaps not intentionally) suggested, recognition of their sovereignty independent of the duration of the truce. It was an unreasonable demand and meant for all intents and purposes that the truce would be equivalent to the peace they had just failed to agree upon. Since the Habsburg delegates were aware that the Dutch could rely on no help from their allies in the event of war, the demand also appeared a little ridiculous.

Spínola had immediately sent word of these developments to the archduke, who, on 31 August, forwarded the Dutch demands to the king for his resolution. In the meantime he expected Spínola to delay the talks as long as possible while they awaited the king's reply. Delays, however, would no longer be accepted by the Dutch, as Spínola informed the archduke on 3 September. What was the States-General's aim? Without allies, and without money, clearly they could not wish to return to war, especially after the people had enjoyed more than a year and a half of peace. From the events that followed, it seems clear they intended to push the archduke into taking his own initiative in the matter. From their long experience of negotiations with him, they no doubt realized that he would give in to their demands if left on his own.[41]

Albert now found himself in a dilemma. Unwilling to permit the negotiations to end, both because if would violate Philip's instructions and because he inherently opposed a return to war, he had to think of some way to extend the discussion. His solution was to use a plan of compromise worked out between Richardot and Jeannin. Arguing that he was complying with Philip's instructions of April 1607 to secure a long-term extension of the cease-fire, Albert now proposed to the States-General a truce of seven years. Since it would be an extension of the existing cease-fire, he argued that no more declaration was needed concerning the point of sovereignty than had already been given in the original eight-month cease-fire of the previous year. Because of this, he suggested, in a clear attempt to arrange things unilaterally, Philip's ratification would be unnecessary (although he expected the States-General to demand it anyway). As for trade, the situation would remain unchanged. In other words, he conceded all their demands for the duration of the truce. Yet again he had proven himself to be willing to sacrifice all of Spain's interests to secure peace.[42]

The archdukes, knowing that such a proposal would not be well received by either Philip or his ministers, wrote worriedly to the court on 20 September to explain their unilateral decision. They argued that it was in no way a binding decision since Philip had the power to refuse to ratify the agreement if it was not to his liking. But, as the marquis of Guadaleste pointed out, this was being disingenuous; by making peace or war dependent upon the king's ratification of the archduke's agreement, Albert had limited Philip's options by eliminating grounds for a compromise plan.[43]

But if the proposal would be unacceptable to the Spanish leadership, it was to prove no less so to the Dutch. They steadfastly refused to make any agreement unless they were granted sovereignty without any condition whatsoever, and in any case would never consider dealing with the archduke alone. Over the objections of a great many of the States-General, Oldenbarnevelt and his followers pushed through a resolution to allow Spínola and the other delegates until the end of the month to receive the king's reply to their own truce plan of 30 August. They would not extend that deadline a minute longer; if the Habsburg deputies had not received word by 30 September, then they were to depart The Hague the following day. Spínola, less than optimistic, wrote the archduke to prepare their forces for war.[44]

Even if Philip had received word of these developments in time to reply, it was clear that he would not be so easily pressured, by either the archduke or the Dutch.[45] At the beginning of September he had given orders that the Spanish troops freed for service after the failure of the attack on Larache should be sent to Flanders immediately, "not delaying as they usually did."[46] That he was perhaps in a martial frame of mind is indicated by a fragment of a document put before him for signature sometime in October: "And it appears to him [unidentified] that it would be a good thing (to show the Rebels that Your Majesty does not want nor need to want peace treaties which are not authorized by him) to make some public demonstration and some demonstration of war that would show that Your Majesty desires it. . . . And Your Majesty ought to consider as a great piece of advice, that however much your royal treasury is consumed and depleted, it still exceeds that of all your enemies, individually or combined."[47] In other words, Philip's financial resources, being greater than his enemies', would allow him to continue the fighting even after they were no longer able to do so. But this is not to say that he was completely unwilling to compromise. On 2 October, still unaware of the archduke's proposed concessions to the states, Philip wrote that he remained adamant that he would concede independence to the states only in return for freedom of worship for the Catholics. Nevertheless, if the deputies were unable to get the Dutch to agree to a seven- or nine-year armistice free of any conditions and of any acts of hostility, then he would be willing to grant them sovereignty in return for freedom of worship *for the duration of the truce.* It was therefore a compromise of method and not of principles. This much granted, he would permit no other alteration of his instructions of 15 July.[48]

Even as this document stood ready for dispatch, the mail arrived from Brussels carrying news of the archduke's proposed concessions to the Dutch in the truce. It sparked an immediate furor at court. The Council of State, including Lerma, held an emergency session in the presence of the king on 9 October to discuss the matter. All the members were in agreement that the archduke would have to be reprimanded. Showing such willingness to agree to either a peace or a long truce did tremendous damage to Philip's bargaining position. Just when Philip had recovered some of the lost ground by his demonstration of firmness in the face of the States-General's proposals—a decision applauded by all the councillors—the archduke had thrown it all away by his eagerness. None of the councillors could believe that Albert and the deputies had put such faith in Jeannin, who, according to Lerma, was "a deputy of the greatest enemy that Your Majesty has!" It was clear to those in Madrid that nothing Jeannin could do would benefit Spanish aims in the talks. Indeed, Jeannin's suggestion that the Dutch demand their independence as a condition of even a truce was designed, they said, to do nothing less than cause the talks to collapse. For Jeannin knew that Philip could never agree to something so unreasonable. Nevertheless, it was done. Now it was up to Philip to try to rectify matters.[49]

This would not be an easy task, especially from Philip's distant vantage point. As he himself wrote, he hoped that the States-General had demanded his ratification of the agreement; this would leave an opening for him to refuse and thus put an end to the unconscionable concessions. If they had not done so, then Philip was unsure of what he would do. Although he urged Albert to follow his earlier instructions to the letter, it was clear that the Spanish had no real plan. Philip could only exhort Albert that he "ought not doubt that if we do what we ought for God and for His honor and glory, He will open a path where we least expect it to achieve our intention." In the meantime he was sending letters of credit to prepare the Army of Flanders for war.[50]

In any case, the king's decision in the matter turned out to be moot. The deadline for the receipt of his resolution had passed, and the peace conference had officially broken up, the delegates from both sides having returned to their homes, dejected that after nine months of intense negotiations they had accomplished nothing. Most people on both sides believed that war was imminent—though neither the French nor the English were willing to let that happen. On the same day that the Habsburg delegates departed, the neutral delegates, backed by Oldenbarnevelt, once more fielded the idea of a long-term truce. Only Maurice and his supporters, the Zeelanders, stood in the way. They were prepared to resume the war rather than give up any of their demands and would do everything in their power to bring it about.

In the early weeks of October, those in favor of war were aided by the chance discovery or theft of some of Richardot's private papers. Among them was a copy of the archduke's secret instructions to his deputies, the very instructions containing the proposal for bringing the northern provinces under the archduke's protection. To those like Maurice, who had argued that the Habsburgs had been duplicitous all along, this seemed all the proof they needed, for they suggested that the Habsburg proposals for a termination of war had been aimed solely at recovering the rebellious provinces. Jeannin's and Oldenbarnevelt's insistence that talks continue could then be viewed in the light of these documents as nothing short of traitorous.[51]

Such claims prompted intense struggles throughout the month of October between the party of peace and the party of war. Pamphlets against the truce flew from the presses, libelous papers were posted against the advocate himself, and Maurice, believing that Jeannin was betraying the intentions of his master, went so far as to send his own envoy to Henry IV to determine if the French king would assist the Dutch in the event of war. Both sides vehemently argued their respective cases before the States-General. On 13 October, Jeannin, aware from his correspondence with Richardot that the Habsburgs were still interested in a settlement, appeared once again before the general assembly on behalf of the ambassadors from France, England, Denmark, Brandenburg, Ansbach, and Hesse to urge the Dutch to accept Albert's proposal of a long truce based upon the cease-fire agreement. The Habsburgs, he argued, would never concede more than they had done, and in any case freedom was won by the sword and was preserved not through treaties but rather by that same sword. In the end, however, it was not Jeannin's arguments that won the day for Oldenbarnevelt and his supporters but a combination of Maurice's inability to drum up widespread support for the conflict and Henry's unequivocal refusal to assist the Dutch in war.[52]

In the last week of October, Henry's letters in response to the embassy sent by Maurice arrived at The Hague. The letter to Maurice was nothing short of the rap on the knuckles that Henry had earlier given the Stadholder's private envoy. In it, the French king reprimanded Maurice for daring to suggest that Jeannin could have been pursuing any other course than that set forth by his master, and he urged the count to see that the truce was the only logical answer to the dispute. Jeannin, delivering the king's separate letter to the States-General, made it clear that Henry would show tremendous regret and displeasure if they insisted on contravening his advice concerning the benefits of a truce. He urged the opponents of the truce to acquiesce in the decision of the majority of the provinces and to strive to maintain the unity of the confederation. Furthermore he advised the States to start putting aside funds for maintaining the garrisons that would still be needed during the truce, doing so in a more equitable manner than heretofore. In short, he was suggesting a revision of the Union of Utrecht to reflect the realities of the new republic. While the speech was perhaps less than persuasive, it did serve to convince the majority of the opponents of the truce, including Maurice, that they could not count on outside support. War was impossible; a truce was the only alternative. All that remained now was to get the king's agreement.[53]

On 23 October, the same day that Henry drafted his letter of reprimand to Maurice, the archduke and Spínola received their own from Philip. It had come too late, however. A few days earlier Albert, in an attempt to draw out the discussion still further, had sent Jeannin word that he could once again offer the Dutch a long-term truce under the same terms as the cease-fire, this time conditional upon Philip's ratification. The neutral ambassadors had duly put this proposal before the States-General and were expecting a reply within two weeks. Since the prospects did not look bright for a Dutch acceptance, however, he urged the king to provide the necessary troops and money for an offensive war, which he estimated would require an enormous expenditure up front, plus an additional three hundred thousand ducats per month. Spínola could see no better course than to await the results of this latest proposition, if for no other reason than it delayed the complete breakdown of negotiations. He clearly did not want to return to war. As he had argued before, the Spanish had proven singularly incapable of either forcing the Dutch out of the Indies or reestablishing Catholicism in the north by means of war. On the contrary, it was because of the war, and its effect on Hispano-Dutch trade, that the Dutch had moved into the Indies; and it was because of the war that the Catholics in the northern provinces were treated so badly, since they were suspected of treachery. A truce was, then, better than nothing. Spínola was confident, he wrote Guadaleste, that the king, when he realized that this new proposal would not not harm his sovereignty, would concede to it despite the fact that it did nothing for freedom of conscience.[54]

The archduke, however, was not so confident. On 28 October, after having discussed the matter with Guadaleste, who urged him to follow the king's instructions to the letter, Albert ordered Spínola to explain to the king once again just what they were proposing with the truce. His express purpose was to demonstrate that they were doing nothing that could be construed as contrary to the king's wishes. It was all so much sophistry, as Guadaleste realized. Shocked to find that both Spínola and Albert still insisted on contradicting the strict orders of the king, Guadaleste wrote to Philip to detail their activities and exculpate himself.[55]

Two weeks later, on 11 November, the Council of State, including Lerma once again, considered these latest actions of the archduke. While the members reiterated the king's resolution not to accept any agreement that conceded independence without getting freedom of conscience in return, they agreed with Spínola that the archduke's proposition at least had the virtue of drawing out the whole process. This delay was critical because their future course depended upon the success or failure of Pedro de Toledo's mission to the French king, a mission that had yet to be resolved. The Spanish, with the encouragement of the papal nuncio, were now offering to grant the Low Countries as a dowry to the infante and Isabel of Bourbon, provided that once the provinces had been ceded, Henry would guarantee the obedience of the rebels to their sovereigns and their return to the Roman Catholic fold! But because Don Pedro had compromised the whole question by his overbearing attitude, the ministers thought it best that such negotiations be continued by the ordinary ambassador, Iñigo de Cárdenas.[56]

While expressing hope that this latest offer would win over the French king, the ministers were not overly optimistic and so suggested that the king prepare his forces for war. But, as Lerma pointed out, this would have to be a defensive war only, since the royal treasury was exhausted and could not afford to pay for more than was "necessary for the conservation of what we possess." Even then, he pointed out, there would have to be significant reforms in the management of military expenditures. The veedor general of the Army of Flanders had recently demonstrated that for every two and a half million ducats sent for the army, only about one and a half million was actually spent on it. Such waste was an unbearable drain on Philip's treasury. To ensure the success of any reforms, all the ministers agreed that Albert would have to keep his nose out of the matter so that the Spanish would not be "throwing good money after bad." As the count of Alba de Liste pointed out, they could no longer even trust Spínola, a man who, by virtue of being Genoese, sought "only his own gain, and [who] when those States were lost, will have lost nothing, and would merely return home."[57]

The archduke was stunned when he received word from the king.

Not only had the king once again rejected his efforts to bring about what he considered to be a reasonable settlement, but it was painfully obvious that Philip had lost all trust in him. He had stripped the archduke and Spínola of their control of the negotiations and would strip them also of their control of the army's finances. Contrary to their advice, the war, if it came, would be a defensive one, following wide-ranging organizational and financial reforms. But the archduke did not give in. Since it was clear that the written word had not been enough to make the king aware of the precarious state of affairs in Flanders, he decided to send a personal embassy. The man he selected was his personal confessor, Father Iñigo de Brizuela. His express purpose, Albert wrote, was "to represent to His Majesty all my opinions in this matter and the inconveniences that would surely follow if His Majesty does not change his resolution, both regarding the truce and the provisions."[58]

Meanwhile Oldenbarnevelt and Jeannin had been doing everything in their power to get the States-General to accept the archduke's latest offer. By 11 November only the province of Zeeland remained opposed to the truce. On that day their representatives finally returned to The Hague, which they had left in early September because of their opposition to any form of truce. On 18 November, Jeannin, along with the delegates from England and the German states, once more proposed their draft version of a truce. This time Jeannin made it clear that if the States-General refused to accept a settlement, Henry would withhold the French subsidies; once again he urged Zeeland to submit to the will of the majority in this issue. It was ridiculous, he said, for one province to try to continue the war while six others wanted peace; Zeeland could not take on the might of the Spanish empire all by itself. Following this speech Oldenbarnevelt soon managed to convince the Zeeland delegation's leader, Malderee, that in the face of French pressure, there was no sense in remaining opposed to a settlement. He hinted, moreover, that the States-General were prepared to abandon the requirement that treaties be made by unanimous vote of the provinces. With that knowledge in hand, the Zeeland delegation left two days later to try to convince the States of Zeeland that they had lost.[59]

Sensing that they would ultimately win over the recalcitrant province, and hearing rumors that Philip had sent a negative response, on 6 December the French and English ambassadors at The Hague sent a representative to Brussels to determine whether the archduke had been acting in good faith. Albert, again against the advice of Guadaleste, still did not tell them of the king's resolution and instead ordered Richardot to request that the English and French representatives propose, as before, a long-term armistice (of twenty to twenty-five years) without any conditions. At the same time he was to tell them that the king had expressed his desire that the talks continue, and to that end he requested a prorogation of the ceasefire beyond the end of the year while they discussed the terms of the truce further. It was indeed a slippery answer, and it stood in direct contradiction to what the king had so recently ordered. Nonetheless it served the purpose of keeping the negotiations going. Not yet ready to commit one way or the other, the States-General accepted even this ambiguous response and Jeannin—who refused to present the archduke's alternative truce plan—had no difficulty procuring the extension of the cease-fire until the middle of February.[60]

But the archduke had exceeded his authority. On 22 December the king wrote again to stress that he would never go back on his July resolution and ordered the archduke to inform the States-General of that position immediately. If the Dutch accepted the resolution but chose not to end all discussions, then, and only then, was Albert to seek a prorogation of the cease-fire for six or eight months. It was nothing more than an attempt to stave off for another year the return to war. An extension of six or eight months would mean that the campaigning season would be over by the time the extension terminated; the Spanish would have managed to obtain three years of respite from the expenses of war. Philip clearly still held out hope for some kind of miracle that would allow the Spanish to resume the war better prepared. Indeed, he fully expected one. At the same time, however, his advisers were pressuring him to take realistic decisions. So, even while proclaiming his unwillingness to compromise and sending three hundred thousand escudos for the projected war, he told Albert that he would wait to see what Brizuela had to say.[61]

At the end of December Albert learned that the neutral delegates had refused to present his proposal for a long-term truce without conditions. Still he did not give up hope. Three weeks earlier, on the orders of Philip, he had sent a special ambassador, Fernando de Girón, to the English court in an attempt to persuade James to intercede in the talks. Although Girón's initial purpose had been to see what the English could do to further Philip's aims, Albert had afterward, again on his own authority, sent orders that Girón instead ask the English king to push the Dutch to agree to a *tregua llana,* or simple treaty, without any conditions.

On 7 January 1609 he finally wrote the Spanish court of his actions and expressed the hope that these would have a beneficial result.[62]

But the archduke was too late. On 11 January the States-General, by unanimous vote, passed a resolution to accept Jeannin's version of a truce. They agreed that the first article of any treaty would have to grant to the United Provinces, clearly and expressly, the status of free countries and provinces over which neither the king nor the archdukes would have any claim. Second, the said treaty could make no ecclesiastical or secular claims that were contrary to the said liberty of the provinces, and if either the archdukes or the king insisted on this point, then the negotiations were to be broken off immediately, and the war resumed. They further voted that the negotiations would be conducted in Antwerp and that the English and French delegates would go there ahead of the rest of the delegation to procure the Habsburgs' commitment to negotiate. The Habsburgs would have to accept these two preliminary points before the Dutch would commit their own delegates to the bargaining table. Meanwhile the States-General and the States of Holland would move en masse to Bergen op Zoom to be close to the talks. The fate of the negotiations now lay in Habsburg hands.[63]

For the first time, not only the attitudes of the two countries but also the decision-making timelines were on converging paths. Less than a week after the States-General decided to proceed with the truce negotiations, the Council of State, in the presence of the king, began its week-long route to the same conclusion. On 17 January the council held its first meeting to examine the letters and opinions brought by Father Brizuela. Its members were strongly divided, Idiáquez, the Constable of Castile, and the cardinal of Toledo strongly favoring a continuation of the war rather than a truce they considered dishonorable and against the will of God. The king's July resolution, Idiáquez suggested, had been an inspiration from the Lord, in whom they had to trust to show them unknown courses of action, and thus "to persevere in that [resolution] is our firmest support, since there are no human councils that are sufficient to get us out of such great difficulties." The other councillors, led by Lerma, favored a conciliatory policy as one that would be more possible in the light of the state of the royal finances. This latter, indeed, was the question upon which the ultimate decision turned.[64]

On 14 January the president of the Council of the Treasury, Juan de Acuña, had forwarded to Lerma the income and expenditure estimates for the upcoming year. It was clear from these not only that the royal treasury was empty but that Philip had pledged payments far in excess of his income. He had consigned 3,303,593 ducats on the promise of the millones for that year, but this looked as if it would bring in only two million at most. In addition he had pledged out of the treasure fleet 444,000 ducats more than it had brought back to Spain. Even after adjustments had been made, there was a shortfall of some 1,038,917 ducats for the coming year. With regard to the current foreign affairs situation, it meant that the archduke would receive no more than 700,000 ducats until the 1609 silver fleet arrived in the autumn—far less than the 150,000 ducats per month the council had anticipated to pay for the Army of Flanders. Acuña suggested that they could perhaps manage to squeeze by if those provisions were reduced to 100,000 ducats per month. Anything above that would mean cutting the provisions needed elsewhere. In view of the archduke's demand for 300,000 per month, plus 400,000 up front, this was a serious problem. Lerma agreed that for once the Council of State would have to examine the figures before deciding their policy.[65]

On 22 January the council met again to consider the options available to the king in light of these figures. Despite the gravity of Acuña's predictions, some of the councillors were not completely won over. Idiáquez argued that the figures reflected only the current state of the treasury and did not take into consideration that 1610 would certainly be a better year for the crown's income. The constable believed that war expenses could be reduced to within thirty thousand ducats of peace-time expenditures merely by instituting the military reforms he and others had suggested so many times before (most notably in the *remedio general* of 1602). Neither of these arguments, however, was able to erase the immediate fact that the king had no money to get into a war that season. Lerma convinced the others, therefore, that they would have to try to make up the shortfall by having recourse to the Genoese and German bankers. In the meantime, there was nothing else for the king to do but entertain the idea of a truce in the form suggested by Brizuela. The best they could hope for would be a long period to ratify the agreement, during which they would see how their negotiations went with the bankers.[66]

Philip was crushed. For six months he had believed he had recovered all the reputation and honor lost by allowing the original cease-fire agreement to stand; now he was again being forced to succumb to the heretic rebels, and by something so incomprehensible as the exigencies of finance. Lerma had tried to soften the blow by arguing that the council, in opposing the truce lest religious freedom be granted, had always labored under the impression that there were many Catholics in the northern provinces. Now, however, three credible informants had told them that in fact very few Catholics lived there. If that was true, Lerma argued, they had certainly not been helped by a continuation of the war, and had probably suffered all the more because of it. The example of England, he argued, had shown that the persecution of Catholics was reduced after peace. Indeed, had not Pedro de Zúñiga, by his presence, not only kept Catholicism alive (by holding the sacraments in his house) but also converted many heretics?[67] On 25 January the councillors tried further to mitigate the effects of the decision by urging Philip to give his assent to Albert's attempt—via Girón—to procure a simple truce without conditions, a course the king happily agreed to take. On 29 January Philip dispatched Brizuela with his alternative orders for the archduke: agree to a treaty for ten years, using the friar's formula concerning independence and omitting any mention of the Indies or the Catholics. Humiliatingly, after so long a struggle the only condition he could add was that he be given eight months in which to ratify the agreement. He hoped, however, that the friar would arrive to find that Girón's mission had been successful and that Albert would have gone ahead with a conditionless treaty.[68]

By the time Brizuela arrived back at Brussels on 8 February, he learned that things had already progressed far toward a meeting of delegates. Girón's mission had come to nothing in the end, but in the third week of January Albert had received word from the English and French negotiators that the Dutch had agreed to discuss terms. Hoping that this development would allow enough time for the king's resolution to return with Brizuela, the archduke had replied that he would send his delegates to Antwerp around the third or fourth of February. For once his initiative was not mistaken; on 9 February his delegates were able to arrive in Antwerp with the king's recently received authorization to open negotiations.[69]

The first meeting took place the following day. The Habsburg negotiators immediately raised objections about the wording of the truce, but when Jeannin threatened to resume the war on 1 March if they refused to come to an agreement, Spínola and the others, knowing full well that they had no other option open to them, yielded and agreed to recognize the independence of the United Provinces in the form requested. By 7 March most of the points in dispute, including the clause concerning the Indies trade, had been hammered out between Jeannin and Richardot in a form acceptable to the States-General. It was agreed that the final treaty would make no mention of the Indies but would instead disallow trade to the king's territories outside of Europe. The clause rather ambiguously stated that the Dutch could trade with other princes outside the limits of Europe without hindrance. Ten days later, the States-General, now in Bergen op Zoom, agreed to send a delegation of nine men to Antwerp to finalize the truce agreement. They arrived in the city on 25 March and immediately agreed to extend the cease-fire until the end of the month. The following day, even before the first meeting of delegates, Spínola wrote the king hopefully that the treaty was on the verge of conclusion.[70]

He was right. In less than two weeks the delegates, working nearly nonstop, had agreed enough on the various points in dispute—borders, the opening of the Scheldt, Nassau estates, fortifications, etc.—to draw up a draft document. The only thing that now lay between it and the delegates' signatures was the eruption of a crisis on the border of the Low Countries. On 25 March the ailing duke of Jülich-Kleve died without any male heirs, and the problem of the succession to his principalities immediately became an international concern. Their strategic location bordering the Rhine made them vitally important to both the Catholic and Protestant powers within and without the Holy Roman Empire. Henry IV, expecting that he might soon end up in a war, decided that it would be better if his allies, the Dutch, were not bound by a truce to refrain from conflict with the Habsburgs' Catholic allies. Eventually, however, the Habsburg delegation's pacific words and Oldenbarnevelt's guarantees that effective support for the French would be forthcoming even after the treaty was signed, convinced the delegates to proceed with the signing of the truce.[71]

And so, on the morning of 9 April 1609, in the town hall in Antwerp, the delegates for Spain, Flanders, and the United Provinces and the mediators from England and France finally put their signatures to a twelve-year truce. The main points were that both parties were allowed to keep the territories they now held, with the exception that captured villages in the jurisdiction of enemy towns would be returned to the control of those towns; that open trade would be allowed within Europe, subject to the normal tariffs and restrictions, though outside of Europe trade to the king's territories would occur only by permission; that for those territories outside of Europe the truce would begin one year after the date of signing; and that the Dutch were to be granted the same rights and privileges within Habsburg territory as had been given to the English in the 1604 treaty.[72]

Spínola was the first to write the king with the news: "Thanks to God on the ninth of this month we finally agreed to a truce for twelve years. . . . I hope that Your Majesty will be very satisfied and served by what has been accomplished in this business, which is what animates me to give to Your Majesty with the utmost pleasure congratulations for seeing you disencumbered of this war, of such labors and expenses, and of the little hope of getting more from it. I hope to God that there follow in Your Majesty's kingdoms on the heals of this success the increase and happiness that I desire."[73] The archduke and the States-General ratified the agreement four days later. By the terms of the truce Philip was given three months to affix his signature. But ratification would not come so easily for the conscience-plagued king. Not until the end of May did he finally, but reluctantly, agree to the truce, and not until 7 July did he actually sign it. By that point he realized that the hopes they all had for an improvement in Spanish finances had come to nothing. Between September 1598 and June 1609 Flanders had cost the Spanish treasury almost 37,500,000 ducats; the damage to the treasury was so great that it would not recover in the near future, nor would the bankers be able to revive Spanish military fortunes.[74] Upon close examination, the war seemed to be over. Nevertheless, a truce is not a peace, and a lack of money still seemed more of a nuisance—perhaps smacking a little too much of a burgher mentality—than a systemic failure warranting a reevaluation of Spanish strategy. As Philip had believed all along, and still believed, the cessation of war would be only temporary, "because, having to choose the lesser of two evils it appeared that it would be this [truce], but deep down in my conscience remains the idea that once this truce is ended it will be suitable to make war, and if the ability should exist, it could be done without scruple, as if it were that these businesses should not be decided by points of law but by arms."[75]

Conclusion:
The Pax Hispanica
in Northwestern Europe

With the ratification of the Twelve Years' Truce, northwestern Europe entered a long period relatively free of major conflict. The significance of this truce depends upon which point of view one adopts. Lerma struggled hard to convince people that Philip III had ushered in a Pax Hispanica comparable to the Pax Romana of Augustus. One of his propagandists, Mattias de Novoa, would write: "Oh happy century, marveled at and sighed over incessantly by the men of the most high and illustrious king, Don Philip III, *the Great,* in which everyone, with a prosperity scarcely ever achieved, settled down and rested from so many impulses and incidents . . . because of the peace of the duke of Lerma, his great favorite, a peace like that of Numa Pompilius and that of Augustus Octavian."[1] Here was a clear attempt to present the peace as a carefully crafted, *activist* (as opposed to reactive) foreign policy. The Spanish monarchy, according to this view, still determined the main lines of European international politics. Many historians, most notably H. R. Trevor-Roper, have continued to apply the concept of a Pax Hispanica to the period between 1609 and 1621, thereby arguing implicitly for the continuing dominance of Spain in seventeenth-century Europe.[2] More recently, though, some have come to disagree with this assessment, arguing that France, and not Spain, was the power most responsible for bringing peace to Europe through the judicious use of threats of force and assistance to enemies of the Habsburgs.[3]

If the actor ultimately responsible for bringing peace to Europe is in dispute, so too are the benefits derived by all parties from the cessation of widespread hostilities between 1598 and 1609, especially in the Low Countries. Although some contemporaries hoped that it might mean a permanent end to war on the continent—as reflected in one contemporary treatise, the *Articles of agreement concerning the cessation of warre . . . with warres testament, or last will, made at his departure out of the . . . Netherlands* (London, 1607)—others, like Cardinal Bentivoglio, the papal nuncio in Brussels, more realistically observed that, far from peace, the truce merely meant the temporary cessation of an endemic conflict: "Thus was the Truce concluded, and thus was the War of *Flanders,* which could not be wholly extinguished, husht for a while."[4] Bentivoglio, who wrote these words with hindsight, was correct; the peace was indeed temporary and extremely precarious. By leaving the issues unresolved, it left Spain and the United Provinces resentful and on edge. Even before the ink was dry on the treaty, both sides, and their respective allies, the Austrians and the French, stood ready to go to war over the disputed succession to the duchy of Jülich-Kleve, a war that would again provide "worke for armourers."[5] Only the chance assassination of Henry IV in 1610 saved Europe from the threat of a European-wide conflagration—and only for a limited time. Because of the failure of the truce to resolve the question of sovereignty of the northern provinces, the Spanish became increasingly concerned over who would succeed Rudolf II on the imperial throne; such a succession would have a tremendous bearing on the Hispano-Dutch conflict because of the Low Countries' connection to the Holy Roman Empire. Fears about the repercussions of these two succession questions shifted the focus of the conflict between the Habsburgs and their opponents from the north-west to the east, that is, to Germany, and marked the beginning of the series of territorial, political, and religious disputes that would eventually culminate in the Thirty Years' War.[6]

If the 1609 truce gave all Europe but a temporary rest, what was its significance for the Dutch? The traditional view has been that 1609 marks the year of independence for the Dutch nation, an independence that was merely confirmed by Spain's eventual complete recognition of it in 1648. Motley's *History of the United Provinces* ends with the truce, as does Pieter Geyl's *The Revolt of the Netherlands,*[7] and even Geoffrey Parker's revisionist work, *The Dutch Revolt,* devotes only thirty pages to the period after 1609, ending his account with the line: "For the Spanish Habsburgs, as for the rest of Europe, the Revolt of the Netherlands had come to an end in 1609."[8] In hindsight this view has much to commend it; by the end of the conflict in 1648, it was clear that all sides felt they were fighting a different kind of struggle and that Dutch independence was no longer in question. But in 1609 this was simply not true. The Spanish government, especially Philip III, still fully expected to resume the struggle and hoped to win:

> Our Lord will be served by the fact that with the gains the rebels get from the trade with my kingdoms they will abandon the navigation to the Indies and with the benefits that redound to them from it they shall relax and not wish to return to the war, since during the period of the truce the alliances they have with the neighboring princes will unravel and they will find it difficult to repay their debts, which as you know are large. And of the people, having enjoyed for so many years the benefit of the trade and commerce with us, and of the freedom from heavy tributes such as they pay now, it can be expected that they will not want to return to the difficulties of war.

This, at least is how the king justified to his ambassador his decision to agree to the truce. As he points out, it was the lack of resources ("pure necessity") and not a lack of desire that forced him to act against his will, to choose, as he put it, "the lesser of two evils." Philip's own statements, therefore, should at least give pause to the scholars who argue that after the failure of Spínola's campaign of 1606, the Spanish never had any intentions of reconquering the rebellious provinces. Given Philip's eventual decision to begin the war anew, I think we must take him at his word and not assume him to be merely putting on a brave face.[9]

The years following the truce showed that Philip's predictions just might come true. The breakdown in the government and society of the United Provinces, which the Spanish had expected, began almost immediately after the signing of the truce, as the particularist tendencies of the individual provinces made themselves increasingly felt now that continual war no longer held them together. To begin with, in 1609 the Dutch army numbered only thirty thousand men, a reduction of 50 percent from previous years. This dealt a significant blow to the segment of the population that earned its living from war, not unlike that produced in the United States by the dissolution of the military-industrial complex after the Cold War. Moreover, those provinces, especially Zeeland, which had profited because of the restrictions placed on their competitors by the war, experienced a dramatic decrease in commerce. This was not all, however; other parts of the economy also experienced significant downswings, mostly affecting the inland provinces. Those most affected by the truce, of course, were the common people. Despite the military reduction, taxes did not noticeably decline during peacetime, and the only benefit the population of the United Provinces could be said to have derived was that no additional taxes were imposed. In addition, as a result of the lifting of restrictions on the export of grain to the Catholic provinces and the increase of exports to Spain and Italy, the cost of food in the United Provinces escalated, rising faster than in any other decade of the century.[10]

As a result of these difficulties, the coalition that had been primarily responsible for bringing about the truce settlement came under heavy attack as the years wore on, and Oldenbarnevelt, the leader of that coalition, found it increasingly difficult to maintain unity within the body politic. As Geoffrey Parker has pointed out, "After the war ended, in 1609, Dutch politics came to be dominated by issues with which Oldenbarnevelt was less familiar and over which he had less control."[11] Eventually he suffered the ultimate punishment for his failure to unify the provinces behind the truce and what it stood for: in 1619 he was executed by the leader of the military party, Maurice of Nassau. With the ensuing concentration of power in the hands of the Stadholder, the federal system, which had relied heavily on the leadership of the States of Holland and Holland's town councils, whose members ensured stability, raised taxes, and financed the army, began to unravel. The new leaders in these structures, having given up so much power, would prove incapable of exercising it when called upon once war resumed.[12]

In addition to these internal problems, the Dutch faced serious difficulties in their traditional alliances with England and France. That they feared the eventual breakdown of these friendships—having witnessed their desertion by both powers in the first years of the century—is borne out by the fact that they launched a massive diplomatic effort to forge new alliances after 1604, eventually securing treaties with the Palatinate (1604), Brandenburg (1605), Morocco (1608), the Ottomans (1611), Algiers (1612), Sweden (1614), and the Hansa (1616). As they well understood, their interests in the Low Countries were not the same as those of France or England. What had kept the three parties together and had allowed them to smooth over their differences was their fear of a common enemy: the Spanish Habsburgs. "The conservation of this State," wrote one observer after the resumption of war in the 1620s, "consisted in the jealousy [worry] of the neighboring kingdoms."[13] The settlements that each of those allies had made with Spain meant those differences would now be central to further relations between the powers. As has been shown, the English and

Dutch already considered themselves to be trade rivals. The goal of Spanish foreign policy after 1609, therefore, was to ensure that such rivalry either increased, or at the very least, caused the Dutch to become isolated from the major powers. Their triumph in this regard was their diplomacy with England, which succeeded in denying the Dutch any significant English aid for almost twenty years.

The Spanish, therefore, had achieved two crucial aspects of their peace strategy of the early years of Philip III's reign: the disruption of the government in the United Provinces—albeit not quite in the manner they had expected—and the isolation of the Dutch from their traditional powerful allies. More important, Philip and his ministers had been able to provide Spanish arms and finances a period of respite lasting more than a decade, another aim of that strategy. Spanish embargoes, reimposed in 1621, effectively strangled Dutch trade from the Baltic to the Mediterranean. Expansion of the Army of Flanders to more than sixty thousand men the same year forced expensive countermeasures by the Dutch and, combined with the necessity of financing the beleaguered Protestant armies in Germany against the Habsburgs, meant the imposition of heavy new taxes, weakening, as the Spaniards had argued it would, the population's resolve to carry on the war. As a result of the Spanish peace strategy, when the war resumed in 1621, the Dutch were in a far weaker position relative to Spain than they had been in 1598.[14] But was it enough, on balance, to proclaim the peace strategy an unmitigated success? Most scholars do not think so, and they instead have agreed with the judgment of Julián María Rubio Esteban that "for history, the Twelve Years' Truce is the first obvious, official, external manifestation of Spanish decline: it is the first crack in the Spanish ideals."[15] Even though Rubio is perhaps a little too harsh and subjective in his suggestion of some kind of betrayal, I believe there is a kernel of truth in his perspective: the treaty does mark a significant change in how traditional Spanish ideals would govern matters of grand strategy.[16]

How then did the grand strategy of Philip III differ from that of his predecessor? Many historians argue that continuity, not change, characterized Spanish strategy in the early years of the seventeenth century.[17] Other authors, like Rubio, argue that a transformation in grand strategy did take place, one that was detrimental to the Spanish empire's ability to maintain its hegemony in Europe. The truth lies somewhere in between and depends heavily on the time frame of the comparisons being made.

As was shown at the outset of this work, by 1598, after repeated failures to complete his designs, Philip II had begun a serious reconsideration of the traditional methods of achieving his foreign-policy goals in northwestern Europe. His foreign policy in the north was based upon three principles: the maintenance of his inheritance; the defense of Catholicism; and his monopoly on trade to the Indies.[18] All three principles were at play to some extent in his wars with England, France, and the Dutch rebels, with the protection of Catholic interests always at the fore. But the strategy he derived from those principles had always been short-term and ad hoc; his "system of government was designed to respond to developments, not to shape them."[19] And by the late 1590s it was clear that such an approach had failed to stop the hemorrhage of the wars. As he neared death, Philip had begun to think in long-range terms and came to the conclusion that he might sacrifice short-term gains for long-term goals. It was a momentous revolution in Spanish foreign policy and signified the birth of a pragmatic "grand strategy" for the monarchy in northern Europe. But it had come too late, and it was left to the next generation to develop these ideas further.

The first moves of Philip III were a conscious reversal of the policy approach favored by his father in his last days; instead of completing Philip II's intentions of withdrawing from the northern theater while Spain recuperated, the new king reverted to war to achieve his strategic aims. Many factors were responsible for this martial response to international issues, most notably the king's desire to emulate the heroic warrior kings of Spain's past and to establish his reputation among princes. As Patrick Williams eloquently put it, "Philip ached for greatness."[20] The new king's desires found support and encouragement within a significant group of ministers who had felt Philip II's compromises to be contrary to the ideals that had made Spain great. In the first year of the reign, the feelings against the old king had been so strong that Iñigo Ibañez, one of Lerma's creatures and a secretary of the Council of State, even thought he could get away with publishing *El confuso é ignorante gobierno del Rey pasado* (The Confused and Ignorant Government of the Late King), which sought to eulogize Philip III's new policies by denigrating those of the immediate past.[21] And the Adelantado of Castile, Martín de Padilla, shortly after the old king's death, went so far as to declare that the world "would see what the Spanish were worth now that they have a free hand, and are no longer subject to a single brain that thought it knew all that could be known and treated everyone else like a blockhead."[22] And they were not alone in those beliefs. Another manuscript from the same date had launched an attack, based on a vast range of classical sources, against the very notion of making peace, especially with heretics and rebels, arguing forcibly that

> whoever counsels making peace with rebels will consider that during them Your Majesty cannot avoid aggravation against your grandeur and authority and that just the very name of peace, even if it is not completed, diminishes the royal authority, which . . . ought not by its acts, assent to the loss of one carat of its solemnity; and moreover, the composition of any peace, even if it be accomplished with such skill and concealment of your few forces that it does not become known why you have been reduced to this point, is different for a powerful king because the minute that he thinks to dissemble a point of his grandeur, conceding to his subjects something of his glory and majesty, he ought in that exact moment to consider that he puts the rest of his kingdoms in danger, inflaming the spirit of those same subjects to desire more, and igniting the hearts of the other vassals to want new things. By this he gives opportunity to the other princes to venture to weaken his forces little by little, until he loses everything.[23]

Thus it certainly appeared that Philip III would receive widespread support for a more militaristic foreign policy than his father had pursued in the last years of his reign.

Very soon, however, social, financial, and psychological realities combined to swing Philip round to the more pragmatic policies advocated by some of his ministers, similar, indeed, to those ultimately outlined by his father. First, it became apparent to the court early in the reign that the goal of winning the support of the aristocracy by appealing to their traditional military function in Spanish society had failed. In 1599 Philip had expanded the Council of War by admitting most of the nobility of note and began to use that organ as a major policy tool; in the first year he convened it more times than the Council of State. By 1600, though, only two of the upper nobility—the count of Fuentes and the duke of Nájera—were attending more than half the time, and it was clear that the aristocracy had rejected the new opportunity to participate in government or resume their traditional role in the social hierarchy.[24] Moreover, this withdrawal of the aristocracy from warfare affected not only the administration of war but its implementation as well. By 1602 the vaunted Spanish Army of Flanders lacked leaders with the necessary stature and ability to command widespread respect (see Chapter 4). As such the army no longer seemed capable either of holding itself together or of winning the necessary victories in the struggle with the Dutch rebels, a problem that seemed to increase with each passing year.[25]

Second, finances failed to match the demands of the young ruler and soon caused him to reconsider his short- and long-term policy goals. At the beginning of his reign, in October 1598, the treasury reported that the king could expect an income of 9,731,405 ducats for the upcoming year. Of that sum, however, some 4,634,293 ducats were assigned for the payment of juros, leaving a liquid capital of a little over five million.[26] But in January a special committee composed of the marquis of Denia (Lerma), the marquis of Velada, and Juan de Idiáquez informed the king that the expenses for the double marriage of Philip and the infanta, plus attendant costs, amounted to no less than one million ducats, and he owed another million for the remaining budget items from the previous year (i.e., expenses for September through December).[27] All this left Philip only 3.4 million ducats for 1599, hardly enough to pay all the expenditures in the peninsula, let alone provide the 3.1 million ducats required in Flanders that year or the enormous sums (2.7 million) necessary to assemble yet another armada for an attack on England.[28] The seriousness of the shortfall forced the government to adopt extreme measures that would have serious long-term consequences. Breaking with a longstanding tradition of sound money, in 1599 Philip debased the coinage, issuing copper money in place of silver, and pocketed the difference. Yet this and others were only temporary measures and did little to alleviate the strains on the Spanish treasury. With the multiple foreign-policy failures of 1601–2, it became clear to his ministers at least that Philip could not continue to fund so many conflicts simultaneously; something would have to give.

Although there were indeed economic and structural incentives for taking certain critical policy decisions, they were not in themselves sufficient reasons for the king to do so. Like his father before him, Philip III believed that the "inscrutable yet benevolent Providence which had created the Habsburg monarchy . . . would in time bring about the recovery of the Netherlands, the humiliation of France, the defeat of England, and the eventual extirpation of Protestantism."[29] Even Philip's ministers believed this to a certain extent. What emerges from an examination of the Spanish documentation for this period is the overwhelming commitment of the majority of the councillors of state to the Catholic cause. In foreign policy matters, Juan de Idiáquez told the king, "two principal matters come across: first, religion; and the other, the temporal state. And in Your Majesty's affairs both issues run together, the first by reason of Your Majesty being 'Defender of the Faith,' and the second by reason of the many kingdoms with which God has entrusted you and which consist of the greatest in all Christendom. Of these two matters, Your Majesty has held and always will hold for the most principal, the first." [30] By 1603, however, after witnessing the complete futility of all attempts to achieve benefits for the Catholics of Europe through the use of force, the councillors, and even Philip himself, had begun to think, like Philip II before them, that perhaps those aims might be better achieved through a combination of tactical retreats and diplomacy. [31]

The transition to this belief was gradual and not always consistent, at least insofar as Philip III was concerned. As early as 1600 the king had already begun to consider such a change in policy, actually consenting to negotiations with Elizabeth of England and deciding to seek an armistice with the Dutch. The turning point, which involved many factors, came during the peace negotiations with England in 1604. Of primary importance was the fact that the Anglo-Spanish war was one from which it was relatively easy to withdraw. In contrast to the wars the monarchy waged with France and the Dutch Republic, Spain engaged no major ground forces against its English opponent; all Philip had to do to stop the war was avoid sending another armada. King James's own pacific and pragmatic actions — such as the unilateral cessation of hostilities at sea declared by him within a month of his accession — made this move entirely feasible. For the first time, Philip took a major step toward realizing that he could sacrifice short-term gains for the higher long-term goals of grand strategy: the *eventual* reduction of Spain's enemies to Catholicism. This willingness to compromise, even if only for a while, meant that negotiation could finally become a viable option of foreign policy; the golden age of Spanish diplomacy was born. [32]

This new direction in policy making necessarily affected Spain's situation in the Low Countries, but only indirectly. Ever since 1600, Philip's ministers had been arguing for the need to settle the dispute with the Dutch by means of a limited peace — a long-term truce — with a view toward resuming the war at some future date when Dutch power might be reduced relative to Spain's. Philip, however, had consistently proven himself intransigent in the face of Dutch demands and, with complete disregard for the weakness of his forces, proposed offensive after offensive to bring the Dutch to their knees. Although these offensives were ostensibly designed to bring the Dutch to the bargaining table so they might make peace with good terms for the Spanish, in reality Philip never intended to let up if he once got the upper hand. Two things finally convinced Philip to follow the same dictates as he had done in the peace with England— short-term compromise for the eventual improvement of the Catholics and settlement of political relationships. The first was the independent activity of the court at Brussels, which consistently thwarted every offensive strategy that came from the peninsula; Albert, through his failures as a subordinate, forced the young king to the necessity of waiting matters out, over the archduke's lifetime if necessary. The second was the utter collapse of the monarchy's finances in 1607, making it impossible to continue providing Spínola with the sums needed to carry on his campaigns in the heart of Dutch territory and force them into submission.

The final treaty with the Dutch represented the climax of the most significant change in Spanish foreign policy. Instead of the ideological intransigence and "strategy of overkill" that had characterized most of Philip II's reign, the Spaniards now aimed to follow a strategy of tactical compromise and diplomatic assaults, hoping that time, or God, would allow them to realize their final goals. But the success of this transformation depended upon many factors, not least of which was the outcome of the truce. The Spaniards had not only wanted to win a respite for their country, both militarily and financially, but had also hoped that Dutch leadership and Dutch military preparedness would suffer by the cessation of hostilities. In fact, the outcome was not what they expected. With Oldenbarnevelt's death in 1619, the Dutch war party gained ascendancy and began gearing up for a renewal of the war; and it was the Spanish, not the Dutch, as one senior commander put it, who found themselves ill prepared militarily when hostilities recommenced at the conclusion of the truce in 1621: "Ever since the end of the war in Flanders, there has been a serious lack of soldiers . . . and there is now a very great difference between His Majesty's forces here in Flanders and those of the enemies of the Crown of Spain. They know this [in Holland] and in other places, and it has encouraged them to attempt things they would not have done twelve or fourteen years ago, and this problem grows every day."[33] Moreover, peace did not even make the financial situation of Spain any better. Even though Spain's expenditures for the Army of Flanders decreased by some 50 percent, the Spanish leadership failed to use the opportunity to accumulate major savings. Instead, owing to deficits and a policy of continued military expenditure in the Mediterranean, the Spanish government's budget remained at pre-truce levels throughout the second decade.[34]

The failure of the truce to achieve the objectives set for it by Philip III's ministers in the first decade resulted in a backlash against the very basis of policy upon which it had been based: compromise instead of intransigence. This was partly a result of structural factors and partly a result of Philip III's inconsistency. While he accepted the principle of compromise as a way to break the deadlock between his empire and the Dutch rebels, he nevertheless clung steadfastly to the belief that he was doing so only temporarily. This was never considered to be a sea change in the direction of Spanish grand strategy but merely a tactical withdrawal. While many of his courtiers, Lerma and Spínola among them, labored to solidify the policy of peace and promote it as a serious and beneficial alternative to the strategies that had been pursued by Philip II, Philip III, and many of his ministers, including those actively engaged in foreign affairs as ambassadors and governors, could not find it in themselves to give up completely the traditional ideals of Spanish foreign policy, chief among them being the protection and propagation of Catholicism. Thus when the truce proved to have many disadvantageous consequences for Catholicism, prestige, military prowess, and the economy, there were plenty of people who felt the king would be willing to hear them out.

The strategy of peace had been a failure. What was called for was a return to the traditional long-term grand strategic aims and the principles that underlay them: protecting Catholicism and defending the Indies trade monopoly. The lesson the Spaniards learned from the Pax Hispanica was that rationalistic, cost-benefit analyses of policy were of no help in preserving those aims and principles. For the remainder of the century, then, Spain's monarchs and ministers would steadfastly reject such reason-of-state approaches to policy in favor of providing solid support for the Catholic cause, even at the expense of Spain's empire. In so doing, they fulfilled to the letter Philip II's pious vow to Pope Pius V that "rather than suffer the least damage to the Catholic church and God's service, I will lose all my states, and a hundred lives if I had them."[35]

Abbreviations

ACC	*Actas de las Cortes de Castilla;* followed by the volume number.
AGS	Archivo General de Simancas, Valladolid; followed by document series, *legajo* (bundle) number, and folio (e.g., AGS Estado 2024:17).
AHE *CODOIN*	Archivo Histórico Español, *Colección de documentos inéditos para la historia de España y de sus Indias,* vol. 4, *Consultas del Consejo de Estado, 1604–06,* edited by M. Alocer (Madrid, 1932).
BL	British Library, London; followed by manuscript number and folio.
BN MS	Biblioteca Nacional, Madrid, *Sala de manuscritos;* followed by the manuscript number and folio.
CODOIN	*Colección de documentos inéditos para la historia de España,* 112 vols. (Madrid, 1842–95); followed by volume number and page references.
CSP Domestic	*Calendar of State Papers, Domestic Series, of the Reign of Elizabeth, 1601–1603, with addenda, 1547–1565, Preserved in Her Majesty's Public Record Office,* ed. Mary Anne Everett Green (London, 1870; Kraus Reprint, Nendeln, Liechtenstein, 1967).
CSP Spanish	*Calendar of Letters and State Papers Relating to English Affairs, Preserved in, or Originally Belonging to the Archive of Simancas,* vol. 4, *1587–1603,* edited by Martin A. S. Hume (London, 1899).
CSP Venice	*Calendar of State Papers and Manuscripts Relating to English Affairs Existing in the Archives and Collections of Venice and Other Libraries of N. Italy;* followed by the volume number and page references.
HMC De L'Isle	Historical Manuscripts Commission, *Report on the Manuscripts of Lord De L'Isle and Dudley, Preserved at Penshurst Place;* followed by volume and page references.
HMC Downshire	Historical Manuscripts Commission, *Report on the Manuscripts of the Marquess of Downshire, Preserved at Easthampstead Park, Berks;* followed by volume and page references. Full biblio-

graphic details for individual volumes can be found in the bibliography.

HMC Salisbury   Historical Manuscripts Commission, *Calendar of the Manuscripts of the Most Honorable Marquess of Salisbury, K.G., etc., Preserved at Hatfield House, Hertfordshire;* followed by volume and page references.

IVDJ   Instituto de Valencia de Don Juan, Madrid; followed by the *envio* (bundle) number and folio.

PRO SP   Public Record Office, State Papers; followed by series and folio number.

Notes

Preface

1. For example, Geyl, *The Revolt of the Netherlands*, 250–59; Parker, *The Dutch Revolt*, 237–40; and Israel, *The Dutch Republic and the Hispanic World*, 28–42.

2. Bierce, *The Devil's Dictionary*, 248. Alberico Gentili, a famed theorist of international law, considered this attitude toward peace a legitimate one and even quotes Philip II to support his view: " 'Negotiations for peace do not suspend hostilities,' says Philip . . . to Sebastian, the late king of Portugal, whom he advised to resort to such means of making the Moorish king careless" (*De iure belli libri tres [1612]*, 2:233).

3. Cf. *HMC De L'Isle*, 3:341, 389.

4. PRO SP 77:201, Edmondes to the Earl of Salisbury, 31 December 1606, quoted in *HMC De L'Isle*, 3:338.

5. AGS Estado 845, Hugh O'Neill to Andrés Velázquez, 23 May 1615, quoted in Micheline Kerney Walsh, *"Destruction by Peace,"* 131. The notion that peace could sometimes be merely a synonym for destruction may stem from Tacitus. In the *Agricola,* chap. 30, Tacitus has the Briton leader Calgacus say of the Romans, "Ubi solitudinem faciunt, pacem appellant" (Where they make desolation, they call it peace).

6. Israel asserts that "the original goal, both in Madrid and the Hague, was not a truce, but a full peace. Despite the deep suspicions that either side harboured with regard to the other, the commitment to a full peace was quite strong on the part of both governments" (*The Dutch Republic and the Hispanic World*, 3). Indeed much of the argument of the first chapter depends upon this erroneous view.

7. AGS Estado 2511:13, consulta, 13 September 1600; AGS Estado 2023:126, consulta, 26 November 1602.

8. William Camden, *The historie of . . . Elizabeth*, 154. On Spanish strategy regarding the renewal of war with the Dutch, see Brightwell, "The Spanish System and the Twelve Years' Truce," 292. Brightwell disagreed with H. R. Trevor-Roper (below, n. 11), who had argued that the Spanish had always intended to renew the war. Among modern historians John Elliott has shown the most willingness to accept the idea that the foreign policy of Philip III may have had more logic about it than previously thought; see his "Foreign Policy and Domestic Crisis."

9. But see García García, *La Pax Hispanica,* for a general overview of Philip III's policy. In addition there are a number of articles on specific episodes in the international relations between Spain and the north, examples of which will be cited in the notes below. On the Dutch view of the period, see the short work by Eysinga, *De Wording van Het Twaalfjarig Bestand van 9 April 1609.*

10. Cf. Kamen, *Golden Age Spain,* 10: "The current decline of interest in diplomatic history has meant that we still do not know enough about the formation of policy and about public opinion, and most of our assumptions about Spanish foreign policy have remained unchanged over the past century." Kamen, however, continues to follow such assumptions regarding a so-called peace party headed by Philip III's chief minister, the duke of Lerma.

11. MacCaffrey, *Elizabeth I,* xi. On Spanish foreign policy in this period, see Elliott, "The Spanish Peninsula, 1598–1648"; Rubio Esteban, *Los ideales hispanos en la tregua de 1609;* Pérez Bustamante, *Felipe III;* Williams, "Philip III and the Restoration of Spanish Government, 1598–1603" and "El reinado de Felipe III"; Trevor-Roper, "Spain and Europe, 1598–1621" (which despite some errors is by far the most intelligent survey of the foreign policy of the reign); Carter, "The Nature of Spanish Government after Philip II" and *The Secret Diplomacy of the Hapsburgs, 1598–1625;* and Alcalá-Zamora y Queipo de Llano, "Iniciativa, desaciertos y posibilismo en la política exterior española bajo Felipe III" and "La política exterior de España en el siglo XVII."

Introduction

1. Parker, "The Making of Strategy in Habsburg Spain," 121–23.

2. Although eventually quelled by Philip's regent, Margaret of Parma, the revolt of 1566 prompted the king to respond with harsh measures. In April 1567 he sent Fernando Alvarez de Toledo, duke of Alba, and an army of ten thousand men to the Low Countries to restore royal authority. But Alba's repressive measures failed to alleviate the problems that had led to the first revolt, and in 1572 a second revolt broke out, led by the *stadholder* (chief magistrate) of Holland, William of Orange. Spanish commitments in other theaters, combined with international support of the rebels, prevented an effective response until the late 1570s and early 1580s, when Philip II's nephew, Alexander Farnese, prince of Parma, managed to reconquer most of the provinces south of the Rhine and east of the IJssel. By 1585 only four northern provinces, dominated by Calvinist burghers, remained in revolt. At that point Spanish commitments elsewhere, this time in France, once again allowed the rebel provinces to regain the initiative. In 1591, Maurice of Nassau, the second (and Protestant) son of William of Orange and the new stadholder of Holland and Zeeland, commanding an enlarged and restructured army and backed by a powerful new government, launched a counteroffensive that by 1595 had recaptured most of the provinces north of the Rhine, bringing the number of United Provinces to seven: Holland, Zeeland, Friesland, Overijssel, Groningen, Utrecht, and Gelderland.

3. Parker, *Spain and the Netherlands,* 188.

4. Historians have been particularly harsh in their assessment of the third Habsburg. The great nineteenth-century historian John L. Motley, for instance, wrote of him that "no feebler nor more insignificant mortal existed on earth than this dreaded sovereign" and that "scarcely a hairdresser or lemonade-dealer in all Spain was less cognizant of the political affairs of the kingdom than was this monarch" (*History,* 4:137). Even John Elliott, the dean of historians of Spain, viewed the young Philip III as a "nonentity" who was "personally incapable of governing" ("The Spanish Peninsula," 443). To this day a historian of the stature of John Lynch can argue that "his mind was empty, his will supine" (*The Hispanic World in Crisis and Change,* 18). Such criticisms, however, have not been limited to English historians. Manuel Danvila y Collado wrote of Philip III that "he showed himself to be detached and indifferent to the fate of our country, and demonstrated to posterity that he did not have the character which the urgent needs of our nation demanded" (*El poder civil en España,* 2:584-85).

5. Danvila y Burguero, *Don Cristóbal de Moura,* 753.

6. To be sure, the prince did little at the meeting of the Council of State but observe and learn. As the papal envoy, Francisco Vendramino, reported, "He attends the Council of State daily, where he remains about an hour. He does not show great acumen for business, but the minds of princes seem to develop with age and experience" (quoted in Pérez Bustamante, *Felipe III,* 25). At fifteen, however, one could hardly expect that he would have taken an active part in the business of the council, and to criticize him—as some contemporaries and not a few historians have done—because he did not is to engage in a display of sheer pettiness. Cf. Henry Kamen's comment that the twelve-year-old prince "appeared to have little intellectual capacity" (*Philip of Spain,* 305).

7. Williams, "Philip III and the Restoration of Spanish Government," 754; Barrios, *El Consejo de Estado,* 110n106 (this work is an essential institutional study of the Spanish Council of State); Cabrera de Córdoba, *Felipe segundo,* 4:263; Parker, *Philip II,* 192; Kamen, *Philip of Spain,* 311.

8. Given such an intimidating array, it is perhaps no surprise that at first the young prince was less than forthcoming with his opinions: "He is unable to give counsel with his tutor present. The poor young lad with his showy uncle and old chamberlain around him; how will he count or with whom will he dare argue?" (BN MS 1439, H 243, fol. 30, Juan de Silva, count of Portalegre to Cristóbal de Moura, December 1593). For a brief, but original and apparently overlooked, treatment of the history of the Council of State and the junta de noche, see Yalí Román Román, "Origen y evolución de la secretaría de estado y de la secretaría del despacho." For additional details on how Philip II initiated the prince into the arts of government, see Parker, *Philip II,* 191-92, and Kamen, *Philip of Spain,* 301-16.

9. Cabrera de Córdoba, *Felipe segundo,* 4:60-69.

10. Ibid., 4:67.

11. Williams, "Philip III," 754.

12. Lynch, *Hispanic World in Crisis,* 18.

13. The secrecy of the council's deliberations could be frustrating to those trying to determine the Spanish monarchy's next moves. In 1605, Sir Charles Cornwallis, the English ambassador in Madrid, wrote the English Privy Council that "their greatest virtue is secrecie in their councells, and what is delivered or committed to them, which I perceive to be exceeding hard here by anie meanes possible to drawe from anie of them" (BN MS 17778:41, Cornwallis to the Privy Council, 9 July 1605). But there is a suggestion that at times there were leaks. On two occasions Philip had to order the count of Miranda to remind the council to keep its deliberations secret (BN MS 18632:37 and 387, notes from Philip III to Miranda, n.d.).

14. AGS Estado 2023:31, consulta, 4 July 1600. And see AGS Estado 634:10, consulta of the junta, 9 November 1601, where Philip wrote that since the whole council could not be present when he was to visit his grandmother, the empress, then he wanted Miranda to accompany him.

15. Jacob Sobieski toured Spain from March through July 1611. The quotation is from the account of his journey in Liske, *Viajes de extranjeros por España y Portugal,* 262.

16. AGS Estado 2024:44, consulta, 10 March 1605. Historians, too, have looked upon such dependence on the councils as a weakness (Elliott, *Imperial Spain,* 301–3), but see the revisionist view expressed by Williams in "Philip III and the Restoration of Spanish Government" and "The Court and Councis of Philip III of Spain," 282–397. My thanks to Geoffrey Parker for providing me his notes on Williams's thesis.

17. Wernham, *The Making of Elizabethan Foreign Policy,* 4.

18. Curiously Philip has forgotten that he elevated Denia to the duke of Lerma at the end of the previous year! (AGS Estado 616:130–31, note from Martín Idiáquez to Philip III, with Philip's reply, 14 January 1600). In 1603 when it looked like Philip III might make a trip to Portugal, the secretary, Andrés de Prada, was instructed to submit dispatches first to the Miranda, who would then decide whether to forward them to the Council (AGS Estado 2023:119, consulta, 12 February 1603).

19. AGS Estado 2511:73, consulta, 8 November 1603.

20. AGS Estado 2024:47, consulta, 13 and 25 August 1605. Cf. Williams, "Court and Councils," 291.

21. García García, "Pacifismo y reformación," 208.

22. For details on the office of *valido,* see Williams, "El reinado de Felipe III"; Feros, "El régimen de los validos," "Lerma y Olivares" (the quotation is from p. 216), and "The King's Favorite."

23. Williams, "El reinado de Felipe III," 425.

24. Williams, "Court and Councils," 60.

25. Román Román, *Secretaría de Estado,* 96–97.

26. See, for example, AGS Estado 2023:101 regarding the move by some

German princes to reincorporate the northern provinces of the Low Countries into the Holy Roman Empire.

27. Williams, "El reinado de Felipe III," 425.

28. BN MS 18546:175, Lerma to the count of Fuentes, 8 May 1602; Cabrera de Córdoba, *Relaciones*, 336.

29. AGS Contaduria Mayor de Cuentas, 3ª epoca, 669, unfoliated, Andrés de Prada to Baltasar de Zúñiga, 29 October 1600.

30. *CODOIN*, vol. 81.

31. Spanish ambassadors continually complained of shortages and arrears in pay. See, for example, Baltasar de Zúñiga's complaints at AGS Estado 2023:104, consulta, 18 May 1602, and CMC, 3ª epoca, 669.

32. Seco Serrano, "Prólogo," in Pérez Bustamante, *La España de Felipe III*, xvi.

33. IVDJ 82:408, Zúñiga to the duke of Sessa, 4 October 1601.

34. AGS Estado 634:9, consulta, 26 September 1601.

35. AGS Estado 2584:17, Villamediana to Philip, 17 March 1605: "Although these are points about which I have written at length, as Your Majesty will have seen by my letters, I will add to and speak again my opinions about this, with the good permission of Your Majesty, supplicating humbly that you pardon me this boldness without holding it against me, excusing it with the fact that I judge myself obliged as much by my conscience as by my honor to give you full account of how I understood and understand this, so that in the future none can put the blame on me."

36. Wernham, *The Making of Elizabethan Foreign Policy*, 3.

CHAPTER 1: *The Failure of the Habsburgs' "Bid for Mastery"*

1. The quotation is from Cabrera de Córdoba, *Felipe segundo*, 4:259. For a masterful synthesis of the international politics that followed the peace at Cateau-Cambrésis in 1559 between France and Spain, see Elliott's *Europe Divided, 1559–1598*. There exist no detailed monographs on the foreign policy aims of Philip II at the end of his reign, and scholars have generally concluded their examination of his policies with the failure of the Gran Armada in 1588; but see Parker, *Grand Strategy*, for a superb treatment of the strategic vision of the whole reign.

2. The royal *decretos*, or bankruptcy decrees, combined with the *remedios generales* (agreements with bankers) that normally followed them, were methods whereby Philip II restructured his debt, converting short-term, high-interest loans directly paid out of yearly crown income into long-term, low-interest bonds.

3. AGS Estado 2855, unfoliated, consulta, 13 November 1596.

4. Cf. Anderson, *Origins*, 193, who points out that Spanish military policy in this period was "remarkable, even heroic, and in part successful."

5. AGS Estado 2855, unfoliated, consulta, 13 November 1596.

6. Ibid., 15 March 1597.

7. As his secretary Mateo Vázquez had once affirmed: "The religious issue involved takes priority over everything" (IVDJ envio 45:452, Vázquez to Philip II, 5 February 1591, quoted in Parker, *Philip II,* 182). See also Parker, *Grand Strategy,* chap. 3.

8. AGS Estado 2224/1:201–2, Philip II to the duke of Sessa, 16 March 1597.

9. AGS Estado 2224/1:5, Philip II to the duke of Sessa, 16 March 1597. Philip, during his brief consortship in England, had considered the restoration of papal authority there to be one of his central policy aims. See especially Rodríguez-Salgado, *The Changing Face of Empire,* 94–100, 198–99.

10. AGS Estado 2224/1:5, Philip II to the duke of Sessa, 16 March 1597.

11. AGS Estado 2224/1:240–42, 1 April 1597. Semple (or Semphill) had been the Scottish commander of a company of mercenaries in Dutch service who, in 1582, betrayed the town of Lier to the Spanish. Thereafter he remained in Spanish service in Brussels, from where he repeatedly forwarded plans for an English invasion to the Council of State in Spain.

12. AGS Estado 2855, unfoliated, consulta, 9 July 1597. Joseph Creswell was the Jesuit priest in charge of the English Catholic College in Valladolid and in general promoted the interests of English Catholics in Spain. Fitzherbert had served as secretary for English letters to Catherine de Médici in the 1580s before entering Spanish service as an informant. In 1603 he went to Rome where he became a priest. For details of their lives and relationships with the Spanish court, see Loomie, *The Spanish Elizabethans,* 108–12, 182–229.

13. According to Henry Kamen, the 1596 armada had Ireland as its target only as a ruse, and it was in fact intended all along for Brittany (*Philip of Spain,* 308). In fact, however, both the 1596 and the 1597 armadas were originally intended to be used against the British Isles, either landing at the southern coast of Ireland or at Milford Haven in South Wales. In both cases Philip II changed his mind at the last minute, ordering the second armada to Brittany (where it would establish a launchpad for an invasion of England the following year) and the third to England, after originally ordering it to Brittany. For a detailed treatment of the armada preparations, see Tenace, "The Spanish Intervention in Brittany," 397–99, 416–24.

14. IVDJ Envio 114:2, Padilla to Philip II, October [1597]; AGS Estado 178, Philip to Padilla, 4 November 1597, quoted in Pierson, *Commander of the Armada,* 216.

15. AGS Estado 615:59, Albert to Philip II, 6 January 1598. For the Franco-Spanish conference and the Treaty of Vervins, see Imhof, *Der Friede von Vervins, 1598.* Charles Paget was an influential member of the English Catholic exiles on the Continent. He disagreed with Fathers Allen and Persons, leaders of the English Catholic exiles in Rome, over the best methods to promote the Catholic faith in England. While plotting against Elizabeth I, he also served as a spy for

her minister, Walsingham. In March 1588 he entered the service of Philip II and moved to Brussels but maintained contact with the English court. In 1599 he became the head of the "Scottish faction" among the English Catholics, favoring the succession of the Scottish king to the throne in opposition to Allen and Persons, who favored the succession of the Spanish infanta, Isabel Clara Eugenia (Stephen and Lee, *Dictionary of National Biography*, 15:46-49). For a detailed treatment of Anglo-Spanish negotiations, based primarily on English sources, in the years before and after the Treaty of Vervins, see Goodman, *Diplomatic Relations*. Despite Goodman's implication that it was Albert who made the first overtures to the English (p. 11), Albert explicitly states that such overtures had been made on the part of the English to Paget first, and it was not until then that Albert let his willingness be known (AGS Estado 615:59, Albert to Philip II, 6 January 1598).

    16. Goodman, *Diplomatic Relations*, 12.

    17. Ibid., 17-20.

    18. It is well known that, in perhaps his last appearance in the Privy Council, Burghley disagreed strongly with Essex over English policy toward Spain. Burghley opened by outlining the reasons why he favored peace, but Essex angrily countered that Spanish practices demanded a continuation of the war, whereupon Burghley reached for a Psalm book and in a dramatic moment of prophetic wisdom silently pointed to a verse that read: "Men of blood shall not live out halfe their dayes." His last gasp for peace having been delivered, Lord Burghley himself died soon afterward on 14 August 1598 (Camden, *The historie of . . . Elizabeth*, 126).

    19. *HMC Salisbury*, 8:13, George Gilpin to the Earl of Essex, 21 January 1598.

    20. Goodman, *Diplomatic Relations*, 21.

    21. By the terms of the Treaty of Nonsuch (20 August 1585), Elizabeth had promised the rebels generous military and financial assistance and an English governor-general. In return the Dutch handed over the ports of Flushing, Brill, and Ostend as "cautionaries" (sureties) until they had repaid Elizabeth's loans.

    22. On the effects of the Spanish embargoes against Dutch commerce, see Israel, *Dutch Primacy*, 39-79, and "Spain, the Spanish Embargoes, and the Struggle for the Mastery of World Trade."

    23. *CSP Venice*, 9:325-326, Francesco Contarini to the oge and Senate, 17 May 1598.

    24. Goodman, *Diplomatic Relations*, 15. There were other considerations motivating Elizabeth to continue aiding the rebels. The French peace with Spain had resurrected English fears of French power. A France at peace with England's enemy and with a newly Catholic king able to influence both the regime in the Spanish Netherlands as well as its former allies in the Northern Provinces posed a grave threat to England. Preventing a unified Netherlands, either as a Habsburg satellite or a French protectorate, was to be the aim of English foreign policy concerning the Low Countries for the next generation.

25. Klarwill, *The Fugger Newsletters*, 306; *HMC De L'Isle*, 2:353.

26. The Treaty of Vervins was signed on 2 May, and the signing of the *donación* of the Low Countries was made on the sixth.

27. Geyl, *Revolt of the Netherlands*, 240.

28. Document no. 1399, dated 6 May 1598, in Lefévre, *Correspondance de Philippe II sur les affaires des Pays-Bas*, 4:465. This secret clause was a direct violation of the terms of the archdukes' oath to uphold the *Edit perpétual*, according to which all foreign troops were to be withdrawn from the Netherlands. See Klingenstein, *The Great Infanta*, 95. This work is one of the few modern biographies of either of the archdukes; unfortunately it is more a romantic tale than a work of scholarship.

29. AGS Estado 2224/1:3, 8 May 1598: "El serenissimo Archiduque Alberto, conforme a su mucho valor, ha de procurar muy de veras la recuperacion o reducion de la parte de aquellos estados que esta desviada de la obediencia de la sancta sede apostolica romana y de su señor natural." In addition there were rumors at the time that Philip knew that the infanta Isabel was unable to conceive children and that the Low Countries would therefore revert back to the Spanish patrimony within a short time (Cabrera de Córdoba, *Felipe segundo*, 4:285).

30. See Matias de Novoa, *Historia de Felipe III*, 60:49. Moura's dismissal may have been due to the bad feelings stemming from an altercation that supposedly took place between him and the prince in 1596 over treating for peace with the French. The prince was indignant over Moura's support for the peace and publicly reprimanded him with the later support of his father. That the two continued to be at odds until the end of the reign is demonstrated by the dispute they had over the keys to the palace the day before Philip II died, Moura refusing to give them up when the prince asked for them (Danvila, *Don Cristóbal de Moura*, 755, 766). For details on Denia and the office of *valimiento*, see Williams, "El reinado de Felipe III"; and Feros, "El régimen de los validos," "Lerma y Olivares," and "The King's Favorite."

31. BN MS E54, fol. 36, letter from Juan de Silva, count of Portalegre, to secretary Esteban de Ibarra, October 1598, quoted in Danvila, *Don Cristóbal de Moura*, 766. Although Moura's treatment seems harsh, such attitudes were to some extent expected upon the accession of a new king. As the third duke of Alba had bitterly remarked in 1559 after Philip II took the throne, "Kings are prone to dislike their father's ministers" (*CSP Venice* 8:113, Michiel to the doge and Senate, 30 July 1559).

32. Williams, "Philip III," 754–55.

33. Ibid., 756–57.

34. Novoa, *Historia*, 56.

35. *HMC Salisbury*, 14:50, the Council of State of Hainault to the archduke Albert, 27 February 1598, emphasis mine.

36. AGS Estado K1460, Archduke Albert to Philip II, 12 August 1598.

37. Israel, *Dutch Primacy*, 56–57. In December, Thomas Edmondes, the English ambassador in Paris, wrote to Robert Sydney that "the late arrests, by the

young King of Spain, of ships of the Low Countries, breeds an opinion that he means some enterprise against us" (*HMC De L'Isle,* 2:357–58).

38. Federico Spínola was the youngest son of the Genoese financier Felipe Spínola, marquis of Sesto and Benafro. Educated at Salamanca in Spain, he soon took service with Alejandro Farnese in the Low Countries, where he conceived the idea of a fleet of galleys that would prey upon Dutch shipping. His exploits in Spanish service would, in 1602, compel his elder brother, Ambrosio, to volunteer to raise a tercio of infantry for the Army of Flanders (see Chapter 4).

39. AGS Estado 621, *Memoria de Federico Spínola,* n.d. Printed in Rodríguez Villa, *Ambrosio Spínola,* 121–28. Spínola petitioned the archduke for permission to raise the troops while the latter was en route to the court. The troops and artillery promised by Albert were not, in fact, provided and the project for the invasion never materialized (AGS Estado 2862, unfoliated, Albert to Philip III, 30 September 1599).

40. Cardinal Andrea explains in a letter dated 25 April 1599 that he entered into negotiations with England only after receiving the king's letter to the archduke Albert and decided to proceed since Albert had already departed for Spain (AGS Estado 616:11). Presumably Albert's letter asking for permission to treat with the English was answered positively—or at least ambiguously enough to permit this interpretation by the cardinal—by Philip III after his father's death. I have not located Philip III's letter to Albert.

41. AGS Estado 616:16, instructions from Cardinal Andrea to Jerome Coomans, 31 December 1598.

42. Attesting to the fact that the negotiation was not a secret to the court in Madrid is the letter of the Venetian ambassador there, Francesco Soranzo, who wrote on 9 December, twenty-two days before Coomans's instructions, that "the Cardinal of Austria is in a very secret treaty with the Queen of England to come to terms. They are desirous to avoid appearing more anxious for this peace than comports with the dignity of the Spanish Crown, and so the negotiations are carried on with the utmost secrecy, though I have had the opportunity to see an abstract of the Cardinal's letter" (*CSP Venice,* 9:350).

43. Williams, "Philip III," 758, and Cabrera de Córdoba, *Relaciones,* 7.

44. By foreign "policy" I mean an overarching and coherent framework within which all actions toward the northern European countries would be fitted. Military activity, while clearly a part of foreign affairs, does not, by itself, constitute a foreign policy.

45. Williams, "Philip III," 759.

46. Ibid. Chinchón's absence was no doubt due to his opposition to the king's traveling so far to meet his bride, which the count considered "indecorous to the Majesty of the king." Pérez-Bustamante, *La España de Felipe III,* 92.

47. The events described in the following paragraphs are derived primarily from the letters written by the Admiral of Aragón to Archduke Albert, printed in *CODOIN,* vols. 41–42, and from Watson and Thomson, *The History of the Reign of Philip the Third,* 1:15–52.

48. Francisco de Mendoza, third son of the marquis of Mondéjar, was born in 1547. In 1584 he married the daughter of the then Admiral of Aragón, Sancho de Cardona, and as a result took the arms and name of his father-in-law. With the latter's death soon afterward, Mendoza assumed the title of admiral. For details on his life and career, see Rodríguez Villa, "D. Francisco de Mendoza, Almirante de Aragón."

49. Roco de Campofrio, *España en Flandes*, 249.

50. Ibid., 259.

51. For the itinerary of the archduke's progress, see Faing, "Voyage de l'Archiduc Albert en Espagne en 1598."

52. *CODOIN*, 42:280, 286–87, 290–91, Albert to Denia, 3 December 1598, 14 and 30 January 1599.

53. Ibid., 294–95, Albert to Denia, 3 April 1599.

54. Ibid., 304–6, Albert to Denia, 3 June 1599.

55. *CSP Venice*, 9:348, Soranzo to the doge and Senate, 23 October 1598.

56. *CODOIN*, 42:305, Albert to Denia, 3 June 1599.

57. I have not been successful in locating the consulta, if indeed there was one, in which the appointment of an ambassador was discussed, nor have I found the instructions given to the ambassador. For the appointment, see the Royal Cedula dated 26 May 1599 in AGS CMC-3^a 669. That there were indeed instructions given to Zúñiga is confirmed by the Council of State's mention of them in their consulta for 2 May 1600 (AGS Estado 840). The Council of State's consultas concerning Flanders (during Philip III's reign), which are housed in the Simancas archive (Estado Flandes), begin only in 1600.

58. Martin and Parker, *The Spanish Armada*, 186, 215. On Zúñiga's later career, see, Elliott, *The Count-Duke of Olivares*.

59. AGS Estado 7038, Libro 381. "Elogio a Don Baltasar de Zuñiga Comendador mayor de Leon . . . de Antonio de Herrera." There is another copy in the Real Academia de Historia, N32, fol. 240.

60. Zúñiga's name is included in the list of those who accompanied Denia to greet the new queen (Cabrera de Córdoba, *Relaciones*, 14).

61. AGS CMC-3^a 669, royal cedula, 26 May 1599.

62. AGS Estado 2851, unfoliated, letter of Joseph Creswell to Philip III, 24 April 1599, quoted in Loomie, *The Spanish Elizabethans*, 195.

63. AGS Estado 2511:54, consulta, 15 June 1599. On the succession question and its place in Philip III's policy, see Loomie, "Philip III and the Stuart Succession."

64. Goodman, *Diplomatic Relations*, 28–31.

65. For an analysis of the incident of Saluzzo, its historical roots, and its impact on the Spanish Road, see Cano de Gardoqui, *La cuestión de Saluzzo*.

66. AGS Estado 616:8, letter of Archduke Albert to Philip III, 25 August 1599.

67. AGS Estado 616:177–78, Baltasar de Zúñiga to Philip III, 25 August 1599.

68. PRO SP 94/6:234, Philip III to Cardinal Andrea, 28 June 1599.

69. Cabrera de Córdoba, *Relaciones,* 35–36, 38; Pérez Bustamante, *La España de Felipe III,* 353.

70. The Irish leaders had been in constant contact with the Spanish court since at least as early as 1593. In 1594 the Spanish had unsuccessfully tried to send two vessels carrying men and money to aid the rebel cause. Spanish interest remained minimal, however, until the powerful Ulster chieftain Hugh O'Neill threw in his lot with the rebels. By the middle of 1595 a good portion of Ireland was in rebel hands and available as a landing site for a new Spanish armada. On the causes of the Irish rebellion and on the career of Tyrone, see Morgan, *Tyrone's Rebellion;* O Faolain, *The Great O'Neill;* and Walsh, *"Destruction by Peace."*

71. Elizabeth, condemning both the truce with Tyrone and his return, placed Essex under house arrest. He was released the following year but was banned from court (MacCaffrey, *Elizabeth I,* 418–30, 514–36; Black, *The Reign of Elizabeth,* 428–41). There were rumors that Elizabeth believed Essex was induced by the French king to make a hash of the Irish expedition in order to upset the ongoing negotiations with Spain (AGS Estado 616:5, Baltasar de Zúñiga to Philip III, 9 November 1599).

72. Goodman, *Diplomatic Relations,* 32–33.

73. AGS Estado 2224/1:300, Philip III to Baltasar de Zúñiga, 10 October 1599.

74. AGS Estado 2224/1:300, Philip III to Baltasar de Zúñiga, 10 December 1599.

75. Watson, *History,* 1:55. By January 1600 some twenty-five hundred troops were in mutiny (Parker, *Army of Flanders,* appendix J, 290–92).

CHAPTER 2: *Setbacks*

1. Parker, "War and Economic Change," fig. 4, 187.

2. *CSP Venice,* 9:354, Francesco Contarini to the doge and Senate, 5 January 1599.

3. *CODOIN,* 42:282–83, Archduke Albert to Denia, 6 December 1598; Klingenstein, *The Great Infanta,* 91. On 23 January 1599, a committee composed of the marquis of Denia, the marquis of Velada, and Juan de Idiáquez, estimated that the archdukes' return journey would cost four hundred thousand ducats (AGS Estado 616:197, *Relacion del dinero que parecio que de presente sera menester . . .*).

4. IVDJ Envio 82:383, Zúñiga to Sessa, 5 January 1600.

5. Ibid. Sessa, placed at the papal court, was Spain's mouthpiece in the Vatican. As such, it was his job to assure the pope that Philip and his ministers were doing all they could for the cause of the Catholic religion

6. IVDJ Envio 82:442, Sessa to Baltasar de Zúñiga, 23 January 1600.

7. PRO SP77/6:104–19, Thomas Edmondes's relation of his mission and reception at Brussels and in France.

8. Quoted in Goodman, *Diplomatic Relations,* 38.

9. Henry IV to Monsieur de Boissise, 11 March 1600, in Laffleur de Ker-

maingant, *L'ambassade de France en Angleterre sous Henri IV*, 2:122. Henry was obviously a much shrewder politician than Edmondes.

10. *HMC Salisbury*, 10:7, Captain Robert Ellyott to Sir Robert Cecil and the Lords of the Council, with enclosure, 23 January 1600.

11. AGS Estado 2023:122, consulta, 22 February 1600.

12. BN Mss. 6170:140, 29 February 1600. The instructions, no doubt drawn up by Philip's secretaries, are nevertheless in the first person and signed by the king; his influence on their contents is undoubtable. I have therefore chosen to represent them as being, indeed, *his* instructions. Zúñiga, besides being a friend to Carrillo, thought it would be good to have a legal expert on the scene. The English, however, thought his appointment hampered the chances of arriving at peace since Carrillo was "knowen to be no great Favourer of Peace, and with-all very haughty and peremptory, like a right Spaniard" (quoted in Goodman, *Diplomatic Relations*, 47).

13. These principles and their effects on Anglo-Spanish relations during Philip II's reign are detailed in Fernández Alvarez, "Felipe II e Isabel de Inglaterra."

14. AGS Estado 617:163, 15 February 1600; Goodman, *Diplomatic Relations*, 40–41.

15. *HMC Salisbury*, 9:93, [Sir R. Cecil?] to Mr. Nicholson, 11 April 1600; Goodman, *Diplomatic Relations*, 44–46.

16. AGS Estado 2023:24, consulta, 21 March 1600.

17. See Parker, "Making of Strategy," 132–35, for a development of this notion as it relates to Philip II.

18. AGS Estado 2023:24, consulta, 21 March 1600.

19. *CSP Venice*, 9:403, 408, 406–7, Francesco Soranzo to the doge and Senate, 8 April, 9 May, and 1 May 1600.

20. Ibid., 404, Francesco Soranzo to the doge and Senate, 13 April 1600. Enríquez de Acevedo, count of Fuentes, had succeeded the duke of Parma as governor of the Low Countries in 1593, where he had stressed the priority of Philip II's war with France over that of the war in the Low Countries.

21. *CODOIN*, 42:338n1.

22. Although Philip did, in fact, in April send Don Martín de la Cerda to Ireland with a thousand arquebuses and ammunition for O'Neill, telling O'Neill that an invasion fleet was being prepared and urging him to keep the rebellion going. For a detailed account of Spanish involvement in Ireland to 1602, see Silke, *Kinsale*.

23. *CSP Venice*, 9:418, Francesco Soranzo to the doge and Senate, 10 July 1600.

24. IVDJ Envio 82:387, Baltasar de Zúñiga to Sessa, 28 April 1600. *CODOIN*, 42:345, Albert to Lerma, 27 May 1600. On the 1600 meeting of the States-General of the obedient provinces, see Gachard, *Actes*.

25. BL *Cotton MSS., Vespasian*, 108, fols. 379–83. "Instructions for our right

trustie and welbeloved servantes, Henry Neville [et al.] . . . appointed by us to
treate with the commissioners from the Kinge of Spaine, and Archdukes of Burgundy for the purposes following." Epitome of the instructions, circa 13 May
1600, printed in *HMC Salisbury,* 9:145–46. For a detailed discussion of the peace
talks in Boulogne, see Hamy, "Conférence pour la paix," which includes some
original documents.

26. AGS Estado 840:72, Baltasar de Zúñiga to Philip III, 13 June 1600. The
English complained that the powers granted by Philip were not as great as those
granted by Elizabeth, since the former's were stamped only with his Privy Seal
and not with his Great Seal. Furthermore there did not seem sufficient power of
delegation nor an assurance that Philip would agree to the conclusions reached
by his appointees as there had been at Vervins. The Spanish replied that the king
did not have a Great Seal since he did not distinguish between a "Privy" and a
"Great" Seal and that there was a clause in the instructions specifically giving the
commissioners power to do what the king would do had he been present (AGS
Estado 2511:20, consulta, 4 July 1600; Goodman, *Diplomatic Relations,* 51–52).

27. MacCaffrey, *Elizabeth I,* 292.

28. One of the aims of the Spanish invasion of Brittany and Normandy in
the 1590s had been to secure good deepwater ports that could harbor Spanish
fleets sailing up the Channel and also provide a base for attacks on England. As
early as 1593, Federico Spínola, a Genoese mercenary, had proposed a scheme
for using Mediterranean galleys in this fashion, but Philip II would not grant
him the commission. Philip III had finally granted Spínola a license to sail galleys into the Channel in 1598. Those in Dunkirk were apparently operating on
their own initiative. By 1601 the English House of Commons was claiming that
Flemish privateers had done more damage to English commerce than the French
navy had done in the whole of the sixteenth century (Stradling, *The Armada of
Flanders,* 11).

29. *HMC De L'Isle,* 2:340–45, Sir William Browne to Sir Robert Sydney,
21 April 1598.

30. Tex, *Oldenbarnevelt,* 1:284–86.

31. Ibid., 1:287; *HMC De L'Isle,* 2:460, George Gilpin to Sir Robert Sydney,
20 May 1600.

32. Tex, *Oldenbarnevelt,* 1:287; *HMC Salisbury* 10:186, Lord Grey to Robert
Cecil, 28 June 1600; ibid., 178–79, Lord Grey to Robert Cecil, 21 June 1600.

33. *HMC Salisbury,* 10:178–79, Lord Grey to Sir Robert Cecil, from Ram-
mikins, 21 June 1600. Robert Dudley, earl of Leicester, had been the English
appointed governor-general of the Netherlands from 1585 to 1588.

34. [Orlers], *The Triumphs of Nassau,* 270–71.

35. The Admiral of Aragón's own account of the battle is quite different. According to him, he was having remarkable successes until he was forced to go to
the aid of the hard-pressed archduke. It was while he was engaged in this operation that the cavalry broke ranks, being leaderless. Afterward Mendoza fought a

rearguard action with two hundred cavalry while the archduke retreated off the field (Admiral of Aragón to Philip III, describing his services, 7 October 1603, in Rodríguez Villa, "Francisco de Mendoza," 525–26).

36. [Orlers], *Triumphs of Nassau*, 279. The exact figures are unknown. According to Mendoza, who saw a burial list in the hands of Maurice, the Dutch buried some eighty-five hundred men in the following days. Of these, two thousand were Spanish. Adding those who had died in the previous day's actions, the admiral estimated Spanish casualties to be twenty-two hundred (Rodríguez Villa, "Francisco de Mendoza," 527).

37. *HMC Salisbury*, 10:197–99, Lord Grey to Sir Robert Cecil, 5 July 1600. This had not been unexpected by some. On 5 July Rowland White wrote to Sir Robert Sydney from the English court that "because here is no newes come from the army since your last from Ostend, yt is feard lest the Prince will quaile in the greatnes of his enterprise and return with the victory of some poore fortes; but [keep] this to yourself" (*HMC De L'Isle*, 2:470–71).

38. *CSP Venice*, 9:419, Soranzo to the doge and Senate, 1600 July 10,

39. AGS Estado 2511:20, consulta, 4 July 1600.

40. Sir Robert Cecil to Sir George Carew, 8 September 1600 in Maclean, *Letters*, 18–23.

41. AGS Estado 2511:2, consulta, 23 July 1600.

42. Ibid. Philip did finally agree to promote the infanta's claim to the English throne on 2 September 1600 (AGS Estado 2511, fol 38, consulta, 2 September 1600).

43. AGS Estado 2511:2, consulta, 23 July 1600. For similar comments by Philip II, see Serrano, *Correspondencia diplomática*, 1:316–17, Philip II to Luis Requeséns, 12 August 1566.

44. *CODOIN*, 42:353, Albert to Lerma, 13 July 1600.

45. On 22 May the Cortes of Castile had tentatively granted the king a *servicio de millones* of eighteen million ducats over six years to be drawn from taxes on wine, vinegar, oil, etc. (*ACC*, 19:673–743).

46. AGS Estado 2023:123, consulta, 4 July 1600; AGS Estado 2023:124, consulta, 20 July 1600.

47. AGS Estado 2511:7, consulta, 29 July 1600; AGS Estado 2023:28, consulta in reply to the king's comments on the previous consulta, 5 July 1600, with a *Relacion de lo que sera menester para el despacho de los mil y quinientos soldados que an de passar a Flandes* and a *Relacion de los navios, armas, municiones, bastimientos que seran menester para las diez mil personas que se han de embarcar*.

48. Novoa, *Historia*, 153.

49. AGS Estado 2023:26, consulta, 1 August 1600.

50. AGS Estado 2023:40, consulta, 13 August 1600. Fernando González, in his dissertation on the high command of the Army of Flanders, argues that it was the attempt during Philip III's reign to put the nobility back into the high command that seriously weakened the effectiveness of that army ("The Road to Rocroi," 45–61). But in placing the blame for the deterioration of the army on

the shoulders of the Spanish leaders, he underestimates the Spanish ministers' attempts to effect thorough reforms in the military. The real culprit was Archduke Albert, who in his capacity as captain-general of the Army of Flanders, consistently refused to implement the reforms proposed by the Spanish court.

51. Gachard, *Actes,* cx–cxiii, 553–70.

52. IVDJ Envio 82:389, Zúñiga to Sessa, 19 July 1600.

53. AGS Estado 2223:139, consulta, 22 June 1600.

54. Gachard, *Actes,* xciii–xcviii, 772–82.

55. Tex, *Oldenbarnevelt,* 1:295.

56. Grimeston, *Generall Historie,* 1253–54; Gachard, *Actes,* xciii–xcviii, 772–82. Grimeston's work is probably a translation or adaptation of the *Nederlandsche Historien* by Emanuel van Meteren, a Dutch merchant who lived in London at the time and whose completed history was printed in the eighteenth century, *Historie van de Oorlogen en Geschiedenissen der Nederlanden,* 10 vols. (Gorcum, 1748–63). On Grimeston's career see Clark, "Edward Grimeston, Translator."

57. AGS Estado 2511:22, consulta, 9 September 1600. "The Islands," or in Spanish "Las Islas," was a common name for the seven provinces of the northern Netherlands that were made up of numerous small islands formed by the sea and the innumerable rivers running through the territory.

58. AGS Estado 2907, "Poderes al Serrinisimo Archiduque Alberto para tratar de paz con los vezinos de las Islas de Olanda y Gelanda, Frisa, Utreque y otros lugares que no estan a obediencia. Con facultad de sostituyr. Dupplicado," 25 September 1600.

59. It will be remembered that Albert had given up Calais to the French, and later he would be willing to have all Spanish troops withdrawn from the Low Countries, a move that represented a serious threat to Spanish power and prestige in the region.

60. On 18 August Zúñiga had written to Sessa of his fears concerning the issue of Saluzzo and its impact on affairs in Flanders: "There are rumors here that the war for Saluzzo has broken out. A great disruption it would be for things here at this point, and it would hinder the passage of men that is so hoped for and so necessary" (IVDJ Envio 82:392).

61. AGS Estado 2511:13, consulta, 13 September 1600; AGS Estado 2023:15, consulta, 17 October 1600. For a modern discussion of factions in wartime government and how it affects the outcome of wars, see Iklé, *Every War Must End,* 59–105.

62. IVDJ Envio 82:444a, Sessa to Baltasar de Zúñiga, 28 September 1600. Cf. similar comments by Martín de Padilla to Philip II, quoted in Kamen, *Philip of Spain,* 307–8.

CHAPTER 3: *Strategic Overstretch*

1. Cabrera de Córdoba reports that on 5 September, after a hard ride from Valladolid the day before, Philip held an emergency meeting of the full Council

of State in his presence (remarkable in itself) specifically to discuss the French king's attack against the duke of Savoy (*Relaciones*, 81). For the background to the Saluzzo dispute, see Chapter 2, this vol.

2. See the discussions of these issues in Cano de Gardoqui, *La cuestión de Saluzzo*, 95–96; "España y los estados italianos"; and "Saboya en la política del Duque de Lerma."

3. For the Spanish Road and its role in the troop movements of the monarchy, see chaps. 2 and 3 of Parker, *Army of Flanders.*

4. *CSP Venice*, 9:424, Francesco Soranzo to the doge and Senate, 28 September 1600. In fact, Henry was sure that given the disaster at Nieuwpoort and the subsequent failure of the Anglo-Spanish negotiations, Philip would find it impossible to throw his weight behind both the archduke and the duke of Savoy and would thus choose to support the archduke (letter of Henry IV, 14 July 1600, quoted in Cano de Gardoqui, *La cuestión de Saluzzo*, 113n193).

5. *CSP Venice*, 9:426, Francesco Soranzo to the doge and Senate, 11 October 1600.

6. AGS Estado 2023:7, consulta, 19 November 1600. This idea of "arming for peace" was a constant theme of the peace strategy pursued by the Habsburgs. As early as 1598 the States of Hainult had told Albert that to put an end to the war "nothing is more necessary than that your highness should use all pressure with his Majesty to get a notable provision of money, so as to astonish the enemy and preserve order among your people. *Peace moreover is never made with more honour and advantage than when a people is well armed*" (*HMC Salisbury*, 14:51, 27 February 1598; my emphasis).

7. AGS Estado 2023:8, consulta, 29 November 1600; AGS Estado 2023:5, consulta, 19 December 1600. The Spanish did not stop Dutch salt smuggling until November 1605, when a fleet commanded by Luis Fajardo surprised Dutch ships in Araya, eventually executing more than four hundred sailors. For Dutch activity in the Caribbean and its effects on Spanish strategy, see Sluiter, "Dutch-Spanish Rivalry," and Hussey, "America in European Diplomacy." A plan to attack the North Sea fishing fleets had been proposed in 1599 by the Biscayan Juan de Guana (AGS Estado 616:181, 24 September 1599). These fisheries would be the subject of Spanish designs for the next forty years; Olivares would refer to them as the Dutch "Indies" to suggest their similarity to that weak area of the Spanish monarchy (quoted in Loomie, "Spanish Faction at the Court of Charles I," 38).

8. AGS Estado 2023:3, consulta, 19 December 1600.

9. *CSP Venice*, 9:470, Marin Cavalli to the doge and Senate, 30 August 1601.

10. IVDJ Envio 82:394, Baltasar de Zúñiga to Sessa, 16 December 1600.

11. *CSP Venice*, 9:437, Francesco Soranzo to the doge and Senate, 16 December 1600; Modesto Ulloa, *La hacienda real*, 695, table 1.

12. *CODOIN*, 42:383, Albert to Lerma, 12 January 1601. Finally, on 1 January 1601, the Cortes officially conceded a servicio of eighteen million ducats. Having granted such an extraordinary sum, however, the delegates then had to

persuade their towns to pay it, which proved to be more difficult than imagined. See also Chapter 2, n. 45

13. Cano de Gardoqui, *La cuestión de Saluzzo,* 139. For a thorough discussion of the place of Milan in the strategy of Philip III, see Fernández Albaladejo, "De 'llave de Italia' a 'corazón de la Monarquía,'" 185–237.

14. AGS Estado K1451:16, consulta, 29 August 1600, quoted in Cano, *La cuestión de Saluzzo,* 144n96.

15. AGS Estado 1897:32, consulta, 16 October 1600, quoted in Cano, *La cuestión de Saluzzo,* 162n160.

16. The French ambassador, Antoine de Silly, count of Rochepot, had arrived in Valladolid at the end of July with the intention of securing Philip III's ratification. For Rochepot's mission, see Laffleur de Kermaingant, *Lettres de Henri IV au comte de la Rochepot.*

17. Cano, *La cuestión de Saluzzo,* 113. By January the Milanese army had some 16,500 troops, 4,000 cavalry, and 12 artillery pieces and were expecting an additional 6,000 infantry from Germany and another 6,000 from Naples (Cano, *La cuestión de Saluzzo,* 193; AGS Estado 1290:8, Fuentes to Philip III, 13 January 1601).

18. *CSP Venice,* 9:440, Francesco Soranzo to the doge and Senate, 20 January 1601; IVDJ Envio 82:398, Baltasar de Zúñiga to Sessa, 24 February 1601. The Treaty of Lyon was signed on 17 January 1601. For details of the treaty and its repercussions, see Parker, *Army of Flanders,* 68–74, and Geisendorf, "Le Traité de Lyon et le pont de Grésin."

19. AGS Estado 2023:3, consulta, 19 December 1600. For the struggle over the succession and English Catholic intrigues during the opening years of the seventeenth century, see Hume, *Treason and Plot,* and Loomie, "Philip III and the Stuart Succession in England, 1600–1603."

20. AGS Estado 2511:56, consulta, 13 January 1601. The Spanish, however, thought that long-range policy aims dictated that the Low Countries be given back to Philip once the archdukes took power in England, "because if those two powers should be united and over time fall subject to someone ambitious and restless, he would have the potential to injure these kingdoms and put the Indies in danger. And although this should not be feared of the archdukes themselves, there is no insurance against those that might follow them." The fact that the Low Countries were to revert to the Spanish crown after the succession was to be withheld from the archdukes until it could be determined how the issue would be resolved (AGS Estado 2023:62, consulta, 10 July 1601).

21. AGS Estado 2023:63, consulta, 10 March 1601; *CSP Venice,* 9:448, Soranzo to the doge and Senate, 15 March 1601; IVDJ Envio 82:399, Baltasar de Zúñiga to Sessa, 10 March 1601. Essex had been released from his house arrest (see Chap. 2, this vol.) by Elizabeth in the spring of 1600. In the autumn, in a demonstration of his continued disfavor, Elizabeth denied him the renewal of his monopoly on the importation of sweet wines. It was a rebuke that neither

Essex's sensitive ego nor pocket could withstand. He began to plot against the Cecil faction (which he believed responsible) and planned to seize possession of the court and bring pressure to bear on the queen. The Privy Council, however, was alerted to the plan and summoned Essex to answer charges. Essex was forced into action. On 18 February he and a band of two hundred armed followers dashed into London with cries of treason, hoping to rouse the populace to revolt. The attempt failed and Essex was captured. Brought up on charges of high treason, he was sentenced to death on 1 March and executed shortly after. See MacCaffrey, *Elizabeth 1*, 418–30, 514–36; and Black, *The Reign of Elizabeth*, 428–41.

22. AGS Estado 2023:61, consulta, 10 March 1601.

23. AGS Estado 2023:110, consulta, 22 April 1601.

24. IVDJ Envio 82:401, Baltasar de Zúñiga to Sessa, 26 May 1601.

25. Isabel Clara Eugenia, *Correspondencia de la Infanta Archiduqesa*, 37, Isabel to Lerma, 12 May 1601.

26. IVDJ Envio 82:402, Baltasar de Zúñiga to Sessa, 2 June 1601 (my emphasis). The Levant enterprise was actually an attack on the city of Algiers. Having decided to put an end once and for all to the continuous Muslim corsair attacks on the coasts of the western Mediterranean, Philip ordered the Genoese captain Gian Andrea Doria to lead a fleet of seventy galleys carrying ten thousand men against the fortified capital city of Algeria. See Rodríguez Joulia Saint-Cyr, *Felipe III y el Rey de Cuco*, 35–40.

27. Don Alvaro de Bazán, the marquis de Santa Cruz, had suggested a similar invasion plan in 1586, in which, although not specified, the southern coast of Ireland may have been the target. His plan was rejected in favor of the duke of Parma's. Previous to this, in 1580, Philip II had sent a small force to Smerwick on the western coast of Ireland to aid a rebel insurgency and await a general uprising. The small army was defeated by combined English naval and land forces (Martin and Parker, *The Spanish Armada*, 90–91, 111–14). On the face of it an invasion of Ireland had much to commend it: it could be invaded directly from Spain using winds from the southwest; English relief efforts might have to wait five weeks for favorable winds from the east; and the populace was sympathetic toward Spain (Falls, "España e Irlanda"). An old English proverb had it that "He who would England win; In Ireland must begin [Qui Angliam vincere vellet; ab Ybernia incipere debet]" (quoted in Froude, *The Reign of Elizabeth*, 4:4).

28. AGS Estado 840, consulta, 9 February 1601, and summary of the estimated cost and details for the expedition to Ireland in *CSP Spanish*, 4:684–85. This sum does not include the cost for upkeep and provisioning of the fleet that would carry the men, estimated to be an additional 197,000 ducats, nor does it cover the costs for the fitting out of Spínola's expedition (AGS Estado 621, consulta, 21 February, 1601).

29. Rodríguez Villa, *Spínola*, 25–27. Spínola's instructions, agreed upon in council two months earlier, were to disembark in England, where he was to

"seize one, two, or more ports and fortify them, from there to prosecute the war and cause offense and damage to the Queen, and to all the heretics and enemies in that kingdom who are disobedient and rebel against the Sacred Apostolic See, and receive beneath His Majesty's protection the faithful and Catholic Christians, and favor and protect them from the oppression and tyranny with which the Queen and her ministers violently force them to follow their schismatic and superstitious sects" (AGS Estado 621, consulta, 21 February 1601, quoted in Rodríguez Villa, Spínola, 30).

30. Silke, Kinsale, 93.

31. Rodríguez Villa, Spínola, 27–28.

32. AGS Estado 2023:48, consulta, 2 June 1601.

33. Rodríguez Villa, Spínola, 28.

34. Isabel Clara Eugenia, Correspondencia, 39, letter of 5 June 1601.

35. CODOIN, 42:402, Albert to Lerma, 21 June 1601. Don Rodrigo Niño y Lasso had served in Flanders under the duke of Parma in the 1580s and 1590s and later under Albert. In 1598–99 he accompanied Albert to Spain and then back to Flanders, where he served as captain of a company of Albert's bodyguard. Albert was to use him on two more such missions to Spain to raise money, in 1603 and 1604. In 1609 he was created count of Añover and served as Philip III's interim ambassador in Brussels until 1611.

36. AGS Estado 2023:42, consulta, 18 August 1601.

37. CSP Venice, 9:456–57, Francesco Soranzo to the doge and Senate, 27 April 1601; Cabrera de Córdoba, Relaciones, 100–101, 105, 110.

38. CSP Venice, 9:466–67, letter to the doge and Senate, 15 July 1601.

39. CODOIN, 42:401, Albert to Lerma, 15 June 1601.

40. MacCaffrey, Elizabeth 1, 293–94.

41. The siege of Ostend, which lasted almost twelve hundred days, is one of the longest in recorded history. There is no modern account apart from the now dated work by Henrard, Histoire du siège d'Ostende, and Belleroche's short, anecdotal account, "The Siege of Ostend." For contemporary accounts of the siege, see Grimeston, True Historie, and Haestens, La Nouvelle Troye.

42. Letter from Sir William Brown to Sir Robert Sydney, 10 July 1601, in Arthur Collins, Letters and Memorials of State, 2:225–26. Sir Robert Sydney was the English governor in Flushing (but resident most of the period in England). and Sir William Brown his deputy commander in charge of the English garrison in the town. The correspondence of Sir Robert Sidney is calendared in HMC De L'Isle, vols. 2–4, but because of the considerable overlap with Collins's work and the difference in editorial policies, the two must be used in conjunction.

43. HMC Salisbury, 11:316 and 335, letters from Captain R. Wigmore to Sir Robert Cecil, 12 and 21 August 1601. The English gunners were even taking advantage of the night to fire long-burning "flare" mortars into the Spanish trenches, which they would then use to sight their regular cannons.

44. HMC Salisbury, 11:358, Captain R. Wigmore to Sir Robert Cecil, 3 Sep-

tember 1601. Nevertheless, despite the assessments of most concerning the strength of the fort and Albert's lack of ability, Cecil, displaying a keener grasp of the resources of the powers involved, was not optimistic about Ostend's chances (ibid., 11:354, letter to the archbishop of Canterbury and Lord Chief Justice Popham, 31 August 1601).

45. The Flemish were then paying upwards of one hundred thousand florins per month to garrison and maintain the eighteen forts with which they had surrounded Ostend in an effort to mitigate the presence of the enemy in their territory (Grimeston, *Generall Historie*, 1266).

46. *HMC Salisbury*, 11:284, Captain J. Holcroft to Sir Robert Cecil, 22 July 1601.

47. Grimeston, *Generall Historie*, 1267.

48. IVDJ Envio 82:403, Baltasar de Zúñiga to Sessa, 27 July 1601; "This situation goes well, thank God, even though . . . not as fast as would be desired; but in the end we expect to succeed in our intention" (*CODOIN*, 42:403, Albert to Lerma, 9 August 1601).

49. *CSP Venice*, 9:472, Marin Cavalli, ambassador in Paris, to the doge and Senate, 30 August 1601; *HMC Salisbury*, 11:336, Captain R. Wigmore to Sir Robert Cecil, 21 August 1601.

50. *CSP Venice*, 9:472, Marin Cavalli to the doge and Senate, 3 September 1601; Cabrera de Córdoba, *Relaciones*, 112, 116; AGS Estado K-1426, A37:22, consulta, 4 August 1601.

51. *HMC Salisbury*, 14:207–8, Sir Robert Cecil to the Master of Gray, 2 March 1602.

52. *HMC Salisbury*, 11:376–77, the Lord Admiral and Sir Robert Cecil to Monsieur Noel de Caron, 12 September 1601; *CSP Venice*, 9:474, Marin Cavalli to the doge and Senate, 4 October 1601.

53. AGS Estado 634:9, consulta of the junta, 26 September 1601.

54. Cabrera de Córdoba wrote in January 1601 that plans were being considered concerning the formation of a special junta similar to the junta de noche that Philip II had used to expedite the business of the councils (*Relaciones*, 93). Although a junta of the Council of State did begin to operate that year, Philip III never granted it the quasi-official status that its predecessor had achieved, and its membership fluctuated. See Román Román, "Origen y evolución de la Secretaría de Estado," 98–102.

55. AGS Estado 634:9, consulta of the junta, 26 September 1601.

56. This was true for the early years of Parma's governorship, but for the period 1585–89 the average subsidy had been over three million ducats per year (3,135,645 escudos). See Parker, *Army of Flanders*, appendix K, 293.

57. AGS Estado 634:9, consulta of the junta, 26 September 1601. The recommendation of the marquis of Poza may have been in order to remove him from court, where he was at odds with Gaspar de Córdoba because of the latter's interference in matters pertaining to the Council of Finance. In February 1602, Poza, because of either mismanagement or the problems with Córdoba, was fired from

his position. See Sepúlveda, *Sucesos,* 129:38, and Cabrera de Córdoba, *Relaciones,* 132, 140.

58. AGS Estado 634:10, consulta of the junta, 9 September 1601.

59. Silke, *Kinsale,* 104–110.

60. *CSP Spain,* 4:690, the Adelantado to Philip III, 10 December 1601; Silke, *Kinsale,* 105;

61. One informant told Cecil that the Spanish forces "want victuals, but are full of money and wealth. They give already three pounds for a cow, two pieces of eight for a mutton, and four reales for a hen" (*HMC Salisbury,* 11:429, enclosure with a letter from Sir Francis Goldolphin to Cecil, 10 October 1601). On the quality of the English forces see *HMC Salisbury,* 11:xviii.

62. Silke, *Kinsale,* 110–23.

63. Ibid., 117. See also Morgan, "Hugh O'Neill."

64. IVDJ Envio 82:405, Zúñiga to Sessa, 9 August 1601; AGS Estado 2023: 109, consulta, 17 November 1601; *CSP Venice,* 9:480, Ottavio Bon and Francesco Soranzo to the doge and Senate, 17 November 1601; IVDJ Envio 82:412, Sessa to Zúñiga, 8 September 1601; *CSP Venice,* 9:477–478, Marin Cavalli to the doge and Senate, 12 November 1601; IVDJ Envio 82:413, Sessa to Zúñiga, 1 December 1601. On the correspondence between James and the papacy, see J. Duncan Mackie, "A Secret Agent of James VI."

65. *HMC Salisbury,* 14:187–88, Sir Robert Cecil to the Master of Gray, 17 October 1601.

66. Rodríguez Joulia Saint-Cyr, *Felipe III y el Rey de Cuco,* 35–40; Braudel, *The Mediterranean,* 1232–34.

67. Grimeston, *Generall Historie,* 1275–76; *HMC Salisbury,* 11:534–35, a spy in the Spanish camp at Ostend, 10 January 1602.

68. Mountjoy had finally been able to invest the entire town on 4 December after receiving three thousand reinforcements from England. On 5 December the half of Mountjoy's army that had been sent to stop O'Neill's advance returned and added an additional two thousand men to the besiegers.

CHAPTER 4: *"Driblets like Sips of Broth"*

1. AGS Estado 840, the Adelantado to Philip III, 10 December 1601, in *CSP Spain,* 4:690–91. The Adelantado had been reduced to the post of Captain-General of the Galleys of Spain—a prestigious position, though it carried fewer responsibilities than he had held previously—after the failure of the 1599 armada.

2. AGS Estado 840, consulta, end of December 1601, in *CSP Spain,* 4:695–99.

3. AGS Estado, 840, the Adelantado to Philip III, 10 December 1601.

4. AGS Estado 840, consulta, 29 January 1602, in *CSP Spain,* 4:701–2. This suggestion attests to their keen understanding of the ramifications of success and failure in foreign affairs since, as they had anticipated, in early January Elizabeth's Privy Council ordered the English fleet to proceed to the Spanish coast

to prevent reinforcements from being sent to Kinsale and to put the Spanish on the defensive (Maclean, *Letters*, 103, 106); however, the fleet did not leave until February.

5. *CSP Domestic*, 9:244, September 1602.

6. AGS Estado 634:12, consulta of the junta of two, 25 January 1602.

7. AGS Estado 2023:91, "Discurso al Conde de Solre." In February the council looked at still another plan to achieve naval superiority, this time involving twenty galleys carrying three thousand men and twenty warships with the same number which were to plague the seaward islands and port towns of Holland and Zeeland. They enthusiastically gave their approval and Philip ordered them to look into how they might increase the number of galleys in Spínola's service (AGS Estado 2023:76, consulta, 14 February 1602).

8. Grimeston, *Generall Historie*, 1277.

9. *CODOIN*, 42:413, Albert to Lerma, 19 January 1602; IVDJ 82:416, Baltasar de Zúñiga to the duke of Sessa, 31 January 1602; AGS Estado 2023:101, consulta, 18 February 1602.

10. AGS Estado 620:27, Baltasar de Zúñiga to Philip III, 20 January 1602; AGS Estado 620:248 and 620:61, letters from Hernando Carrillo and the archduke Albert to Philip III, 20 January 1602. The noble in question was the duke of Bouillon, who was married to the sister of Maurice of Nassau.

11. AGS Estado 2023:101, consulta, 18 February 1602; AGS Estado 2224/2:281, Philip III to Baltasar de Zúñiga, 13 Mar 1602. The dates here are a fine example of the dilatory nature of Spanish policy making. The difference between the date of Zúñiga's letter to the court and his receipt of their reply was over ninety days!

12. AGS Estado 2023:77, consulta regarding Zúñiga's letter of 6 March, 1 April 1602.

13. *HMC Salisbury*, 14:207–9, Sir Robert Cecil to the Master of Gray, 2 March 1602; *CSP Domestic*, 9:151–52, instructions to Sir Richard Leveson, admiral of the fleet against Spain, 26 February 1602. Once there, following what R. B. Wernham calls the "final maturing of Elizabethan naval strategy," the fleet was supposed to establish a full-time blockade by patrolling the coastal and sea lanes, taking whatever opportunities were offered to inflict damage on Spanish shipping and troop movements, and remaining on station until the return of the Spanish silver fleet (Maclean, *Letters*, 103, 106; Wernham, *Return*, 393–94).

14. Cabrera de Córdoba, *Relaciones*, 137; *CSP Venice*, 9:498, Ottaviano Bon and Simon Contarini to the doge and Senate, 21 March 1602.

15. AGS Estado 2023:77, consulta, 1 April 1602; *HMC Salisbury*, 12:33, Sir Robert Cecil to George Nicholson, 7 February 1602; *HMC Salisbury*, 12:86, Thomas Edmondes's memorandum on the Treaty of Boulogne, 28 March 1602.

16. *CODOIN*, 42:420, Albert to Lerma, 21 April 1602; Rodríguez Villa, *Spínola*, 50. While Albert blamed Fuentes for the delay, it was actually a result of the French destruction of the Pont de Grésin, the bridge over the Rhône, which had been left to the duke of Savoy as part of the settlement with France

in the Treaty of Lyons and which was used by the reinforcements destined for Flanders (Parker, *Army of Flanders,* 69). The reason for the bridge's destruction was French suspicion of Spanish involvement in the conspiracy of Charles, marshal of Biron. Biron was the provincial governor in Burgundy and a favorite of Henry IV, who had become disillusioned with the king and, during the war with Savoy, had conspired to assassinate him. By May 1602 he was gathering disaffected nobles about him, and Henry finally arrested and executed him. For details of the conspiracy, see Zeller, "La conspiration du maréchal de Biron," and Cano de Gardoqui, *La conspiración de Biron.*

17. Tex, *Oldenbarnevelt,* 318.

18. AGS Estado 2023:104, consulta, 18 May 1602.

19. AGS Estado 2023:97, consulta, 1 April 1602.

20. AGS Estado 2023:104, consulta, 18 May 1602.

21. Ibid.

22. That James would be a dangerous opponent was certainly not a mistaken judgment on the part of the Spanish ministers. Throughout the 1580s and even as late as 1596 he had been actively trying to construct a grand Protestant alliance with the northern powers. There were even attempts to unite the other Catholic powers against Spain. See Mackie, "A Secret Agent of James VI."

23. AGS Estado 2023:104; AGS Estado 2511:57, consulta, 18 May 1602; AGS Estado 2224:246, Philip III to Zúñiga, 8 June 1602. In August the two hundred thousand ducats for Zúñiga had still not been sent. Eventually the council decided that negotiating with James VI would be harmful to Philip's reputation unless James first requested assistance or discussion from Philip, in which case Philip could bargain his assistance for James's promise of obedience to the Catholic (AGS Estado 2023:72, 17 August 1602).

24. AGS 2224, Philip III to Baltasar de Zúñiga, 11 June 1602, quoted in Rodríguez Villa, *Spínola,* 51; AGS Estado 2224, Philip III to Archduke Albert, 11 June 1602, quoted in Rodríguez Villa, *Spínola,* 52. On 13 May the council had looked at an every more grandiose plan for an invasion of England from the Adelantado of Castile. He wanted to unite some fourteen thousand additional troops with Spínola's fourteen thousand, all of whom would then cross the Channel in a fleet of fifty galleys under his command. He thought that Flanders would provide everything necessary and that he would need only an additional two million ducats for a reserve. Naturally the council had to point out that it was virtually impossible for them to come up with either the men or such extraordinary sums, and they showed little trust in the Spínola brothers' promises (AGS Estado 840, consulta, 13 May 1602, in *CSP Spain,* 4:713–15).

25. Grimeston, *Generall Historie,* 1278–79; Charles Dalton, *Life and Times,* 1:87. Dalton's *Life* contains the letters of Sir Edward Cecil (nephew of the secretary of state, Sir Robert Cecil) covering the years 1572–1637. Cecil was part of the eight-thousand-man English contingent of Maurice's army. The admiral, it will be remembered, had been held prisoner by the Dutch since the Battle of Nieuwpoort. In the interval he had been engaged in lengthy negotiations for his

release, finally obtaining it after twenty-three months of imprisonment, a ransom payment of over seventy-five thousand florins, and a Spanish agreement to exchange Dutch prisoners held in Spain. His release had come just twenty-five days before this campaign (Rodríguez Villa, "Francisco de Mendoza," 527–29, 595–99).

26. Letter from Edward Cecil to Sir Robert Cecil, 19 July 1602, in Dalton, *Life,* 1:89–92. Grave was an important river crossing that was well worth taking because it was on the south—"Spanish"—side of the Maas. The quotation is by Buzanval, the French envoy to the States, on the occasion of a visit to the site of Grave; quoted in Motley, *History,* 4:97.

27. *CODOIN,* 42:111–14, 121–26, the Admiral of Aragón to Albert, 10 and 12 July 1602; Rodríguez Villa, "Francisco de Mendoza," 529. The quotation is by Novoa, *Historia,* 194.

28. AGS Estado 2224, Philip III to Spínola, 9 July 1602, quoted in Rodríguez Villa, *Spínola,* 54; AGS Estado 620, Philip III to Zúñiga, 4 September 1602, printed in Rodríguez Villa, *Spínola,* 59n1 (emphasis mine). Toward the end of July, the archduke even told Philip that such exigencies meant that he could not guarantee he would not use Federico's forces, although he would try to keep them separate unless it was absolutely necessary (AGS Estado 2023:72, consulta, 17 August 1602).

29. *CSP Venice,* 9:503, Marin Cavalli to the doge and Senate, 20 May 1602.

30. Cabrera de Córdoba, *Relaciones,* 140; *HMC Salisbury,* 12:183–85, Sir Richard Leveson to "Right Honorable" [Sir Robert Cecil], 15 June 1602. The Saõ Valentin's cargo, however, when sold brought almost forty thousand pounds to the English treasury, an amount equivalent to the cost of the queen's navy for a whole year! (My thanks to Geoffrey Parker for this information.)

31. *CSP Domestic,* 9:220, "Instructions given to Sir Wm. Monson . . . ," 19 July 1602; Wernham, *Return,* 398.

32. Letter from Sir Robert Cecil to Carew, 17 August 1602 (Maclean, *Letters,* 121).

33. Letter from Sir William Browne to Sir Robert Sidney, 22 August 1602; quoted in Dalton, *Life,* 1:93.

34. Letter from Sir Robert Drury to Sir Robert Cecil, 7 August 1602 (*HMC Salisbury,* 12:259; my emphasis).

35. AGS Estado 2288:2, Zúñiga to Philip III, 18 July 1602.

36. AGS Estado 2023:72, consulta, 17 August 1602. In June, Philip had promised to provide the needed money "even if it meant pledging and selling [his] own jewels" (AGS Estado 2224, Philip III to Zúñiga, 11 June 1602, quoted in *ACC,* 20:v–vi).

37. AGS Estado 2023:72, consulta, 17 August 1602; AGS Estado 620:131–32, Philip III to Baltasar de Zúñiga with enclosed "Poder a don Baltasar de Çuñiga para la suspension de armas con rebeldes," 10 September 1602.

38. *CODOIN,* 42:427–32, Albert to Lerma, 23 September 1602; AGS Es-

tado 2023:45, consulta, 28 September 1602; Grimeston, *Generall Historie*, 1280–81; AGS Estado 620:139, Baltasar de Zúñiga to Philip III, 29 September 1602.

39. *CODOIN*, 42:427–30, Albert to Lerma, 23 September 1602. He received seven hundred thousand ducats.

40. Grimeston, *Generall Historie*, 1282–84, 1289. Letter of Edward Cecil to Sir Robert Cecil, 24 September 1602, printed in Dalton, *Life*, 1:95. Frangipani's correspondence during the years he spent as nuncio in Flanders has been published; see Essen, *Correspondance d'Ottavio Mirto Frangipani*.

41. AGS Estado 2023:45, consulta, 28 September 1602.

42. Cabrera de Córdoba, *Relaciones*, 148; *ACC*, 20:575–97, disputes and voting on 31 October 1602.

43. *ACC* 20:587. For the Adelantado's similar remark, see the epigraph to this chapter.

44. On the fiscal problems of Castile and their effects on domestic policy, see Fortea Pérez, "Reino y Cortes," and Jago, "Taxation and Political Culture in Castile, 1590–1640."

45. Grimeston, *Generall Historie*, 1290–92; *CSP Domestic*, 9:243, [blank] to Lord [blank], 7 October 1602; *CSP Venice* 9, Marin Cavalli to the doge and Senate, 21 October 1602.

46. Spanish arms were suffering setbacks not only in the north but in the Mediterranean theater as well. On 8 November the fleet that had been sent against Algiers in October returned without effecting anything after merely hearing that the enemy was entrenched and waiting for them (Cabrera de Córdoba, *Relaciones*, 158–59).

47. AGS Estado 2023:70, consulta, 22 October 1602.

48. Jorge Basta was born in 1550 and later went to Flanders to fight in Farnese's army. By 1580 he had risen to the post of General of the Cavalry. Afterward he went to France and then to Transylvania to fight in Emperor Rudolf's war against the Turks. In 1606 he published *Il Maestro di Campo Generale* in Venice. He died, count of Huste, in Vienna in 1607. He had been proposed for the second-in-command position by the archduke in April 1602, but the council thought him too rough a man to be given the position of mayordomo mayor and the responsibility of civil administration in the event of Albert's death. In any event he refused to leave the emperor's service, claiming his wife wanted him to stay in Germany (AGS Estado 2023:104, consulta, 18 May 1602; AGS Estado 2023:72, consulta, 17 August 1602).

49. Albert to Lerma, 22 November 1602, *CODOIN*, 42:vol. 42, 432–34.

50. AGS Estado 2023:126, *Sobre el remedio general de Flandes*. The date of the actual consulta is 26 November 1602, but it is made clear that the decisions the members reached were the result of a conference in which each member presented his opinions, beginning with the Constable of Castile. The count of Chinchon's opinion paper (AGS Estado 621:43) is dated 20 November 1602, suggesting that this was the starting date of the conference, or at least their con-

sideration of the matter. Present in this session of the Council of State were the constable; Juan de Idiáquez, the *comendador mayor* of León; the count of Chinchón; the count of Miranda; the marquis of Velada; the marquis of Poza; Friar Gaspar de Córdoba; and the count of Olivares. Lerma, noticeably, is absent from this list.

51. A similar proposal had been offered to Philip II in 1574 but had been rejected as inhumane. See Parker, *Grand Strategy*, 136–38.

52. In 1600 the army was composed of some seven thousand Spaniards, seven thousand Germans, and three thousand Italians, plus an additional fifty-five hundred foreign troops of various nationalities (Gachard, *Actes*, xli). Since then only four thousand *Spanish* reinforcements had been sent to Flanders (Parker, *Army of Flanders*, 278).

53. Although there is no date for the king's decisions, he himself stated that he had taken "these days" to think about the matters, and a consulta by the Council of State on 12 December suggests that he had still not taken a decision regarding the "remedio general" (AGS Estado 2023:75).

54. To provide such sums the king was rumored to be negotiating a loan of twelve million ducats from his financiers (Cabrera de Córdoba, *Relaciones*, 158).

55. And in fact in January of the following year not only was the number of members in the Council of Finance increased, but new personnel were added in every section of the finance hierarchy (Cabrera de Córdoba, *Relaciones*, 164). The previous month (16 October) Philip had ordered that the Consejo de Hacienda (Council of the Treasury and the Contaduría Major (Accounts Department be united into a single body to alleviate the bottleneck in the flow of money caused by their separate financial functions (Danvila y Collado, *El poder civil*, 2:573–74).

56. Pedro Ernesto, count of Mansfelt, had been the interim captain-general in the Netherlands between December 1592 and February 1594 (Parker, *Army of Flanders*, 281). Later Philip agreed to the council's recommendation that Basta be tricked into returning to the king's service by telling him that he needed to attend to the problems of his estate (AGS Estado 2023:60, consulta, 18 January 1603).

57. The Admiral of Aragón, who had held this post, was ordered back to Spain after his failure to prevent the capture of Grave. Upon arriving in Burgos, in northern Spain, he was humiliatingly banished to his estates and ordered not to come within ten leagues of the court (*CODOIN*, 42:449, note). The news of this treatment was not well received in Flanders (IVDJ 82:439, Baltasar de Zúñiga to the duke of Sessa, 8 March 1603).

58. For Philip II's rhetoric in 1574, see Parker, "[The Laws of War in] Early Modern Europe," 46–47. The words used by both rulers are strikingly similar.

CHAPTER 5: *The English Succession and the Hope for a Settlement*

1. AGS Estado 2023:75, consulta, 12 December 1602.

2. Ibid. Baltasar de Zúñiga, upon learning of this, wrote to Sessa that, while

it was a good sum of money (seven million over three years), still more would be needed if they wished to wage the war suitably (IVDJ 82:424, 3 January 1603). The letters of credit for the two hundred thousand ducats arrived on 20 January, and the archduke wrote thankfully to Lerma, for, as he said, he knew that the duke was responsible for procuring the money for Flanders (*CODOIN*, 42:441, 20 January 1603).

3. AGS 840, Report of the Council of State on the memorial from Friar Florence Conroy, 13 January 1603, *CSP Spain*, 4:719. Immediately after the defeat at Kinsale in January 1602, Hugh O'Donnell had set out for Spain on a mission to request further aid for the rebellion. Once in Spain he had been successful at convincing Philip to begin assembling a new Spanish expedition. O'Neill, meanwhile, had retreated to northern Ireland and continued to beat off the English forces hounding him. By August, however, it had become clear to him that he could expect no help from Spain that year; the Spanish had been unable to put together a fleet in time to send it before the autumn storms. Hugh O'Donnell, who had been overseeing the preparations in La Coruña, decided to return once again to the court to plead for immediate help but died en route in the castle of Simancas, outside Valladolid. O'Neill's plight was now serious. While he continued to write to Spain requesting either more assistance or ships to take him and his followers to Spain, he began making peace overtures to the English. Not until 17 February 1603, however, did Elizabeth write to Mountjoy allowing him to begin negotiations. On 30 March 1603 (o.s.), O'Neill, unaware that the queen had died six days earlier, humbly submitted to Mountjoy in Mellifont, henceforward promising loyalty and obedience to the queen and her laws. Shortly afterward the new king, James, confirmed the settlement (Walsh, *"Destruction by Peace,"* 13–28; Wernham, *Return*, 398–406).

4. AGS Estado 2511:88, consulta, 1 February 1603, printed in *CSP Spain*, 4:720–29 but without Philip's reply.

5. Although outwardly Elizabeth was in excellent health as late as 13 February, when the newly appointed Venetian secretary wrote that she was "in perfect possession of all her senses" and that everyone believed "her life is much further from its close than is reported elsewhere" (*CSP Venice*, 9:529), within a couple of weeks she had once again fallen into a deep melancholy, and the bitterly cold winter of that year began to take its toll (Neale, *Queen Elizabeth*, 389).

6. AGS Estado 2023:119, consulta, 13 February 1603. The figures for the garrisons represent only Spain's contribution; the archduke was responsible for providing the approximately 10,500 remaining garrison troops.

7. Ibid.

8. Ibid.

9. The archduke may indeed have extracted such sums from his subjects, but according to a relación presented to the council on 25 February, only two thirds of this money actually reached the army (889,447 ducats for the previous year; AGS Estado 634:65, 25 February 1603). In a report given to Andrés de Prada by the count of Solre on 4 December 1604, it was estimated that the

provinces of the Spanish Netherlands would need to provide 118,704 escudos per month for the 10,485 garrison troops that were their responsibility. By comparison the Spanish court would need to spend 403,300 escudos per month to maintain 41,950 soldiers (a field army of 25,000 plus additional garrisons). Effectively Philip III was expected to be paying four-fifths of the total war costs (AGS Estado 2868, unfoliated, *Relacion general del gasto necessario del exercito y de las guarniciones*). The paymaster general, Gabriel de Santisteban, estimated that the crown had already paid out no less than 3,734,339 escudos between 2 April and 30 November 1602 (AGS Estado 2023:116, consulta, 18 February 1603); it must be pointed out, however, that Santisteban was recalled in disgrace in 1603 and charged with fraud, and his figures should not, therefore, be considered definitive (Parker, *Army of Flanders,* 283). Spínola later figured that 120,000 of the 200,000 ducats sent monthly from Spain were used just at Ostend. This effectively left the archduke with only 80,000 ducats per month with which to fund the remaining field army (Spínola to Philip III, 7 October 1603, printed in Rodríguez Villa, *Spínola,* 67–70).

10. Meanwhile in Flanders there were already rumors that the Dutch were making "great levies of troops" and were preparing to begin campaigning as soon as the weather improved. Zúñiga feared that they would enjoy a tremendous success since the archduke's forces were so reduced (IVDJ 82:436, Baltasar de Zúñiga to Sessa, 28 February 1603).

11. AGS Estado 2023:86, Royal Cédula, 27 February 1603; AGS Estado 622:295, draft of the cédula, signed by Philip III and annotated "Reduzion del comercio con los estados de flandes, yslas de olanda, zelanda y con los subditos de los Principes y Republicas amigos y neutrales." The edict was popularly called the "Placard of Juan de Guana" after its supposed inspirer. Because it applied equally to French trade, Henry IV, on 5 November 1603 (o.s.), published his counterdecree, which imposed a 30 percent duty on Spanish Habsburg goods entering France and on all French goods for sale in Spanish territories. Four months later, in February 1604, Henry broke off all commercial relations with Spain and the Spanish territories (*HMC De L'Isle,* 3:76n1).

12. AGS Estado 2224/2:448, 449, Philip III to Baltasar de Zúñiga and to Archduke Albert, 27 February 1603. For documents concerning the effect of these actions on trade between France and the Low Countries, see Sturler, "Documents diplomatiques."

13. *HMC Salisbury,* 14:256–57, Richardot to Hurtado, 2 March 1603.

14. Ibid.

15. AGS Estado 2511:64, consulta, 2 March 1603, printed in *CSP Spain,* 4:729–37, but without Philip III's comments.

16. Ibid., 734. It is clear from their desire to use the pope to broker with the French over a candidate that Philip and his ministers were unaware that the pope was engaged in ongoing negotiations with James VI for the latter to convert to Catholicism in order to win his support. The pope would probably not have been willing to help the Spanish when there was still hope that a Catholic

could be put on the English throne without their help (Mackie, "A Secret Agent of James VI," 385–86).

17. *CSP Spain*, 4:735.

18. Both Federico and Ambrosio Spínola were busy levying new troops in Flanders, Germany, and Italy for the invasion force (Rodríguez Villa, *Spínola*, 60–61).

19. *CSP Spain*, 4:739–41, Joseph Creswell to Lerma and Philip III, 18 March 1603 and undated.

20. AGS Estado 2557:1, consulta, 21 April 1603. For a detailed treatment of Spanish policy regarding the succession, paying special attention to the Catholic angle, see Loomie, "Philip III and the Stuart Succession."

21. The military preparations that could be undertaken given the Spaniards' current financial situation had recently been thoroughly discussed in a session of the full Council of War.

22. *CODOIN*, 42:446, Albert to Lerma, 19 March 1603.

23. AGS Estado 2023:38, consulta, 8 April 1603.

24. Ibid.

25. See Montpleinchamp, *Histoire de l'Archiduc Albert*, 307–8n2.

26. Osuna remained, however, in service in Flanders until 1608, when he returned to the court. From 1611 to 1616 he was viceroy of Sicily and in 1616 was made viceroy of Naples, where he gained notoriety for advocating a staunch Spanish foreign policy independent of the court in Madrid. He was recalled in 1620 and died in disgrace in 1624.

27. Grimeston, *Generall Historie*, 1298; *CODOIN*, 42:446, Albert to Lerma, 19 March 1603. On the general collapse of discipline within the Army of Flanders during this period, see González de León, "The Road to Rocroi," 36–87.

28. Isabel Clara Eugenia, *Correspondencia*, 83, Isabel to Lerma, 16 April 1603.

29. *CSP Venice*, 10:5, Marin Cavalli to the doge and Senate, 14 April 1603.

30. Tex, *Oldenbarnevelt*, 1:326–27; Motley, *History*, 4:147–48.

31. Grimeston, *Generall Historie*, 1295; *HMC De L'Isle*, 3:16, Sir William Browne to Sir Robert Sydney, 14 April 160; Collins, *Memorials*, 2:269–70, Sir William Browne to Sir Robert Sydney, 16 April 1603.

32. *HMC Salisbury*, 15:38–40, the Lords of the Council to King James, 18 April 1603.

33. There exists only one monograph concerning the foreign policy of James immediately after his accession to the English throne: Lee, *James I and Henri IV.* For James's relations with the Habsburgs, however, there are a number of articles that merit attention. See in particular Cuvelier, "Les préliminaires du traité de Londres," based on state papers in the Belgian archives; Mackie, "James VI and I and the Peace with Spain, 1604," showing that James's policies were less the result of personal pacifism than the logical outcome of Elizabethan policies; Loomie, *Toleration and Diplomacy* and "Sir Robert Cecil and the Spanish Embassy"; and Adams, "Spain or the Netherlands?" In addition there are two excellent articles

concerning the effect of American issues on Anglo-Dutch-Spanish diplomacy: Hussey, "America in European Diplomacy," and Andrews, "Caribbean Rivalry and the Anglo-Spanish Peace of 1604."

34. In Oldys and Birch, *Works*, 8:299–316. For details concerning the presentation of the manuscript to James I, see Thompson, *Sir Walter Ralegh*, 189–90; and Lacy, *Sir Walter Ralegh*, 283.

35. Ralegh, "A Discourse Touching a War with Spain," in Oldys and Birch, *Works*, 8:309–10.

36. Mackie, "A Loyall Subiectes Advertisment," 1–2, 7. Some of the Howards were, however, heavily involved in the navy and privateering, e.g., Lord Thomas Howard and Charles Howard, lord of Effingham. See especially Wernham, *The Return*. There were additional critiques of James's foreign policy in circulation, both in England and abroad. See, e.g., John Askham's discourse against the peace, BL, Harleian MSS. 35, C.18; and Dominici Baudi, "Oratio . . . ad potentisimum Britanniarum Regem Iacobum I, Fidei defensorem, de non ineundo foedere cum Hispano."

37. The date 24 April was the one-month anniversary of James's accession. Although all the letters of marque had technically lapsed at Elizabeth's death, the cessation of hostilities was made official by proclamation on 23 June (o.s.), and those found committing acts of hostility after 24 April (o.s.) were to be treated as pirates and to have all their goods and property confiscated. *CSP Venice*, 10:14, 37, Simon Contarini to the doge and Senate, 1 and 24 May 1603.

38. Cuvelier, "Les préliminaires," 283; AGS Estado 2511:90, consulta, 31 May 1603; Grimeston, *Generall Historie*, 1298; *HMC Salisbury*, 15:73, Archduke Albert to King James, 14 May 1603; *CODOIN*, 42:447–50, Albert to Lerma, 16 April 1603.

39. AGS Estado 2511:93, consulta, 29 April 1603.

40. Churton, *Gongora*, 1:150–51. It had been Raymond de Tassis who had informed Philip II of the attempted flight of his son Carlos (Prescott, *History of the Reign of Philip the Second*, 2:486). Juan de Tassis is not to be confused with his uncle Juan Baptista (or Bautista) de Tassis, then ambassador to France, nor with his son Juan de Tassis Peralba, second count of Villamediana, the famous poet.

41. Allen, *Post and Courier Service*, 30. For the route from Brussels to Burgos (via Paris), for example, a distance of over three hundred leagues, the Tassis contracted to deliver mail within seventeen days, with an extra day allowed for winter travel.

42. It could not have hindered his appointment that he also had the favor of Lerma. In 1595, during Lerma's viceroyalty in Valencia (meant to isolate him from the court), Tassis had been instrumental in helping him maintain close contact with Prince Philip (Pérez Bustamante, *Felipe III*, 90). Along with his father, Juan de Tassis had also been among the thirty-six gentlemen to accompany Lerma on the initial journey to the eastern kingdoms in 1599 (Cabrera de Córdoba, *Relaciones*, 14).

43. Philip was disturbed by the conflicting reports he had been receiving

from various members of the Brussels court and in January had ordered Zúñiga to return to court and give a trustworthy account (AGS Estado 2023:60, consulta, 18 January 1603). Zúñiga would not return to his post. In August 1603 Philip appointed him ambassador to Henry IV in France, where he served until 1607 before being sent in May 1608 to Prague as ambassador to the emperor.

44. BN MS 2347:70–77, "Instruccion que el Rey nuestro Señor Don Phelipe 3° dio a Don Juan de Tassis su Correo mayor, quando su Magistad le embio por embajador de Inglaterra: año de 1603: Instruccion secreta," 29 April 1603. Later Philip sent word that Tassis should not take time out to discuss this with the archdukes but rather proceed immediately with his mission to England (AGS Estado 2571:20, Philip III to Juan de Tassis, 5 May 1603). On the importance of the election of the king of Romans to the international relations of this period, see Gindely, *Rudolf II und seine Zeit*.

45. BN MS 2347:70–77.

46. Tassis took the latter to heart. During his almost two years in England he spent nearly half a million ducats on bribes to English ministers and courtiers, plus another thirty-three thousand to facilitate various persons entering and exiting the British realms (AGS CMC 2ª 42, "Memoria de lo que yo Don Juan de Tassis Conde de Villamediana he gastado por quenta del Rey Nuestro señor en la jornada que por su Real Orden y mandado hize al Reyno de Inglaterra [Gastos secretos]," 15 May 1607. His secret expenses amounted to 702,982 ducats.

47. A checklist of the letters given to Tassis by the king is at AGS Estado 2571:16, dated 3 May 1603. As Pérez Bustamante points out, Tassis was not an official ambassador and therefore carried no credentials other than as agent of Philip III to congratulate James on his accession (Pérez Bustamante, *La España de Felipe III*, 357).

CHAPTER 6: *The Policy of Rapprochement*

1. BN MS 2577; Sepúlveda, *Sucesos*, 128:180. On the attribution of the epigraph to the duke of Alba, see Sir Charles Cornwallis's statement that "an old Saying and *Wish* of the Duke of *Alva (that* Spaine *might have Peace with* England, *and then would not care though they had Warrs with all the World,)* hath nowe gotten *the Force and Reputation of a generall Rule and Maxime amongst them;* and soe settled, that I think it will not leave them; which moves my Lord to beleeve, that plainly and faithfully they intend to use all Meanes to conserve and increase their Amitie with *England*" ("Private instructions delivered [by Sir Charles Cornwallis] to Mr. Hawkesworth for his business in England [1605]," in Sawyer, *Memorials of Affairs of State*, 2:168–69. The version I have translated comes from Castro, *Felipe III*, 97.

2. *CSP Venice*, 10:17–18, Giovanni Scaramelli to the doge and Senate, 1 May 1603.

3. *CSP Venice*, 10:20, Scaramelli to the doge and Senate, 8 May 1603.

4. The count of Basigny, son of Lord Boxtel, had written to the United

Provinces for a passport to come in person to present an offer on behalf of the States of Brabant. The Dutch urged Basigny to put his commission in writing so that they might consider it. As was to be expected, however, these approaches never developed into a real dialogue, Basigny continuing to request permission to bring his commission in person, and the States-General just as stubbornly refusing his request (ibid., 10:21; Grimeston, *Generall Historie,* 1298).

5. Quoted in Motley, *History,* 4:169n75.

6. *CSP Venice,* 10:38, Marin Cavalli to the doge and Senate, 25 May 1603.

7. *HMC Salisbury,* 15:77, Sir Anthony Shirley to the king, 19 May 1603. For details concerning the extraordinary life and adventures of Sir Anthony Sherley during this period, see Davies, *Elizabethans Errant,* esp. chaps. 8 and 10.

8. *CSP Venice,* 10:107, Scaramelli to the doge and Senate, 22 October 1603.

9. AGS Estado 2511:90, consulta, 31 May 1603; Cuvelier, "Les préliminaires," 284; Grimeston, *Generall Historie,* 1297. The Dutch in Flushing, upon hearing about James's attitude in these preliminary audiences, staged a riot against the English garrison fearing that James intended to side with the archduke. The riot itself, of course, did nothing to ease English feelings of ill will toward the Dutch (*HMC De L'Isle,* 3:30, Sir William Browne to Lord Sydney; Collins, *Letters and Memorials,* 2:273, Sir William Browne to Sir Robert Sydney).

10. Grimeston, *Generall Historie,* 1296. There is some dispute over the date of the engagement, and I have found no contemporary source that gives a specific date, other than Grimeston (who says the event occurred on 27 May). I have chosen here to accept the date given by Rodríguez Villa.

11. *CSP Venice,* 10:43-45, Scaramelli to the doge and Senate, 4 June 1603; *CSP Venice,* 10:50, Scaramelli to the doge and Senate, 12 June 1603.

12. AGS Estado 2511:90, consulta, 31 May 1603.

13. Tex, *Oldenbarnevelt,* 1:329; *CSP Venice,* 10:49, Scaramelli to the doge and Senate, 12 June 1603; AGS Estado 840:257, copy of the council that the Dutch gave to the king of England on 12 June 1603.

14. Cuvelier, "Les préliminaires," 285. Neither Béthune nor the French (he brought with him ninety gentlemen and three hundred servants) were welcomed by all the English. On Béthune's passage across the Channel, the commander of the English escort fleet fired across the bow of his ship to let the French know that the English had precedence in those waters (Motley, *History,* 4:154; *CSP Venice,* 10:54, Scaramelli to the doge and Senate, 26 June 1603).

15. *CSP Venice,* 10:54-56, Scaramelli to the doge and Senate, 26 June 1603; Tex, *Oldenbarnevelt,* 1:331-32.

16. Among other provisions, the treaty stipulated that the parties pledged mutual military assistance in the event of Habsburg attack (Motley, *History,* 4:178-80).

17. Tex, *Oldenbarnevelt,* 1:333; Larkin and Hughes, *Stuart Royal Proclamations,* 1:30; *CSP Venice,* 10:66, Scaramelli to the doge and Senate, 17 July 1603; *CSP Venice,* 10:67, Scaramelli to the doge and Senate, 23 July 1603.

18. Juan de Tassis arrived in Paris on 7 June and in Brussels at the end of

June (*CSP Venice,* 10:51, Cavalli to the doge and Senate, 16 June 1603; *CODOIN,* 42:459, Albert to Lerma, 3 July 1603).

19. AGS Estado 2511:79, consulta, 22 July 1603.

20. AGS Estado 2557:2, consulta, 26 July 1603. Regarding Robert Taylor's negotiations, see Cuvelier, "Les préliminaires," 487–89, and Loomie, *Toleration and Diplomacy,* 17–22.

21. AGS Estado 2557:2, consulta, 26 July 1603.

22. *CODOIN,* 42:460–62, Albert to Lerma, 12 July 1603.

23. AGS Estado 2557:2, consulta, 26 July 1603, Philip's remarks. He sent Tassis letters of credit for an additional one hundred thousand ducats to be used for bribes and four hundred thousand to buy the cautionary towns in James's possession (AGS Estado 2557:4, instructions from Philip to Juan de Tassis, 23 August 1603).

24. AGS Estado 2023:53, consulta, 26 July 1603; Parker, *Army of Flanders,* 189; *HMC De L'Isle,* 3:38–39, Nicolas de Blocq to Sir William Browne, 3 July 1603; Collins, *Letters and Memorials,* 2:274, Sir William Browne to Robert Sydney, 10 July 1603. The rivers may have been easy to cross because of low water levels due to one of the hottest and driest summers in memory (Isabel Clara Eugenia, *Correspondencia,* 84–85, Isabel to Lerma, 1 June 1603).

25. Collins, *Letters and Memorials,* 2:271, Sir William Browne to Lord Sydney, 17 May 1603; *HMC De L'Isle,* 3:43, and Collins, *Letters and Memorials,* 2:276, Sir William Browne to Lord Sydney, 28 July 1603.

26. *HMC De L'Isle,* 3:43, and Collins, *Letters and Memorials,* 2:276, Sir William Browne to Lord Sydney, 28 July 1603. Soon afterward, however, Pompeo Targone, a Roman military engineer in the Spanish employ, invented new floating and wheeled batteries to bombard the fort, thus rekindling Albert's optimism (*HMC De L'Isle,* 3:45, Sir William Browne to Lord Sydney, 17 August 1603; *CSP Venice,* 10:69, Anzolo Badoer [new Venetian ambassador in France] to the doge and Senate, 25 July 1603; and esp. Motley, *History,* 4:184–85). Collins, *Letters and Memorials,* 2:277, Sir William Browne to Lord Sydney, 10 August 1603; Collins, *Letters and Memorials,* 2:278, and *HMC De L'Isle,* 3:49, under letter of 10 August 1603 (o.s.), Edward Vere to Sir William Browne, 14 August 1603; *HMC De L'Isle,* 3:49, Sir William Browne to Lord Sydney, 27 August 1603.

27. AGS Estado 2511:76, consulta, 21 August 1604. William Watson, a Catholic priest, and a fellow priest named Clarke had planned to kidnap James and force him to change his ministers and policies. James had earlier promised Watson that he would extend religious toleration to the Catholics once he assumed the throne. When he did not keep his promise, Watson and Clarke planned to seize him at Greenwich on 24 June 1603 and hold him until he declared toleration. The plot was revealed by Jesuits. It soon became linked to what George Brooke, one of the conspirators, called the "Main Plot," which involved Henry Brooke, Lord Cobham and (allegedly) Sir Walter Ralegh in a conspiracy to put Arabella Stuart on the throne using money provided (unwittingly) by the count of Aremberg. Watson, Clarke, and Brooke, along with Ralegh and Cob-

ham, were arrested on charges of high treason. All were found guilty. Watson and Clarke were disemboweled and castrated. George Brooke, brother-in-law to Cecil, lost his head to the axe. At the last minute Cobham's and Ralegh's sentences were commuted to imprisonment in the Tower of London. Ralegh, unjustly convicted in a manner reminiscent of Stalin's show trials of the 1930s, was to remain there for the next thirteen years—in reality for daring to oppose Cecil and for promoting the cause of war (Akrigg, *Jacobean Pageant*, 38-47; Cuvelier, "Les préliminaires," 491-96).

28. Sawyer, *Memorials*, 2:1, James I to the States-General, 10 August 1603; *CSP Venice*, 10:82-84, Scaramelli to the doge and Senate, 20 August 1603; *HMC Salisbury*, 15:237-38; *CSP Venice*, 10:82-84, 85-87, Scaramelli to the doge and Senate, 20 and 27 August 1603.

29. AGS CMC 2ª Epoca:42, unfoliated, *Memoria de lo que yo Don Juan de Tassis, Conde de Villamediana he rezebido para los gastos . . . [Gasto de correos y otras cossas]*, 15 May 1607.

30. *HMC Salisbury*, 15:243-44, 245-46, Lord Cecil to Sir James Elphinstone, secretary of state for Scotland, 12 September 1603, and Sir Lewis Lewkenor to Lord Cecil, 16 September 1603.

31. *HMC Salisbury*, 15:243-44, Lord Cecil to Sir James Elphinstone, secretary of state for Scotland, 12 September 1603; *HMC De L'Isle*, 3:55-56, Sir William Browne to Lord Sydney, 8 September 1603 (two letters).

32. AGS Estado 622, Albert to Philip III, 29 September 1603, printed in Rodríguez Villa, *Spínola*, 66-67; *CODOIN*, 42:463-64, Albert to Lerma, 28 September 1603; Parker, *Army of Flanders*, 249. Spínola hoped to finish off the siege quickly so that he would have in his hands the artillery and veterans that had been lacking in the army's endeavors in previous years (AGS Estado 622, Spínola to Philip III, 7 October 1603, printed in Rodríguez Villa, *Spínola*, 67-70). The agreement called for Spínola to take over direct payment of the expenses for the siege in return for letters of credit for 720,000 escudos, the cost of the siege for six months. Philip, however, was unable to fulfill the terms of the contract and told Spínola that he would have to take the repayment out of the ordinary provisions for Flanders, "since to send more from here is impossible and it is enough just to continue the provisions that are sent to Flanders" (AGS Estado 2023:91, consulta, 2 November 1603).

33. *HMC De L'Isle*, 3:66-67, 67-68, Sir William Brown to Lord Sydney, 14 and 16 October 1603; Motley, *History*, 4:181-84; Montpleinchamp, *Histoire de l'Archduc Albert*, 334.

34. Sir Thomas Edmonds to the Earl of Shrewsbury, 21 September 1603, in Lodge, *Illustrations*, 3:21; *CSP Venice*, 10:96-97, Scaramelli to the doge and Senate, 28 September 1603.

35. Lodge, *Illustrations*, 3:39-41, The earl of Worcester to the earl of Shrewsbury, 4 October 1603; AGS Estado 2557:8, consulta, 8 November 1603.

36. AGS Estado 840:253, *Copia de la platica que el Conde de Villamediana hizo al*

rey de ynglaterra en la audiençia secreta; AGS Estado 840:254, *Repuesta que El Rey de Inglaterra dio a voca a Don Juan de Tassis en la audiençia secreta de ocho de ottubre 1603;* AGS Estado 2557:8, consulta, 8 November 1603.

37. AGS Estado 2557:8, consulta, 8 November 1603.

38. Cabrera de Córdoba, *Relaciones,* 174, 190. In February the council had finally selected the constable as the person to go to Flanders to watch over things, to which he had humbly replied that "in the appointment of general for Flanders the Council has today rendered me more honor than I am due; I think the passion of colleagues has blinded them" (AGS Estado 634:43, constable to His Excellency [Lerma?], 18 February 1603).

39. AGS Estado 2557:8, consulta, 8 November 1603; AGS Estado 2557:7, Philip to Villamediana, 30 November 1603. The constable had actually already departed from Valladolid on 31 October accompanied by Baltasar de Zúñiga, who had been appointed as ambassador to France to replace Juan Baptista de Tassis. He arrived in Brussels two months later. Presumably the full powers were sent to him en route. See the *Relacion de la jornada que hizo á Inglaterra el Constable de Castilla . . . ,* printed in *CODOIN,* 71:467–94. For bibliographic and historical details concerning this and other manuscript reports of the constable's journey, consult Ramirez de Villa Urrutia, "La jornada del condestable de Castilla á Inglaterra para las paces de 1604."

40. Collins, *Letters and Memorials,* 2:280–81, Sir William Browne to Lord Sydney, 26 October 1603; *CODOIN,* 42:464–65, Albert to Lerma, 14 November 1603; *HMC De L'Isle,* 3:73–75, Sir William Browne to Lord Sydney, 10, 12, and 18 November 1603. Browne reported that Albert had put some five thousand troops into the town. On 16 September Nicolas de Blocq, the Dutch agent for the English in Flushing, had written to Sir William Browne concerning the face-off between the two leaders and how it would be determined. "Whichever is stronger," he said, "will compel the retirement of the other and will carry off the prize. It is a new fashion of besieging towns" (*HMC De L'Isle,* 3:58).

41. *CODOIN,* 42:467–69, Albert to Lerma, 5 January 1604; *HMC De L'Isle,* 3:80–81, Nicholas de Blocq to Lord Sydney, 18 December 1603; *HMC De L'Isle,* 3:81–82, Sir William Brown to Lord Sydney, discussing captured letters between Aremberg and Villamediana, 26 December 1603.

42. AGS Estado 842:84, note to Villamediana from a confidant, 14 November 1603; AGS Estado 842:138, *avisos* (news) from England, 28 December 1603.

43. AGS Estado 2511:73, consulta, 8 November 1603. Even today, however, relations between states depend in large part upon the personal relationships between leaders; one has only to think of the rapport that developed between Ronald Reagan and Mikhail Gorbechev, which was responsible in large measure for the peaceful end of the Cold War.

44. Villamediana's problems, according to Thomas Edmondes, stemmed from the fact that he had not paid all his bills to vendors. When he tried to leave Salisbury, the townspeople attacked his entourage, killing one of his retainers

(Lodge, *Illustrations,* 3:83–85, Sir Thomas Edmondes to the earl of Shrewsbury, 23 December 1603 [o.s.]).

45. AGS Estado 842:146, Villamediana to Philip, 9 January 1604; AGS Estado 842:10, advice from a confidante [1604]. For the importance of hats in the protocol of respect in the ceremonies of foreign service, see Jansson, "The Hat Is No Expression of Honor."

46. AGS Estado 2023:129, consulta, 10 February 1604.

47. AGS Estado 2557:12, consulta, 25 March 1604.

48. Ibid.

49. Ibid.

50. Ibid; AGS Estado 2024:74, consulta, 10 February 1604.

51. AGS Estado 2024:75, consulta, 6 April 1604; *CODOIN* 42:488–89, Albert to Lerma, 17 June 1604. The constable's figures curiously take no account of the sums supposed to be provided by the provinces themselves, perhaps because these were exhausted just to provide garrisons.

52. Motley, *History,* 4:199.

53. Grotius, *De rebus belgicis,* 795.

54. Collins, *Letters,* 2:282–83, Sir William Browne to Lord Sydney, 15 March 1604, with enclosed letter from Captain Thomas Poyntz, dated 11 March 1604, printed in *HMC De L'Isle,* 3:91; Grimeston, *Generall Historie,* 1304–5; Tex, *Oldenbarnevelt,* 1:337; Motley, *History,* 4:200; *HMC De L'Isle,* 3:94–96, Sir William Browne to Lord Sydney, 25 April 1604.

55. Some of the defenders, probably because they were unpaid, just walked out of their forts without firing a shot!

56. Motley, *History,* 4:201–9; *HMC De L'Isle,* 3:94–109, letters from Sir William Browne to Lord Sydney, dated 25 April through 29 May 1604.

57. Motley, *History,* 4:209–10; *HMC De L'Isle,* 3:102, and Collins, *Letters,* 2:283–84, Sir William Browne to Lord Sydney, 18 May 1604.

58. AGS Estado 2024:130, consulta, 8 May 1604; AGS Estado 2024:84, consulta, 22 June 1604; Parker, *Army of Flanders,* appendix J, p. 292.

59. AGS Estado 2024:85, consulta, 25 May 1604; AGS Estado 2512:2, consulta, 25 May 1604; AGS Estado 2512:15, copy of *relación* of pensions given to English courtiers, 20 July 1604; AGS Estado 2571:83, Philip to Villamediana, 10 June 1604.

60. *Relación de la jornada, CODOIN* 71:467–94.

61. Both the constable and Albert believed they could not keep the towns even if they were to get them from the English, "the enemy being more powerful on the sea than we ourselves are, and that whoever should be so will always be the masters of those towns" (AGS Estado 841:56–58, constable to Philip, 22 June 1604).

62. AGS Estado 2557:18, consulta, 15 July 1604.

63. AGS Estado 2557:17, consulta, 1 July 1604. Throughout the spring, Philip was taking up to four months to respond to Tassis's letters. By July this had

been reduced to a month (AGS Estado 2571:71, Philip to Villamediana, 8 April 1604, responding to letters dated 30 November through 9 February; AGS Estado 2571:97, Philip to Villamediana, 22 July 1604, responding to letters of 13 and 16 June).

64. *CODOIN* 42:494–95, Albert to Lerma, 28 July 1604.

65. AGS Estado 2571:98, Philip to Villamediana, 26 July 1604.

66. AGS Estado 2557:18, consulta, 15 July 1604. As early as March the constable, knowing that the English would never agree to a clause expressly forbidding them from navigating to the Indies, asked Philip for further instructions concerning this point. If such instructions were not forthcoming, he would carry out Philip's initial instructions to demand such a clause, even if it meant war between the two countries (AGS Estado 841:10–11, constable to Philip, 24 March 1604).

67. AGS Estado 841:77, paper sent to the constable by Villamediana; AGS Estado 841:98–99, constable to Philip, 20 July 1604.

68. AGS Estado 841:92, "Capítulos de paz," included with AGS 841:91, Villamediana to constable, 16 July 1604; emphasis in the original. The wording— "debeat commercium liberum, in quibus ante bellum fuit commercium iuxta et secundum usum, et observantian antiquorum foederum et tractatuum"—remained virtually identical in the final treaty (clause 9).

69. AGS Estado 841:100, Villamediana to the constable, 23 July 1604.

70. AGS Estado 841:98–99, constable to Philip, 20 July 1604; AGS Estado 841:112, constable to Philip, 30 July 1604. Secretary Cecil, the earl of Dorset, the lord treasurer, the admiral of England, the earl of Devonshire, and the earl of Suffolk were each to receive three thousand felipes annually, plus a gift payment in jewels. The earl of Northampton was to receive five thousand felipes in pension and six thousand in a lump-sum payment. Later, after they realized his influence with the new king, it was suggested that Cecil's pension be raised to six thousand annually. Moreover they thought it wise to give gifts of between sixteen and twenty thousand escudos to James and his son Prince Henry via the conduit of the countess of Suffolk (AGS Estado 841:99, "Memoria de lo que al Conde de Villamediana y al senador Rovida pareçe que conviene hazer en materia de dadivas y pensiones"; Senator Rovida was professor of law at the College of Milan and was assisting Villamediana with legal technicalities). See also the payments recorded in AGS CMC 2ª 42, *Memoria de lo que yo Don Juan de Tassis Conded de Villamediana he gastado por quenta del Rey Nuestro señor en la jornada que por su Real Orden y mandado hize al Reyno de Inglaterra [Gastos secretos]*, 15 May 1607. On the plan to buy toleration for the Catholics through payment of recusancy fines, see Loomie, *Toleration and Diplomacy*, 32–36.

71. AGS 841:106, instructions for Don Blasco de Aragon for his mission to the archduke, 21 July 1604; *CODOIN* 42:493–94, Albert to Lerma, 22 July 1604; Motley, *History*, 4:211–12.

72. Loomie, *Toleration and Diplomacy*, 36.

73. AGS Estado 841:123, Villamediana to Philip, 3 September 1604; *CODOIN* 71:467–94, *Relación de la jornada*. For the treaty in Latin with a Spanish translation, see Abreu y Bertodano, *Colección de los tratados de paz*, 243–82.

74. Although English troops and money were free to be deployed privately to the Low Countries.

75. On Anglo-Spanish commerce after the peace, see Taylor, "Price Revolution or Price Revision? The English and Spanish Trade after 1604," which points out that the benefits of this reopening of trade were neither as clear-cut nor as widespread as the English had expected (or been led to believe).

76. Weldon, *Court and Character of King James*, 9–10. Weldon, a courtier at James's court, had written a nasty satire on the Scots, which, when revealed to James, cost him his job at the Board of Green Cloth. He never forgave the king and wrote this unflattering portrait of the court in revenge (Akrigg, *Jacobean Pageant*, 262–63).

77. Between December 1603 and September 1604 Ostend had had six governors; all except the last were either killed or wounded while in office. For a list of the governors, see *HMC De L'Isle*, 3:119n1).

78. Grimeston, *Generall Historie*, 1317; Motley, *History*, 4:214–16. Modesto Lafuente, in his *Historia general de España*, puts the figures at forty thousand deaths for the Spanish and seventy thousand for the Dutch, based on Spanish and Dutch sources (15:335). The exact figures are unknown. It must, of course, be remembered that many of these casualties were a result of sickness and not of battle.

79. Motley, *History*, 4:215–16.

80. This image was made explicit in a copper engraving by C. de Passe, which showed Spínola, in full armor, removing a thorn from the foot of the Belgian lion. See Muller, *Onze gouden eeuw*, 1:43.

CHAPTER 7: *"Blood and Fire"*

1. *CSP Venice*, 10:178, Nicolo Molin, Venetian ambassador in England, to the doge and Senate, 1 September 1604.

2. Quoted in Motley, *History*, 4:223–24.

3. *CSP Venice*, 10:174–75, Nicolo Molin to the doge and Senate, 18 August 1604.

4. Ibid., 179–80, 184–85, Nicolo Molin to the doge and Senate, 8 September and 6 October 1604.

5. Ibid., 190, Nicolo Molin to the doge and Senate, 3 November 1604.

6. AHE *CODOIN*, 4:94–97, consulta, 18 September 1604. Only four hundred thousand escudos were actually sent, but even this was, according to Philip, "more than I had thought possible according to the state of my treasury" (AHE *CODOIN*, 4:99–100, consulta, 30 September 1604).

7. *CSP Venice*, 10:179–80, 190, Nicolo Molin to the doge and Senate, 8 Sep-

tember and 3 November 1604. For the constable's objections to such a move, see Chap. 6.

8. AGS Estado 634:16–31, various papers concerning the mission of Rodrigo Nino y Lasso, 8–16 August 1604.

9. *CODOIN* 42:496–99, Albert to Lerma, 23 August 1604; ibid., 504–15, *Relación de la desembarcación del enemigo en Flandes y de su progreso.* The archduke placed much of the blame for the Sluis fiasco on the shoulders of Luis de Velasco, the Spanish commander of the cavalry who apparently refused to obey his orders. It is even possible that Velasco had been behind the latest mutiny, which took place in the ranks of the cavalry and which was quelled temporarily by a promise to pay them two months' salary and put them into garrison (ibid., 500–502, Albert to Lerma, 6 September 1604).

10. The constable argued that Philip had four options concerning the archdukes: (1) that Albert withdraw to a portion of his territories and leave off prosecuting the war; (2) that the archdukes leave Flanders altogether, perhaps receiving Sicily as compensation; (3) that Philip remove the Spanish army from Flanders; or (4) that Philip abandon the Low Countries to their fate so as not to lose the rest of the monarchy's territories in an effort to save those. When the junta of the Council of State finally considered the matter, Juan de Idiáquez persuaded the others to wait and see how well the changes in the command structure went. If all went well, there would be no need to remove the archdukes from power (AGS Estado 634:59, consulta of the junta, 24 December 1604).

11. AGS Estado 634:50, consulta of the junta of two, 28 September 1604. Even during the negotiations with the English, the Spanish had shown a noticeable willingness to exclude the archduke's ministers from setting Habsburg priorities. In June, Richardot, one of Albert's representatives at the peace talks, had complained to his master that the archdukes' interests were not being looked after "as if everything came from the King, and nothing from your Highness" (quoted in Loomie, *Toleration and Diplomacy,* 30). Richardot had good reason for believing so; on 16 September the junta of two had told the king, "The worst of all is that the Archduke does not obey Your Majesty or believe what he is told to him by us, and instead he believes the greatest enemies of himself and of the greatness of Your Majesty, like Richardot and others" (Lonchay, Cuvelier, and Lefèvre, *Correspondance,* 1:201). According to Nicolo Molin, the Venetian ambassador in London,, it was for these reasons that the archduke decided to post his own ambassador to the court of England: "Anyway there is a rumour that the Archduke has opinions concerning Flanders very different from those of Spain, and that he finds he must keep his own Envoy at this Court to look after his interests; all the more so as rumour is rife that there will be a match between the Prince of Wales and the Infanta [Philip III's daughter, Ana], who will bring the Low Countries as her dower. . . . The rumour has reached the ears of the Archduke, who naturally is annoyed at any suggestion of touching the Provinces during his lifetime" (*CSP Venice,* 10:202–3, Nicolo Molin to the doge and Senate, 30 December 1604).

12. *CODOIN* 42:516–19, Albert to Lerma, 5 October 1604.

13. As Philip, writing in reply to Spínola's description of the fall of Ostend, himself acknowledged: "I thank you very much for the service you have done me in that enterprise, which has been very special; and in that respect I will remember your person and house and give you the honor and reward that you deserve for this action and for the zealousness of your service to me" (AGS 2224, 22 October 1604, quoted in Rodríguez Villa, *Spínola*, 90).

14. Rodríguez Villa, *Spínola*, 91–92.

15. This treaty was a direct outcome of the peace with England. The arch-dukes' representatives had stipulated that a settlement with England over trade matters would have to be accompanied by a similar agreement with France. The constable used his authority to agree to such a treaty in Paris on 12 October 1604. For the treaty itself, see Abreu y Bertodano, *Colección de los tratados de paz,* 1:286–93.

16. AGS 2868, unfoliated, *Relación general del gasto necessario del exército y de las guarniciones,* 4 December 1604; AGS 2024, unfoliated, *Relación particular de las ayudas que cada provincia obediente da a sus Altezas desde la junta de los estados generales del año 1600 y en que se gastan* [December 1604]; AGS Estado 2024, unfoliated, papers brought by the count of Solre, 26 December 1604.

17. AGS Estado 634:59, consulta of the junta of two, 24 December 1604.

18. AGS Estado 2023:133, consulta, 6 January 1605. Philip's detailed instructions on how to conduct the offensive are at AGS Estado 2023:134, consulta, 6 January 1605.

19. AGS Estado 624, conference between D. Pedro de Franqueza and the marquis Spínola, referred to Lerma, 3 February 1605, quoted in Rodríguez Villa, *Spínola*, 96–99.

20. Rodríguez Villa, *Spínola*, 99, 101. For his two positions, Philip awarded Spínola an annual salary of 12,600 ducats, equivalent to the yearly income of many of the Spanish aristocracy. The function of the *superintendente general* was to decide upon the priority of items of expenditure for the army and determine which *libranzas* (authorizations of payment) would be paid first. This, of course, gave the office holder considerable discretionary power with regard to finances and therefore with regard to the whole direction of the army (Parker, *Guide to the Archives of the Spanish Institutions,* 93–94).

21. AGS Estado 2571:117, Philip to Villamediana, 3 February 1605. Since Philip still had not sent an ambassador to Brussels to replace Baltasar de Zúñiga, Villamediana had the responsibility of acting as go-between to the Dutch representatives. Moreover, he was desperately trying to enlist James to put pressure on the Dutch to come to terms.

22. AHE *CODOIN*, 4:184–85, consulta, 17 March 1605.

23. On the burdens of taxation the war placed upon the Dutch populace, see the superb recent contribution by 't Hart, *The Making of the Bourgeois State.* By 1622 the ordinary taxation in Holland, exclusive of the stamp duties, customs, extraordinary duties, and local taxation, amounted to more than ten florins

per head; the actual taxes paid were probably significantly higher (cf. 138–39). This was the equivalent of one month's wages for ordinary seamen and soldiers (Israel, *The Dutch Republic: Rise and Fall,* 352). As was nearly always the case in the early-modern period, the poorer classes paid the majority of the taxes, including those on corn, buckwheat, sugar, copper, starch, spices, beer, cattle, textiles, fish, vinegar, candles, salt, cheese, and butter.

24. Israel, *The Dutch Republic: Rise and Fall.* This book, in which Israel argues that "the Revolt can be said to have widened, and reinforced, a duality which had long existed in politics and economic life" (Preface, vi), is an extended examination of the ways in which the northern and southern provinces became divided in their culture and ideologies after the beginning of the revolt. For another, and shorter, treatment of the same issue, see Rowen and Harline, "The Birth of the Dutch Nation."

25. AHE *CODOIN,* 4:186–93, consulta, 22[?] March 1605; AGS Estado 2225, unfoliated, Philip to Albert, 5 April 1605.

26. Grimeston, *Generall Historie,* 1321–22.

27. AGS Estado 2571:123, Philip to Villamediana, 5 March 1605. The clause of the Anglo-Spanish treaty concerning notification of such ship movements posed some problems for the Spanish. If they gave advance notice to the English in order to secure permission from James, they risked compromising the fleet if the English should inform the Dutch of the movement. Philip tried to avoid this problem by requesting permission well in advance but without stipulating an exact date for the fleet's departure (see also AGS Estado 2584:21, Villamediana to Philip, 19 April 1605).

28. Tex, *Oldenbarnevelt,* 2:346.

29. AGS Estado 634:59, consulta of the Junta, 24 December 1604. In March the count of Villamediana pointed out that it was the unanimous opinion in the English court that putting pressure on the Dutch by sea was necessary (AGS Estado 2584:17, 17 March 1605). One of Albert's subjects went so far as to propose a detailed financial plan for two fleets totaling 170 ships and more than 13,000 men, to be paid for over a seven-year period (AGS Estado 624:234, 5 April 1605).

30. AGS Estado 2571:117, Philip to Villamediana, 3 February 1605. James did, indeed, issue orders to put a stop to the piracy in the Channel, but he was merely paying lip service to the notion. No real effort was made to prevent the Dutch prowling (AGS Estado 2584:01, Villamediana to Philip, 17 March 1605).

31. Cabrera de Córdoba, *Relaciones,* 242.

32. *CSP Venice,* 10:223, Francesco Priuli to the doge and Senate, 19 February 1605.

33. AGS Estado 2584:21, Villamediana to Philip, 19 April 1605.

34. Cabrera de Córdoba, *Relaciones,* 243–45. In August, Cornwallis repeatedly told the Venetian ambassador that "before the peace the Spanish treated my master like a mistress, now they treat him like a wife; then they did all they could to please him, now they neglect him altogether" (*CSP Venice,* 10:264, Francesco Priuli to the doge and Senate, 6 August 1605). Cornwallis's secretary, Francis

Cottington, likewise had little sympathy with the Spanish, something of which the Spanish themselves were well aware. They intercepted a letter he wrote to the English Privy Council shortly after his arrival in which he delineated his impressions: "This kingdom consisting only nobilitie, merchants, and labourers, the latter estate is verie poore, the second with warres almost utterly exhausted, the nobilitie in a manner all exceedingly indebted and their lands ensaged [mortgaged]; yet much is it to be admired for their expense in outward appearance is not proportionable to the reconning of their revenues, but I suppose that the account of their manie ducketts is not unlike the tallie they use to make by their rosaries of their prayers, for as the one serves them to make themselves great in opinion without the effect, soe doth the other to give an appearance of pietie and devotion without the working power of either" (BN MS 17778:27–28, 31 May 1605 [o.s.]). For some cultural responses to the new Anglo-Spanish relationship, see Johnson, "La Española inglesa."

35. Zúñiga's correspondence from the English court is replete with discussions of the hunts he enjoyed with James. The ability to attend these hunts and therefore be close to the king gave Zúñiga a significant diplomatic advantage in the years to come.

36. AGS Estado 2863:3,9, instructions to Don Pedro de Zúñiga for the embassy to England, 20 April 1605. For a detailed look at the content of these instructions, see Carter, *Western European Powers*, 48–63.

37. Although, as we have seen, he was not averse to making such concessions as such. Even as late as March he had conceded the English the right to treat Noel Caron, the Dutch representative in London, as an ambassador, equal in status to those of the other foreign states; Philip granted this concession to James despite the fact that treating Caron as an ambassador was tantamount to admitting Dutch independent sovereignty. As Philip tactfully allowed, "The reason that he [James] has taken this resolution is so that it may act as a demonstration of his good will and desire to preserve peace and thus I have chosen to understand it" (AGS Estado 2571:130, Philip to Villamediana, 20 March 1605).

38. *CSP Venice*, 10:242, 247, Francesco Priuli to the doge and Senate, 31 March and 14 June 1605; Cabrera de Córdoba, *Relaciones*, 245–50.

39. Tex claims that the plan was betrayed by indiscretions for which Oldenbarnevelt was blamed, but it is clear that nearly everyone knew of the plan well in advance, since the Admiral of Zeeland discussed it with Sir William Browne almost a full month earlier (Tex, *Oldenbarnevelt*, 1:349; HMC De L'Isle, 3:155–56, Sir William Browne to Lord Sydney, 20 April 1605).

40. Grimeston, *Generall Historie*, 1341–47; Tex, *Oldenbarnevelt*, 1:349; Motley, *History*, 4:232–33. There are superbly detailed engravings of all Spínola's battles and encampments in Pompeo Giustiniano, *Delle guerre di Fiandra, libri VI*. Complete itineraries, from manuscript *relaciones*, of Spínola's 1605 and 1606 campaigns, with a detailed map, are printed in Montpleinchamp, *Histoire de l'Archiduc Albert*, appendices 2–3, pp. 575–600.

41. Grimeston, *Generall Historie*, 1347; *CSP Venice*, 10:254–56, 258–59, Nicolo Molin to the doge and Senate, 29 June and 13 July 1605; Motley, *History*, 4:229–30. On the use of this sea route after 1604, see Parker, *Army of Flanders*, 52–53, 58, 279.

42. Collins, *Letters and Memorials*, 2:313–14, Sir William Browne to Robert, Lord Viscount Lisle, 25 July 1605; *HMC De L'Isle*, 3:182–84, Sir William Browne to Viscount Lisle, 29 July 1605; Grimeston, *Generall Historie*, 1347–48; Montpleinchamp, *Histoire*, appendix 2, pp. 578–85.

43. Motley, *History*, 4:234–35; Grimeston, *Generall Historie*, 1351; Montpleinchamp, *Histoire*, appendix 2, pp. 585–88.

44. Motley, *History*, 4:235–39; Grimeston, *Generall Historie*, 1352–53; Montpleinchamp, *Histoire*, appendix 2, pp. 578–85.

45. *HMC De L'Isle*, 3:194–95, John Throckmorton to Viscount Lisle, 14 September 1605.

46. AHE *CODOIN*, 4:226–29, consulta, undated, but probably 3 September 1605.

47. AHE *CODOIN*, 4:229–42, consulta, 3 September 1605. The Armada del Almirantazgo was most likely the name applied to Spínola's galley fleet. I have been unable to find any further information concerning it.

48. The reference to Spínola points to the esteem in which Juan de Idiáquez held him. As the commendador mayor pointed out, "Even though it is usually the opinion that those who carry arms are not suitable to discuss peace, you should believe of his zeal that he will undertake it with utmost seriousness, without respect to his own individual end, because his intention is to serve Your Majesty and win honor, and he can as easily achieve this through peace as through war, and at less cost or danger to himself. Besides, he that carries arms can put an end to things that [the Archduke] alone could not do." Thus Idiáquez laid the groundwork for Spínola's future efforts in securing the truce with the Dutch.

49. AHE *CODOIN*, 4:247–54, consulta, 24 September 1605.

50. Akrigg, *Jacobean Pageant*, 69–78. For the Spanish role in the affair, see Loomie, *Guy Fawkes in Spain*. For a popular account, see Fraser, *Faith and Treason*. Whether or not the Spanish were aware of the exact nature of the plot is debatable, but their support of the Catholics' secret plots is not. On 2 July, Philip wrote to Spínola giving him secret instructions to hear the proposals of the English Catholics who had first approached Philip in 1602 and to consider giving them one hundred thousand ducats if Spínola thought something would come of it (AGS Estado 2225:18).

51. AGS Estado 2584:77, Pedro de Zúñiga to Philip, 21 November 1605; AGS Estado 2512:101, consulta, 4 December 1605.

52. *Letters of King James VI and I*, ed. Akrigg, 275–77.

53. AGS Estado 2584:88, Pedro de Zúñiga to Philip, 15 December 1605. On the English reaction to the Gunpowder Plot and its effect on the Anglo-

Habsburg entente, see Loomie, "Sir Robert Cecil and the Spanish Embassy," and Croft, "Serving the Archduke," which, based on English figures, I think over-estimates the importance of the English troops to Spínola's campaigns.

54. AHE *CODOIN*, 4:275-78, 279-82, consultas, 22 November 1605 and 10 January 1606.

CHAPTER 8: *Exhaustion*

1. Tex, *Oldenbarnevelt*, 350; 't Hart, *Making of a Bourgeois State*, 55, 100-12, esp. figs. 2.2, 4.1, and 4.2.

2. See Giustiniano, *Delle guerre di Fiandra*, 228-29 and figs. 14 and 25, for a description and illustrations of the fortifications. Fig. 25 is printed in Parker, *Military Revolution*, 39. See also Parker's *Army of Flanders*, 16-17, for a discussion of these fortifications and their role in Dutch defensive strategy.

3. Tex, *Oldenbarnevelt*, 1:350, 352; Parker, *Dutch Revolt*, 237; t'Hart, *Making of a Bourgeois State*, 59-63 (esp. figs. 2.3, 2.4, pp. 60, 61), 125-26, 145, 165-67.

4. Sluiter, "Dutch-Spanish Rivalry," 186-91. Some 130 private vessels re-portedly sallied forth from Dutch ports in the early months of 1606 in order to prey upon Spanish shipping.

5. The payment of this and the other examples of subsidies that follow were the excuses Lerma gave to Louis Verreyken (who had been sent by the archduke to represent the negative effects of the Spanish embargoes on trade in the southern Netherlands) for not acceding to his request for financial assistance. Verreyken's report to Albert is in Lonchay, Cuvelier, and Lefèvre, *Correspondance*, 6:102-4. For a general discussion of political developments within the empire during this period, see Parker, *Europe in Crisis*, 76-94; Chudoba, *Spain and the Empire;* and the older, but still valuable, work of Gindely, *Rudolf II und seine Zeit.*

6. On Archduke Ferdinand's policies in the Adriatic, and especially his sup-port of the Uskoks of Croatia, see Bracewell, *The Uskoks of Senj.* On Spanish involvement there, see Ciriaco Pérez Bustamante, "El dominio del Adriatico y la política española."

7. The dispute between the papacy and the Venetians is covered in detail by Bouwsma, *Venice and the Defense of Republican Liberty*, 339-482. On Christ-mas day of 1605 the papal nuncio in Venice had delivered a brief from the new pope, Paul V, ordering the Senate to revoke several laws that he considered an infringement of his rights and liberties as head of the Catholic Church, upon pain of excommunication of themselves as a body and of interdiction of all the republic's territories. When the Venetian government refused, the excommuni-cation and interdict were subsequently effected, on 17 April 1606, prompting the two sides and their allies to prepare for war. For Spain's involvement in the dispute and its effects on Spanish policy, see Pazos, "Del conflicto entre Paulo V y Venecia"; Corral Castanedo, *España y Venecia (1604-07);* Seco Serrano, "Venecia, Roma, España." On the decision to move the court, see Cabrera de Córdoba,

Relaciones, 268–69; and Williams, "El reinado de Felipe III," 433–34, and "Lerma, Old Castile, and the Travels of Philip III of Spain."

8. AHE *CODOIN*, 4:186–93, consulta, 21 March 1605.

9. Rodríguez Villa, *Spínola*, 119.

10. Ibid., 120.

11. AHE *CODOIN*, 4:304–06, consulta, 18 February 1606.

12. Ibid., 307–15, consulta, 23 February 1606.

13. *HMC De L'Isle*, 3:243–44, Sir William Browne to Viscount Lisle, 10 February 1606.

14. For the details of the proposal and English reactions to it, see the documents printed in Sawyer, *Memorials*, 2:160–69,176–78,199–202.

15. On the lives and careers of these two men, see Loomie, *Spanish Elizabethans*, 52–93.

16. On Stanley, see ibid., 129–81.

17. *HMC De L'Isle*, 3:242*n*1; AHE *CODOIN*, 4:288–92, consulta, 15 January 1606.

18. AGS Estado 2585:12–13, Pedro de Zúñiga to Philip III, 28 February 1606. Philip did not even finalize San Germán's instructions until 4 February (AGS Estado 2571:160, Philip to the marquis of San Germán).

19. *CSP Venice*, 10:328–29, Zorzi Giustiniani (Venetian ambassador in England) to the doge and Senate, 23 March 1606; AGS Estado 2585:21, Pedro de Zúñiga to Philip III, 16 March 1606. It should be noted that Zúñiga was having some difficulty paying the pensions owed to the English ministers, who were theoretically supposed to mitigate such feelings (AGS Estado 624:173, consulta, 18 March 1606); AGS Estado 2585:29–31, Pedro de Zúñiga to Philip III, 5 April 1606; AGS Estado 2585:25, Pedro de Zúñiga to Philip III, 31 March 1606.

20. Tex, *Oldenbarnevelt*, 1:352–55. Henry, viscount of Turenne and duke of Bouillon, had been implicated in the Biron conspiracy and afterward had fled to Geneva and his independent territories. In April 1604, he and a group of other French nobles had begun to conspire against Henry, but the king discovered the attempt and sent an army to suppress it, quickly taking most of Bouillon's strongholds. Bouillon, however, held out until April 1606, finally surrendering only after Henry launched a powerful siege train against him (Greengrass, *France in the Age of Henri IV*, 231–32).

21. Cabrera de Córdoba, *Relaciones*, 276–77; Cuvelier and Lefèvre, *Correspondance*, 6:109, 110–11, Luis Verreycken to Albert, 23 March 1606, and Juan Carillo to Albert, 1 April 1606; "Instructions for you, Ambrosia Spínola, marquis of Venafro, knight of the Order of the Golden Fleece, and my Councilor of State and War," 16 April 1606, printed in Rodríguez Villa, *Spínola*, 124–32.

22. Isabel Clara Eugenia, *Correspondencia*, 145.

23. *HMC De L'Isle*, 3:260, 263, Sir William Browne to Viscount Lisle, 10 April 1606, and N. de Blocq to Viscount Lisle, 18 April 1606. The dispute between the town of Brunswick and the duke of Brunswick had begun in 1587 when the

former refused its allegiance to the duke and insisted instead that it was directly subordinate to the Holy Roman Emperor. By 1600 the quarrel had erupted into violence. In 1605, after a suprise attack, the duke laid siege to the town, which then enlisted the aid of the other remaining towns of the Hansa. The Brunswick and Hansa forces managed to hold out against the duke until the following year, at which time he called off the siege and went to Prague, in the hopes of winning a favorable ruling and military assistance from the emperor. Once there, Brunswick became one of Rudolf's most trusted advisers, remaining in that position until his unexpected death in 1613. The town of Brunswick was still defiant at his death. On his life and works (he wrote a number of well-received plays), see Knight, *Heinrich Julius, duke of Brunswick*.

24. *HMC De L'Isle* 3:267-68, Sir William Browne to Viscount Lisle, 3 May 1606.

25. Rodríguez Villa, *Spínola*, 122-23; *CODOIN* 42:565-68, Albert to Lerma, 9 June 1606. The details of the campaign that follows have been reconstructed from the following sources: Grimeston, *Generall Historie*, 1355-65; *CODOIN* 42:569-74, 43:5-14, Albert to Lerma, 1 July-6 October 1606; *HMC De L'Isle* 3:278-80, 292-328; the *relación* of Spínola's campaign printed in Montpleinchamp, *Histoire*, 593-600; Motley, *History*, 4:259-68; and Rodríguez Villa, *Spínola*, 135-45. I have depicted the campaign in some detail because it demonstrates the considerable role played by luck in the implementation of political and military strategy.

26. Solre is also called Sora in many of the documents of this period. William Shaw, editor of *HMC De L'Isle* 3, goes to great lengths to show that these are not in fact the same man and that Sora is perhaps related to the Italian dukes of Sora (286*n*1), but Solre is clearly listed as a member of Spínola's command in the *relación* of the 1606 campaign cited above, and in the archduchess's correspondence with Lerma she invariably refers to the count of Sora when she clearly means Solre, who was at that time on a mission for the archdukes to the Spanish court (Isabel Clara Eugenia, *Correspondencia*, 121, 124). See also Brants, "Une mission à Madrid de Philippe de Croy, comte de Solre, envoyé des archiducs en 1604." Finally, Spínola himself wrote that he had given the orders to cross at Zwolle to the count of Solre (AGS Estado 8814:73, Spínola to the marquis of Villena, Spanish ambassador in Rome, 21 November 1606).

27. *HMC De L'Isle*, 3:293-94, N. de Blocq to Viscount Lisle, 23 July 1606.

28. *HMC De L'Isle*, 3:302-3, Sir William Browne to Viscount Lisle, 22 August 1606.

29. *CODOIN* 43:15-16, Albert to Lerma, 18 October 1606; Isabel Clara Eugenia, *Correspondencia*, 158-59, 10 November 1606; Motley, *History*, 4:265; AGS Estado 8814:73, Spínola to the marquis of Villena, 21 November 1606.

30. *HMC De L'Isle*, 3:327-28, N. de Blocq to Viscount Lisle, 19 November 1606; *CODOIN*, 43:23-24, Albert to Lerma, 22 November 1606; Motley, *History*, 4:266-75.

31. AGS Estado 634:89, note from Lerma to Villalonga concerning the secret resolutions of the junta, 17 September 1606.

32. AGS Estado 634:93, consulta of the junta, 14 December 1606.

33. As if this example is not enough to demonstrate Philip's preoccupation with regaining control of his patrimony, on 31 December 1606 Philip sent the marquis of Guadaleste, his new ambassador to the archdukes, instructions concerning the dispositions he was to take in the event of the death of either archduke to insure the return of the Netherlands to the Spanish crown (AGS Estado 2226:237).

34. HMC De L'Isle, 3:330–32, Sir William Browne to Viscount Lisle, 25 and 26 November 1606; Tex, Oldenbarnevelt, 2:363.

35. HMC De L'Isle, 3:334–36, N. de Blocq and Sir William Browne to Viscount Lisle, 29 and 30 December 1606.

36. AGS Estado 2289:233, extract from the instructions given to Walrave van Wittenhorst by Archduke Albert, 6 May 1606; CODOIN 43:27–31, Albert to Lerma, 21 December 1606, discussing Wittenhorst's earlier mission; AGS Estado 2289:234, paper sent to the United Provinces via Father Creswell; HMC De L'Isle, 3:269, Sir William Browne to Viscount Lisle, 14 May 1606; Tex, Oldenbarnevelt, 2:359–61. The secret committee (secreete besoigne) was made up of key members of the states of Holland who were sworn to secrecy in an attempt to prevent the opponents of the peace from knowing about Oldenbarnevelt's contacts with the archduke. According to an institutional change introduced in 1585, all issues that were to be discussed in the full assembly had to be approved in advance by the standing committee, the Gecommitteerde Raden, and circulated to the eighteen voting towns. This meant that all important issues were discussed in the town councils as well as the states, with final decisions being a process of consultation among all eighteen councils, the Council of State, the standing committee, and the full states. Oldenbarnevelt clearly could not have pushed his plans through all of these institutions without stiff opposition; the secret committee allowed him to bypass them. See Tex, Oldenbarnevelt, 360–61; Israel, The Dutch Republic and the Hispanic World, 30–31; and Israel, The Dutch Republic: Rise and Fall, 278–79.

37. CODOIN, 43:27–31, Albert to Lerma, 21 December 1606.

38. Tex, Oldenbarnevelt, 2:362–63; Motley, History, 4:296.

39. CODOIN, 43:27–31, Albert to Lerma, 21 December 1606; AGS Estado 2289:170, Spínola to Philip, 22 December 1606.

CHAPTER 9: Warrior Diplomacy

1. The most succinct account of the negotiations of 1607–9 in English is in Israel's The Dutch Republic and the Hispanic World, 1–42. His account suffers, however, from its reliance, for the Spanish side of the issues, on the work of Cardinal Guido Bentivoglio, the papal nuncio, who did not have direct access to the Spanish decision-making process, and on the relaciones of Cabrera de Córdoba,

who is not always accurate, especially when he discusses the decision making of the king's councillors. This leads Israel to erroneous conclusions, such as when he states that "the original goal, in both Madrid and The Hague, was not a truce, but a full peace" (3), something even Motley knew was untrue (see his *History*, 4:435), or when he argues that Lerma was the person responsible for the initiative on the Spanish side. Additionally, I believe Israel overemphasizes the role that Dutch incursions in the Spanish Indies had on the actual decisions that the court took with regard to the peace talks. The decision to effect a peaceful settlement with the rebels had been taken long before the Dutch made any serious gains in the Indies; the gains themselves were not decisive but were merely one more factor that reinforced the direction of Spanish policy but did not decide it.

2. Nicolson, *Diplomacy*, 3d ed. (Oxford, 1963), 25–26; *CODOIN*, 43:32–33, Albert to Lerma, 6 January 1607.

3. *CODOIN* 43:32–33, Albert to Lerma, 6 January 1607; Motley, *History*, 4:296; Grimeston, *Generall Historie*, 1371. Motley is clearly in error when he gives the date of the presentation to the States-General as 10 January.

4. The states' reply is printed in Rahlenbeck, *Considérationes d'Estat*, 75–77. There is an English translation in *HMC Salisbury*, 19:13–14. A Spanish copy is in AGS Estado 2289:232.

5. AGS Estado 2289:32, Spínola to Philip III, 3 February 1607. So troubling was the dispute to the Spaniards that strange visions seen by ordinary peasants in their fields were interpreted by authorities as signs of the dispute. On 3 December, just before dawn, two servants of Don Fernando Beltrán, *vecino* (citizen) and *regidor* (chief official) of the village of Ledesma, witnessed a giant black cloud appear out of nowhere. Just then a giant black serpent with a long tail came forth from the cloud and made its way toward Salamanca, where it disappeared into a colored sky. The whole matter having been reported and brought before council, the verdict was that the black cloud represented Venice, its dark color symbolic of the excommunication and censure of the pope, and the serpent the sin the Venetian people had committed in not obeying the pope. That the serpent (sin) had left the black cloud (Venice) behind meant that the Venetians were seeking absolution in the colored sky (the red-colored body of Rome and her church) (BN MS 18698:37, *Relación de lo que se vio en el cielo . . . 3 de diziembre deste presente año de 1606*).

6. The request, signed by both Spínola and Father Neyen, is printed in Deventer, *Gedenkstukken van J. van Oldenbarnevelt*, 3:106. I do not believe that the condition regarding the Indies can be construed as indicating that this was the most significant issue for the Habsburg side. Rather, this was for Albert the most equivalent long-term concession he could request from the Dutch.

7. Motley, *History*, 4:301–2; Tex, *Oldenbarnevelt*, 363–64. Tex gives the date of Cruwell's arrival at The Hague as 6 January, but this is clearly an error since it was Wittenhorst's failure in late January that sparked Cruwell's mission. Tex's dates are often in error and should be checked against other accounts.

8. AGS Estado 2289:31, Spínola to Philip III, 15 February 1607.

9. Tex, *Oldenbarnevelt*, 364; Motley, *History*, 4:302.

10. On 8 April 1606 the governor of the Philippines, Don Pedro de Acuña, landed before the fort of Ternate with a force of Spanish soldiers that had left Spain in 1604. After a five-day siege, Acuña took the fort. The operation had been proposed by the junta of the Council of War for the Indies in January 1602. Owing to the distances involved, it took four years before it could be concluded (Torres y Lanzas, *Catálogo de los documentos relativos a las Islas Filipinas*, 4:173, 5:108–9). On 9 March 1607 Andrés de Prada wrote to Spínola that they had learned of the victory the previous afternoon (AGS Estado 8796:311, minute).

11. There is an English translation of this text in Grimeston, *Generall Historie*, 1372–73. According to Cardinal Bentivoglio, Father Neyen convinced Albert to sign the documents after arguing that the passage in which the archduke said he would treat with the United Provinces as free was "to be always understood with a sense of similitude . . . as *if they were free*, and not with a signification of true and legitimate liberty," but his view may have been tainted by hindsight (Bentivoglio, *Relaciones*, 11).

12. AGS Estado 2138:79, minutes of the council meeting, 13 March 1607.

13. Grimeston, *Generall Historie*, 1372; Motley, *History*, 4:308–10.

14. *HMC De L'Isle* 3:361–63, Sir William Browne to Viscount Lisle, 27 March 1607.

15. Motley, *History*, 4:310; *HMC De L'Isle* 3:364–65, Sir William Browne to Viscount Lisle, 4 April 1607; AGS Estado 2289:54, Spínola to Philip III, 18 April 1607; AGS Estado 2289:49, Spínola to Lerma, 18 April 1607; AGS Estado 2289:58, Albert to Philip III, 18 April 1607; Isabel Clara Eugenia, *Correspondencia*, 169–70, letter to Lerma, 17 [*sic*] April 1607.

16. AGS Estado 8796:304, Niño y Lasso to the marquis of Villena, 20 April 1607; AGS Estado 8795:203, count of Bruay to the marquis of Villena, 27 April 1607.

17. AGS Estado 8796:167–68, Juan Vivas to marquis of Villena, 27 April 1607. This is perhaps the first instance in which the peace that was to follow was expressly compared to the Pax Romana. An accord had been reached between the pope and Venice when Cardinal de Joyeuse arrived in Venice in early April with a brief revoking the papal interdict against that city. The interdict and excommunication were officially lifted on 21 April (Bouwsma, *Venice and the Defense of Republican Liberty*, 413).

18. Grimeston, *Generall Historie*, 1374; Motley, *History*, 4:317; Harline, *Pamphlets, Printing, and Political Culture*, 8, 112.

19. AGS Estado 2586:17, Pedro de Zúñiga to Philip III, 30 April 1607. Although the English court had known that the States were engaged in discussions with the archduke's representative, everyone fully expected that the Dutch would inform them of the status of the talks before committing themselves to anything (*HMC De L'Isle*, 3:359–60, Sir William Browne to Viscount Lisle, 26 March 1607; *CSP Venice*, 9:487, Zorzi Giustinian to the doge and Senate, 5 April 1607).

20. *CSP Venice*, 9:494, Zorzi Giustinian to the doge and Senate, 2 May 1607.

21. AGS Estado 2025:2, consulta of the junta of two, 20 February 1607; *CODOIN*, 43:52–57, Albert to Lerma, 31 May 1607; AGS Estado 2289:92, Diego de Ibarra to Philip III, 8 June 1607, discussing the king's letter to Spínola. The news of the cease-fire arrived on 30 April. For a stirring account of Heemskerk's battle, see Motley, *History*, vol. 4, chap. 47.

22. Cabrera de Córdoba, *Relaciones*, 305.

23. According to José Luis Cano Sinobas, in his entry for Diego de Ibarra in Bleiberg's *Diccionario de Historia de España*, 2:418, Ibarra had been appointed inspector general (*veedor general*) of the Army of Flanders in 1590. This is the date also given by William Shaw in his note on Ibarra in *HMC De L'Isle*, 3:375, who adds that Ibarra had also held this post with the Spanish forces in Sicily. From 1591 to 1593, however, he served as a Spanish representative in Paris, charged with exerting Spanish influence over the Catholic League in order to procure the nomination of Isabel Clara Eugenia to the French throne. From 1593 to 1599 he actually served in his post as inspector general of the Army of Flanders (Parker, *Army of Flanders*, appendix E, p. 282) and as mayordomo to Archduke Albert; he returned to Spain in 1600.

24. BN MS 1492:305, "Copy of a letter that the secretary Andrés de Prada wrote to Lerma in Madrid on 6 May 1607, and his reply in the margin from the palace on the same day, in the same month and year." This document demonstrates the most subtle of manipulations. As under Philip II, only the king and his closest advisers had complete knowledge of the events and decisions that shaped Spanish policy (see Parker, "Making of Strategy," 135). In this case, even the secretary of the council, Andrés de Prada, was privy to more information than the council members themselves. By selectively feeding the council information, Prada and Lerma could obtain the recommendations from the council members that they desired. Moreover, by merely posing the question they want answered — "the king is making up his mind whether . . ." — the secretary and the minister could limit the terms of the debate and thus once again guarantee the outcome.

25. The draft of this consulta, in Prada's hand, is at AGS Estado 2025:30, 12 May 1607. On the dorsum someone has written, "This was emended as will be noticed." The clean copy of the consulta is at AGS Estado 2025:28–29. On this copy the individual votes of the council members, as well as their final recommendation, have been crossed out, and Prada has written new general recommendations, without individual votes, in the margin.

26. Cabrera de Córdoba, *Relaciones*, 305; AGS Estado 2138:82, consulta concerning Diego de Ibarra's instructions, 12 May 1607. Ibarra's instructions, both public and secret, dated 17 May, are printed in *Noticias históricas*, ed. Berwick y Alba, 129–33. They are the only place I have seen where Philip actually writes that he believes they were winning the war. The king did not send his official reply to the archduke's notification of the cease-fire until 29 May (AGS Estado

2226:282), although, as will be seen below, they received word in Brussels of Spanish reactions through other correspondents. Even the English were aware of Ibarra's mission by the end of May and hoped to take advantage of any discord it sowed among the Habsburgs (Sawyer, *Memorials*, 2:307–8).

The six hundred thousand ducats was a windfall, given the state of Spanish finances. Philip had taken extraordinary steps to procure the necessary sums, going so far as to pack the Cortes with his henchmen: Lerma stood for Madrid — in the belief that "where he steers others will follow"; Calderón for Valladolid; and Alba for Zamora. Eventually (on 22 August) the Cortes granted the king a *servicio de los millones* of 17.5 million ducats for a period of six years (2.5 million per year), in addition to conceding ordinary and extraordinary *servicios* of three hundred thousand ducats annually (each), and donated an additional six hundred thousand for the redemption of part of the debt for ten years. In April, however, none of these sums were guaranteed, and Lerma himself had to provide one hundred thousand ducats from his own estate for the defense of the southern Spanish coast against the Dutch (Cabrera de Córdoba, *Relaciones*, 299, 305; *ACC*, 23:336–52, 629). In fact it would take until September for the letter of credit to be sent.

27. AGS Estado 2289:86, Jan Neyen to Archduke Albert, 9 May 1607; Tex, *Oldenbarnevelt*, 2:370–71; Motley, *History*, 4:313.

28. AGS Estado 2289:87, Neyen to Albert, 17 May 1607.

29. AGS Estado 2289:88, Spínola to Philip III, 19 May 1607; *CODOIN*, 43:49–51, Albert to Lerma, 19 May 1607. The news had been forwarded by Carlo Strata, one of Spínola's correspondents at the Spanish court.

30. *CODOIN*, 43:52–57, Albert to Lerma, 31 May 1607. This letter, a response to the news that Lerma had not liked the conditions of the negotiations, belies the notion that Lerma had been the foremost exponent of the peace from the outset.

31. Jeannin's instructions, dated 22 April 1607, are printed as part of the *Négociations*, 63–89. On the life of Pierre Jeannin and his important role in French government under Henry IV and his successors, see the recent biography by Ballande, *Rebelle et conseiller de trois souverains*. For the activities of the French envoys and their English counterparts during the treaty negotiations, see Lee, *James I and Henri IV*, 79–141.

32. Tex, *Oldenbarnevelt*, 2:373–74.

33. In fact the States-General merely decided to keep the French envoys on hand while they themselves continued their negotiations with the archdukes (Grimeston, *Generall Historie*, 1375; Tex, *Oldenbarnevelt*, 2:372–74). For a lengthy discussion of the Franco-Dutch meeting, see Motley, *History*, 4:383–90 (mainly an attempt to exculpate Oldenbarnevelt of any wrongdoing during the negotiations).

34. Grimeston, *Generall Historie*, 1374; Tex, *Oldenbarnevelt*, 2:370–71, 374.

35. AGS Estado 2289:90, Spínola to Philip III, 5 June 1607.

36. AGS Estado 634:70, "Por si se tratare de lo de Flandes," a draft advice paper on the peace talks, unsigned and undated, but probably early May 1607; *Noticias históricas*, ed. Berwick y Alba, 131–33, Ibarra's secret instructions.

37. *Noticias históricas*, ed. Berwick y Alba, 131–33, Ibarra's secret instructions.

38. AGS Estado 2138:86–87, minutes of the Council of State, 19 June 1607.

39. AGS Estado 2138:76–78, opinion of the Constable of Castile, 21 June 1607, regarding the powers to be sent to the archduke. Contrast this with Lerma's views on the matter in January 1609 (see Chapter 10).

40. AGS Estado E2289.109, Diego de Ibarra to Philip III, 24 June 1607. That Philip thought a loss of reputation as a result of concessions would engender further wars shows how little we in the twentieth century have advanced in our thinking over our seventeenth-century forebears, for the idea smacks of modern notions of the problems of appeasement. Donald Kagan, an opponent of appeasement or concessions, argues in *On the Origins of War and the Preservation of Peace* that great powers can maintain peace only if they project strength in all their dealings with rival states (just as the Spanish tried to do). This argument, however, fails to address Paul Kennedy's contention—using the Spanish monarchy as one of his models—that great powers tend to be weakened or destroyed by overextension and overcommitment (*The Rise and Fall of the Great Powers*).

41. AGS Estado 2025:35–36, Spínola to Philip III, 25 June 1607; AGS Estado 2289, Spínola to Philip III, 26 June 1607, quoted in Rodríguez Villa, *Spínola*, 177.

42. Both versions of the ratification are printed in Rahlenbeck, *Considérations d'Etat* appendix 4, pp. 78–79.

43. *CODOIN,* 43:63, Albert to Lerma, 11 July 1607; AGS Estado 2289, Ibarra to Philip III, 11 July 1607, quoted in Rodríguez Villa, *Spínola,* 191. Neyen's report to the Council of State, given on 6 August 1607, is at AGS Estado 2289:226. Rodríguez Villa, *Spínola,* 188.

44. Isabel Clara Eugenia, *Correspondencia,* letter to Lerma, 20 July 1607, 177–78. Ibarra did not, however, actually depart the Low Countries until 20 September (*CODOIN,* 43:77, Albert to Lerma, 20 September 1607). Ibarra's angry letter to the king is printed in Rodríguez Villa, *Spínola,* 194–95.

45. *HMC De L'Isle,* 3:385–86, Sir William Browne to Viscount Lisle, 25 July 1607, and unsigned copy of Spínola's letter to the States-General, 16 July 1607.

46. *HMC De L'Isle,* 3:389–90, Sir William Browne to Viscount Lisle, 30 July 1607; AGS Estado 2289:173, report of the audiencier Luis Verreyken concerning his negotiation in Holland, 18 August 1607; Grimeston, *Generall Historie,* 1375–76; Tex, *Oldenbarnevelt,* 2:376; Motley, *History,* 4:392–94.

47. AGS Estado 2289, Spínola to Philip III, 31 July 1607, printed in Rodríguez Villa, *Spínola,* 189–90.

48. AGS Estado 2289:173, report of the audiencier Luis Verreyken concerning his negotiation in Holland, 18 August 1607; Grimeston, *Generall Historie,* 1376; Tex, *Oldenbarnevelt,* 376–77; Motley, *History,* 4:396.

49. These drafts are at AGS Estado 2289, fols. 177 and 178.

50. AGS Estado 2289:173, report of the audiencier Luis Verreyken concern-

ing his negotiation in Holland, 18 August 1607; Grimeston, *Generall Historie,* 1376; Tex, *Oldenbarnevelt,* 376- 77; Motley, *History,* 4:396.

51. See the report delivered by Lerma to the Cortes on the afternoon of 5 November: *Relación de lo que la real hacienda debe a diferentes hombres de negocios y otras personas y de gajes de los criados de las casas reales y sueldo de la gente de las guardas y de la que sirve en los presidios, fronteras, armadas y otras cosas, en 30 de Octubre de 1607.* The actual debt stood at 22,748,971 ducats and 100 maravedís, of which 20,748,971 was the principal (*Actas de las Cortes de Castilla,* 23:551–59).

52. Rodríguez Villa, *Spínola,* 192; AGS Estado 2289:187, Guadaleste to Philip III, 21 August 1607. The crown had agreed to pay the mutineers 292,000 escudos in monthly installments. Their final settlement, on 27 November 1607, was 372,000 escudos (Parker, *Army of Flanders,* appendix J, p. 292). According to Spínola's report in August, he was receiving only 135,000 escudos a month from the Spanish, 30,000 of which went to the mutineers. Thus he was trying to support his army on only 105,000 escudos per month, one-third of the budget he had had the year before (AGS Estado 625:38, consulta, 20 September 1607).

53. *CODOIN,* 43:68–70, Albert to Lerma, 21 August 1607. In September the archduke was reportedly reduced to the position of attempting to pawn the infanta's jewels to a Paris banker (*HMC Downshire,* 2:32, John Beaulieu to William Trumbull, 19 September 1607).

54. AGS Estado 2586, fols. 51 and 58, Pedro de Zúñiga to Philip III, 24 July 1607 and 5 August 1607.

55. AGS Estado 2138:75, consulta, 12 August 1607.

56. *CODOIN,* 43:71–74, Albert to Lerma, 7 September 1607; AGS Estado 2289:202, Spínola to Philip III, 8 September 1607. The Spanish were optimistic regarding the fleet, because the cessation of hostilities at sea meant that the Dutch would no longer threaten it. When news of the cessation arrived in Spain, Philip ordered ships to be sent out to escort the fleet into Spanish waters, where it arrived in mid-September (*CODOIN,* 43:79, Albert to Lerma, 10 October 1607, referring to Lerma's letter of 18 September containing the news of the fleets arrival). The official figure for the silver brought by the fleet was 6,929,030 ducats, of which the crown received 2,084,349 (Martín Acosta, *El dinero americano,* 270).

57. AGS Estado 2289:172, Spínola to Philip III, 21 August 1607.

58. *CODOIN,* 43:79–80, Albert to Lerma, 10 October 1607; AGS Estado 2289:217, Spínola to Philip III, 11 October 1607.

59. Grimeston, *Generall Historie,* 1383; AGS Estado 2289:235, Spínola to Philip III, 11 October 1607.

60. AGS Estado 2289:257, "Summary of the letters of the Father Commissioner General and of the Audiencier, written in The Hague, 29 and 31 October 1607"; Grimeston, *Generall Historie,* 1384; Motley, *History,* 4:403–5.

61. Copies of the French version of the ratification document are printed in Rahlenbeck, *Considérationes d'Etat,* 79–84, and Jeannin, *Négociations,* 1:465–70.

62. Translations are from Motley, *History,* 4:405–6, with slight modifications of syntax.

63. Grimeston, *Generall Historie*, 1385; Tex, *Oldenbarnevelt*, 2:378–79. AGS Estado 2289:262, "Report that the Father Commissioner General and the Audiencier gave to His Highness of all that passed this last time that they were in the Islands," enclosed with AGS Estado 2289:260, Spínola to Philip III, 12 December 1607.

64. Lee, *James I and Henri IV*, 88–89; *HMC De L'Isle*, 3:405–6, Sir William Browne to Viscount Lisle, 23 September 1607.

65. Jeannin, *Négociations*, 1:470–71.

66. The States-General had first taken up the West Indies project on 27 June 1606 and had approved it as a "laudable, honorable, and very useful" measure. After the cease-fire, consideration of the project was stopped until February 1608, when it once again surfaced as a means of putting pressure on the Spanish during the peace negotiations. For the debates, see Jameson, "Willem Usselinx," 22–47.

67. AGS Estado 2289:262.

68. Ibid.

69. For the details of Tyrone's story after 1601, see Walsh, *"Destruction by Peace,"* which not only gives a narrative of the events of O'Neill's later life but also includes (in translation) almost all the Spanish documents from the archives at Simancas bearing on Spain's relationship to the Irish leaders.

70. Ibid., 17–20, 30.

71. Ibid., 37–45, 61–63; Lee, *James I and Henri IV*, 92–93.

72. Walsh, *"Destruction by Peace,"* document 39, pp. 181–82; AGS Estado 2586, Pedro de Zúñiga to Philip III, 3 October 1607. In reality, the fleet was intended for a strike against Algiers. James had even reportedly said that "the King of Spain had gone too far and that if he once caused him [James] to don the harness, he would never leave it off until he had shown him that he can cause him more damage than he thinks"(Walsh, *"Destruction by Peace,"* document 38, p. 181, extract of a letter from La Boderie, French ambassador in London, to Puisieux, Henry IV's minister of foreign affairs, 26 September 1607); Lee, *James I and Henri IV*, 91–92; *HMC De L'Isle*, 3:411, 414, Sir John Throckmarton to Viscount Lisle, 3 October 1607, and N. de Blocq to Viscount Lisle, 11 October 1607.

73. AGS Estado 2289:262, report of the Father Commissioner General and the audiencier. A résumé of the emperor's letter is in Grimeston, *Generall Historie*, 1386–87. A similar letter had been sent to Albert and forwarded to the Spanish court by Guillen de San Clemente, the Spanish ambassador in Prague, but the Council of State did not get around to discussing the letters until December, far too late to help Verreyken during his awkward moments with Oldenbarnevelt (AGS Estado 2323:23, consulta, 6 December 1607; AGS Estado 2138:62–63, consulta, 13 December 1607). This was not the only pressure that Oldenbarnevelt and the other Dutch leaders tried to bring against their enemies. In October the Dutch had fielded a plan for a defensive triple alliance between France, England, and the Dutch. Disputes among the parties over financing had delayed the measure and caused some changes in the terms of the alliance, but in principle all

three sides had agreed by December that it would benefit the Dutch cause. The French actually managed to sign a bilateral treaty with the Dutch on 23 January 1608 (Lee, *James I and Henri IV*, 99–104; *HMC Salisbury*, 19:328, earl of Salisbury to Sir Thomas Edmondes, 28 November 1607).

74. AGS Estado 2289:262.

75. Ibid.

76. Quoted in Motley, *History*, 4:412.

77. Cabrera de Córdoba, *Relaciones*, 319. The most comprehensive examination of Philip III's finances to date is Pulido Bueno, *La real hacienda de Felipe III.* The last chapter of the work covers the various attempts to free up crown income through 1608.

78. Martín Acosta, *El dinero americano*, 237–38; Pulido Bueno, *La real hacienda*, 252ff; Cabrera de Córdoba, *Relaciones*, 320; AGS Estado 8796:222–23, Juan Vives to the marquis of Villena, 23 November 1607; AGS Estado 2226:312, Philip III to Albert, 11 November 1607.

79. The same strategy had been employed in 1599, but with some adverse reactions; many of the mutineers deserted to the Dutch. See Parker, *Army of Flanders*, 194–95. The ban on the mutineers of Diest is printed in Brants, *Receuil des ordonnances des Pays*, 1:371, 374.

80. AGS Estado 2290:50, translation of the letter from the states of the United Provinces written to their highnesses the archdukes, 23 December 1607, and the archdukes' reply, 31 December 1607 (both are printed in Rodríguez Villa, *Spínola*, 203–5); Grimeston, *Generall Historie*, 1388; Motley, *History*, 4:413–14 (Motley gets the date of the General Assembly of the States-General wrong; it was 20 December, not 13 December).

81. AGS Estado 2025:5, consulta of the junta of three, 16 January 1607. Here again, Lerma belies his reputation as a pacifist.

82. Ibid. On 19 January, while returning from a party at the palace, Villalonga was arrested by Hernando Carillo (the king's former negotiator in the Boulogne peace talks) and charged with embezzling vast sums of money from the treasury. The first of Lerma's creatures had fallen (Pérez Bustamante, *La España de Felipe III*, 133).

83. Grimeston, *Generall Historie*, 1388–89.

CHAPTER 10: *The Search for the Advantage*

1. AGS Estado 2138:48–50, consulta, 7 January 1608; AGS Estado 2290:80, *La minuta del poder que se embio ultimamente de Flandes . . . dada en Madrid a 10 de henero 1608;* AGS Estado 2290:25, States-General to Father Neyen and Audiencier Verreyken, 11 January 1608. On the career of Mancicidor, see Lefèvre, "Don Juan de Mancicidor."

2. AGS Estado 2290:129, *Instruccion que S.A. ha dado para los que van a Olanda a tratar lo de la paz*, 26 January 1608.

3. Rodríguez Villa, *Spínola*, 207, 213.

4. Birch, *The Court and Times of James the First*, 1:73–74, John Chamberlain to Dudley Carleton, 21 February 1608; Grimeston, *Generall Historie*, 1395–96; AGS Estado 2290:130, Albert to Philip III, 21 February 1608; Spínola to Philip III, 5 March 1608, in Rodríguez Villa, *Spínola*, 216–17.

5. Spínola to Philip III, 5 March 1608, in Rodríguez Villa, *Spínola*, 217; Tex, *Oldenbarnevelt*, 2:385–86. Birch, *Court and Times*, 1:73–74, John Chamberlain to Dudley Carleton. For the Dutch merchants' arguments against abandoning the Indies trade, see Grimeston, *Generall Historie*, 1396–99, and *A Briefe Declaration of the . . . Peace*. In April the marquis of Guadaleste forwarded to Madrid a copy of a Dutch pamphlet which argued that the Dutch engaged 180 ships and 8700 men per year in the West Indies trade alone, a trade that was worth some 14 million florins (AGS Estado 2290:88, Guadaleste to Philip III, 7 April 1608, enclosing *Memorie vande gewichtige redenen die de Heeren Staten generael behooren te beweghen om gheensins te wijcken vande handelinghe ende vaert van Indien*, with a Spanish translation). See also the documents printed in *HMC Downshire*, 2:466–73.

6. Grimeston, *Generall Historie*, 1396–97; Spínola to Philip III, 5 March 1608, in Rodríguez Villa, *Spínola*, 217.

7. Spínola to Philip III, 5 March 1608, in Rodríguez Villa, *Spínola*, 218–21. The French and Dutch had signed a mutual defensive league on 23 January.

8. AGS Estado 2025:87, consulta, 28 February 1608.

9. AGS Estado 2290:68, Richardot to Albert, 4 March 1608.

10. AGS Estado 2290:140, Spínola to Philip III, 30 March 1608, in Rodríguez Villa, *Spínola*, 222.

11. The lists of propositions (AGS Estado 2290:75 and 77) were included in Spínola's letter to the king of 30 March 1608 (AGS Estado 2290:140). An English translation of both lists is given in Grimeston, *Generall Historie*, 1401–3. The other Spanish points were (3) commerce out of the provinces; (4) the issue of monetary adjustments; (5) the position to be taken in the matter of the privileges granted to the English nation; and (7) the issue of neighboring princes. The County of Charolais was part of the Habsburgs' Burgundian inheritance that was now inside French territory.

12. Grimeston, *Generall Historie*, 1404–05. The Scheldt waterway to Antwerp had been closed to maritime traffic since 1585 and was a major factor in the decline of that city's commerce (Israel, *The Dutch Republic and the Hispanic World*, 30).

13. *HMC Downshire*, 2:23, Samuel Calvert to William Trumbull, 12 March 1608. Grimeston reported that many of the foreign representatives, seeing that the negotiations were taking far longer than expected, left for their own countries (Grimeston, *Generall Historie*, 1409).

14. Motley, *History*, 4:450; *HMC Downshire*, 2:46–47, Jean Beaulieu to William Trumbull, 27 March 1608.

15. Grimeston, *Generall Historie*, 1405–7. For the details of the proposals see: AGS Estado 2290:76, "Appuntamientos sobre las dos escrituras que estas diputa-

dos nos dieron a 29 de este mes de marzo de año 1608; tocante a las Indias"; AGS Estado 2290:78, "Papel de las Islas tocante a las Indias que pretenden haya de entrar en le tratado principal de la paz"; and AGS Estado 2290:85, draft concerning the intra-Netherlands trade, all of which were enclosures to Spínola's report to Philip III, 30 March 1608 (AGS Estado 2290:140).

16. AGS Estado 2290:72, Hurtuño de Urizar to Philip III, 7 April 1607; AGS Estado 2290:88, Guadaleste to Philip III, 7 April 1607.

17. *HMC Downshire*, 2:44–45, Cottington to Trumbull, 16 March 1608.

18. Cabrera de Córdoba, *Relaciones*, 317, 322, 345, 347; *HMC Downshire*, 2:77, Cottington to William Trumbull, 17 October 1608. Lerma clearly felt himself to be in trouble during this period, and his actions suggest he was trying to stem the tide of criticism directed toward him. In an attempt to shore up his power with the king, in 1608 he would keep Philip on progress from 19 May to 3 October, much of the time either in the town of Lerma or in Valladolid, where the duke's influence could be particularly strong. As Patrick Williams has demonstrated, Lerma's long slide from power begins at this point. By 1611, after a struggle for power with the queen that ended only when she died, one of his creatures, Calderón, would be tried for murder and eventually banished from court. Philip III then began to look more to Lerma's son, the duke of Uceda. Even the royal cédula of 23 October 1612 that Lerma obtained from Philip, ordering all the councils to obey Lerma, failed to stop his slide, and in 1617 he asked to be dismissed (Williams, "Lerma, Old Castile, and the Travels of Philip III," 393–97).

19. BN MSS 11124:18–29, consulta of the Council of State (copy), 26 March 1608. This bound volume of manuscripts, formerly of the Osuna collection, contains the most significant consultas of the Council of State concerning the negotiations with the Dutch, covering the years 1602–22. The volume appears to have been made for Don Pedro de Toledo (the volume contains manuscript letters to and from him), probably begun on the occasion of his embassy to France in 1608, where he was sent to secure the assistance of Henry IV in the Hispano-Dutch negotiations. Spínola's reply to Philip's instructions (sent out on 6 April) is at AGS Estado 2290:202, 29 April 1608; Albert's is at AGS Estado 2290:73, 29 April 1608.

20. Cabrera de Córdoba, *Relaciones*, 336–37. Tex's suggestion that Lerma and Philip would not see Neyen because they had chilled toward him is misleading (*Oldenbarnevelt*, 2:388). *HMC Downshire*, 2:51, Cottington to Trumbull, 12 April 1608; Grimeston, *Generall Historie*, 1409; *CODOIN*, 43:96–99, Albert to Lerma, 3 May and 14 May 1608; AGS Estado 2138:33, Spínola to Albert, 8 May 1608.

21. Cabrera de Córdoba claims that some high-ranking court members even paid Lerma for some of the let blood by offering him jewels worth forty thousand ducats (*Relaciones*, 336). Significantly, despite his attempt to control influence on the king by constant travel, Lerma was separated from Philip for much of the spring because of his illness and the negotiations with the Cortes for the

millones. This, of course, makes it difficult to see how Lerma could have been influencing Philip's decisions in these matters directly (Williams, "Lerma, Old Castile, and the Travels of Philip III," 395).

22. BN MSS 11124:30-41, consultas of the Council of State (copies), 10 May 1608. The friar's papers, with Lerma's annotations, are found at AGS Estado 2290:198-99; Lerma's note is dated 6 May, but Neyen probably delivered the papers to Lerma much earlier. The two issues upon which Neyen had delivered his opinions were the Indies trade and the Spanish demand for freedom of worship for the Catholics in the provinces.

23. BN MSS 11124:37; Cabrera de Córdoba, *Relaciones*, 337; Pérez Bustamante, *La España de Felipe III*, 254-55.

24. *CODOIN*, 43:100-101, Albert to Lerma, 21 May 1608.

25. Tex, *Oldenbarnevelt*, 2:387, 389-90; Motley, *History*, 4:453. The latter part of the agreement was supposed to have been kept secret from the Habsburg negotiators, but Spínola learned soon afterward of its existence (see AGS Estado 2290:223 and 271, Spínola to Philip III, 21 May and 16 June 1608).

26. AGS Estado 2290:223, Spínola to Philip III, 21 May 1608.

27. Cabrera de Córdoba, *Relaciones*, 336, 341; Martín Acosta, *El dinero americano*, 239; Braudel, *The Mediterranean and the Mediterranean World*, 1:510-17.

28. AGS Estado 2025:117, consulta, 28 June 1608; *HMC Downshire*, 2:64-65, 67, Jean Beaulieu to William Trumbull, 25 June 1608 and Cottington to Trumbull, 2 August 1608; Cabrera de Córdoba, *Relaciones*, 345, 348; Martín Acosta, *El dinero americano*, 239. And it was not just military spending that diverted funds from Flanders. On 28 June the king authorized the marriage of the queen's sister, María Magdalena, to the prince of Florence, and promised a dowry of five hundred thousand to the grand duke of Tuscany (Cabrera de Córdoba, *Relaciones*, 343).

29. AGS Estado 2290:271, Spínola to Philip III, 16 June 1608; *CODOIN*, 43:105-07, Albert to Lerma, 21 June 1608. The annotated list of the States-General's twenty-eight points is at AGS Estado 2290:267, with another copy at fol. 274.

30. AGS Estado 2586:115, Pedro de Zúñiga to Philip III, 26 June 1608.

31. The treaty is printed in Rymer and Sanderson, eds., *Foedara*, 16:667-70. For details concerning the negotiations for the treaty, see Lee, *James I and Henri IV*, 97-117.

32. Spínola's letter informing Philip of the treaty did not arrive until 14 July (see AGS Estado 2290:291, Spínola to Philip III, 1 July 1608). A copy of the instructions sent to the archduke is at E2226:94, sent from Lerma, 15 July 1608. Spínola's instructions are at E2226:105 with a letter from Philip III to Albert, 15 July 1608. The underlining is present in the copy of the text.

33. Cabrera de Córdoba, *Relaciones*, 342. The council's look at the instructions is at BN MS 11124:42-43, copy of consulta, 19 July 1608.

34. AGS Estado 2226:105, Philip III to Albert, 15 July 1608; AGS Estado 2138:30, consulta, 10 July 1608.

35. The king's letter of explanation to Neyen is at AGS Estado 2226:159, along with his reply to Neyen's opinions concerning the two issues of religion and trade (both are enclosed with fol. 94).

36. Philip's instructions arrived at The Hague on 27 July, where they were greeted with elation by Juan de Mancicidor (AGS Estado 2290:298, Juan de Mancicidor to Philip III, 28 July 1608). Albert's letter to Lerma, dated 6 August 1608 is printed in *CODOIN,* 43:113–18.

37. Jeannin, *Négociations,* 2:321–23, Jeannin to Villeroy, 15 August 1608; Tex, *Oldenbarnevelt,* 2:393; AGS Estado 2290:325, Juan de Mancicidor to Philip III, 21 August 1608; Grimeston, *Generall Historie,* 1409–10.

38. AGS Estado 2290:111, Spínola to Philip III, 21 August 1608; Tex, *Oldenbarnevelt,* 393–94.

39. AGS Estado 2290:276, *Papel que dieron los estados de Olanda a los diputados de Su Magestad en La Haya a 23 de Agosto 1608.*

40. AGS Estado 2290:144, Spínola to Philip III, 7 October 1608; AGS Estado 2290:279, *Papel que los embaxadores de Principes que estan en la Haya dieron a los estados de Olanda sobre la tregua;* Tex, *Oldenbarnevelt,* 396.

41. AGS Estado 2290:144, Spínola to Philip III, 7 October 1608; AGS Estado 2290:277, Albert to Philip III, 31 August 1608; *CODOIN,* 43:125–26, Albert to Lerma, 31 August 1608; Tex, *Oldenbarnevelt,* 2:397; Motley, *History,* 4:467–70; Grimeston, *Generall Historie,* 1412.

42. AGS Estado 2290:174, Albert to Philip III, 20 September 1608; AGS Estado 2290:144, Spínola to Philip III, 7 October 1608; Grimeston, *Generall Historie,* 1411–12.

43. AGS Estado 2290:174, Albert to Philip III, 20 September 1608; *CODOIN* 43:129–30, Isabel to Lerma, 20 September 1608 (also printed in Isabel Clara Eugenia, *Correspondencia,* 194–95, incorrectly dated 10 September); AGS Estado 625:119, Guadaleste to Philip III, 20 September 1608.

44. Tex, *Oldenbarnevelt,* 2:397; AGS Estado 2290:144, Spínola to Philip III, 7 October 1608; AGS Estado 2290:178, Spínola to Albert, 15 September 1608. The Dutch resolution, dated 13 September, is printed in Grimeston, *Generall Historie,* 1412. Grimeston's history ends at this point on a note of uncertainty over the future of the negotiations.

45. The mail from Brussels of 20 September did not arrive until 4 October.

46. Cabrera de Córdoba, *Relaciones,* 348; AGS Estado 2025:144, consulta of the grand commander of León, 13 September 1608.

47. AGS Estado 2138:60, *Para firmar de Su Magestad: Despachos de officio para diferentes partes.*

48. AGS Estado 2226:137, Philip III to Albert, 2 October 1608.

49. BN MS 11124:75–86, copy of consulta, 9 October 1608.

50. AGS Estado 2226:146, Philip III to Albert, 9 October 1608.

51. Motley, *History,* 4:488–99; Tex, *Oldenbarnevelt,* 2:398–99.

52. The text of Jeannin's speech is printed in Jeannin, *Négociations,* 2:457–63. For details concerning the dispute within the Dutch ranks and its effect

on their negotiating stance, see Motley, *History*, 4:470–515; Tex, *Oldenbarnevelt*, 2:397–413.

53. The letters of Henry IV to Maurice and to the States-General, dated 23 October, are printed in Jeannin, *Négociations*, 2:521–30; Jeannin's speech is on 541–44. On the provincial quota system by which the expenses of the Generality were provided, see Israel, *The Dutch Republic: Rise and Fall*, 285–91, and t'Hart, *The Making of a Bourgeois State*, chap. 3, passim. The system remained largely unchanged after the signing of the truce, with the exception of a reduction in the sums paid by the province of Zeeland.

54. AGS Estado 2290:143, Albert to Philip III, 24 October 1608; AGS Estado 2290:170, Spínola to Philip III, 25 October 1608; AGS Estado 2290:144, Spínola to Philip III, 7 October 1608; AGS Estado 2290:138, Spínola to Guadaleste, 26 October 1608.

55. AGS Estado 2290:169, Spínola to Philip III, 28 October 1608; AGS Estado 2290:139, Guadaleste to Philip III, 28 October 1608.

56. BN MS 11124:140–53, copy of consulta, 11 November 1608.

57. Lerma had already explained to Philip that he had very little money to undertake war the following year. Out of the silver fleet that had recently arrived the king had received only two million ducats, of which a million would have to go to pay the ordinary and extraordinary expenses. This left only a million for Flanders, or less than 150,000 ducats per month, and did not include the sums necessary to pay for their naval expenses (BN MS 11124:124–39, copy of consulta, 27 October 1608).

58. *CODOIN*, 43:144,146,148, Albert to Lerma, 29 & 30 November, and 2 December 1608. Father Brizuela was accompanied by his nephew, Don Iñigo de Brizuela, one of Albert's gentlemen of the table.

59. Tex, *Oldenbarnevelt*, 2:412–13; Motley, *History*, 4:511–13; Jeannin, *Négociations*, 2:573–80.

60. AGS Estado 2290:11, Spínola to Philip III, 12 December 1608; AGS Estado 2290:07, Guadaleste to Philip III, 12 December 1608.

61. AGS Estado 2226:171, Philip III to Albert, 22 December 1608. On 16 December the council had told the king that even after reforms the Army of Flanders, if it were to go on the offensive for only six months of the year, would cost 2,275,963 ducats per year; and this figure did not include other military expenditures like the navy. The council had advised, therefore, that a defensive posture might be a better route to take if there must be war (AGS Estado 625:102, draft of consulta).

62. *CODOIN* 43:150–51, Albert to Lerma, 27 December 1608; AGS Estado 2291:52, copy of a billete of Juan de Mancicidor, 30 December 1608; AGS Estado 2291:54, Albert to Philip, 7 January 1609.

63. "Act containing the resolution of the States about the principal articles of the long-term truce," in Jeannin, *Négociations*, 3:120–22; Motley, *History*, 4:516–17; Tex, *Oldenbarnevelt*, 2:416–17.

64. BN MS 11124:156–77, copy of consulta, 17 January 1609. Brizuela's report is at AGS Estado 626:56.

65. This budget, along with Acuña's letter of explanation, is printed in *CODOIN,* 36:545–61.

66. BN MS 11124:178–95, copies of consultas, 22 January 1609. Brizuela had argued that since Philip was not treating with the rebels as free people but as people *held* to be free, he would only be granting them limited sovereignty, dependent upon their continuing to be held to be free by the granting party, i.e., for the duration of the truce. The king would, therefore, be fully justified in returning to war after the expiration of the agreement, without having given up any of his rights of sovereignty.

67. BN MS 11124:156–77, copy of consulta, 17 January 1609. Contrast this with the council's view of this issue in 1607.

68. BN MS 11124:206–09, copy of consulta, 25 January 1609; AGS Estado 2227:unfoliated, verbal instructions for Brizuela, 27 January 1609; AGS E2227:16, Andrés de Prada to Guadaleste, 28 January 1609; AGS Estado 2227:12, Philip to Guadaleste, 29 January 1609.

69. AGS Estado 2291:33, *Relacion del viaje que ha hecho don Hernando de Girón a ynglaterra,* n.d.; AGS Estado 2291:40, Spínola to Philip III, 20 January 1609.

70. Motley, *History,* 4:516–18; Tex, *Oldenbarnevelt,* 2:417–20; AGS Estado 2291:30, Spínola to Philip III, 26 March 1609; AGS Estado 2291:50, Albert to Philip III, 28 March 1609.

71. AGS Estado 2291:75, Guadaleste to Philip III, 3 April 1609; *CODOIN,* 43:158–59, Albert to Lerma, 3 April 1609; Tex, *Oldenbarnevelt,* 2:421. For details concerning the Jülich-Kleve succession, see Anderson, "The Jülich-Kleve Succession Crisis (1609–20)."

72. These are the main points of the treaty; for a complete text of the thirty-eight articles, in the original French with a Spanish translation, see Abreu y Bertodano, *Colección de los tratados de paz,* 458–76. Abreu also prints (484–85) a secret addendum to the treaty supposedly signed by the Habsburg delegates which guaranteed that the Dutch would not be molested if they chose to trade to the Indies. Effectively this meant the exclusionary article was gutted. Jeannin's *Negociations* is the original and, as far as I can ascertain, the only source for this secret treaty. The Spanish ministers make no mention of any such secret addendum in their discussion of the treaty's ratification later that year, a surprising fact given their insistence that the Dutch be excluded from the Indies. The treaty was also printed in English: *Articles, of a treatie of truce. Made and concluded in the towne . . . of Antwerp, the 9. of April 1609. . . .* (London, 1609). For a modern translation of the main articles, see Rowan, *The Low Countries in Early Modern Times,* 112–13.

73. AGS Estado 2291:71, 15 April 1609.

74. AGS Estado 2138:11, *Lo que se voto en pressencia de Su Magestad a 30 de Mayo de 1609 en lo de la ratificación de la tregua y provision de dinero para Flandes;* AGS Estado

2291:90, *Forma de la ratificación de la tregua con los de Olanda y Zelanda*, signed 7 July 1609; *Relación del dinero remitido á Flándes . . . desde 13 de setiembre de 598 . . . hasta 20 de junio de 609*, 20 June 1609, printed in *CODOIN*, 36:509-44.

75. AGS Estado 2227:12, Philip III to Guadaleste, 29 January 1609.

Conclusion

1. Matias de Novoa, *Historia de Felipe IV, Rey de España*, in *CODOIN*, 77:653-54.

2. Trevor-Roper, "Spain and Europe, 1598-1621," 267-82; this is still the best discussion of the years of truce.

3. See, for example, Greengrass, *France in the Age of Henri IV*, chap. 9: *"Pax Gallicana,"* 236-50.

4. Bentivoglio, *Historical Relations*, 35.

5. Cf. Dekker, *Worke for armourers.*

6. See Sutherland, "The Origins of the Thirty Years War," who argues that the Thirty Years' War can be subsumed within the third of four phases in the anti-Habsburg struggle, a phase that began in 1609-10. For the increasing involvement of Spain in the internal affairs of the Empire, culminating in the formation of a Catholic League to counterpoise the Protestant League formed in May 1608, see Chudoba, *Spain and the Empire*, 196-200.

7. Both authors did, however, go on to write further volumes dealing with the later history of the United Provinces, but it is clear that 1609 marked a division in that history between countries struggling *for* independence and countries struggling to *retain* independence. See Motley, *The Life and Death of John of Barneveld*, and Geyl, *The Netherlands in the Seventeenth Century*.

8. Parker, *Dutch Revolt*, 266.

9. AGS Estado 2227:12, Philip III to the marquis of Guadaleste, 29 January 1609. Cf. Jonathan Israel's remark that "there can no longer be any doubt that the Spanish crown had come to accept the principle of Dutch political and religious independence by 1606, and that there was never subsequently any Spanish ambition or plan for reconquering the break-away northern Netherlands" (*The Dutch Republic and the Hispanic World*, xiv).

10. For details see Oestreich, *Neostoicism and the Early Modern State*, 76; Israel, *The Dutch Republic and the Hispanic World*, 42-65; Israel, *The Dutch Republic: Rise and Fall*, 420-49; and Parker, *Dutch Revolt*, 240-70.

11. Parker, *Europe in Crisis*, 142.

12. Israel, *The Dutch Republic: Rise and Fall*, 480-81.

13. Quoted in Roland Hussey, "America in European Diplomacy, 1597-1604," 2.

14. Israel, *The Dutch Republic and the Hispanic World*, 42-64; Israel *The Dutch Republic: Rise and Fall*, 478-85; and Parker, *Europe in Crisis*, 145.

15. Rubio, *Ideales hispanos*, 122.

16. Other authors too have suggested that 1609 marks a change in Span-

ish grand strategy, but they have argued that it was a change in focus, from the northern theater back to the Mediterranean theater. (Cf. Lynch, *The Hispanic World,* 56; and Israel's comment: "Ever since 1606, and possibly even before, Lerma had been preparing to engineer a major shift in the imperial ambitions, expenditure, and priorities of the Spanish crown away from northern and central Europe, away so to speak from the Habsburg connection, towards the Mediterranean and against the Islamic world" [Israel, *The Dutch Republic and the Hispanic World,* 12]). To support their claims such authors usually cite the decision, taken on the same day that the Habsburg delegates signed the truce with the Dutch in Antwerp, to expel the Moriscos (converted Muslims) from Spain. The timing of the expulsion order is significant, though purely accidental. While Philip and his ministers had no way of knowing when the final treaty would be signed, the decision was a result of a conjuncture of circumstances of which that signing was a part. First, it was clearly a move meant to affirm that Philip had not forgotten that his principal duty was to defend the Catholic faith on all sides. Second, one cannot discount the fact that the Spanish ministers knew that they would have more resources available to carry out the plan now that they would have reduced commitments in the north. But the argument that this act represents a new focus in Spanish policy on the problems of the Mediterranean is clearly contradicted by the facts. Philip III had been sending expeditions into the Mediterranean early in his reign, beginning in 1601, and in 1602 had signed a treaty with the Persians against the Ottoman Turks. Simultaneously he had launched major offensives in the northern theater of operations. In fact the expulsion, far from representing a new concentration of Spanish attention on the Mediterranean, was merely the climax of a long debate on the merits of the move that had begun as early as 1582. Under Philip III, the idea had been given serious attention as early as January 1599, when the Council of State advised the king to expel all moriscos between the ages of fifteen and seventy beginning in the winter of that year. As Manuel Danvila argued more than a hundred years ago, "It seems to me clear that, after these deliberations and affirmations by the Council of State [on 30 January and 2 February 1599], the morisco question was already resolved; that already the die had been cast; that the expulsion had been decided, and that the only thing that now occupied the Council was the manner and terms by which the expulsion would be realized." The expulsion marks a change of focus for the monarchy, but that change came in 1599–1600, not in 1609, and it was not from a northern to a Mediterranean strategy(Danvila y Collado, *La expulsión de los Moriscos Españoles,* 239–40). In his letter to Archduke Albert explaining the expulsion decision, the king himself points out that the debate over the issue had taken years but that the moriscos obstinate refusal to submit to the Catholic faith and their constant plotting against his kingdoms had finally convinced him to order their expulsion (AGS Estado 2227, unfoliated, Philip III to Albert, 3 November 1609). That the Spanish feared some sort of insurrection among the moriscos, possibly aided by North African Muslims, is indisputable. In 1608 Alonso de Contreras, a former lieutenant then passing as a hermit, was arrested, accused of being the "King of the Moriscos," and charged with providing muskets and leadership for a rising in New Castile, for which he was later tortured before being able to prove his innocence (Contreras, *Adventures,* 94–110).

17. See Parker, "Spain, Her Enemies, and the Revolt of the Netherlands," 37; Cano de Gardoqui, "Saboya," 41–42; and Chudoba, *Spain and the Empire,* 174.

18. Fernández Alvarez, "Felipe II," 20.

19. Parker, "Philip II, Paul Kennedy and the Revolt of the Netherlands," 69.

20. Williams, "Philip III," 756.

21. The climate was not, however, *that* favorable. Ibañez was arrested in January 1600 and was not officially pardoned until May 1605 (Cabrera de Córdoba, *Relaciones,* 60, 243).

22. Quoted in Williams, "Philip III," 755.

23. BN MS 18721⁵⁸, *Como se deve qualquier Principe poderoso guiar en los consejos de pazes con sus enemigos y en admitir reconciliacion a sus subditos rebeldes,* fol. 70. Cf. Luis Valle de la Cerda's *Avisos de estado y guerra.*

24. Williams, "Philip III," 755–59.

25. See also González de León, "The Road to Rocroi," for a detailed discussion of the *falta de cabezas* (lack of leaders) syndrome in the Army of Flanders.

26. Domínguez Ortiz, *Política y hacienda de Felipe IV,* 5.

27. AGS Estado 616:198, *Relacion del dinero que parecio que de presente sera menester,* 23 January 1599.

28. For the sums sent to Flanders, see fig. 2, this vol. On the estimated cost of the 1599 armada, see the reports submitted by Bernabé de Pedroso, *proveedor general* (quartermaster general) of the Armada, in AGS Guerra Antigua 653.

29. Parker, "Philip II, Paul Kennedy, and the Revolt," 69.

30. AGS Estado 2511:79, consulta, 22 July 1603.

31. To be sure, many of Philip's councillors, like Idiáquez, had been vocal and influential advocates of peace even under Philip II, but it was only after 1603 that their ideas began to carry determinative weight in the council.

32. Philip II's failure to have alternative strategies to his war plans had prevented a similar development in the previous reign. See Parker, "Philip II, Paul Kennedy, and the Revolt," 69.

33. Quoted in González de León, "Road to Rocroi," 44–45.

34. Israel, *The Dutch Republic and the Hispanic World,* 42–43. In 1617 the crown estimated that its receipts would total 5,357,000 ducats but that expenditures would exceed 12 million, and in 1621, with liquid funds amounting to only 1,601,000 ducats, it expected to have to pay out 2,738,000 for defense costs alone (Domínguez Ortiz, *Política y hacienda,* 7–8; Lynch, *Hispanic World,* 49–50).

35. Serrano, *Correspondencia diplomática,* 1:316–17, Philip II to Luis de Requeséns, 12 August 1566. Requeséns was to deliver this vow to Pius V.

Bibliography

This book is based primarily upon manuscript material, full citations of which are given in the notes.

Primary Sources

Abreu y Bertodano, Joseph Antonio de. *Colección de los tratados de paz, alianza, neutralidad . . . hechos por los pueblos, reyes, y príncipes de España . . . : Reynado del Señor Rey Don Phelipe III.* Part 1. Madrid, 1740.

Actas de las Cortes de Castilla. Vols. 18–27. Madrid, 1893–1907.

Alamos de Barrientos, Baltasar. *Discurso político al rey Felipe III al comienzo de su reinado.* Edited by Modesto Santos. Madrid, 1990.

Albert, Archduke. "Cartas del archiduque Alberto á don Francisco Gomez de Sandoval y Rojas, marqués de Denia y duque de Lerma, desde 1598 hasta 1611." In *CODOIN.* Vols. 42–43. Madrid, 1863.

Archivo General de Indias. *Catálogo de los documentos relativos a las Islas Filipinas.* . . . Edited by Pedro Torres Lanzas and Francisco Navas delle Valle. Barcelona, 1925–36.

Archivo Histórico Español. *Colección de documentos inéditos para la historia de España y de sus Indias.* Vol. 4, *Consultas del Consejo de Estado, 1604–06.* Edited by M. Alocer. Madrid, 1932.

Articles, of a treatie of truce. Made and concluded in the towne . . . of Antwerp, the 9. of April 1609. . . . London, 1609.

Articles of agreement concerning the cessation of warre . . . with warres testament, or last will, made at his departure out of the . . . Netherlands. London, 1607.

Baudi, Dominici. "Oratio . . . ad potentisimum Britanniarum Regem Iacobum I, Fidei defensorem, de non ineundo foedere cum Hispano." In *Espistolae.* Amsterdam, 1662.

Bentivoglio, Cardinal Guido. *Historical Relations of the United Provinces* and *of Flanders.* London, 1652.

Berwick y Alba, duque de, ed. *Noticias históricas y genealógicas de los estados de Montijo y Teba según los documentos de sus archivos.* Madrid, 1915.

Birch, Thomas. *The Court and Times of James the First.* 2 vols. London, 1848.

———. *An Historical View of the Negotiations Between the Courts of England, France, and Brussels, from the Year 1592 to 1617.* London, 1749.

A Briefe Declaration of the . . . Peace that is now intreating of . . . Together with an abstract of divers weighty Reasons and Arguments alledged by the Netherlanders, to prove the the Generall States ought not by any meanes to grant unto the discontinuance of their trade and trafficke into the East-Indies. London, 1608.

Cabrera de Córdoba, Luis de. *Felipe segundo.* 4 vols. Madrid, 1877.

—————. *Relaciones de las cosas sucedidas en la corte de España desde 1599 hasta 1614.* Madrid, 1857.

Calendar of Letters and State Papers Relating to English Affairs, Preserved in, or Originally Belonging to the Archives of Simancas. Vol. 4, *1587–1603.* Edited by Martin A.S. Hume. London, 1899.

Calendar of State Papers, Domestic Series, of the Reign of Elizabeth, 1601–1603 . . . Preserved in Her Majesty's Public Record Office. Vol. 9. Edited by Mary Anne Everett Green. London, 1870.

Calendar of State Papers and Manuscripts Relating to English Affairs Existing in Archives and Collections of Venice and Other Libraries of N. Italy. Vols. 7–11. London, 1890–1904.

Camden, William. *The Historie of the Most Renowned and Victorious Princesse Elizabeth.* London, 1630.

Campofrío, Juan Roco de. *España en Flandes: Trece años de govierno del Archiduque Alberto (1596–1608).* Madrid, 1973.

Colección de documentos inéditos para la historia de España. 112 vols. Madrid, 1842–95.

Collins, Arthur. *Letters and Memorials of State . . . written and collected by Sir Henri Sydney, . . . Sir Philip Sydney, and his brother Sir Robert Sydney.* 2 vols. 1746. Reprint. London, 1973.

Contreras, Alonso de. *The Adventures of Captain Alonso de Contreras: A Seventeenth Century Journey.* Translated by Philip Dallas. New York, 1989.

Dekker, Thomas. *Worke for armourers; or, the peace is broken. Open warres likely to happen this yeare 1609; God help the poor, the rich can shift.* London, 1609.

Faing, Gilles du. "Voyage de l'Archiduc Albert en Espagne en 1598." In *Collection des voyages des souverains des Pays-Bas.* Edited by L. P. Gachard. Vol. 4. Brussels, 1882.

Giustiniano, Pompeo. *Delle guerre di Fiandra, libri VI.* Antwerp, 1609.

Grimeston, Edward. *A Generall Historie of the Netherlands.* London, 1608.

—————. *A True Historie of the Memorable Siege of Ostend.* London, 1604.

Grotius, Hugo. *De rebus belgicis: or, The annals, and history of the Low-Countrey-warrs.* London, 1665.

Haestens, H. *La Nouvelle Troye, ou mémorable histoire du siège d'Ostende, le plus signalé qu'on ait veu en l'Europe.* Leiden, 1615.

Het Secreet des Conincx van Spaengnien, Philippus den tweeden, achterghelaten aen zijnen lieven Sone Philips . . . . N.p., 1599.

Historical Manuscripts Commission. *Calendar of the Manuscripts of the Most Hon. the Marquis of Salisbury.* Vols. 8–21. London, 1902–70.

—————. *Report on the Manuscripts of Lord De L'Isle andDudley Preserved at Pens-*

hurst Place. Vols. 2–4. Edited by C. L. Kingsford and William Shaw. London, 1934–42.

———. *Report on the Manuscripts of the Marquess of Downshire.* Vol. 2, *Papers of William Trumbull the Elder, 1605–1610.* Edited by E. K. Purnell and A. B. Hinds. London, 1936.

Isabel Clara Eugenia. *Correspondencia de la Infanta Archiduquesa . . . con el Duque de Lerma y otros personajes.* Edited by Antonio Rodríguez Villa. Madrid, 1906.

James I of England. *Letters of King James VI and I.* Edited by G. P. V. Akrigg. Berkeley, 1984.

Jeannin, Pierre. *Négociations diplomatiques et politiques du Président Jeannin,* 3 vols. Paris, 1819.

Klarwill, Victor. ed. *The Fugger Newsletters, Second Series.* London, 1926.

Laffleur de Kermaingant, P. *L'ambassade de France en Angleterre sous Henri IV: Mission de Jean de Thumery, sieur de Boissise (1598–1602).* Vol. 2, *Pièces justificatives.* Paris, 1886.

———. *Lettres de Henri IV au comte de la Rochepot, ambassadeur en Espagne, 1600–01.* Paris, 1889.

Larkin, James F., and Paul L. Hughes, eds. *Stuart Royal Proclamations.* Vol. 1. Oxford, 1973.

Lefèvre, Joseph. *Correspondance de Philippe II sur les affaires des Pays-Bas.* 4 vols. Brussels, 1940–60.

Lodge, Edmund, ed. *Illustrations of British History, Biography, and Manners, in the Reigns of Henry VIII, Edward VI, Mary, Elizabeth, and James I.* 2d ed. 3 vols. London, 1838.

Lonchay, Henri, Joseph Cuvelier, and Joseph Lefèvre, eds. *Correspondance de la Cour d'Espagne sur les affaires des Pays-Bas au XVIIe siècle.* 6 vols. Brussels, 1923–37.

Machiavelli, Niccolò. *Discourses on the First Ten Books of Titus Livius.* Translated by Christian E. Detmold. New York: Modern Library, 1940.

Novoa, Matias de. *Historia de Felipe III, Rey de España.* In *CODOIN.* Vols. 60–61. Madrid, 1875.

———. *Historia de Felipe IV, Rey de España.* In *CODOIN.* Vols. 69, 77, 80, 86. Madrid, 1876–86.

Oldys, W., and T. Birch. *The Works of Sir Walter Ralegh.* 8 vols. 1829. Reprint. New York, 1963.

[Orlers, Jan Janszen.] *The Triumphs of Nassau, translated out of the French by W. Shute.* London, 1613.

Relacion de la jornada que hizo á Inglaterra el Constable de Castilla . . . In *CODOIN.* Vol. 71. Madrid, 1881.

Rymer, Thomas, and R. Sanderson, eds. *Foedara, conventiones, litera, et conjuscunque generis acta publica, inter reges Anglicae et alios quovis imperatores, principes, vel communitates ab . . . anno 1101, ad nostra usque tempora . . . .* 20 vols. London, 1704–32.

Sawyer, Edmund, ed. *Memorials of Affairs of State . . . from the Original Papers of the Right Honorable Sir Ralph Winwood.* 3 vols. London, 1725.

Sepúlveda, Jerónimo de. *Sucesos del reinado de Felipe III.* Edited by J. Zarco Cuevas. In *Ciudad de Dios,* vols. 128–130. Madrid, 1922.

Serrano, Luciano. *Correspondencia diplomática entre España y la Santa Sede durante el pontificado de San Pio V.* 4 vols. Madrid, 1914.

Sully, Maximilen de Béthune, Duke of. *Memoirs of the Duke of Sully, Prime Minister to Henry the Great.* Translated by Sir Walter Scott. 4 vols. London, 1856.

Torres y Lanzas, Pedro. *Catálogo de los documentos relativos a las Islas Filipinas existentes en el Archivo de Indias de Sevilla.* Vol. 5. Barcelona, 1929.

Valle de la Cerda, Luis. *Avisos de estado y guerra para oprimir rebellones y hacer paces con enemigos.* Madrid, 1599.

Weldon, Anthony. *The Court and Character of King James.* 1650. Reprint. London, 1817.

Zarco Cuevas, J. *Documentos para la historia del Monasterio de San Lorenzo el Real de El Escorial.* 4 vols. Madrid, 1916–24.

Secondary Sources

Adams, Simon. "Spain or the Netherlands? The Dilemmas of Early Stuart Foreign Policy." In *Before the English Civil War.* Edited by Howard Tomlinson. New York, 1984.

Akrigg, G. P. V. *Jacobean Pageant, or the Court of King James I.* New York, 1967.

Alcalá-Zamora y Queipo de Llano, José. "Iniciativa, desaciertos y posibilismo en la política exterior española bajo Felipe III." *Estudios* (Departamento de Historia Moderna, Zaragoza) (1976): 191–223.

———. "La política exterior de España en el siglo XVII." *Estudios* (Departamento de Historia Moderna, Zaragoza) (1980–81): 135–57.

Allen, E. John B. *Post and Courier Service in the Diplomacy of Early Modern Europe.* The Hague, 1972.

Anderson, Alison D. "The Jülich-Kleve Succession Crisis (1609–20): A Study in International Relations." Ph.D. diss., University of Illinois at Urbana-Champaign, 1992.

Anderson, M. S. *The Origins of the Modern European State System, 1494–1618.* London, 1998.

Andrews, K. R. "Caribbean Rivalry and the Anglo-Spanish Peace of 1604." *History* 59 (1974): 1–17.

———. *Trade, Plunder, and Settlement: Maritime Enterprise and the Genesis of the British Empire, 1480–1630.* Cambridge, Eng., 1984.

Ballande, Henri. *Rebelle et conseiller de trois souverains: Le Président Jeannin, 1542–1623.* Paris, 1981.

Barrios, Feliciano. *El Consejo de Estado de la Monarquía Española, 1521–1812.* Madrid, 1984.

Belleroche, Edward. "The Siege of Ostend; or the New Troy, 1601–1604." *Proceedings of the Huguenot Society of London* 3 (1888–91): 427–539.

Black, J. B. *The Reign of Elizabeth, 1558–1603.* 2d ed. Oxford, 1959.

Bouwsma, William. *Venice and the Defense of Republican Liberty.* Berkeley, 1968.

Bouza Alvarez, Fernando J. "Monarchie en lettres d'imprimerie: Typographie et propagande au temps de Philippe II." *Revue d'histoire moderne et contemporaine* 41–42 (1994): 206–20.

Bracewell, Catherine W. *The Uskoks of Senj: Piracy, Banditry, and Holy War in the Sixteenth Century Adriatic.* Ithaca, 1992.

Brants, Victor. "Une mission à Madrid de Philippe de Croy, comte de Solre, envoyé des archiducs en 1604." *Bulletin de la Commission Royale d'Histoire* 77 (1908): 185–203.

———. *Receuil des ordonnances des Pays Bas: Règne d'Albert et d'Isabelle, 1597–1621.* Vol. 1. Brussels, 1909.

Braudel, Fernand. *The Mediterranean and the Mediterranean World in the Age of Philip II.* 2 vols. New York, 1972–73.

Brightwell, Peter. "The Spanish System and the Twelve Years' Truce." *English Historical Review* 89 (1974): 270–92.

Cano de Gardoqui, José Luis. *La conspiración de Biron (1602).* Valladolid, 1970.

———. *La cuestión de Saluzzo en las comunicaciones del imperio español (1588–1601).* Valladolid, 1962.

———. "España y los estados italianos independientes en 1600." *Hispania* 92 (1963): 524–55

———. "Saboya en la política del Duque de Lerma: 1601–1602." *Hispania* 101 (1966): 41–60.

Carter, Charles Howard. "The Nature of Spanish Government after Philip II." *Historian* 26 (November 1963): 1–18.

———. *The Secret Diplomacy of the Habsburgs, 1598–1625.* New York, 1964.

———. *The Western European Powers, 1500–1700.* Ithaca, 1971.

Castro, Cristóbal de. *Felipe III.* Madrid, 1944.

Chudoba, Bohdan. *Spain and the Empire.* Chicago, 1952.

Churton, Edward. *Gongora: An Historical and Critical Essay on the Times of Philip III and IV of Spain.* 2 vols. London, 1862.

Clark, G. N. "Edward Grimeston, the Translator." *English Historical Review* 43 (1928): 585–98.

Corral Castanedo, Alfonso. *España y Venecia (1604–07).* Valladolid, 1955.

Croft, Pauline. "Serving the Archduke: Robert Cecil's Management of the Parliamentary Session of 1606." *Historical Research* 64 (1991): 289–304.

Cuvelier, Joseph. "Les préliminaires du traité de Londres (29 août 1604)." *Revue Belge de Philologie et d'Histoire* 2 (1923): 279–304, 485–508.

Dalton, Charles. *Life and Times of General Sir Edward Cecil, Viscount Wimbledon.* 2 vols. London, 1885.

Danvila y Burguero, Alfonso. *Don Cristóbal de Moura, primer marqués de Castel Rodrigo (1538–1613).* Madrid, 1900.

Danvila y Collado, Manuel. *La expulsión de los Moriscos Españoles.* Madrid, 1880.

————. *El poder civil en España.* Vol. 2. Madrid, 1885.

Davies, D. W. *Elizabethans Errant: The Strange Fortunes of Sir Thomas Sherley and His Three Sons.* Ithaca, N.Y., 1967.

Deventer, Marinus Lodewijk van. *Gedenkstukken van J. van Oldenbarnevelt, zijn tijd,* 3 vols. The Hague, 1860–65.

Diccionario de Historia de España. Edited by Germán Bleiberg. Madrid, 1979.

Domínguez Ortiz, Antonio. *El Antiguo Régimen: Los Reyes Católicos y los Austrias.* Vol. 3 of *Historia de España.* Edited by Miguel Artola. Madrid, 1988.

————. *Política y hacienda de Felipe IV.* Madrid, 1960.

Echevarría Bacigalupe, Miguel Angel. "Recursos fiscales y guerra en Europa: Flandes, 1615–1622." *Manuscrits* 2 (1995): 273–307

Elliott, John H. *The Count-Duke of Olivares: The Statesman in an Age of Decline.* New Haven, 1986.

————. *Europe Divided, 1559–1598.* London, 1968.

————. "Foreign Policy and Domestic Crisis: Spain, 1598–1659." In *Spain and Its World, 1500–1700.* New Haven, 1989.

————. *Imperial Spain.* 1963. Reprint. New York, 1966.

————. "The Spanish Peninsula, 1598–1648." In *The Decline of Spain and the Thirty Years War, 1609–48/59.* Vol. 4 of *The New Cambridge Modern History.* Cambridge, 1970.

Essen, Léon van der. *Correspondance d'Ottavio Mirto Frangipani, premier nonce de Flandre (1596–1606).* Analecta Vaticano-Belgica, 2d ser.: Nonciature de Flandre, vols. 1–3. Brussels, 1924–42.

Eysinga, W. J. M. Van. *De Wording van Het Twaalfjarig Bestand van 9 April 1609.* Verhandelingen der Koninklijke Nederlandse Akademie van Wetenschappen, n.s., vol. 66, pt. 3. Amsterdam, 1959.

Falls, Cyril. "España e Irlanda durante el reinado de Isabel de Inglaterra (1558 a 1603)." In *Segundo curso o Superior de Metodología y Crítica Históricas del Servicio Histórico Militar, Estado Mayor Central del Ejército.* Madrid, 1950.

Fernández Albaladejo, Pablo. "De «llave de Italia» a «corazón de la Monarquía»: Milán y la Monarquía Católica en el reinado de Felipe III." In *Fragmentos de Monarquía.* Madrid, 1992.

Fernández Alvarez, Manuel. "Felipe II e Isabel de Inglaterra (Una paz imposible)." *Revista de historia naval* 23 (1988): 19–35.

Fernández Alvarez, Manuel, and Ana Díaz Medina. *Los Austrias mayores y la culminación del imperio (1516–1598).* Vol. 8 of *Historia de España.* Edited by Angel Montenegro Duque. Madrid, 1987.

Feros Carrasco, Antonio. "Lerma y Olivares: La práctica del valimiento en la primera mitad del seiscientos." In *La España del Conde Duque de Olivares.* Edited by John Elliott and Angel García Sanz. Valladolid, 1990.

————."Política interior: El régimen de los validos." In *La crisis del siglo XVII.* Vol. 6 of *Historia de España.* Planeta ed. Barcelona, 1988.

Fortea Pérez, José Ignacio. "Reino y Cortes: El servicio de millones y la reestructuración del espacio fiscal en la corona de Castilla (1601–1621)." In *Política y hacienda en el antiguo régimen*. II Reunión científica de la Asociación española de historia moderna, vol. 1. Murcia, 1992.

Fraser, Antonia. *Faith and Treason: The Story of the Gunpowder Plot.* New York, 1996.

Froude, James A. *The Reign of Elizabeth*. 5 vols. London: n.d.

Furber, Holden. *Rival Empires of Trade in the Orient, 1600–1800*. Minneapolis, 1976.

Gachard, L. P. *Actes des Etats Généraux de 1600*. Brussels, 1849.

García García, Bernardo. "Pacifismo y reformación en la política exterior del duque de Lerma (1598–1618). Apuntes para una renovación historiográfica pendiente." *Cuadernos de Historia Moderna* 12 (1991): 207–22.

———. *La Pax Hispanica: Política exterior del Duque de Lerma*. Louvain, 1996.

Gardiner, Samuel R. *History of England from the Accession of James I to the Outbreak of the Civil War, 1603–1642*. 10 vols. London, 1904–5.

Geisendorf, P.-F. "Le Traité de Lyon et le pont de Grésin, ou d'une cause parfois méconnue des troubles des Grisons au 17e siècle." *Mémoires et Documents publiés par la Société d'Histoire et d'Archéologie de Genève* 40 (1961): 279–86.

Geyl, Pieter. *The Netherlands in the Seventeenth Century, 1609–1648*, 2d ed. (originally published as *The Netherlands Divided*). 1936. Reprint. London, 1961.

———. *The Revolt of the Netherlands, 1555–1609*. 2d corrected ed. New York, 1962.

Gindely, Anton. *Rudolf II und seine Zeit, 1600–1612*. Prague, 1863.

Gómez-Centurión, Carlos. *La Invencible y la empresa de Inglaterra*. Madrid, 1988.

González de León, Fernando. "The Road to Rocroi: The Duke of Alba, the Count Duke of Olivares and the High Command of the Spanish Army of Flanders in the Eighty Years War, 1567–1659." Ph.D. diss., Johns Hopkins University, 1991.

Goodman, Nathan G. *Diplomatic Relations between England and Spain, with Special Reference to English Opinion, 1597–1603*. Philadelphia, 1925.

Goslinga, Cornelis. *The Dutch in the Caribbean and on the Wild Coast, 1580–1680*. Assen, Netherlands, 1971.

Greengrass, Mark. *France in the Age of Henri IV.* 2d ed. London, 1995.

Hamy, L. "Conférence pour la paix entre l'Angleterre et l'Espagne tenue à Boulogne en 1600." *Société Académique de Boulogne-sur-mer Bulletin* 7 (1906): 434–60.

Harline, Craig. *Pamphlets, Printing, and Political Culture in the Dutch Republic*. Dordrecht, 1987.

Henrard, P. *Histoire du siège d'Ostende 1601–4*. Brussels, 1890.

Hume, Martin A. S. *The Court of Philip IV.* London, 1907.

———. *Treason and Plot: Struggles for Supremacy in the Last Years of Queen Elizabeth.* New York, 1901.

Hussey, Roland. "America in European Diplomacy, 1597–1604." *Revista de Historia de América* 41 (1956): 1–30.

Iklé, Fred C. *Every War Must End.* Rev. ed. New York, 1991.

Imhof, Arthur E. *Der Friede von Vervins 1598*. Aarau, 1966.

Israel, Jonathan I. *Dutch Primacy in World Trade, 1585–1740*. Oxford, 1989.

———. *The Dutch Republic: Its Rise, Greatness, and Fall, 1477–1806*. Oxford, 1995.

———. *The Dutch Republic and the Hispanic World, 1606–1661*. Oxford, 1982.

———. "Spain, the Spanish Embargoes, and the Struggle for the Mastery of World Trade, 1585–1660." In *Empires and Entrepots: The Dutch, the Spanish Monarchy, and the Jews, 1585–1713*. London, 1990.

Jago, Charles. "Taxation and Political Culture in Castile, 1590–1640." In *Spain, Europe and the Atlantic World: Essays in Honour of John H. Elliott*. Edited by Richard L. Kagan and Geoffrey Parker. Cambridge, 1995.

Jameson, J. F. "Willem Usselinx." *Papers of the American Historical Association* 2 (1887).

Jansson, Maija. "The Hat Is No Expression of Honor." *Proceedings of the American Philosophical Society* 133 (1989): 26–34.

Johnson, C. B. " 'La Española inglesa' and the Practice of Literary Production." *Viator* 19 (1988): 377–416.

Kagan, Donald. *On the Origins of War and the Preservation of Peace*. New York, 1995.

Kamen, Henry. *Golden Age Spain*. Atlantic Highlands, N.J., 1988.

———. *Philip of Spain*. New Haven, 1997.

Kennedy, Paul. *The Rise and Fall of the Great Powers*. New York, 1987.

Kissinger, Henry. *Diplomacy*. New York, 1994.

Klingenstein, L. *The Great Infanta: Isabel, Sovereign of the Netherlands*. New York, 1910.

Knight, A. H. J. *Heinrich Julius, Duke of Brunswick*. Oxford, 1948.

Lacy, Robert. *Sir Walter Ralegh*. London, 1973.

Lafuente, Modesto. *Historia general de España*. Vol. 15. Madrid, 1855.

Lee, Maurice. *James I and Henri IV: An Essay in English Foreign Policy, 1603–1610*. Urbana, 1970.

Lefèvre, Joseph. "Don Juan de Mancicidor, secrétaire d'Etat et de Guerre de l'archiduc Albert, 1596–1618." *Revue Belge de Philologie et d'Histoire* 4 (1925): 697–714.

Liske, Javier. *Viajes de extranjeros por España y Portugal en los siglos XV, XVI, y XVII*. Madrid, 1878.

Loomie, Albert J. "Guy Fawkes in Spain: The 'Spanish Treason' in Spanish Documents." *Bulletin of the Institute of Historical Research*, special suppl. 9. London, 1971.

———. "Philip III and the Stuart Succession in England, 1600–1603." *Revue Belge de Philologie et d'Histoire* 43 (1965): 492–514.

———. "Sir Robert Cecil and the Spanish Embassy." *Bulletin of the Institute of Historical Research* 42 (1969): 30–57.

———. *The Spanish Elizabethans: The English Exiles at the Court of Philip II*. New York, 1963.

———. "The Spanish Faction at the Court of Charles I, 1630–1648." *Bulletin of the Institute of Historical Research* 59 (1986): 37–49.

————. "Toleration and Diplomacy: The Religious Issue in Anglo-Spanish Relations, 1603–1605." *Transactions of the American Philosophical Society*, n.s., 53:6 (1963).

Lovett, A. W. "The Castilian Bankruptcy of 1575." *Historical Journal* 23 (1980): 899–911.

Lynch, John. *The Hispanic World in Crisis and Change, 1598–1700.* Oxford, 1992.

————. *Spain, 1516–1598: From Nation State to World Empire.* Oxford, 1991.

MacCaffrey, Wallace T. *Elizabeth I: War and Politics, 1588–1603.* Princeton, 1992.

Mackie, J. Duncan. "James VI and I and the Peace with Spain, 1604." *Scottish Historical Review* 23:92 (1926): 241–49.

————. "'A Loyall Subiectes Advertisment' as to the Unpopularity of James I.'s Government in England, 1603–4." *Scottish Historical Review* 23:89 (1925): 1–17.

————. "A Secret Agent of James VI." *Scottish Historical Review* 9 (1912): 376–86.

Maclean, John, ed. *Letters from Sir Robert Cecil to Sir George Carew.* London, 1864.

Markham, Clements R. *The Fighting Veres: Lives of Sir Francis Vere, General of the Queen's Forces . . . and of Sir Horace Vere, General of the English Forces in the Low Countries . . . .* Boston, 1888.

Martin, Colin, and Geoffrey Parker. *The Spanish Armada.* London, 1988.

Martín Acosta, Maria Emelina. *El dinero americano y la política del imperio.* Madrid, 1992.

Mattingly, Garrett. *The Armada.* Boston, 1959.

————. *Renaissance Diplomacy.* 1955. Reprint. New York, 1988.

Mendoza, Francisco de. "Cartas del Almirante de Aragon, Don Francisco de Mendoza al Archiduque Alberto, relativas en su mayor parte á la guerra de Flándes, desde 1596 á 1602." In *CODOIN.* Vol. 42. Madrid, 1863.

Merriman, Roger B. *The Rise of the Spanish Empire in the Old World and the New.* Vol. 4, *Philip the Prudent.* 1918. Reprint. New York, 1962.

Montpleinchamp, Jean Bruslè de. *Histoire de l'Archduc Albert.* Edited by A.L.P. de Robaulx de Soumoy. Collection de Mémoires relatifs à l'Histoire de Belgique. Brussels, 1870.

Morgan, Hiram. "Hugh O'Neill and the Nine Years War in Tudor Ireland." *Historical Journal* 36 (1993): 21–37.

————. *Tyrone's Rebellion: The Outbreak of the Nine Years War in Tudor Ireland.* Woodbridge, 1993.

Motley, John Lothrop. *History of the United Netherlands.* 4 vols. 1867. Reprint. New York, 1898.

————. *The Life and Death of John of Barneveld, Advocate of Holland.* 2 vols. New York, 1874.

Muller, Pieter L. *Onze gouden eeuw: De republiek der Vereenigde Nederlande in haar bloeitijd geschetst.* 3 vols. Leiden, 1896–98.

Neale, J. E. *Queen Elizabeth.* London, 1934.

Nicolson, Sir Harold. *Diplomacy.* 3d ed. Oxford, 1963.

O Faolain, Seán. *The Great O'Neill.* 1942. Reprint. Dublin, 1986.

Oestreich, Gerhard. *Neostoicism and the Early Modern State.* Cambridge, 1982.
Palacio Atard, Vincente. *Derrota, agotamiento, decadencia en la España del siglo XVII.* 3d ed. Madrid, 1966.
Parker, Geoffrey. *After Columbus: Spain's Struggle for Atlantic Hegemony.* The Lawrence F. Brewster Lecture in History, 11. Greensville, N.C., 1992.
————. *The Army of Flanders and the Spanish Road, 1567–1659.* Cambridge, 1972.
————. *The Dutch Revolt.* Rev. ed. London, 1985.
————. "Early Modern Europe." In *The Laws of War: Constraints on Warfare in the Western World.* Edited by Michael Howard, George J. Andreopoulos, and Mark R. Shulman. New Haven, 1994.
————. *Europe in Crisis, 1598–1648.* London, 1979.
————. *The Grand Strategy of Philip II.* New Haven, 1998.
————. *Guide to the Archives of the Spanish Institutions in or Concerned with the Netherlands (1556–1706).* Archives et Bibliothèques de Belgique, no. 3. Brussels, 1971.
————. "The Making of Strategy in Habsburg Spain: Philip II's 'Bid for Mastery,' 1556–1598." In *The Making of Strategy: Rulers, States, and War.* Edited by Williamson Murray, MacGregor Knox, and Alvin Bernstein. Cambridge, 1994.
————. *The Military Revolution: Military Innovation and the Rise of the West, 1500–1800.* Cambridge, 1988.
————. *Philip II.* 3d ed. Chicago, 1995.
————. "Philip II, Paul Kennedy and the Revolt of the Netherlands, 1572–76: A Case of Strategic Overstretch?" In *Clashes of Cultures: Essays in Honour of Niels Steensgaard.* Edited by Jens Christian V. Johansen, Erling Ladewig Peterson, and Henrik Stevnsborg. Odense, Denmark, 1992.
————. "Spain, Her Enemies and the Revolt of the Netherlands, 1559–1648." In *Spain and the Netherlands, 1559–1659: Ten Studies,* 17–43. Rev. ed. London, 1990.
————. "War and Economic Change: the Economic Costs of the Dutch Revolt." In *Spain and the Netherlands: Ten Studies.* Rev. ed. London, 1990.
————. "Was Parma Ready? The Army of Flanders and the Spanish Armada in 1588." In *Beleid en Bestuur in de Oude Nederlanden: Liber Amicorum Prof. Dr. M Baelde.* Edited by Hugo Soly and René Vermeir. Ghent, 1993.
Pazos, Manuel R. "Del conflicto entre Paulo V y Venecia: El embajador de la Serenísima en España y el entredicho." *Revista de Estudios Historicos del Archivo Ibero-Americano* 13 (1944): 32–61.
Pérez Bustamente, Ciriaco. "El dominio del Adriático y la política española en los comienzos del siglo XVII." *Revista de la Universidad de Madrid* 2:5 (1953): 57–80.
————. *La España de Felipe III.* Vol. 24 of *Historia de España.* Edited by Ramón Menéndez Pidal. 3d ed. Madrid, 1988.
————. *Felipe III: Semblanza de un monarca y perfiles de una privanza.* Madrid, 1950.
Petrie, Charles. *Don John of Austria.* New York, 1967.

Pierson, Peter. *Commander of the Armada: The Seventh Duke of Medina Sidonia.* New Haven, 1989

Pillar, Paul R. *Negotiating Peace: War Termination as a Bargaining Process.* Princeton, 1983.

Prescott, William H. *History of the Reign of Philip the Second, King of Spain.* 2d ed. 3 vols. London, 1860.

Pulido Bueno, Ildefonso. *La real hacienda de Felipe III.* Huelva, 1996.

Rahlenbeck, Charles, ed. *Considérationes d'Etat sur le traicté de la paix avec les Sérénissimes Archiducz d'Austriche.* Collection de Mémoires Relatifs a l'Histoire de Belgique. Brussels, 1869.

Ramirez de Villa Urrutia, Wenceslas. "La jornada del condestable de Castilla á Inglaterra para las paces de 1604." *Revista Contemporánea* 35 (Sept.–Oct. 1881): 163–81.

Ramsay, G. D. *The Queen's Merchants and the Revolt of the Netherlands.* Manchester, 1986.

Ranke, Leopold von. *The Ottoman and the Spanish Empires in the Sixteenth and Seventeenth Centuries.* Philadelphia, 1845.

Read, Conyers. "Queen Elizabeth's Seizure of the Duke of Alba's Payships." *Journal of Modern History* 5 (1933): 443–64.

Rodríguez Joulia Saint-Cyr, Carlos. *Felipe III y el Rey de Cuco.* Madrid, 1954.

Rodríguez Villa, Antonio. *Ambrosio Spínola, primer marqués de los Balbases.* Madrid, 1904.

———. "D. Francisco de Mendoza, Almirante de Aragón. In *Homenaje á Menéndez y Pelayo en el año vigésimo de su profesorado.* Edited by Juan Valera. Vol. 2. Madrid, 1899.

Rodríguez-Salgado, M. J. *The Changing Face of Empire: Charles V, Philip II, and Habsburg Authority, 1551–1559.* Cambridge, 1988.

Rowen, Herbert H., ed. *The Low Countries in Early Modern Times: A Documentary History.* New York, 1972.

Rowen, Herbert H., and Craig E. Harline. "The Birth of the Dutch Nation." In *Politics, Religion, and Diplomacy in Early Modern Europe: Essays in Honor of De Lamar Jensen.* Sixteenth Century Essays and Studies 27. Edited by Malcolm R. Thorp and Arthur J. Slavin. Kirksville, Miss., 1994.

Rubio Esteban, Julián. *Los ideales hispanos en la tregua de 1609.* Valladolid, 1937.

Russell, Joycelyne G. *Peacemaking in the Renaissance.* London, 1986.

Seco Serrano, Carlos. "Asti: un jalón en la decadencia española." *Arbor* 29:3 (1954): 277-91.

———. "Venecia, Roma, España: El conflicto de 1606–1607 y sus consecuencias." In *Homenaje a Jaime Vicens Vives.* Vol. 2. Barcelona, 1967.

Seeley, John. *The Growth of British Policy.* 2 vols. Cambridge, 1895.

Silke, John J. *Kinsale: The Spanish Intervention in Ireland at the End of the Elizabethan Wars.* New York, 1970.

Sluiter, Engel. "Dutch-Spanish Rivalry in the Caribbean Area, 1594–1609." *Hispanic American Historical Review* 28 (1948): 165–96.

Stephen, Leslie, and Sidney Lee, eds. *Dictionary of National Biography.* 22 vols. London, 1885–1901.

Stewart, Richard W. "The 'Irish Road': Military Supply and Arms for Elizabeth's Army during the O'Neill Rebellion in Ireland, 1598–1601." In *War and Government in Britain, 1598–1650.* Edited by Mark C. Fissel. Manchester, 1991.

Stradling, R. A. *The Armada of Flanders.* Cambridge, 1993.

Sturler, J. de. "Documents diplomatiques et administratifs relatifs aux différends commerciaux et maritimes survenus entre les Pays-Bas et la France de 1599 à 1607." *Bulletin de la Commission Royale de l'Histoire* 104 (1939): 73–150.

Sugden, John. *Sir Francis Drake.* New York, 1990.

Sutherland, N. M. "The Origins of the Thirty Years War and the Structure of European Politics." *English Historical Review* (July 1992): 587–625.

't Hart, Marjolein C. *The Making of the Bourgeois State: War, Politics, and Finance during the Dutch Revolt.* Manchester, 1993.

Taylor, Harland. "Price Revolution or Price Revision? The English and Spanish Trade after 1604." *Renaissance and Modern Studies* 12 (1968): 5–32.

Tex, Jan Den. *Oldenbarnevelt.* Translated by R. B. Powell. 2 vols. Cambridge, Eng., 1973.

Thatcher, Margaret. *The Downing Street Years.* New York, 1993.

Thompson, Edward. *Sir Walter Ralegh: Last of the Elizabethans.* New Haven, 1936.

Thompson, I. A. A. *War and Government in Habsburg Spain, 1560–1620.* London, 1976.

Trevor-Roper, H. R. "Spain and Europe, 1598–1621." In *The Decline of Spain and the Thirty Years War, 1609–48/59.* Vol. 4 of *The New Cambridge Modern History.* Edited by J. P. Cooper. Cambridge, 1970.

Turba, Gustav. *Beiträge zur Geschichte der Habsburgen.* Vienna, 1898.

Ulloa, Modesto. *La hacienda real de Castilla en el reinado de Felipe II.* 3d ed. Madrid, 1986.

Walsh, Micheline Kerney. *"Destruction by Peace": Hugh O Neill after Kinsale.* Monaghan, 1986.

Watson, Robert, and William Thomson. *The History of the Reign of Philip the Third, King of Spain.* 2d ed. 2 vols. London, 1786.

Wernham, R. B. *After the Armada: Elizabethan England and the Struggle for Western Europe, 1588–1595.* Oxford, 1984.

———. *The Making of Elizabethan Foreign Policy, 1558–1603.* Berkeley, 1980,

———. *The Return of the Armadas: The Last Years of the Elizabethan War against Spain, 1595–1603.* Oxford, 1994.

Williams, Patrick. "The Court and Councils of Philip III of Spain." Ph.D. diss., University of London, 1973.

———. "Lerma, Old Castile and the Travels of Philip III." *History* 3 (1988): 379–97.

———. "Philip III and the Restoration of Spanish Government, 1598–1603." *English Historical Review* 88 (1973): 751–69.

———. "El reinado de Felipe III." In *Historia general de España y América*. Vol. 8. Rialp ed. Madrid, 1987.

Yalí Román Román, Alberto. "Origen y evolución de la secretaría de estado y de la secretaría del despacho." *Jahrbuch für Geschicte von Staat, Wirtshaft und Gesellschaft Lateinamerikas* 6 (1969): 41–142.

Zeller, Berthold. "La conspiration du maréchal de Biron." *Compte rendu des séances et travaux de l'Académie des sciences morales et politiques* 111 (1879): 130–59.

Index

Acuña, Juan de, president of the Council of the Treasury, 229
Acuña, Pedro de, commander in the Philippines, 175, 295n10
Adelantado of Castile. *See* Padilla, Martín de
Admiral of Aragon, Francisco de Mendoza: appointed to negotiate with England, 28; background, 256n48; banished to estates in Spain, 272n57; at the battle of Nieuwpoort, 47, 259n35; commands Habsburg forces in Brabant, 21, 84–85; negotiates his own release, 269n25
admiralties, Dutch, 156
Aerssen Cornelius van, recorder for States-General, 174, 177
Aguila, Juan de, commander of Spanish forces in Kinsale, 75
Alba, Fernando Alvarez de Toledo, duke of, 248n2, 254n31, 277n1
Alba de Liste, Antonio Enríquez de Guzmán, count of, 82
Albert of Austria, archduke of the Netherlands: appeals to loyal provinces for funds, 42, 51, 193; appoints Ambrosio Spínola commander of the Army of Flanders, 143; appoints Ambrosio Spínola delegate to Hispano-Dutch peace talks, 201; awaits reinforcements, 60; commands forces at battle of Nieuwpoort, 45; costs of marriage trip, 257n3; defends negotiations with the Dutch, 182; distrust of Dutch motives, 173; expeditures for trip to Spain, 30; factions at court of, 83; and Fedrico Spínola, 6, 20; granted sovereignty of the Netherlands, 2, 17; independent activities of, 15, 24, 27, 51, 70, 82, 88, 89, 121, 169,

270n28; instructions to delegates for Hispano-Dutch peace talks, 203, 223; instructions to Louis Verreyken in talks with England, 38; and the invasion of England, 63; justifies negotiations to Lerma, 170; membership in Junta de Noche, 3; military strategy of, 122; and mutineers in Army of Flanders, 133, 201; negotiations with England, 20, 38; negotiations with the Dutch, 70, 80, 169; at Ostend, 139; pleads for resources from Spain, 191; policies of, 19; pressures Spanish court, 93, 107; proposes protectorate of the United Provinces, 204; proposes seven-year truce, 221, 225; reform of Army of Flanders, 108, 260n50; refuses to hand over suspects in Gunpowder Plot, 160; role in policy making, 19; sends envoy to James I, 111, 228; stripped of military influence, 98; willing to concede sovereignty of the northern provinces, 174
ambassadors, role in policy making, 10, 11, 251n35. *See also under individual ambassadors*
Andrea of Austria, Cardinal, regent of the Netherlands (1598–99): 20, 23, 255nn40,42
Antwerp, Truce or Treaty of. *See* Twelve Years' Truce
Araya, 157
Aremberg, Karel van, 111, 119, 128
Armada de Barlovento, 215
Armada del Almirantazgo, 153, 289n47
armistice: as goal of Hispano-Dutch negotiations, 53, 80; versus peace, 218
Army of Flanders: composition of, 272n52; costs of, 145, 273n9, 306n61; defensive

WITHDRAWN